Our Brethren are on the Field

Chattanooga in the Civil War

Letters, Diaries and Remembrances From those Who Fought and Campaigned for Chattanooga

MOUNTAIN ARBOR
PRESS

Alpharetta, GA

ISBN: 978-1-63183-532-2

Library of Congress Control Number: 2019933474

Printed in the United States   0 2 1 1 1 9

∞ This paper meets the requirements of ANSI/NISO Z39.48-1992 (Permanence of Paper)

Book Cover: Battle of Missionary Ridge by Alfred Waud, Library of Congress. No restrictions on publishing

Disclaimer: Much of the material in this book falls into the public domain, otherwise, rights and permissions have been secured. All phots, unless otherwise noted are obtained from the library of Congress.

Dedication

First, and foremost, we want to dedicate this effort to all those who have served in all branches of the United States military and those that have given their lives for our freedom. However, this book was specifically written to support the opening of a museum and history center dedicated to all the humble, quiet men who are Medal of Honor Recipients. They wear this medal not thinking of their own deeds but with a conviction that those who did not return are the true heroes. We want to thank Jason Rusk, Alisa Rusk and David Brannon, who contributed time and money to this fund-raising project for the Charles Coolidge Medal of Honor History Center that will open February 2020 in Chattanooga Tennessee. The Charles Coolidge Medal of Honor Heritage Center is an important personal project for me. My father Paul Quinlin was a World War II veteran serving in the 32nd Infantry Division, 118th regiment, Company F, second Platoon. My father turned 18 in June 1944 and enlisted in the 32nd Division (The Red Arrow Division) and was shipped off to the Pacific Theater. The 32nd fought in a number of crucial battles in the Pacific theater including Burma, New Guinea and the Philippines.

My father was a runner and when communications were cut my dad would run out back and forth from the front to the Command Post (CP) with critical information regarding the conditions on the front and returning with orders from the CP. On March 31, 1945 while in the Philippines on the Vella Verdi Trail, he had just returned from such a mission to a fox hole occupied by his platoon sergeant William Dominquez and Michael Nichols. A Japanese grenade was thrown into the fox hole whereupon Michael took off his helmet and jumped on the grenade. When it exploded it killed Michael and wounded William and my father. William would write to me in 1985 that "I saw the Japs coming near our position and knew they were going to kill us as by that time in the war they were not taking wounded American prisoners. Then a BAR (Browning automatic rifle) started to fire to my rear. It killed, wounded or pinned down the Japs so I could drag your dad back to a field hospital. William Shockley was the man behind the BAR and he remained at the position until the Japs killed him." Michael and the two Williams saved the life of my father.

iii

I personally want to dedicate this project to these three men and the chance they gave my father to live his life. I have dedicated my life to honoring these men, as well as those before and after them, that have given the last full measure of devotion so that others may share our way of life in a free world that can only survive through their sacrifices and commitment to others. I hope that my humble efforts reflect the full measure of gratitude I feel for their sacrifices and the opportunity that was provided for me and all of us who benefit from their dedication to freedom and the pursuit of happiness.

Brad

Introduction

Few people outside of devout historians fully understand the role of Chattanooga, Tennessee in the American Civil War. Two major battles took place in the neighborhood: Chickamauga and the consequent battles for Chattanooga including Lookout Mountain and Missionary Ridge. But why were these major battles fought with such sacrifice in this mostly rural border area between Tennessee and Georgia? Chattanooga's significance to both sides during the conflict cannot be overestimated. In *Our Brethren Are on the Field* we share a narrative about Chattanooga's strategic value and the nearly two years spent trying to secure it by the Union while the Confederacy conducted two campaigns attempting to keep it from falling by pushing north towards the Ohio River and central Tennessee.

The narrative provides a story line that describes the actions of Federal and Confederate armies in the state of Tennessee as well as Georgia and Alabama. It begins with the fall of Nashville and culminates in the final Union victory that secured Chattanooga as the launching point for its invasion of the Deep South and the ultimate defeat of the Confederacy.

Our text supplements the letters, diary entries and regimental histories sighted here, telling the story of the men who fought for both sides during the contests to control the city. History comes to life when you hear the thoughts and experiences of those who were living that history in the moment of its happening.

This book hopes to both broaden the reader's understanding of this crucial region in the western theatre of the war and why holding or taking Chattanooga was one of the key objectives of the entire war. This, of course, was evidenced by the human and material sacrifice made by both the Union and the Confederacy to control Chattanooga.

The other purpose of this book is to help the reader understand why Chattanooga was selected for the "Charles Coolidge Medal of Honor Heritage Center". The Medal of Honor was created and first bestowed upon those deemed worthy during the Civil War. There have been some 3,500 Medals of Honor awarded since its inception. The first recipients of the Medal of Honor were nineteen of the twenty-four men that comprised Andrew's Raiders. Their story is reviewed in this book's narrative and four of those recipients are buried here at the Chattanooga National Cemetery. While these four men are the only Medal of Honor recipients from the Civil War buried at Chattanooga National Cemetery, 33 of the Medals were awarded to Union soldiers who fought here during Chickamauga and the battle for Chattanooga. Three Medal of Honor recipients from later wars are buried here as well; they are Master Sergeant Ray E. Duke for action in the Korean War, Corporal Desmond Doss, for action in World War II and Private William F. Zion, for action in the Boxer Rebellion.

Of the thirty-seven soldiers whose letters, diaries or memoirs are used in this book, twenty-one of them were either killed outright or died during the war. Twelve of those men are buried in the Chattanooga National Cemetery.

It is fitting that Chattanooga was selected for this important site and we are proud to offer all the proceeds from this book to the support of the Charles Coolidge Medal of Honor Heritage Center.

Dick and Brad

Contents

Maps

All maps used in Our *Brethren Are on the Field* were generously provided by Hal Jespersen and sourced through his web site, cwmaps.com.

Engagements in Hamilton County and Its Vicinity after September 8, 1863 to the End of the War

Union troops entered and occupied Chattanooga on Sept 9, 1863

1863

Fryars's Island -- Sept 9
Lookout Mountain, GA --- Sept 9
Peavine Creek, GA -- Sept 10
Blue Bird Gap, GA -- Sept 11
Rossville, GA -- Sept 11
LayFayette, GA --- Sept 11
Ringgold, GA --- Sept 11
Lee and Gordon's Mill, GA --- Sept 11-13
Leet's Tan-Yard, GA --- Sept 12
LaFayette, GA -- Sept 14
Catlett's Gap, GA, Pigeon Mountain ------------------------------- Sept 15-18
Lee and Gordon's Mill, Ga --- Sept 16
McLemore's Cove, GA -- Sept 17
Ringgold, GA --- Sept 17
Owen's Ford, Chickamauga Creek, GA ------------------------------ Sept 17
Jay's Mill, GA -- Sept 18
Pea Vine Ridge, GA --- Sept 18
Alexander's Bridge, GA -- Sept 18
Reed's Bridge, GA -- Sept 18
Dyer's Ford, GA --- Sept 18
Chickamauga, GA --- Sept 19-20
Sequatchie Valley -- Sept 21
Missionary Ridge --- Sept 22
Stevenson's Gap --Sept 22
Shallow Ford Gap -- Sept 22
Chattanooga Valley --- Sept 22
Siege of Chattanooga --Sept 22 – Nov 25
Lookout Mountain --- Sept 23
Hiwassee -- Sept 26
Cotton Port Ford -- Sept 30
Anderson's Gap --- Oct 1
Valley Road near Jasper -- Oct 2

"The battle of Chickamauga was one of the best illustrations of the pluck, endurance, and prowess of the American soldier which the War afforded. Measured by the percentage of losses and the duration of the fighting of the various portions of each army, it was the deadliest battle of modern times. Its strategy will always be notable in the history of wars." - General H. V. Boynton.[1]

Our Brethren are on the Field

Part One

Chapter One

Chattanooga's Beginning

The Chattanooga area was originally settled and occupied for thousands of years by various Native American groups. Eventually the area became part of the homeland of the Cherokee in the later part of the 18th century. In 1816 John Ross settled in the area and established Ross's Landing on the Tennessee River. Ross's father had been a Scotsman and his mother was part Scottish and part Cherokee. As the settlement grew, Ross's Landing became a key center for the Cherokee and their trading partners.

As his status with the Cherokee nation rose, Ross sold his Rossville property in 1826 to Nicholas Dalton Scales, a Methodist minister and missionary. He sold his Ross's Landing Ferry to Scales and Pleasant H. Butler. Ross sold his Landing holdings in order to move to the headwaters of the Coosa River near present day Rome, Georgia, as this was the political center of the Cherokee Nation where he intended to take a more active role in the nation's leadership. Two years later Ross became the Principal Chief of the Cherokee Nation. He would continue in that role during the forced relocation of the Cherokees to lands west of the Mississippi and on through the rebuilding of the nation in Indian Territory.

The Cherokee established a government modeled after that of the United States and Ross presided over the Cherokee people through the development of the nation in the Southeast. Government wasn't all the Cherokee adopted from their white neighbors. They built homes and towns in the same fashion as whites and wore similar clothing as well.

Terms had been established in the 1785 Treaty of Hopewell that made the Cherokee Nation off limits to whites except for traders and missionaries. Nonetheless, white squatters continued to encroach on Cherokee lands. Having been educated at South West Point Academy in Tennessee, Ross was a believer in the principles of the Constitution and trusted in the U. S. Supreme Court. It was Ross's leadership that had persuaded the Cherokee nation to model its government on the standards and principals of the United States. As such, he felt that he could negotiate with Federal authorities who would treat the Cherokee as a sovereign nation thus preserving their homelands.

This was not to be the case at all. The demand of the white population for the land was a growing tidal wave and the Federal Government was determined to move the Cherokee and all Native Americans westward to accommodate that wave. Ross was equally determined to save the homeland of his people. Ross legally opposed the will of Washington, using the Treaty of Hopewell to keep the U.S. government from their objective.

However, there was another faction within the nation that represented a smaller number of Cherokees. This faction believed the only solution was to move west, creating distance between the white settlers and Indians. The leaders of this faction were Major Ridge and his sons, John and Buck. In order to circumvent Ross's opposition, President Andrew Jackson and others in Washington developed a scheme to grab the land by dealing with this minority group. Inviting Ross and his representatives as well as Ridge and his people to Washington, the government chose the leaders that were favorable to relocation as the "voice" of the Cherokee Nation.

On December 29, 1835, a small number of Cherokees, led by John Ridge and Elias Boudinot signed the Treaty of New Echota. Its legitimacy was so questionable it passed authorization by only a single vote in the U. S. Senate. This treaty opened the way for the forced removal of approximately 250,000 Cherokee, Chickasaw, Choctaw, Muscogee (Creek) and Seminole Indians, known collectively as the Five Civilized Tribes in what was to become known as the Trail of Tears.

In May of 1838 the Federal government sent General Winfield Scott and 7,000 troops to round up and forcibly remove the Native Americans from the southeastern states and begin relocating them to lands designated as Indian Territory west of the Mississippi River. Ross's Landing was used by the military as one of three large staging areas for this relocation to the west. Thus, somewhat ironically, Ross's original business endeavor became a key component for the evacuating Cherokees via the "Trail of Tears".

In 1839 Ross Landing was incorporated as Chattanooga, growing rapidly due to its desirable location and ease of transit using the navigable Tennessee River.   The original town consisted of about 240 acres and Ross's Landing was the focal point of the community and surrounding region. By 1850 the railroad arrived in Chattanooga. Not just one but three. The Western & Atlantic Railroad, the Knoxville & Chattanooga Railroad and the Nashville & Chattanooga Railroad enhanced Chattanooga's importance. These three rail lines opened a new economic system and Chattanooga became somewhat of a boom town. This role as a key transit hub would make Chattanooga a focal point throughout the Civil War.

Chapter Two

Chattanooga, a Strategic Linchpin

Colonel J. E. MacGowan commanded a regiment in the Federal Army that occupied Chattanooga during the war. He left detailed records regarding the town during the occupation including this passage describing the importance of the town to the Union.

"From 1861 forward to the end there were two main lines of invasion followed by every Federal Army that sought to penetrate the Confederacy to the southward of the Ohio. One we may call the overland line which ran to and through Chattanooga, and depended on the railroads and army wagon trains for transportation. The other, three hundred miles to the westward, we may call the water route and it depended largely on the Mississippi River and its tributaries for moving both men and supplies. In all movements on the easterly of these lines of invasion and attack Chattanooga was the major objective and when it was finally gained, at the fearful cost of Chickamauga in September and Missionary Ridge in November, 1863, a Federal loss of not less than 30,000 men killed and permanently disabled, and enormous destruction of war material, the position was regarded for its war uses and the moral effect of its transfer to the invaders as worth the sacrifice. It lay in what may be called the Middle Western section of the Confederate territory. It could be, when properly fortified, held against a great army by a single division of men. It provided a snug base from which invasion could proceed farther south. Its occupancy flanked the Confederate forces holding East Tennessee and South West Virginia, forcing them to retire in Georgia or fall back toward Richmond."

To fully understand the efforts behind both sides' efforts to control Chattanooga, one must examine more than the ultimate campaign that ended in its permanent occupation by the Union. MacGowan's quote limits the cost to the Union to those specific to Chickamauga and Missionary Ridge. The greater truth regarding the efforts to hold and capture Chattanooga began in 1862 and includes the Huntsville, Alabama campaign, the Perryville Campaign in Kentucky and the New Year's conflict of 1863 at the battle of Stones River. Additionally, from

September of 1863 through the end of the war in 1865 there were 64 separate engagements fought in the Chattanooga region.

In early 1862 the Union controlled Nashville while Chattanooga beckoned as the doorway to the Deep South. As MacGowan pointed out, the railroads were the key to moving supplies and munitions for armies that numbered as many as 100,000 men or more. By the time of the Civil War, a fourth rail line coming from Vicksburg to the east also intersected with the three original lines. Controlling these vital lines of communication was critical for both sides. By holding Chattanooga, the Confederates could block the Union invasion into Georgia while protecting one of its most important transportation routes for arms, munitions, textiles, and supplies of every nature and so vital to the Confederacy's existence. Conversely, the North could use Chattanooga as a key staging area and transportation center to support military action that would bring the South to its knees while depriving the south of these crucial supplies.

The efforts that ultimately decided Chattanooga's fate consisted of six primary campaigns and battles related to the fall of Chattanooga to the Union and its ultimate control of the city in order to use it as the necessary springboard for the invasion of the Deep South.

The first phase was the attempt of Union Major General Don Carlos Buell to approach from the west following the capture of Corinth, Mississippi. When Buell's Army of the Ohio reached Huntsville, Alabama the Confederacy responded by sending General Braxton Bragg's Army of Mississippi to Chattanooga for its defense. Bragg determined, with much prodding from fellow General Kirby Smith, that the best way to protect Chattanooga and remove the threat from Buell was to invade Kentucky and threaten the Ohio River cities of Louisville and Cincinnati, thus forcing Buell to move north in their defense. This led to the first significant conflict related to Chattanooga, the Battle of Perryville in October of 1862.

The second battle related to the Union advance on Chattanooga was the Battle of Stones River on December 31, 1862 and January 2nd, 1863. Union Major General William Rosecrans' strategic defeat of Bragg forced Bragg to withdraw from the Nashville vicinity and move further south and east in order to winter around Shelbyville and Tullahoma, Tennessee.

In the summer of 1863, General Rosecrans resumed his advance on Chattanooga. This third phase featured an almost bloodless campaign of brilliant maneuver that forced Bragg to evacuate his positions in middle Tennessee and eventually evacuate Chattanooga, retreating into the North Georgia Mountains.

The fourth phase of the campaign was the battle of Chickamauga. As Bragg retreated into north Georgia, he sent "deserters" into the Union lines to claim that the Confederate Army was in full retreat and completely demoralized. Rosecrans took the bait and quickly pursued his prey without consolidating his forces which were on three different approach avenues. Meanwhile, the First Corps of the Army of Northern Virginia, commanded by Major General James Longstreet, was arriving in north Georgia to reinforce Bragg. Additional reinforcements arrived from Mississippi to swell the ranks of Bragg's army. Now, with numbers in his favor, Bragg reversed his course and struck Rosecrans. Anything but bloodless, Chickamauga was fought over two days generating over 34,000 total casualties on both sides. That compares to 53,000 casualties during the three days of battle at Gettysburg. Had Chickamauga extended to a third day of fighting with the same casualty rate as the first two, it may have eclipsed Gettysburg as the bloodiest battle of the war. After being driven from the field by this bloodbath, Union forces retreated to Chattanooga setting the stage for the fifth phase.

Bragg moved slowly following his victory at Chickamauga. While many feel an opportunity was lost to complete the destruction of Rosecrans' demoralized and badly bruised army by a rapid pursuit and attack, Bragg's army was equally shaken and battered by the intense fighting of the battle. Instead of a hard pursuit, Bragg opted to besiege Chattanooga and starve Rosecrans' army into submission. In order to do so he positioned his army in a semi-circle around the city, anchored by the heights of Lookout Mountain on his left and Missionary Ridge on his right as he faced the city from the south. Positioned to deny resupply of the Union Army via the Tennessee River and blocking access by rail, Bragg was sure it was only a matter of time before Chattanooga would once more be in Confederate hands.

The sixth phase in this series of definable efforts is the Union breakout, engineered by General Ulysses S Grant in November of 1863. Through assaults on Lookout Mountain and Missionary Ridge Grant's forces broke Bragg's lines and sent him scurrying back into Georgia for good.

As a result of these last three actions for the control of Chattanooga, both Rosecrans and Bragg were relieved of their commands. Tens of thousands of troops were killed, wounded or missing as a consequence of the actions from September to November here.

After the Federals secured the town in November, it served as a significant military warehouse, staging area and hospital for the balance of the war. Throughout the Atlanta Campaign of 1864, Major General William T. Sherman's three armies were supplied via the Western and Atlantic railroad from the newly secured depot. This included everything from arms, munitions, rations for men, fodder for animals and everything his armies needed to support their missions. Chattanooga hospitals treated every Union soldier severely wounded during the Atlanta Campaign and continued to serve the wounded, sick and dying until the end of war.

Chapter Three

Peace to War (Under the Stars and Bars)

While the Atlantic Coastal region saw some action during the war, a majority of the conflict in the Eastern Theatre of the Civil War was confined primarily to Virginia with the exception of General Robert E. Lee's two forays into Maryland in 1862 and Pennsylvania in 1863. The Western Theatre of the war encompassed a vast landscape covering more than four hundred miles from Memphis to Knoxville, in Tennessee alone. Confederate forces were stretched thinly attempting to cover the important strategic positions In Tennessee, Alabama and Mississippi. Emphasis had to be placed on protecting the railroads and Mississippi River crossing at Vicksburg that constituted the vital lifelines of the Confederacy. The geo-political situation around Chattanooga and Knoxville added to the complexities of this requirement.

The agricultural economy surrounding Chattanooga and Eastern Tennessee was much different than the lower south where large plantations growing cotton generated significant capital and profits. The narrow valleys surrounded by rough mountainous ridges in the Chattanooga region were small and diversified in their products. Slave labor was for the most part unprofitable in eastern Tennessee so the economic forces and politics of the lower south were mostly ignored by the outlying districts of Chattanooga. However, the product of the rural community was still important due to the needs of processing plants and industry that relied on the forest and mineral resources of the region that had been developed in the 1840s.

Hence, the eastern Tennesseans found themselves more in favor of the Union and the northern cause than the slave owning powers and considerations of the lower south. Since many Tennesseans felt more aligned with Northern sentiments and had no qualms with the Union, this represented another potential threat to the Confederate cause. That sentiment would manifest itself as civil unrest and active support for the Union cause. In fact, eastern Tennessee raised a number of regiments for the United States army during the war.

Following the Tennessee state vote to secede on June 8, 1861 eastern Tennessee held its own "Union" convention on June 28, 1861 chaired by Thomas A. R. Nelson. A litany of charges including coercion, ballot tampering and worse, were lodged against the pro-secession government.[1] The convention resolved to secede from Tennessee and remain with the Union. Ironically, Confederate President Jeff Davis had to send troops to quell the potential rebellion.

In November of 1861 William Clift, a magistrate for Hamilton County and longtime member and leader of the local militia, declared himself for the Union and organized the 7th Tennessee Federal Regiment, who in turn elected him Colonel. While they had no official Federal authority they commenced guerrilla activities around the Chattanooga region. Clift was a key participant in the November plan to burn nine railroad bridges from Bristol, Tennessee to Bridgeport, Alabama on the same evening. Five were actually destroyed. On November 14, 1861 Governor Isham G, Harris issued orders for Clift's capture along with his men.

Chattanooga was clearly ill prepared to defend itself against such attacks and the bridge burning had inflamed supporters of both sides in the region. The Confederate Army sent reinforcements to better secure this key transportation hub and maintain order. The first of these was Colonel Sterling A. M. Wood and his 7th Alabama regiment. Upon arrival he immediately set out with 650 men to capture Clift and the approximately 500 men encamped with him up river on the Tennessee. As soon as Wood disembarked his troops in the area suspected of Clift's camp, he ran into another armed group and a brief engagement ensued. A number of men in both groups were wounded before Wood discovered that this other group of men was actually Home Guard troops on the same mission. Joining forces, the group moved on to Clift's camp. When they arrived they found it abandoned. Many of the Northern sympathizers had left for Kentucky to enlist in the Federal Army and Clift and some others had retreated to the mountains for safety.

Upon returning to Chattanooga on the 16th of November Wood wrote in his report to General Braxton Bragg:

"This morning (I) have moved the regiment out to the burned bridges, 15 miles, so as to get out of the way of whiskey, and to encamp among the Lincolnites. When I arrived... a Tennessee regiment without arms was just arriving all in Confusion; a general panic; everybody running up and down, and adding to the general alarm. I issued an order taking command; put the town under martial law; shut up the groceries; forbade any exit, by railroad or otherwise, without a permit from provost marshal; had every avenue guarded; arrested about twelve persons who were talking Lincolnism before I came... I have relieved all our friends in this country. All were alarmed; all are now resting easy. I have run all the Lincolnites."

Wood and his troops were withdrawn in December, as the authorities believed that his previous action had been enough to subdue the Federalists. For a period of time things returned to a more normal pattern for the town and its inhabitants.

In early 1862, after the fall of Forts Henry and Donelson, Nashville was abandoned by the Confederates. General Albert Sydney Johnston, commanding the Western forces of the Confederacy, simply didn't have the men and resources to protect the vast area he was charged with defending and, of necessity, constricted his lines to guard against losing vital communications lines. This left Nashville to the Union Army becoming the first Confederate State Capital to fall on February 25th.

Consequentially, refugees began to pour into Chattanooga on every rail car and they were soon joined by over a thousand sick and wounded Confederate soldiers being evacuated from Nashville. The army had not sent surgeons or attendants with these troops and for eight days after the first train had arrived the Confederate quartermaster for transportation, Charles W. Anderson, struggled to care for them even though the community had risen to the challenge and was doing all they could to accommodate the soldiers' needs. Anderson reported:

"When the first train arrived with some three hundred on board, they were in a most pitiable condition. They had been stowed away in box and cattle cars for eighteen hours, without fires, and without any

attention other than such as they were able to render each other. Tears filled the eyes of many at the depot when these poor fellows were taken from the cars, so chilled and benumbed that a majority of them were helpless. Two other trains came the following day with men in the same condition. Three soldiers were found dead in the cars, one died in the depot before removal, and another died on the way to the hospital.

"The removal of these soldiers from the hospitals at Nashville was a military necessity; but why they were sent, unaccompanied or preceded by a proper corps of surgeons, medical supplies, and hospital attendants, I never knew. It was eight days after their arrival in Chattanooga before I was relieved of the responsibility for them. In that time, six more were buried, and the number of deaths would have been far greater, but for the attendance of Chattanooga physicians, among who I specially remember, Dr. P. D. Sims and Dr. Milo Smith. It was not until General Floyd's Division reached Chattanooga that the hospitals were taken charge of by any army surgeons."[2]

Mrs. Benjamin Hardin Helm was a refugee who had stayed on in Chattanooga during this time. She was the sister-in-law of Abraham Lincoln and wife of a Confederate General. Mrs. Helm immediately enlisted herself with the task of gathering materials and securing volunteers to sew cloth to cots so that wounded Confederate soldiers didn't have to sleep on the floors of the makeshift hospitals. Years later she described her experiences:

"The refugees came from the trains into the little dingy reception room (at Chattanooga) to wait, sometimes for hours, for a room, looking so worried, with baskets, bundles and dilapidated valises surrounding them. Sometimes there would be a mother with a sleeping child in her arms, and others on the hard floor, with little or nothing to eat, ennuied to death. As they waited, I would go in, with brass thimbles, needles and threads, and cotton sacks on my arm and inquire if there was anyone among them who would sew a little on the cots so much needed for the suffering soldiers. Every fagged woman would brighten up at the idea of being useful, and sew diligently until time for them to continue their journey. A great deal was thus accomplished. Among the ladies who passed through I remember Miss Henrietta Johnston,

daughter of General Albert Sidney Johnston, and his daughter-in-law, Mrs. William Preston Johnston, on their way to Virginia, who willingly lent helping hands. A lady in the hotel helped greatly, I am so sorry I cannot remember her name – I went to her room one morning to cut out the sacks; the little (stale) room, combined with the poor food I had tried to eat for breakfast, made me faint. There was no stimulant at hand, so Mr. Brooks, after tearing around the hospital in great fashion, found a man with a bottle of Hostetter's Bitters, which without the ceremony of adding water, they poured down my throat. It would have resuscitated the dead. I think we cut out about twelve hundred sacks."[3]

While the mountainous topography surrounding Chattanooga was a deterrent to the movement of large armies and their requisite supplies, the city was still vulnerable to attack from Nashville. General John B. Floyd was ordered with 2,500 troops to defend the town, arriving there March 8th 1862. He reported to his superiors that it would require at least 6,000 men to make the approaches to the town invulnerable. Those troops weren't available so, still fearing attack from Nashville, Generals Johnston and Kirby Smith (commander of eastern Tennessee troops) ordered that the approaches be carefully guarded while supplies held in the town at that time were transferred by rail to Atlanta.

At this specific point in the war, the Union Command was primarily focused on capturing the Confederate stronghold of Corinth, Mississippi, another crucially important rail junction. Major General Ulysses S. Grant's Army of the Tennessee was to lead the attack on Corinth from his base at Pittsburg Landing 135 miles southwest of Nashville on the Tennessee River. To prevent rebel reinforcements in the southeast from reaching the Corinth area, Major General Don Carlos Buell, U. S. commander of the Army of the Ohio devised a plan to have General Ormsby B. Mitchell move toward and capture Huntsville, Alabama and hold that place if possible. Occupying Huntsville, approximately midway between Chattanooga and Corinth, would block rail access to Mississippi and engage Confederate forces along the Alabama, Tennessee and Georgia borders.

Another component of the plan to disrupt Confederate reinforcements from Atlanta involved a group of 22 Union soldiers in civilian clothes and a civilian named William Hunter Campbell. These men were led by another civilian, Federal scout and spy, James J. Andrews. The story of the Andrews' Raiders and the "Great Locomotive Chase" was one of the most daring missions of the war.

Before the Federal plan to capture Corinth could be executed, the Confederates, under Albert Sidney Johnston, attacked Grant's forces at Pittsburg Landing resulting in the battle known more familiarly as Shiloh. Hard fought over the two days of April 6 and 7, the bloodiest battle of the war to that point was won by Grant and the Union. Not only were the Confederate forces beaten back by the end of the fighting, they lost General Albert Sidney Johnston who was mortally wounded on the first day of the battle. The man thought by many to be the most talented military leader in the Confederacy might have been saved had his attendants applied the tourniquet he had in his own pocket. With his femoral artery severed by a Union bullet Johnston died within minutes. The enormity of the casualties from this battle was stunning. In this one fight the combined losses of over 23,000 killed, wounded or missing were greater than the totals for the entire Revolutionary War. As a result the Northern forces moved much more cautiously and deliberately toward Corinth, digging in and fortifying each day after modest advances. Corinth wouldn't be captured for almost two months. Ultimately, the outnumbered Confederates abandoned the town on May 29th, 1862.

Axel Reed was a member of the 2nd Minnesota Volunteer Infantry, USA. The day after Corinth was captured he wrote the following in his diary providing a sense of frustration at having not actually attacked the enemy:

...The siege of Corinth, Mississippi, where nearly a hundred thousand rebels had gathered under able generals and as many union troops gathered under Generals Grant, Halleck, Buell, Thomas, Pope, Logan, McCook, Sherman and others, to conquer our rebellious citizens and take the inland city, and, after nearly two month's skirmish fighting, building breast works, trenches, nearly two months the rebel army, under Gen. Bragg, evacuated Corinth and sneaked away one night,

May 29th, and that evening the rebels kept up a beating of drums which sounded close to our lines. A brass band came out to our front about 11 o'clock at night and played "Dixie Land." May 30th, the morning was bright and warm as summer; the soldiers waked without reveille, as no drums were allowed to beat on our side; a little after daylight a number of reports were heard to the southwest of bursting shells, some thought it meant a day of bloody work, but in our part of camp it was thought to be the blowing up of magazines within the rebel lines and that evacuation was taking place. Our true General, Rob. McCook, ordered the 18th Regulars and the 35th Ohio forward to feel of the enemy and the 2nd Minn. and the 9th Ohio in reserve, and in a few minutes came orders for us to march. Every man felt that he had a great duty to perform and that he might not see another so bright a morning, but for all that some were laughing and seemingly feeling joyous and joking among themselves and unconcerned, but there was an inward feeling that no one but those who have experienced such occasions know. (We) Marched by the flank, passing through woods until we came to a creek that had been contended for by rebels on account of water. Now we came to the foot of a ridge with the timber all felled for an 'abattis' or an obstruction to an enemy approaching the breastworks. We formed in line of battle and passed on toward the noted town of Corinth, passing the rubbish of a rebel camp piled up in piles and torpedoes placed inside so they might explode. One or two of them exploded, hurting one of our men. Thus after a siege of nearly two months with Gen. Grant's and Buell's army combined, a poor empty town is our reward. The siege of Corinth has proved a great mistake on the part of our generals. The enemy should have been attacked by all means. Reports were brought in by negroes that the rebels were shipping big black guns off on the cars a week before the evacuation, but our generals would not hear to a negro. What is Corinth or any other place as long as a rebel army exists ready to strike us a fatal blow and kill many of our men? Nothing. Their army is what we want to conquer, then we can secure the union as it was when good men will rise up in the south and form a Union; that the whole desire is not to enslave the negro race.

Prior to the fall of Corinth on April 11th, General Mitchell had captured Huntsville, Alabama, severing the Memphis and Charleston

Railroad, the only line at that time that ran from the Mississippi River to the east. In order to better secure his position Mitchell used the 15 locomotives and numerous cars he captured there to begin extending his control of the railroad. In the coming weeks his troops moved almost 70 miles to the east and west on the line prohibiting Confederate reinforcement by rail.

On April 12th, Andrews and his "Raiders" captured a train and cars on the tracks at Big Shanty (now Kennesaw, Georgia) and began their mission to destroy rails and burn bridges between that place and Chattanooga.

The execution of the Raiders part of the plan had begun to unfold a few days before all the excitement. The group of twenty four participants, having broken up into groups of 2 or 3, made their way to Chattanooga where they were to buy tickets and proceed south to Marietta, Georgia. The men assembled at the depot in Chattanooga. If challenged, their cover story was that they were from Kentucky and on their way to join Confederate forces.

Upon reaching Marietta the men checked into the hotel and went to sleep immediately. Early the next morning Andrews briefed them all on the plan and instructed them to buy tickets to numerous stops along the way to Chattanooga. This would avoid the potential suspicion that might be conjured up by a large group of men traveling to the same destination.

When the train stopped for breakfast at Big Shanty the passengers and crew departed but Andrews' men remained on board. Once the others were clear, Andrews and another of the Raiders climbed into the General, the train's engine. The others uncoupled the cars behind the first three and they were off, but their plan was about to start unraveling.

The group's first setback was minor but perhaps a harbinger of things to come. No sooner were they out of sight of the depot but the General started to slow. The departing engineer had closed the dampers when he left for breakfast. Discovering the problem, the dampers were quickly opened and the General was off again.

In the meantime, the original conductor of the General, William Allen Fuller, had begun his pursuit of his stolen locomotive with two others. At first they were on foot. Within a short distance of Big Shanty they came across a work crew and commandeered their hand car. While the likelihood of catching a locomotive using these methods of pursuit seemed highly improbable, the route between Atlanta and Chattanooga was quite hilly and the average speed was just 15 miles an hour for a locomotive. Combined with stops and delays along the way, Fuller was confident of catching up.

At Etowah, Fuller commandeered the small locomotive Yonah, which was on a siding and under full steam. Andrews had failed to destroy this engine as they passed. This error would become the key to his ultimate undoing. Now with a locomotive of his own and recruiting others to aid in his pursuit of the Raiders, Fuller moved up the line in rapid pursuit.

The first major delay for Andrews occurred when the General got to Kingston, Georgia. To this point he had been able to tell small station masters that he had an urgent ammunition train that had been ordered to Chattanooga as quickly as possible by General Beauregard. This story had worked until he reached Kingston where the station master, having telegraph communication with Chattanooga, had been ordered that all additional southbound trains were to have priority. While Andrews had planned for the normal southbound train schedule from Chattanooga, he did not know of these additional emergency southbound trains being generated due to Mitchell's capture of Huntsville. He was delayed at Kingston for over an hour.

By the time he was on the move north again Fuller was only minutes behind him. Arriving at Kingston, Fuller switched to the engine William R. Smith which was on a sidetrack leading west to Rome, Georgia. In no time he was again speeding north in pursuit. Once north of Kingston Andrews had stopped briefly to tear up the rail behind him in order to slow his pursuers. When Fuller reached the breach, two miles south of Adairsville, he was forced again to move on foot until he came across the locomotive Texas which was heading south from Calhoun. Commandeering Texas, he began the pursuit again while running the locomotive in reverse.

The Raiders were too inexperienced and, lacking the proper equipment or training, struggled to do severe damage to the rails behind them. It had also begun to rain. This meant their efforts to burn bridges were likewise in vain. By now, the pursuers were so close that attempts to tear up the tracks were impossible. They couldn't stop for wood so the sides and floors of the cars were used for fuel in the firebox. As things became more desperate, the last two cars were uncoupled in successive order in hopes that they might derail Texas. Fuller masterfully engaged the cars and pushed them out of the way. Finally the last car was set afire and uncoupled on one of the bridges in hopes that it would start the barnlike cover ablaze.

This, too, failed and the Raiders, who had lost all confidence, were afraid that the entire countryside had been alerted to their actions. Knowing that the mission had failed, Andrews burned his papers in the firebox and told the Raiders to abandon the train with each man "on his own". As a last resort as they were abandoning, the General was put in reverse and sent back toward Texas in hopes that it might wreck the pursuing locomotive, but to no avail. The Raiders then split up and fled into the countryside.

News of Mitchell taking Huntsville, less than 100 miles to the west, combined with an urgent telegraph from the conductor of the stolen locomotive headed north with an unknown number of Yankees as part of the scheme to cut Chattanooga off from the rest of the south, had sent a nervous population into a near panic. Every able bodied man was pressed into service and every means possible was put to use in order to evacuate civilians to the countryside and mountains.

Some sense of relief came when word was received in Chattanooga of the capture of the train being operated by the Raiders, just over a dozen miles south of town. Now a posse was organized to hunt down the Union Raiders who had abandoned the stalled train near Graysville, Georgia. Even though the Raiders had split up in order to enhance their chances of individual escape, all were eventually captured.

Upon capture they were brought to Chattanooga for questioning before being sent south to Atlanta. In the end, eight of the Raiders including Andrews were hanged in Atlanta. Eight others escaped and six were ultimately exchanged as prisoners of war. Nineteen of the Raiders were the first United States soldiers to be awarded the new Medal of Honor.

Chattanooga's first sincere introduction to combat came less than two months later on June 7, 1862 when Brigadier General James Negley's 7th Brigade of the Department of the Ohio appeared on the north bank of the Tennessee across from the city. He unlimbered artillery and opened fire on the town. The Confederate batteries returned fire. This continued until dark. The next morning the bombardment recommenced for several hours before Negley withdrew his troops.

Confederate D. M. Key participated in this action and wrote to his wife on June 10th:

"In my last I believe I told you that the cavalry of the enemy and perhaps other forces were on the opposite bank of the river. On the morning of the day on which I wrote their infantry made its appearance in range of our cannon and it opened fire upon them. This was about 5 o'clock P. M. No sooner did it find three batteries of the enemy artillery opened on our batteries...

"The cannon played on each other from then till dark the sharpshooters of both armies in the meantime firing at each other across the river. Night ended the conflict. We had 3 men wounded and none killed. The wounded will get well. Our folks, it is said, killed one Colonel and one Captain and some four or five others. The next morning Maj. Genl. Smith having arrived we were ordered to move from our camp near Col. Brabsons on to Cameron Hill and to support our batteries. This we did about 9 o'clock A.M. At 9:12 o'clock the cannon of the enemy again opened upon our camp near Brabsons and on the town (in) general.

"They threw shells and balls all through Market Street and over the town and far beyond the Crutchfield House. Our guns remained in perfect silence Gen. Smith having ordered them not to fire until he ordered them to do so. The enemy ceased firing about 12 o'clock and commenced a hasty retreat. They are said to have crossed Walden's Ridge and to be marching up Sequatchie Valley.

18

"Our Cavalry has crossed the River and been sent in pursuit. The enemy are said to have numbered 7,000 by the most reliable accounts. Some put them at 15,000. On this side we had at the commencement of the firing one artillery Co. and Regiment of Cavalry besides my own command and some cavalry. On Sunday, notwithstanding they thundered their cannon on the town and camps. No one was so much as scratched. Several houses were hit by their balls, but no considerable damage was done. No notice was given for women and children to leave, still most of them left without telling. They threw shot and shell all over the camp we had occupied near Brabsons, but fortunately for us they had fired after we left it. In short the enemy fled in haste, having done very little damage. They robbed and stole everything belonging to citizens on the other side of the River, took all Southern men prisoners and carried them off with them.

"We are still on Cameron Hill without tents or baggage. We roll up on the hill side and sleep as we can having nothing in the world but bread and meat to eat. Yet the boys do not complain and seem in fine spirits."[4]

Following the Union occupation of Corinth, General Don Carlos Buell moved his Army of the Ohio east with expectations that he would capture Chattanooga and liberate eastern Tennessee. During the last week in June he had established his headquarters at Huntsville. This close proximity of the Army of the Ohio was cause for much concern in Chattanooga. Confederate General Kirby Smith was not at all optimistic about being able to hold a line from Chattanooga to the Cumberland Gap with a mere 5,000 men.

Our Brethren are on the Field

Part Two

Chapter Four

The Confederate Kentucky Campaign and Perryville

Smith was responsible for the defense of Chattanooga while headquartered in Knoxville. He also sought glory and fame, something that was not available in the eastern Tennessee region south of the Cumberland Gap. He had bombarded both Richmond and General Bragg, in Mississippi, with continuous pleas for reinforcements in order to hold Chattanooga against the imminent attack of Buell not far to the west of the city. Richmond had sent 6,000 reinforcements and Bragg a few thousand as well, but Smith insisted that unless Bragg could arrive with his Army of Mississippi, there would be no chance of saving the town. The 34th Georgia Infantry had been formed in May, 1862 and ordered to Chattanooga as part of the troops to reinforce Smith. George H. Burns was a member of that new regiment and wrote home early in the month of June not even a month after having enlisted:

From Jefferson Tenn early June 1862

> *Dear wife and children, I am well though much worn out with our late travails. We have been on a mighty stretch of late trying to keep out the yankeys from you. We have to guard this place & reinforce up above when necessary. If I get my bounty money shortly I will get a 24 hours furlow & come home and see you. When you write again, write how you are getting along & how my truck looks and all about it. I want to see you all very bad. We are getting nearly mad enough to fight good. They have dragged us about lately until we are getting good mad. I hope we will see a better time soon when we will live at home in peace and be free again. Be sure and write. I expect I will have the measles. We are ordered to Knoxville I will write from there.*

In Huntsville a Union soldier, Adelbert Childs, of the 33rd Ohio wrote home about the same time. The 33rd had marched through Kentucky and Tennessee arriving to reinforce Buell's force when Childs wrote to his sister:

June 18th 62
Camp Tailor Huntsville Alabama

Dear sister I reseved your leter of the 5th yesterday. Im glad to here that you are all well. Im still among the living. We have bin on a scouting expedition for the last 16 days. We are nearly worn out. I don't know when we wil get back to camp again. It is very warm here and We sleep in the the woods. It sootes first rate. The rebels are like snakes in the grass. They get behind trees logs stumps and branches and shoot our pickets and strip them of everything and leave them for the fouls to devour. We are on one side of the Tennessee River and them on the other. We shoot at one nother curse one nother then one steped out from behind a tree shot at me and then asked me to come over and dine with him. We exchanged fire a few times but the river is (so) wide that it does no good Mutch. Tell miss hale not to be backward but write to me and I will anser it. Some how I undersand that you got the $35 that I sent. Tell Fred he had beter be in hell than to take old Bill. I will have the ___ list in time for him. Well I got the nice verse you sent. It was very well. You must learn to write so you can write to me, So take good care of mi horse until I come home.

I can't think of any more so no more now. So Good by
Direct to Huntsville Alabama
33 Reg Co. H
Oh you must take you care of mary mi sweet little sister.

George H Burns of the 34th Georgia wrote again to his wife on the 22nd of June to let her know he had "seen the elephant":

Chattanooga June the 22nd, 1862

Dear wife, I can inform you that I am well & hope this will find you well. As I wrote to you that we had marching orders, we left hear Fryday evening & went down the Nashville road about 18 miles. We were marched down the hill to the edge of the river bottom and here we rolled up in our blankets & spent the night not knowing what the next day would bring. We got up the next morning expecting to fight soon. We could hear the sharp crack of the rifles. The picket guards were firing across the river about a half mile below us. We were then formed in line and marched down the river three quarters of a mile. We then halted to await further orders. While we were hear our men brought one poor fellow by us, shot in the thigh. I think he will die shortly. After this we heard sharp firing across the river. In a few minutes our pickets came by with a yankey captain & two privates prisoners & one yankey shot 5 or 6 times. I begin to think this was the elephant I had heard of. We thought the enemy were about 12 thousand strong. We had our battery planted on this side of the river to protect us as we crossed over. Two regiments crossed below & came up the other side. They charged the enemies batteries & took them. They fell back to Jasper without firing a cannon. At this time Gen. Ledbetter received a dispatch from General Smith at Knoxville that our forces had fell back from Cumberland gap & for him to bring his forces back hear & await further orders. So we are expecting orders to go to Knoxville. If we had not got this order we would have broken up the den of them. They have ruined the country over there. They have taken all the poor peoples provisions & left them to suffer. This is in Marion county Tennessee where we went. We got back hear last night about 12 o'clock. Jeff has got about well. He came down to us yesterday morning & stayed with us until we came back. I think the chance for me to get off is a bad one but I will do all I can to get off. Nancy you don't know how bad I want to see you. I dreamed of you and father's folks the other night while I lay under the boughs of a tree far from home & in the enemies country. I felt bad when I awoke as you may suppose. Then I prayed for protection & that it might be impressed on all you to pray the next day for my protection. Then I knew I was on a just cause fighting for you and my old father, mother, and sisters. I must close. Farewell Dear wife.

Your own dear G. H. Burns.

Six days later, Burns had already marched to Knoxville and back to Chattanooga. Homesick and exhausted he had this to say:

Chattanooga Tenn.

June 28th 1862

My Dear wife, father, mother, brother, sisters, We are well & hope this will find you all well. We came back hear last Thursday from

Knoxville. We only stayed there two nights and one day. The enemy fell back from where they were. We got a dispatch that the enemy was reinforced by five thousand and were marching on Chattanooga. We are hear waiting for an attack from them. I don't think there will be any fight hear soon, though we heard fire of cannon yesterday evening in the direction of Shellmound, about 18 miles below hear. We did not (see) any of William's or Bob's folks as we went or came. We got a letter from Jane a few days ago. She wants us to come up some day to take dinner. I am going to get a pass one day for 24 hours and go up & see her. She said her & Robert was going down to your house about the 16th of next month. We sent our things to Dalton from Knoxville. They are at Frank Jackson's. Some of you go up the first chance you have & get a key that will unlock the box & get them. I sent my satchel, Jeff sent two shirts, a pair of pants and a pair of drawers.

We are beginning to see the Elephant. We got to sleep last night for the first good nights sleep in a week. I feel much worn out after so much running about. Its no use to tell you that I want to see you for I can't tell you anything about it when I think back of the last happy days and then of my present condition. I wonder Oh shall I ever live happy anymore. May God help me through this struggle & to live in peace with you again. Nancy I don't know whether I will get to come home or not. I will do all in my power to come. You need not send me any more socks. We are not allowed anything more than we can carry. Write to me. We have not had any letter in over a week. I must close for the present. Farewell dear wife.

G H Burns

Our things are in O.D. Keith's box at Dalton

To discourage Buell from advancing on Chattanooga by disrupting his supply communications, two daring cavalry raids were commenced by the Confederates.

John Hunt Morgan was to lead 900 troopers out of Knoxville into Kentucky disrupting Federal lines of communication and dispensing healthy doses of panic among the population. He was also to recruit as many southern men as he could to his brigade from among the Kentuckians. Morgan was tremendously successful in accomplishing his mission. Between July 4th and the 9thth Morgan's men road through Sparta, Tennessee, then Lebanon, Kentucky reaching Tompkinsville, Kentucky. There they surrounded the 400 man Federal garrison and captured them all. Thirty miles north of Tompkinsville he reached the Louisville and Nashville telegraph line where he sent false information stating that he intended to attack Louisville and Cincinnati, Ohio. On the 17th of July he approached Cynthiana, Kentucky a rail depot south of Cincinnati. Here he captured the garrison and 300 much needed horses. Panic was spreading throughout the region with cries for reinforcements and recruits in Louisville and Cincinnati reaching a crescendo.

Concurrently, Nathan Bedford Forrest was on his own mission. With 1,000 cavalrymen he left Chattanooga on July 6th bent on disrupting Buell's supply lines with the ultimate target being the large Federal depot at Murfreesboro, Tennessee. On July 13th he implemented a three pronged attack on that place. Combining tactics and a little chicanery, he convinced the 1,200 man garrison to surrender, including Brigadier General Thomas T. Crittenden. He also bagged 50 wagons, their teams and approximately $250,000 in valuable supplies.

Still Buell maintained his position, feeling out the advances to Chattanooga.

Finally, Bragg capitulated to the constant calls for reinforcements by Kirby Smith and moved his 35,000 man army to Chattanooga, the advance units arriving on July 27th. When Smith and Bragg met to plan their strategy, Smith had taken a stance that he should move through the Cumberland Gap and into northern Kentucky as a way to capture some of the glory he sought. Bragg thought it best to combine forces and get behind Buell's army in central Tennessee. On the 31st the two ultimately agreed to support each other and begin a vague campaign with Bragg's objective remaining Buell's army and Smith's objective the Ohio River.

Captain Charles Swett commanded the Warren Light Artillery Battery, attached to Hardee's Corp in Bragg's army. The battery had been formed in Vicksburg and began service in August of 1861 serving with the Army of Mississippi and Army of Tennessee through the duration of the war. After retiring from the siege of Corinth, Swett wrote in his memoirs:

> On July 24th 1862, the battery and other artillery of Hardee's command started for Chattanooga, (infantry going by rail) which place we reached August 19th. On the 26th, the battery was assigned to Liddell's Brigade, and remained with it until he was sent to Mobile, and Col. D.C. Govan was made a Brigadier, with whom the company remained until the "Closing scene".

On August 9th, 1862, Smith began to implement his plan of moving rapidly into Kentucky. He informed Bragg of his intention to move past the flank of the 10,000 Union forces in the gap under General George W. Morgan, cutting him off from Lexington. He marched out of Knoxville on the 13th of August with 9,000 men, leaving Carter Stevenson's Division to face Morgan's troops at the gap. By the 18th he had flanked Morgan and placed his forces squarely in Morgan's rear at Barboursville. Morgan, realizing he was precariously positioned, withdrew from the gap. Smith informed Bragg of his success and that he would proceed directly to Lexington in order to resupply and create a diversion for Bragg's movements.

By the time Smith approached Richmond, Kentucky, twenty miles south of Lexington, he had already encountered more resistance than he thought he might. Prisoners also informed him that heavy reinforcements were expected by August 23rd. In spite of an expected hostile reception, Smith was in need of resupplying his army and pushing on to Lexington was the only way he could achieve that resupply.

On the 24th of August he sent a message to Bragg, suggesting that he move his army north through the Cumberland Gap and join him in an advance to the banks of the Ohio, thus distracting Buell from eastern Tennessee. Bragg complied, moving his forces out of Chattanooga on the 29th of August.

While headed north into Kentucky, Bragg's headquarters remained in Chattanooga. The post commandant, General Sam Jones, was responsible for gathering needed supplies and forage for the Army of Mississippi as well as repairing, maintaining and protecting the rail lines. He also was responsible for providing additional army hospital capability. The Crutchfield House, once the largest hotel accommodation in Chattanooga, had been serving as a hospital since the abandonment of Nashville, but was now officially taken over by the army and renamed Ford Hospital. Further increasing hospital capabilities, several large warehouses were commandeered and the upper floors were converted into hospitals. The open doors and windows between the warehouse buildings provided for significant airflow on the upper floors making conditions more bearable for the wounded and sick.

During the month of August a Confederate newspaper was also established and the people of Chattanooga were buoyed by reports of successes such as Lee's victory at Second Manassas (Bull Run) in Virginia and Bragg's advance into Kentucky.

On August 30th, Smith's command did battle with Brigadier General Mahlon D. Manson's forces about 7 miles south of Richmond, Kentucky. The fight lasted the entire day, with Federal Major General William "Bull" Nelson arriving midafternoon to take charge of Manson's troops. Most of Manson's troops were raw recruits who had been cobbled together in Louisville for the defense of the state when Smith began his invasion. Although green, the Union boys fought hard and gave ground grudgingly until late in the afternoon when two Confederate brigades were able to turn both Federal flanks routing them through Richmond and beyond toward Lexington. During the fight "Bull" Nelson was wounded and taken captive among the 4,000 troops Smith claimed to capture, along with 10,000 stands of arms, nine artillery pieces and a complete wagon train full of supplies.

The result of this fight was that there were no effective units left to resist Smith in eastern Kentucky. He moved his headquarters to Lexington and sent cavalry troops to occupy Frankfort, the state capital. To this point Kirby Smith had been aggressive and successful.

Now he went on the defensive to await Bragg and see how Buell would respond.

By mid-August Buell had determined that Confederate cavalry raids had damaged his vital rail lines to a degree that he could no longer maintain his position in the Huntsville and Decatur, Alabama area. He consequently determined to move north to McMinnville, Tennessee. This way he could block any movement by Bragg toward Nashville. When Bragg moved north from Chattanooga on the 29th marching up the Sequatchie Valley headed for Kentucky he was only 20 miles east of McMinnville. This was easy striking distance for Buell. Confused as to Bragg's intentions, instead of moving to close with him Buell headed northwest to Murfreesboro, arriving there on September 5th. He was now just 35 miles south of Nashville but his communication lines were still tenuous. Confederate cavalry Raiders had broken the rails north of Nashville that ran from that city to Louisville making resupply difficult. He now retired to Nashville, even further from Bragg's north bound army, before continuing north towards Louisville.

Recruiting efforts in the north continued to bring fresh troops to the armies of the Union, including Buell's army of the Ohio. The 117th Illinois regiment had been newly formed and was in their camp of instruction at this point of the campaign. It would soon join Buell's ranks. One of its new recruits, Vincent Messler, wrote home to his parents explaining why he closed his business and volunteered.

Camp Butler Sep 6 1862

Dear Father & Mother and to all. I am well or nearly so and hope this may find you all enjoying good health. I Rec a letter from you day before yesterday. It was sent from Rosemond here by the post master. You need not send any more letters to Rosemond. I also see a letter from Charles. I am in camp now near Springfield, Illinois called Camp Butler. You said you was sorry that I enlisted. I don't want any body to feel sorry for me for I think I ought to go. My life isn't worth any more than anyone else is and I go to my countrys call for I think it needs me.

I started the 12th day of August. I don't know how long we will be here but not long. I guess we had a election day before yesterday to elect a few more officers. They were most all elected the first day but the company wasn't quite full then and elected the rest since. They elected me drummer so I suppose I will have to beat the drum. I told you I would send you some money but haven't sent it yet. I let a fellow have one hundred dollars in Rosemond. The man I left my business with to settle up. He is a good fellow. I have known him for 4 years.

I just shut up my shop and started off. I would like very well to (have) seen all my folks first but I was afraid it would be to late if I undertook to go to NI for I wouldn't be drafted for anything. I made up my mind long ago they never would have the chance to draft me. There is about 6 or 8 thousand men here comeing and leaving all the time. I suppose our Regiment will leave soon for dixie. It is the 115th Regiment Illinois Volunteers. We drill every day morning and afternoon.

I have nearly $300 comeing to me in Rosemond. I would like to send it to you if I could conveniently. There is or has been about 2,500 Rebels prisoners here but they say they are all going to leave tomorrow. It is raining a little now but it has been very dry here for 6 or 8 weeks.

Write soon

Direct to Vincent Messler
115th Regiment Ills. Vounteers
In care of Captain J. W. Lapham
Camp Butler Illinois

I hope we will all meet again on earth but we cant all expect to live through the war and I think it has just commenced the way things look now and if it is my fate to be one of the killed I hope to live again in a better world (where) War is no more forever.

From your affectionate son
Vincent Messler
Excuse poor writing for I have to write on the ground.

Meanwhile, Bragg continued north to Glasgow, Kentucky arriving there on the 14th of September. Staying parallel to Bragg's force, Buell arrived in Bowling Green Kentucky 30 miles to the west on the same day. Now Bragg determined that Smith should join him and together strike out to capture Louisville. If they could gain this crucial Ohio River City before Buell could reinforce the garrison it would not only cripple Buell's army but send a terrible panic through the north.

He began his movement in that direction on the 15th but a stubborn Union commander, John T. Wilder of the 17th Indiana Volunteer Infantry stationed at Fort Craig, Munfordville, Kentucky, delayed his advance for two days. Captain Swett recalled the events of Bragg's capture of the garrison of Fort Craig on September 17th:

Sept. 16th, at Rowlett's Station, near Woodsonville, we found a Federal Fort and troops, commander's name not remembered. Bragg demanded surrender of Fort Craig, as it was called, which was refused, and we were ordered to open on the fort at day-light Sept. 17th. Our position was very elevated, being on a ridge, and every shot would have plunged into the enclosure. This was nine months to the day since we had a brush with Siegel, and on almost the exact spot. Daylight came and we were waiting to hear artillery fire, being satisfied we were not the only company with instructions like our own. The sun appeared and perfect quiet was in possession, still we thought best to burn no powder. In a few minutes an officer on horseback rushed up and gave the information that the fort surrendered at 1 O'clock A.M.!! We thought things, said nothing and joined our brigade without the stain of murder on our hands.

Bragg seemed to be in no hurry, believing Buell still to be in Bowling Green. It was not so. Buell had been on the move again. The now close proximity of the armies to each other presented another opportunity to strike a powerful blow by one or the other. Bragg held a strong defensive position and Buell had numerical superiority but neither seemed to want to engage the other.

While Buell and Bragg continued their evasive dance of maneuver Swett wrote of the 20th:

Sept. 20th, we were in line of battle expecting Buell, till 3 P.M. Buell failed to put in an appearance and we again took up the line of march northward.

Bragg now moved northeast toward Bardstown and Buell rapidly marched on to Louisville, arriving there on the 25th. He had beaten Bragg to the key river city, assuring its security against Confederate attack. Buell was lauded in the northern press for saving the day. Bragg had, for his part, drawn Buell out of Alabama and central Tennessee, away from Chattanooga, earning some laurels of his own at this point.

When Bragg reached Bardstown the supplies he had requested sent from Lexington were not there. In fact, Smith had not left Lexington to join him as ordered. Smith had determined that Bragg could take Louisville on his own and stayed put. Now with only three days' supply and operating in a parched countryside due to a summer long draught, Bragg was forced to send troops on far ranging missions to forage for sustenance. He left his troops in place at this point and rode to meet with Smith in Lexington in order to decide what they should do next. Both Bragg and Smith had expected that the southern sympathizers in Kentucky would welcome them with open arms and enlist in their army to swell the ranks. While welcomed by many sympathetic Kentuckians, recruits did not materialize in anything like significant numbers. Bragg decided that since Frankfort was currently in their hands he would install the provisional officials that had been appointed by the Confederacy in 1861 prior to being run out of the state by Union forces. This way he could claim Kentucky for the southern cause followed by creating a conscription act in order to enlarge his army.

Buell also had to contend with some troublesome circumstances himself. When he arrived in Louisville he was no longer in his Department of Tennessee where he commanded. He was now in the district commanded by General H. G. Wright and it took a number of days to sort out who would assume command. In the end, the war department weighed in on the side of Buell. In Washington, Lincoln had been furious that Buell had done nothing to prohibit Bragg and Smith from roaming unopposed in the state of Kentucky. In fact,

General in Chief Halleck had written the order relieving Buell of command but the public sentiment for Buell at this point was running very high. He was the hero who just saved Louisville and Cincinnati from falling to the Confederacy. Again, Buell received a reprieve. There was also a shakeup in command within his forces when General Jefferson C. Davis (no relation to the Confederate president) shot and killed "Bull" Nelson in an argument. (Nelson had been released after his earlier capture and rejoined the Army of the Ohio.) Davis was arrested and turned over to the civil authorities and Nelson was gone creating two significant leadership gaps.

A few days settled these issues. Buell was now reenergized in his efforts to bring Bragg to battle and eliminate the Confederate presence in Kentucky. He set out on October 1st to bag the Confederates by cutting off their line of retreat to the south trapping them between his army and the Ohio River.

Axel Reed of the 2nd Minnesota penned these lines in his diary regarding Buell's movements from Corinth to Louisville and on to Perryville:

"... General Buell's army separated from General Grant's and marched east through northern Alabama to east Tennessee, nearly two hundred miles, to capture or disperse Gen. Bragg's rebel army, concentrated at Chattanooga, which gave our army the slip and got several days head start by forced marches to the north, passing through the entire states of Tennessee and Kentucky, to within a few miles of Louisville, and we marching a few miles west and behind our enemy, passing through Nashville, Bowling Green, Ky., where we came up to the rebel army and it was said that Gen. Thomas and other Union generals wanted to fight there and then; but General Buell would not and let the invading army of Bragg's escape, going further north to capture Louisville and Cincinnati. Marching forty miles a day in a more northwesterly direction to the Ohio river and taking boats, we arrived at Louisville in time to save that city from capture. We then marched against the enemy in a leisurely manner, allowing the rebel army to gather all the forage, provision and plunder they desired until one of our divisions, commanded by a fighting general, overtook them at Perryville, Ky., and brought on that memorable battle. "

On October 2nd, Bragg learned of an advance toward Frankfort via a route through Shelbyville northeast of Bragg's main force bivouacked at Bardstown. Buell's main force, in fact, was headed south toward Bardstown in order to attack Bragg there. Bragg ordered Smith to leave Lexington and bring his 10,000 men to Frankfort while ordering Polk, in charge of the troops at Bardstown, to move north and strike the Federal flank as they proceeded east.

Polk's cavalry patrols had informed him of Buell's true intent. Knowing the very real risk at hand he withdrew toward Bryantsville where a supply depot had been established rather than expose his own flank by following orders. Meanwhile Bragg continued to be consumed with the attempted installation of the provisional government in Frankfort. Finally, the heavy skirmishing to the west of the city convinced him that he could not protect the provisional government. At that point everything quickly fell apart. Now Bragg retreated south from Frankfort to join Polk. Kirby Smith was ordered to stop his retreat at the Kentucky River near Versailles. Polk and Hardee remained divided by more than 20 miles and both were ordered to consolidate near Harrodsburg. Bragg would then rejoin his now united force, turn back to the north, combine with Smith and do battle with Buell somewhere near Versailles.

Troops on both sides were desperate for water which made the hilly and ragged country even more difficult to traverse. The long draught had dried up many a creek and pond, causing both armies to suffer greatly. Water was to become one of the reasons that Perryville became the location for the battle that was coming. Here, Hardee's men were being pushed by lead elements of the Federal army as they approached Perryville. Polk ordered him to halt and determine the enemy's strength.

Thus Hardee placed Major General Simon Bolivar Buckner's Division along the hills to the west and north of Perryville. Buell's force was approaching in three columns from the west. The lead column in the center was Major General Gilbert's corps marching on the Springfield Pike. To his north and some miles behind him marched Major General McCook's corps on the Mackville Pike. Behind Gilbert on the Lebanon Pike was Crittenden. Confederate and Union cavalry had skirmished all day on October 7 and by evening the Confederate cavalry had retired behind the two regiments of Brigadier General St. John Liddell who was positioned on a ridge overlooking the mostly dry Doctor's Creek. A few muddy pools of water were still to be had and now both armies were focused on securing that water for their empty canteens.

Gilbert's lead elements under Brigadier General Philip Sheridan were the first infantry to reach the creek bed around 11 PM. The confederates put up a spirited fight through the night but eventually were forced to withdraw toward Perryville to the east.

During the night Polk had arrived in Perryville with Cheatham's Division to reinforce Hardee. Bragg had given Polk orders to attack the next day. Neither army commander had a grasp of the actual situation. Polk had 16,000 men and was preparing an attack on what would soon be close to 60,000 men of the Army of the Ohio. Bragg, still anticipating that the fight would materialize in the Versailles area, had 36,000 men preparing to meet the single Federal division of 12,000 men that had been sent by the northeastern route as a diversion.

Back in Perryville, General Hardee sensed the dangerous situation and sent a message to Bragg strongly suggesting that he consolidate his forces and strike one or the other of the Federal columns. Bragg now rode to Perryville to take command there and quickly eliminate what he erroneously assumed to be the smaller of the two Federal forces. Arriving mid-morning he began rearranging troops from defensive to offensive positions and instructed Polk with Cheatham's Division in the van to attack the Federal left at 1:00PM.

On the Federal side, Buell had ordered McCook and Crittenden to advance through the early morning hours in order to catch up and join with Gilbert for an attack he planned to make at 10:00. This message was delayed in reaching the two corps commanders so they were late in moving that morning. By mid-morning Buell assumed that he would have to wait until the following day to launch his attack.

At noon on the 8th Cheatham's artillery opened fire on Gilbert's opposing artillery to prepare for the attack but this attack was delayed because Polk saw McCook's corps advancing on the Mackville Pike and didn't want to jeopardize his men by moving into a position where he could be easily flanked. Bragg arrived on the scene, accepting Polk's explanation for the delay in the attack. Now he ordered Polk further to the right to avoid any flanking attempt. As McCook's troops left the Pike to form on a ridge to their left Polk unleashed his attack before they could get into position and prepare a defense.

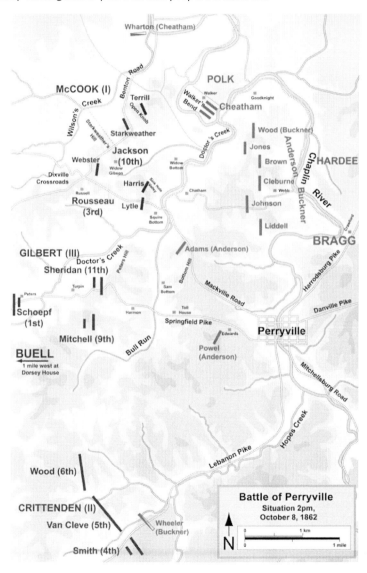

The Confederates were initially caught in a deadly artillery crossfire that took a severe toll on the lead elements but reinforcements and the addition of another two brigades enabled the attack to overrun the artillery and press into the Federal infantry. Much of the Union force was comprised of green recruits who fought well for a short period but were overwhelmed and driven back by Cheatham's veterans. A mile into their retreat McCook's men again tried to make a stand but they were again broken by two of Cheatham's brigades. McCook's corps was almost cut completely in half before a brigade under Brigadier General John C. Starkweather made a stand that stopped the assault and began to push it back.

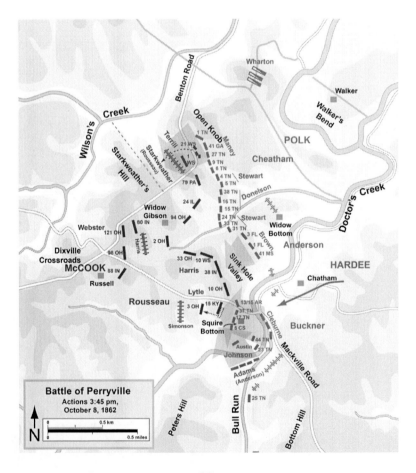

Gilbert's left had become engaged with Anderson's Confederate brigade and a desperate fight continued until darkness to hold the lines that were being pressed to the breaking point. Late in the day Sheridan aggressively counter attacked Anderson's brigades and drove them back toward Perryville. Not wishing to compromise his success as darkness was approaching he consolidated his gains and fortified his position just west of town.

It was late in the day before Buell even realized that a fight had occurred. A rare condition known as acoustic anomaly had created an environment where the sound of the battle could not be heard even though he was only a few miles away. Crittenden's corps was just 2 miles south of the battle and could have easily turned the Confederate left had he or Buell been aware of the engagement.

There was a bright and full moon that night and skirmishing continued long after dark. Buell determined to press the attack the next morning. Bragg on the other hand had finally become convinced of the true situation and realized he was fighting the entire Army of the Ohio. He ordered Polk and Hardee to withdraw immediately to Harrodsburg where he could consolidate his forces and block any attempt by Buell to cut off his line of retreat.

The day had gone to the Confederates but only due to the failings of the Union command aided by the acoustic anomaly. Buell had lost 845 dead, 2851 wounded and 515 missing for a total of 4,211 casualties. Bragg's total losses were 3,396.

Axel Reed's 2nd Minnesota was engaged at Perryville as part of Brigadier General Albin Schoepf's First Division of Gilbert's III Corps. His diary described their experience with the acoustic anomaly and their eventual action as follows:

Oct. 8th "Fighting commenced early in the day and the reports of small arms and cannon was plainly heard, but we thought it nothing more than skirmishing with the rear guard. As we were in the advance the day before we had to go in the rear today, but trains passed on while we lay under arms, talking and laughing as though all was well, little dreaming that such a conflict was raging at the front and many of our fellow comrades lay bleeding and weltering in their blood upon the *battle field. Not until afternoon did we hear that a battle was actually being fought. We could see the Signal Corps on the hill. About 3 o'clock p.m. we were ordered to march with two days' rations; marched a short distance and halted; stragglers came back telling us that our force had been victorious, having driven the enemy in all directions; that they were retreating in disorder, but the peals of cannon and sound of musketry opened louder to the ear which proved the reports a mistake. It appears that our forces first drove the enemy a mile but they were reinforced and recovered all the lost ground. Moved forward again about a mile, passing troops standing in line of battle, filed to the left just before reaching 'Chapel Hill' and passed through a low piece of ground that was filled with smoke of the battle field. The enemies' batteries were playing upon us, balls and shells were flying over our heads, the hill to our right was protecting us from them. We took position on the top of the hill, close behind 'Loeder's battery', which opened a deadly fire upon the enemy. A rise of ground to our front was lined with the enemies' batteries. They charged upon our battery to (the) left, but 'Loeders' put in such a fire that they had to fall back. A battery at our right did good execution. We could hear the enemy yell as they charged. The balls fell thick around us one grape shot striking close to the flag staff close to my right. The 15th regulars, 9th and 35th Ohio were at our left and the 87th Indiana behind us. A Heavy fire was kept up until dark, when firing ceased and we moved to the right. The enemy retreated during the night and left us victors of the field and (to) bury their dead and take care of their wounded. Our army followed them slowly to Crab Orchard, and when it was learned that "Bragg's army" was well across the Cumberland River into Tennessee, we marched back to near Lebanon, Ky., where our teams came from Louisville with knapsacks and blankets. Nearly every officer and enlisted man became disgusted if not enraged at the supine action of Gen. "Don Carlos" Buell, as he was openly accused of being a "rebel sympathizer," " a brother-in-law" of Gen. Braggs, and all the evil names that a lot of loyal soldiers could think of....*

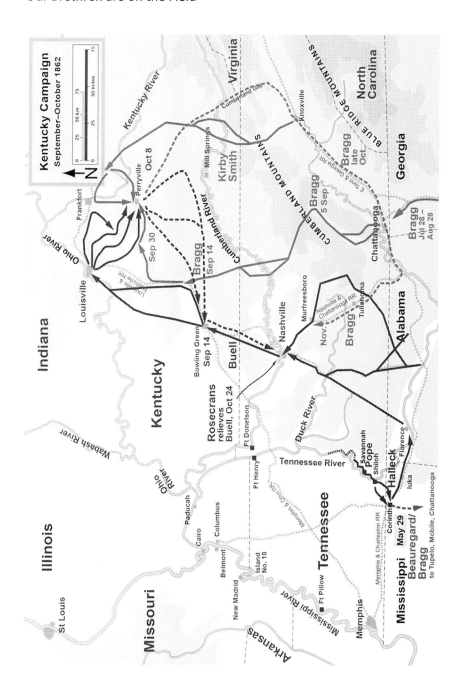

Battle of Perryville Illustration from Harpers Weekly

Major General Braxton Bragg   Major General Wm. Kirby Smith

Confederate States of America

(all images courtesy of the Library of Congress

Major General William J. Hardee   Lt. General Leonidas Polk

Confederate States of America

Major General Don Carlos Buell   United States of America
(all images courtesy of the Library of Congress)

Chapter Five

Both Armies Regroup in Middle Tennessee

Once Bragg could reunite his forces he retreated south towards Tennessee. The 200 mile march was grueling and costly to his army. By the time he reached Knoxville, 15,000 men were suffering from typhoid, dysentery and other ailments while the rest were near starvation. His commanders and troops alike were bitter and demoralized by the difficult and costly campaign for Kentucky that netted nothing but misery. There were public cries for his removal. Confederate President, Jefferson Davis, called Bragg to Richmond to discuss the campaign, hear Bragg out and determine if Bragg should remain in command and what the next strategy would be.

Back in Chattanooga the recently established Confederate newspaper reported the retreat of Bragg and Smith. Combined with the earlier news of General Robert E. Lee's failed invasion of Maryland, the populous was understandably dejected.

Earlier in September, Kate Cuming and two other volunteers from Mobile Alabama had been instrumental in helping improve the care for the troops. She worked tirelessly in a 600 bed hospital and rallied the local women to the assistance of the hospitalized soldiers. Now they prepared for the influx of wounded and sick soldiers of Bragg's army.

At the same time, in Washington, President Lincoln beseeched Buell to pursue and destroy the Confederates. Buell had refused. He argued that the roads were too rough and the country too dry and barren for his Army of the Ohio to advance on Bragg's retreating troops. Instead, he began moving his troops toward Nashville where he intended to rest and refit his army before returning to the original strategy of taking Chattanooga and eastern Tennessee via the southern approaches from Alabama. By now, Lincoln had had enough of Buell's temerity. On October 23rd he relieved Buell of command and replaced him with Major General William Stark Rosecrans. Rosecrans had been successful in driving Sterling Price out of Iuka, Mississippi in September and defeating Earl Van Dorn at Corinth in October. He seemed to be the type of fighter Lincoln needed.

Rosecrans took command of what was now to be called the Army of the Cumberland and, instead of moving directly south as hoped by the war department, he concurred with Buell's orders to move to Nashville. When the army eventually arrived there the problem of supply still plagued him. Due to the draught, the Cumberland River was too low for navigation and the rail lines from Louisville were still in disrepair from Confederate cavalry raids. Thus, Rosecrans would have to rely heavily on wagons to resupply his army while he rested and trained his men for the next campaign.

During their meeting, Bragg had managed to retain Jefferson Davis' confidence by sharing his plan to move the army to Murfreesboro, Tennessee and from there attack Nashville. On October 28th, Bragg's lead elements under command of General John C. Breckinridge arrived in Murfreesboro. He immediately ordered Forest and Morgan to make cavalry raids on Nashville attacking the garrison simultaneously from the north and south. On November 6th both cavalry units skirmished with the Federals in the works around Nashville doing little more than harassing fire. The next day, November 7, Rosecrans arrived at Nashville with the Army of the Cumberland. Any opportunity the Confederates may have had to take the lightly guarded city was gone.

The balance of Bragg's army reached Murfreesboro after another grueling route south to Chattanooga from Knoxville then northwest to Tullahoma and finally up the Stones River valley. Here they finally began to recover and resupply from their fall of despair.

Overall command of the Confederate forces in the west was given to General Joseph E. Johnston on November 24th in order to have a more localized and informed decision maker in that theatre rather than relying on Richmond entirely. Johnston determined to place Kirby Smith's men in Bragg's command and designated the combined force as the Army of Tennessee.

Chattanooga's role for the Confederacy's military effort was once again ratcheted up. General Johnston established his headquarters in the city in early December. President Jefferson Davis soon scheduled a meeting in the town to confer with Johnston and review the troops.

Shortly afterwards, on December 11th , Davis arrived in Murfreesboro to inspect Bragg's troops and determine if it might be possible to send one of his divisions to Lieutenant General Pemberton in defense of Mississippi and Vicksburg. Bragg insisted that if a quarter of his troops were sent to Mississippi he would have no chance against Rosecrans' army of 65,000 holding Nashville. Davis told Bragg to fight and if necessary retreat behind the Tennessee River, but the troops needed to be sent to Pemberton. On the 13th after having enjoyed an early Christmas celebration with the citizens of Murfreesboro, Davis left for Chattanooga to confer once more with General Johnston.

Chapter Six

Stones River

Confederate Cavalry continued to patrol and make raids on the Federal lines of communication during the month of December. On December 25th, Rosecrans brought his commanders together. Based on the enemy cavalry raiding and being separated from Bragg's army as well as intelligence stating that Bragg had lost a division to the Mississippi front, he told his commanders that in the morning they would strike out for Murfreesboro. The Confederates were at their most vulnerable and he intended to whip them and drive them out of middle Tennessee.

On the day after Christmas, following a heavy rain the night before, half of the Army of the Cumberland marched out of Nashville in three columns. The left column under Crittenden contained three divisions and moved down the Nashville Pike. In the center, McCook marched three divisions and one cavalry brigade down the Nolensville Pike toward Triune. Upon reaching that point he was to turn east toward Murfreesboro. On the right, George Thomas had one division and three brigades on the Franklin Turnpike. He was to proceed to Brentwood, then turn east and come in to Murfreesboro in the rear of McCook. Rosecrans had approximately 44,000 men advancing toward the enemy, leaving almost half of his strength in Nashville or guarding the railroad from Louisville.

As soon as Rosecrans' army advanced past his outposts the Confederate Cavalry began skirmish actions in earnest, delaying his progress toward Murfreesboro and giving Bragg time to pull together his spread out forces, which he now consolidated in a defensive position north and west of the town.

Late in the day on December 29th, Crittenden's corps approached Murfreesboro, sending a single brigade across Stones River to push the Confederate pickets back into the town. Soon that brigade faced Breckinridge's entire division and wisely withdrew to take a defensive position while awaiting the rest of the army.

The following day, Bragg sent Wheeler's cavalry to harass the Federal rear. At noon on the 30th Wheeler's command came across McCook's supply train in Lavergne, Tennessee. Storming them he capturing all 300 wagons, bagged 700 prisoners and destroyed over a million dollars of Federal supplies. Continuing on, Wheeler caught another 150 wagon supply train at Nolensville. By the time his raid had finished he returned to Confederate lines having captured and paroled 1,000 soldiers and brought back enough weapons to equip a brigade as well as many fresh horses for his command.

Captain Silas S. Canfield was selected by his comrades on September 8, 1892 to write the full history of the 21st Ohio Volunteer Infantry during the war. In 1893 his work was published in Toledo. He took great care to confer with fellow soldiers and officers regarding all the actions of the regiment which was to become a much honored unit of the Army of the Cumberland. He wrote the following about the advance of Rosecrans' army to Murfreesboro:

On the 26th of December, the army marched from its several camps to meet the enemy in deadly conflict on the field of Stone's River, with full confidence in its leaders, and high hopes and anticipations of victory.

The left wing marched by the Murfreesboro pike, the right wing by Nolensville, Knob's Gap and Triune, and the center to threaten Hardee, and thence to Nolensville, where it would be in position to support either wing in case of attack.

The regiment marched to the sound of cannon nearly all day, and reached Nolensville, from which the enemy had been driven, about dark, and bivouacked for the night. The roads were very bad, so that our train did not arrive until late at night, and the next morning before starting, everything was thrown out of the wagons not absolutely necessary to be carried along, and much of value to the officers was left, which was never recovered by them.

On account of a heavy fog the next morning, the divisions started late with the 21st in advance. Hardee having fallen back from Triune, we marched from Nolensville across to Stewartsboro, on the Murfreesboro pike, with the rebel skirmishers in our front most of the way, stubbornly resisting our progress. Being unacquainted with the country, General Negley pressed a citizen into the service as guide; his life depended on his piloting us safely across. We bivouacked near Stewartsboro, where we remained the 28th, it being Sunday, and General Rosecrans being averse to fighting on the Sabbath; yet there was skirmishing throughout the day. On the 29th we moved forward to Overall's Creek, driving the enemy's skirmishers. Here we were in plain sight of the enemy's works, near the Murfreesboro pike. The 30th was spent skirmishing, cutting roads through the cedars, and getting the army in position before the enemy, and at night we lay on our arms in line of battle....

As Canfield stated, the Federal army spent the 30th in deploying and redeploying for favorable position to attack the Confederates. After a miserable day of movement by wet and weary soldiers the Federal line extended from Crittenden on the far left through Thomas in the center and ending with McCook on the far right. The line was approximately 2 ½ miles long and positioned west of Stones River with Crittenden's corps split in two. Half were on the east side of the river and half on the west. Rosecrans' plan was to attack Bragg's right with his left wing, that being Crittenden's corps. Thomas was to support Crittenden's attack while McCook was to hold his ground against any Confederate attack. If that attack was not forthcoming he was to push the Confederates to keep them in place but be careful not to over commit. In order to deceive Bragg as to his intentions, he ordered McCook to extend his line building many fires so that the Confederates might think the strength of the Federal Army was on McCook's end rather than Crittenden's.

Bragg determined that he would not only strengthen his left but attack the Federal right where they appeared to be strongest. The Confederate Army of Tennessee spent the evening redeploying into these assault positions. Hardee was moved from the right of the Confederate line behind Polk and into position on the Confederate left leaving only Breckinridge's Division protecting the Confederate right along with a cavalry brigade.

As it turned out quite by happenstance, both opposing generals had come up with the same strategy. They would vigorously attack the other's right the next day. As both armies settled in for the night a Federal regimental band played northern favorites. Soon a Confederate band returned the favor playing songs loved in the south. To end the impromptu concert both bands played "Home Sweet Home" as both armies did their best to get some sleep. The stage was set for one of the most brutal fights of the war.

While both commanders depended on surprise as a crucial component of their attack plans, it was most critical for the Confederates. Bragg's entire army was in place with no chance for reinforcement so he needed to act quickly and decisively in order to win. Even though both armies were approximately the same size, Rosecrans could be reinforced from Nashville.

In the center of the Union line, about 2 AM on the 31st, Brigadier General Joshua W. Sill awakened his division commander, Brigadier General Philip Sheridan. Being informed of large enemy troop movements toward their right, Sheridan proceeded to Corps Commander Major General McCook and warned of an impending attack. At first McCook dismissed the news but prior to dawn he alerted his other two division commanders to be prepared for an attack. Division commanders Davis and Johnson passed the alert to their subordinates. Brigadier General August Willich commanded the brigade on Johnson's far right. Earlier he had sent a patrol to check on the Confederate lines. When they reported nothing unusual he let down his guard. At 5:30 AM his troops were preparing their coffee and breakfast as per their routine. To Willich's left and front, Kirk's brigade, maintaining their diligence, was up and under arms and consequently better prepared for an attack.

At 6:00 AM 11,000 Confederates of McCown's and Cleburne's divisions of Hardee's corps formed in the fog in front of the cedars facing Johnson's division. They moved silently across the open fields until they came within close range of the Federal troops. They then increased their speed to the double quick and let out the shrill Rebel yell. Kirk's men put up a valiant fight for as long as they could. Johnson sent a request for help to Willich but Willich had gone to find Johnson, leaving his command leaderless and confused. The fight to

Kirk's front lasted only a few minutes more before the Confederates reached and overwhelmed his line. The men panicked, broke and fled.

By this time the Confederate line had reached Willich's brigade and hit them just as they were taking arms. All was confusion and a sea of men, both Confederate and Union, surging past them to their rear. Willich's men likewise broke and fled the onslaught. Within the first 30 minutes of the battle two Federal brigades had been broken and disorganized with a loss of over 2,000 casualties.

The Federal right had been completely flanked and Johnson's Division was breaking, brigade after brigade, to the Army of the Cumberland's rear. To the left of the broken Union brigades was the division of Jefferson C. Davis (Union). Davis ordered his right most brigade to refuse its flank forming an angle where half his men faced the original front while the balance were turned back at 90 degrees to face the Confederates to their right.

Davis' troops fought grudgingly and refused to yield to the Confederate assault, slowing their momentum. To Hardee's right, Polk's corps was becoming engaged with Sheridan and Davis' divisions. However the attacks of his brigades under Vaughan and Maney's were made piece meal and became ineffective, further slowing the Confederate momentum.

As Bragg was unleashing his attack on the Federal right, Rosecrans was at the Federal far left, commencing an assault of his own. He had just ordered Generals Van Cleve and Wood to move forward against Breckinridge's Division on the east side of the river. Upon setting them in motion he had returned to his headquarters where sometime around 7:00 he became aware of the intense battle being fought on his right.

He immediately sent orders for Van Cleve to stop his advance and return to the west side of the river while sending reinforcements from Thomas and Wood to McCook. The Confederates continued to hammer the Federal right flank but a stout defense by Sheridan and a counterattack by one of his brigadiers thwarted the attack. Sill paid a high price in halting the brigades of Vaughan, Loomis and Maney.

Polk ordered General Cheatham to re-form his four brigades and resume his attacks on Sheridan and Davis. To Cheatham's left, Cleburne, who had now outflanked Davis, drove into the Federal right and rear at the same time. Davis' men could no longer resist the pressure and they broke for the rear exposing Sheridan's flank. The entire Union army was in danger of being rolled up.

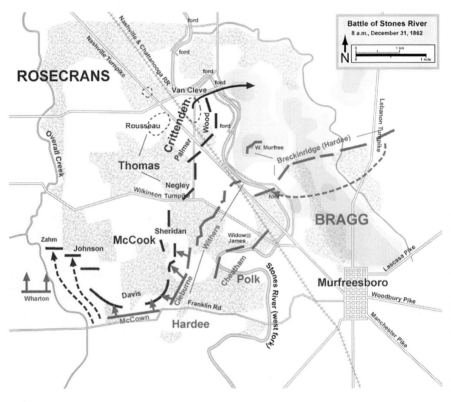

Acting quickly, Sheridan swung his entire line to the right at a 90 degree angle to his original line. Reinforcements in the form of Major General Lovell Rousseau's division were now arriving and took position on Sheridan's new right. By 10:00 the Federal line had been hammered into a V shape with Sheridan's division at the point of the V on the left and Negley's division of Thomas' corps at the point on the right.

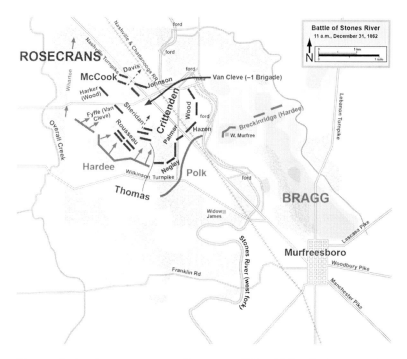

The confederate pressure on the apex of the V finally became too much for Sheridan's men to resist and he was forced to make a fighting withdrawal of approximately one half mile behind the Wilkinson Pike.

On the Confederate left, Hardee was urgently seeking reinforcements from Bragg. The morning had cost him a third of his command and he needed more men to continue an effective assault. Polk in the center was heavily engaged and had lost perhaps 30 percent of his corps so there was no help for Hardee to be had there. To the far right Breckinridge had not been engaged but he told Bragg that a large Union force was about to attack him and Bragg determined not to take the two brigades from him which he had been considering.

Still the Confederates continued to push the Federal line. Union Division Commander Rousseau ordered the brigade of Colonel John Beatty to hold a position in a grove of Cedars to the right of Sheridan's battered brigades at all costs. Beatty positioned his four regiments accordingly. He was immediately engaged and blunted the initial

Confederate attack before being further pressed by McCown's Confederate division. While he had been told to hold the position "until hell freezes over" Beatty saw that Sheridan on his left was withdrawing and Shepherd to his right was likewise pulling back. Assuming that hell had indeed frozen over he ordered his troops to withdraw.

Sheridan had retreated, not because he was beaten, but because his men had run out of ammunition. The Confederate cavalry raids in the days preceding the battle had caused McCook's supply train to move back further from the front. Consequently Sheridan fell back beyond the Nashville Pike, yet another half mile to his rear in order to have his cartridge boxes replenished. This created a gap between Negley's division on Sheridan's left and Rousseau to his right. While Hardee's Confederates attempted to leverage the gap, Negley and Rousseau were able to pull back while closing the gap and keeping the Confederates at bay. Crittenden's Third Division under Van Cleve, having been recalled from the Federal left where Rosecrans had originally planned to attack Breckinridge's Division, was now falling in on the Federal right, repelling Hardee's nearly exhausted troops.

The movement of the Union right and center corps to positions in the rear of the Nashville Turnpike left Palmer's brigades of Crittenden's corps exposed in a 4 acre cedar wood known to locals as the Round Forest. His troops were formed in a salient in the Forest. Polk thought the position looked vulnerable so he ordered his last two brigades under Generals James Chalmers and Daniel S. Donelson to break the salient.

First Chalmers' brigade was foiled in their attack then Donelson's men attacked and were also beaten back. Their fierce attacks resulted in massive casualties with two of Donelson's three regiments losing over 50 percent of their strength. Colonel William B. Hazen's brigade had been positioned in this apex at the Round Forest all morning. Supported by a variety of reinforcements he had held his position undauntedly. It was now noon and the battle had been raging for six hours.

Bragg, notified of reinforcements to the Federal Right, determined that their left must now be weak. Hardee was completely stalled and Polk should have an opportunity to smash Rosecrans' now depleted left. He ordered Breckinridge to send 4 brigades at once in order to make the winning assault. At this point the infantry attacks subsided while Bragg awaited the arrival and positioning of these fresh troops.

During the lull, Rosecrans' commanders were able to solidify their lines, replenish ammunition and move artillery to a ridge above the Round Forest in support of Hazen's brigade. It was now late in the afternoon and the light was beginning to fade. At about 4:00 Polk ordered the first two brigades from Breckinridge to attack the Round Forest. They were pounded by the massed artillery behind and above Hazen's troops. Hazen held his fire until the Confederates were at close range then unleashed a single murderous volley. It was enough to repulse and break the Rebel line.

As the broken brigades fell back to Polk's line the second two brigades of Breckinridge's Division arrived and were immediately ordered to take the Round Forest. By now 50 Federal artillery pieces were massed and supporting Hazen's position. The result of the second wave was the same as the first with heavy casualties and nothing gained. As darkness approached a cease fire was ordered and the fighting ended for the day.

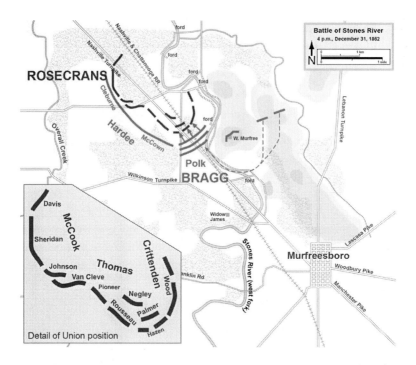

Much like the earlier battle of Shiloh, the Confederates had made a brilliant initial attack that caught the unprepared right of Rosecrans' army much as it had Grant's. Before that assault eventually lost steam it had pushed the Federal right nearly three miles from where it had begun the day. Far from being disordered though, Rosecrans' army held a strong defensive position with good interior lines of communication by the end of the day.

Although they had ultimately held their ground and were now in strong defensive positions, Rosecrans didn't consider the day a success. He called a council of war with his commanders asking if it was their opinion that they should retreat. McCook advised retreat as did Rosecrans' cavalry commander. Crittenden and Thomas were non-committal but would support Rosecrans' decision either way. Rosecrans dismissed the group without a decision before personally scouting a possible route of retreat behind his army. When he returned he announced that they would hold their ground. He then ordered a train of wagons to take as many wounded as possible back to Nashville and return with as many rations and supplies as possible.

Bragg, on the other hand, thought that he had won a great victory. Upon hearing that Federal wagons were moving rearward toward Nashville he wired Richmond that the enemy had given up their strong position and were retreating. He didn't bother preparing orders to reorganize his own shattered brigades or make any changes in his army's current dispositions.

Rosecrans spent the entire night repositioning his troops and encouraging officers and men alike to have faith the battle would be won the next day. All through that night the temperature dropped and rain added to the misery of the wounded, dying and exhausted troops of both armies.

In Chattanooga, it was reported that Federal and Confederate forces were once again engaged in mortal combat at Murfreesboro. Initial reports were positive but everybody tensely awaited the final outcome.

Canfield continued his description of the battle from the perspective of the 21st Ohio during the first day's fight and the night that followed:

> Early on the morning of the 31st the battle opened by the enemy making a furious attack on the right of General McCook's command. We were not long in determining by the receding sound of musketry, that the right was being driven. The rebels had been ordered to attack, commencing on their left, by divisions, successively to their right. General Sheridan on the right of General Negley, disposed his division to meet the altered conditions made by the right being swung back, and when attacked repulsed the enemy, who returned to the assault, but he continued to hold them at bay until the enemy had passed his right, and his ammunition was exhausted, when he was obliged to fall back.

> Withers massed his division by brigades, and moved to the attack of General Negley's division, about the time Sheridan's men became engaged. A corn field was in front of the 21st O., and as soon as the rebels came in range, the infantry opened a deadly fire on them.

More persistent courage on the one hand, or greater coolness on the other, could hardly be displayed. Openings through their serried ranks were several times made by canister shot, still they came boldly on. Men fell at every step, and still they pressed forward.

"Cap, do you want to see that man come out of that saddle?"

"Yes" – and the horse was without a rider.

"Gosh! I had a dead one on him." "He'll never kill any more Yanks." "This gun never deceives me." "I know right where she carries." Such are some of the expressions made by the men of the 21ˢᵗ during the heat of battle.

When the enemy was only about thirty yards distant, the order was given to "fix bayonets;" but about this time they broke and fled, followed by a volley as a parting salute. It was said the bayonets were used on some parts of the line, but not on the left of the regiment. Our front clear, we had a chance to view the ghastly sight. A deserter and a rebel major captured later, are my authority for saying seven hundred and forty lay dead on the field before us. Shortly after the repulse, Lieutenant Colonel Neibling came along the regiment and said, "My G-d boys! We gave 'em H-ll; didn't we?" The enemy having passed us on both flanks he called out, "Fall back, we are surrounded!" How we got back through the cedars I can never tell, except that we walked – we didn't run. The rebels were behind us and on either flank. Many of the men of the 21ˢᵗ were fighting, and several were killed on the retreat. In falling back the men of the Regiment became badly scattered, and mixed with other commands, but a portion of them was collected, who procured ammunition and took position in support of the Board of Trade Battery, near the pike, which was being worked with telling effect on the advancing rebels. Again and again rebel officers tried to get their men to charge this battery, but were unable to get them to advance beyond the woods, about one hundred yards distant.

Night closed the conflict, the right having been driven back a mile and a half and the right and center occupying a position along the pike, at a right angle to its position in the morning.

Soon after dark a small fire was built, and several of the men of the 21st had gathered about it, trying to get a little warmth.

General Rosecrans came up and said, "You are my men and I don't like to have any of you hurt. Where the enemy see a fire like this, they know twenty-five or thirty men are gathered about it, and are sure to shoot at it. I advise you to put it out." Scarcely was he done speaking, when sure enough a line shot came just high enough to miss the heads of the party, and a shell exploded just beyond.

About eleven o'clock we were permitted to go back out of range of the enemy's guns, build fires and get supper, of which we were sorely in need; a hasty and scanty breakfast being the only sustenance we had had that day.

The regiment with its brigade then took position in support of General Haskel. Early the next morning we were ordered to the support of General McCook's right....

The next morning, New Year's Day, Bragg was shocked to learn that the enemy was still in place in their lines. He had been certain Rosecrans would be gone and he had no plan or strategy prepared. Throughout the day he had his men collect Federal supplies that had been abandoned the day before and tinkered with his lines. Polk advanced his line to the Round Forest and Breckinridge returned to the east side of Stones River to his original position.

The Federal Army of the Cumberland awaited the return of Confederate attacks all day long, anxiously expecting the horrors of the previous day to return. It never happened. Rosecrans and Thomas rode the lines encouraging the boys to have heart and they in return were proud and pleased with Rosecrans determination to stay and hold the ground.

On January 2nd Bragg sent skirmishers to see if the enemy was still in place. Upon learning they were indeed still there, he ordered artillery to probe their positions. The Federal artillery responded with vigor. It was clear that Rosecrans had no intention of leaving.

On the far right of the Confederate line there was a commanding ridge on the east side of the river. If Confederate artillery could be placed on this ridge it would be able to lay down enfilading fire on the Federal line making it untenable. Bragg sent scouts to reconnoiter the ridge. Upon returning with the news that a Federal division already held that ridge, Bragg determined to have Breckinridge remove them in order to execute this plan.

The brigade Bragg's scouts had spotted on the high ground belonged to Colonel Samuel Beatty who had spent the previous day fortifying his position on what he knew to be crucial ground at the far left of the army. Just to the west of his position on the other side of the river were an additional 6 guns of the 3rd Wisconsin Artillery. Between Beatty and these guns the open field to their front was completely covered against any assault.

Having scouted these positions himself, Breckinridge was appalled when Bragg ordered him to attack the ridge and secure the high ground east of the river. He objected vehemently. Bragg was resolute that his orders would be obeyed. A week prior to this order Bragg had upheld the execution of a Kentucky soldier for desertion despite Breckinridge's pleas for his life. A quarter of the troops of Breckinridge's Division were Kentuckians and they felt Bragg had a distinct disrespect and disliking for them; first this execution and now orders to make a suicide charge. The commander of the 1st Kentucky Brigade, known as the orphan brigade since their state was occupied by the Federals, was Brigadier General Roger W. Hanson. Hanson now offered to ride to Bragg's headquarters and kill him personally.[1] Breckinridge refused the offer and prepared an attack for 4:00 that afternoon as he had been ordered.

Observing Breckinridge's preparations, Rosecrans reinforced Beatty's forces including the massing of 58 artillery pieces on the hill on the west side of the river.

At 4:00 Polk's artillery west of the river opened on the Federals in support of Breckinridge's attack. Shortly after Breckinridge ordered his men to charge. Hanson's orphan brigade and Gideon Pillow's Tennesseans advanced across the 600 yards of open field ignoring the heavy casualties they were suffering under the Federal artillery. Due to sheer determination they had gained the crest of the hill within 30 minutes and were routing Beatty's men who were falling back in disorder.

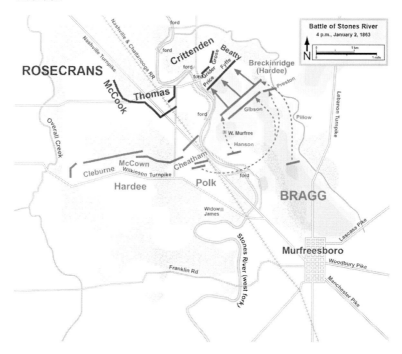

Had they stopped there and consolidated their gains the story may have turned out differently. The Confederate troops had suffered immensely over the past six days and wanted to end this battle immediately. They kept pushing forward to the river as Beatty's men fled before them. Their officers couldn't recall them from their excited advance. As they descended the reverse slope of the hill in pursuit of Beatty's men the Confederates exposed themselves to the 58 guns massed on the other side of the river. The slaughter was more than they could withstand and they began to withdraw back up the hill.

Colonel John F. Miller of Negley's division was positioned on the west side of the river. Seeing the Confederates being dismantled by the artillery barrage, Miller ordered his brigade to counterattack across the river. Soon other regiments joined Miller as the tide of battle had turned and the Confederates were now in full retreat. The

Confederate officers attempted to stop and reform them on the crest they had just won but to no avail. By 4:45 the attack that had started with such promise was a complete rout streaming back to their original lines. Once the crest was secured the Federals ceased their counterattack, having thwarted the Confederates thoroughly.

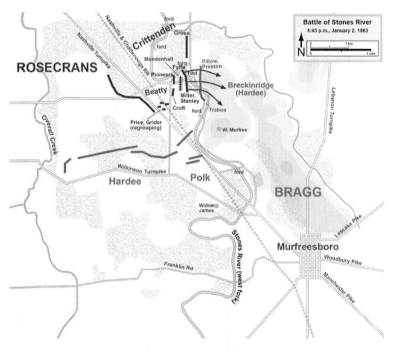

Canfield wrote of the 21st Ohio's involvement on the climactic day of the battle:

> *About noon on January 2nd a part of a ration of flour was issued to the men, with the admonition to prepare and eat it as soon as possible. Some made paste, sweetened and drank it; others made dough, and in every conceivable way without utensils, tried to bake it. Some ate the dough partly baked, and when the order "fall in" was given, some snatched theirs from the fire and others went away dinnerless, leaving theirs behind unbaked. The regiment, with the rest of Negley's division, went on the "double quick" about a mile and a half, filled their canteens, and laid down on the right bank of Stone's River, to await the assault of the enemy.*

At precisely four o'clock, the gun at Bragg's headquarters was fired as the signal to attack. Immediately the enemy's batteries along their whole front opened fire on the Union line, and Breckenridge with 7,000 men and two batteries, moved forward to the assault of the left wing.

When they came in range, fifty-eight pieces of artillery, which had been placed in a commanding position in anticipation of the attack, opened on the advancing foe. Nothing daunted by this they swept on.

Van Cleves division which had been stationed over the river, terrified at the onslaught of the rebels, delivered their fire, and retreated in haste, and great disorder. Men and horses a commingled mob; horses with riders and horses without, men with guns and men without, all making haste to escape, the enemy pursuing vigorously and pouring a destructive fire into the retreating mass. "My G-d!" said Colonel Neibling, "it was the most heartrending sight I ever saw." General Negley and Colonel Miller were busy endeavoring to instill calm courage into the men. Colonel Neibling instructing the regiment to messure out the sulphurous regions to the rebels "by the acre," and Colonel Moody urging the 74th Ohio, not to be out done by the 21st.

Much of this, if not most of it, was altogether unnecessary.

The men who had so completely routed the enemy on the 31st of December, had full confidence in their ability to overcome them on the 2nd of January.

The rebels elated with their supposed victory, reached the bank of the river, to be met with a destructive volley, and charge from the troops in reserve, when they recoiled, but made a stubborn resistance to the advance of the 2d division. After being driven half a mile, they retreated precipitately to their entrenchments.

A battery of four guns, in capture of which the 21`st participated, was a part of the fruit of the victory. Being relieved, we fell back over the river, and took position in support of the artillery, which had done such excellent service during the battle. This ended the fighting of the 21st Ohio at Stone's River.

Things had finally turned completely for the Army of the Cumberland. Rosecrans was about to receive reinforcements from Nashville and he had beaten back a concerted attack on his left. Rosecrans ordered another ruse conducted to threaten Bragg. Many fires were built and troops moved about to make it appear that he already had those reinforcements and was extending his left far to the east. Bragg ordered a strong reinforcement of his right to counter this perceived threat then told all commanders to hold their ground at all costs.

By the morning of the third, Bragg realized that his situation was becoming very precarious and that the strain on his army had been so severe that it was about to dissolve. By that afternoon his wagons were headed south toward Shelbyville. Later that evening Polk pulled out and moved toward Shelbyville. The next morning Hardee left the line and proceeded to Tullahoma.

Stones River had been a costly battle for both sides. Bragg's Army of Tennessee numbered approximately 35,000 men going into the fight. He lost over 9,200 killed or wounded, 27% of his total. Rosecrans had just over 9,500 casualties or 23% of his 41,400 troops engaged. Yet Stones River was a major strategic victory for the north. It secured Kentucky from possible further threat and assured that Nashville would become a major supply center for the Federal armies in the south. It also encouraged those loyal to the Union in eastern Tennessee.

Our Brethren are on the Field

Major General William S. Rosecrans   Major General Thomas L. Crittenden

Major General Alexander McCook   Major General George H. Thomas

United States of America.

(all images courtesy of the Library of Congress)

Our Brethren are on the Field

Part Three

Chapter Seven

Tullahoma

Bragg now reestablished a line behind the Duck River. The Army of Tennessee wintered in the area of Shelbyville while Rosecrans' Army of the Cumberland established its base of recovery at Murfreesboro. Six months were to pass before Rosecrans was ready to take the offensive towards the prize, Chattanooga.

Shortly after the Battle of Stone's River, Vincent Messler of the 115th Illinois Infantry wrote to his parents on the 30th of January having been moved to Louisville, Kentucky on his way to the front. He mistakenly assumed that the unit would continue on to Vicksburg but the 115th would in fact participate in Rosecrans' campaign against Bragg and the taking of Chattanooga.

Jan 30, 1863

Camp Near Louisville Ky

Dear Father & Mother I just rec a letter from you and very glad to hear from you. I also Rec. one from Davis and Sarah a few days ago on our march. I wrote to you a few days before we started. We started 26th of Jan & arrived here today at 1 ½ oclock P.M. 85 miles. We take the boat tomorrow morning. I suppose but don't know where they will land us. We never know where we are going until we get there. I told you in my other letter that we would go to Vicksburg and I think so yet but not sirtain. There is a great many troops here now. There was two Brigades of us come from Danville and I don't know how many came other ways.

The first day we marched we came 16 miles. The next 18. The next 20. The next 17 & the next 14. One thing favored us. We had our knapsacks halled (hauled) on this march. I carried my drum. I haven't rode in a wagon half a mile in all our marches. I feel very tyred tonight. I think I can let you have the money you spoke about by the time you mentioned. I have only $21.50 with me and I don't know when we will draw on uncle Sam again. Settling up my accounts in

Rosemond Ills will have it ready for me. I guess I will write to him and tell him to express $100, one 100, to you if it is possible to do so. I expect this will be the last time I will get a chance to write for a long time if we go to Vicksburg and it will be very unsirtain weather you get the letters regular or not. It is almost bed time and I am tyred. My breast hirts me some. I have the Rheumatism somewhat. I suppose it is on account of laying on the damp ground. You had better direct your letters to Louisville Ky. They will follow up the Regt. Please write as often as convenient.

My love and best wishes to you all. Your son V. Messler.

The 26th Ohio had seen action at Corinth, Mississippi and been part of Buell's march through northern Alabama. Following that they were part of his pursuit of Bragg through Tennessee and Kentucky. Having fought at Perryville and now Stone's River, they were becoming a veteran unit. As they waited to advance, one member, Joseph Vangundy, wrote home about money he had sent but had apparently not been received by his father. The absence of a son who contributed to the family's financial survival was an oft experienced hardship for those at home. Soldiers sent whatever they could, however they could, to support their loved ones.

Camp near Murfreesboro
Feb 28th 1863
Mr Jonathan Vangundy

Respected father I take this opportunity to write you a few lines in reply to yours of January 26. I was glad to hear that you were all well. My health is good at present and hope these few lines may find you all enjoying good health. Well Pap you spoke something about me sending you some money. Well we were only payed off for two months the last time and I owed the Sutler some for tobacco but I will send you five dollars in this letter. I sent you 80 dollars last October while I was at Louisville. I sent it in Francis name and told him to give it to you but I have failed to receive an answer as to whether you have got it or not. I will tell you how to proceed to get it. Go to Frank and sea if he has got it and if he has not got it you go to Major Plarsin in Chillicothe and ask him about it as we all sent it to him. That is those that sent money home. He can tell you all about it and as soon as you get this and sea about the other write and let me know all about it. We are yet encamped near Murfreesboro and I don't think we will make a forward movement very soon as the roads are very bad yet. Well when you write tell me how much that piece of land sold for. I got a letter from Sam a few days ago. He was well. I wish you would send me – cents worth of postage. Please write soon. Direct as before. My love to you all

Joseph Vangundy

Benjamin Mason's 137th New York Volunteers were still in the east as part of the Army of the Potomac during this period but would later participate in the battles for Chattanooga as part of Joseph Hooker's corps. He shared his thoughts about the shifting rationale of the war from strictly fighting for the Union to abolition.

Aquia Landing VA
March 12, 1863
Dear Mother

Wrote to you to let yo know that I was in the hospital and was getting beter and was goin to my regiment. I wrote that I would send yo a check of 28.00. I have neglect writing to yo. Yo mosent (mustn't) think hard of me. I am tuff as a bare. Our camp is hon a rising knole. We have fare vue of the Potomac. We can see the ships and steambotes sail up and down the river for a mile or more. We have ben bilding some fortifications. The weather is quite nise know (now). We haven't much rain know (now). I suppose that it is quite cold up there know (now). I am in hopes this war will play ought (out) son (soon). I came down here to fight for the stares (stars) and stripes but I see that is plaid (played) ought (out). We are fighting for the nigers.

I can't think of much more at presant. Write as soon as yo get this.

Direct

137 Regt NYI V
Washington D C
This is from

> *Your son B F Mason*
> *To Mary Mason*

Adelbert Hannom and the 104th Illinois had been captured in December of 1862 at Hartsville, Tennessee. Paroled upon capture they were stationed in Chicago at Camp Douglas waiting for their "exchange" and return to the army in Murfreesboro. He wrote to his father in mid-March suggesting that they may instead be sent to Utah to fight Mormons.

March 15 1863

> *My dear father it is with pleasher that I take my pen in hand to let you know that I am well and ihope (I hope) that these few lines will find you and all of my friends enjoying the same blessing. We hav got very fine weather up hear at this time. It is dry and nise. It is rumored that we are agoing to Utow (Utah) to fight the Mormons and if we do if iliv (I live) threw it i am a going to Calaforny (California) to try my luck. John Melon and me bout (bought) a can of oysters last night. Wished that you could hav ben hear to help us eat them. We had a fun time. Isent (I sent) thurty five dollars by express to you. Kenny Harm and me sent ours to gather and you can get it any time. Ihave (I have) no more to write at present. Iwill (I will) close by saing good by. Iyet (I yet) remain your son.*

> *Adelbert Hannom*

> *Write often*

Camp Douglas was a prisoner of war camp and three days after his earlier letter Hannom had this to say about the enemy prisoners in Chicago:

March 18, 1863

> *My dear father it is with pleasher that itake (I take) my pen in hand to let you know that I am well and ihope (I hope) that these few lins willfind you enjoying the same blessing. I got your letter today and I was glad to hear from you and to hear that you and all of the family was well. You sed that times was purty hard with you at this time.*

Isent thurty five dollars to gave Kenny for you and you can get it at any time. these rebbles up hear is a takeing the oath like everything. There is to thurds (2/3) of them that say that they will not go back to the south agen. Never will they fight against the union. My dear father iwould like to be to home this spring to help Thad and Fred to grab and clear up that land but father you nead not think that I am tired of the surfice (service) at tall. I hav not got much to write this time. Ihas got to go on dress perade purty soon.

Write often for ilike to hear from home. Iwill close by saing good by. Giv my luv to all of my friends. Iyet remain yours,

> *Adelbert H. Hannom*

> *To elder G. B. Hannom*

Joseph Vangundy wrote on the 20th of March describing the fine spring weather and dry roads while telling his father that he will follow up on the thirty dollars he sent to Chillicothe.

Camp ner Murfreesboro
Tennessee March the 20 1863

Der (Dear) Father and Mother I take the opertonety to right you a few lines to let you know I am still up and around as usual. Ive got my helth good as ever I had in my life. Well when these few line comes to hand I hope the(y) will find you in the same good helth and enjoying good times as well as I am. I receive your letter today and was very glad to her from hom. Also I fond a small leter in side of it which I injoying myself very much when I was readin it. Well I don't know when I shall get to come home or not before the war is over or my time is out but the talk is now they are going to give five men out of hundred furlows this sumer and if that is sow I will stand a good bit for getin home this somer (since) I haven't been home since I have been out in surves (service). Father, you need not mind that thirty dollars I sent to you. Not till I right agin for I intend to right to Chillicothe in a few days myself to find out where it is and if I find out what become of it I will right Back to you. Then you go and lift it for me. I think we have very nice wether here now. The peach trees is out in bloom. All we have dusty rodes and I don't think you can tell me you have dusty rodes. Well I think I will have to close by saying I aint got anything to right to you any more at present but your with respeck father an mother. No more but right soon. From Joseph Vangundy

In early April Robert Woody, a Union cavalryman, wrote of a resent scouting expedition he was returning from. The weather continued to improve and more patrols and preparations were being made, but Rosecrans was still not ready to advance.

Murfreesboro April the 10, 1863

>*Dear Father and Mother*

>>*I take my pen in hand (to) inform you that I am well at present and hoping that these few lines may (find) you all well. I received your letter yesterday and was glad to hear from you and to hear you was all well. We have being on another skout (scout). We was 9 days. We whent way down on the Cumberland river but we did not git (into) no fight. Took 50 or 60 prisoners and several horses. It (is) dusty weather and windy weather. tolable (tolerable) warm in day time and cold at night. When we was out on the skout lots (of) people planting corn but they no body planting corn around Murfressboro. They (aren't) doing any thing 7 miles from Murfreesboro. We are going (to be) payed some more money before long. 2 months more pay. I thought I would tell how much paper (costs). 2 sheets for 5 cents. Postage stamps I have not seen any of them lately. Want to send about 8.00 dollars home yet first chance I git. I don't know where wood be safe or not to send in a letter but I would not risk more (than) 5 dollars. I believe that I (might) risk five dollars more. Most all (the) boys all well. Bill Wicker I han't (heard) from for four days or (more) but when we heard from him he was no better nor no worse. If anybody wants (to) git in to this Company now is the time. if they will go (to) Indianoplis they can git transportation.*

>>*Murfreesboro is prettist a place that I seen in Tennessee but this country is to hilly for me. I guess that I have told you all that I can think of so I must conclude. So good Bye. You must write soon. Tell me all the news. From your son*

Robert Woody Lindsey Woody

I will send you 5 more dollars and risk it.

Dennis Murphy was another member of the 104th Illinois. At the end of April an erroneous report had twenty-five thousand rebels about to attack Franklin, Tennessee. His regiment was quickly mobilized and sent out as pickets to warn of any potential attack. The miserable weather expressed highlights the difficult conditions soldiers on both sides experienced.

Camp Brintwood April 30th 63

Dear Brother,

I received your letter in due time wich gave me and all the Boys the gratist of pleasure in hearing from you and to know that you and Father and Mother and James and Mary is injoying good health which leave me at present. Thank God for it. Dear Brother we all morn the fait of jim Ryan. Your letter was the first that brought the news about him but since that there has been a dossen letters stating that mornfull news of poor Jim. I have received the paper yesterday and I am thankfull to you for it. Dear Brother Last Wednesday knight Gen Granger of Franklin sent us news that there was 25 thousand Rebels advancing on Franklin and would atact this place and Franklin to geather. At half past eleven we was all ordered to pack Napsacks strike tents and then they gave us 40 rounds of extra catrages so we had 80 rounds to carry. Then at 1 oclock we Marched over and took our place in side the fort lay in there all knight. Niset (next) Morning our company went out on picket. It commenced raining that afternoon and rained all night. We had no shelter and of corse we got wet as we could be. Friday morning it rained. We came back. We had to go to work and put up our tents in a bout 2 inches of blue mud. It rained all day Friday and knight. This morning it dus not rain but we are all wet and no dry clothes to put on. I would not rite this morning only there is a rumer that we cannot send no more mail for 10 days. I don't bleave it. Tom feels very Bad for the downfall of his brother and also for Marys bad luck with there children. We are expecting to get paid in a week or so. Let me know how father and mother and James and Mary is getting along. I don't know as I have any more at present but we all

join in sending you and Father and Mother and James and Mary and
Mr and Mrs Wolf and Pat and Jo Jinell and wife and M. Ryan and all
friends to numerus to mention.

So no more at
Present from your beloved Brother
D J. Murphy
Be shure and send me you picture

Joseph Vangundy wrote to his father in mid-May from the camp of the
26th Ohio near Murfreesboro. He was excited to hear that General
Burnsides had arrested the Copperhead, Clement Vallandigham, for
seditious speeches and anticipated an attack by the Confederates
soon.

Camp Ner Murfreesboro
Tenn May the 9 1863
Der father I take my pen in hand to let you no that I am well at present
and hope when these few lines comes to hand they may find you (and)
the rest of the family in fine spirits. Well father we have had some
purty bad wether for three or for days back. It has bin raining all the
time and came like winter to us here for we aint bin ust (used) to such
cold wether here in the south like it had ben for a while. I am afered
(afraid) our fruit is gone under down here. If it is I don't know what we
will do for aples an peaches this somer. It will go purty ruff with us for
last somer we had plenty of them. It done us great deal of good for we
was very cares (scarce) of rashings (rations) at that time. Well father
we herd some purty good news today. We herd that old burn sides
(Burnsides) had old verlanddingham (Vallandingham) arrested for
making Buternut speaches. Well all that I wish that they may hand
him and all his crew for that is what I am out here in surves (service) is
to conker (conquer) the dam rebels sons of bitches so it makes me mad
to here tell of such scondles (scoundrels) at home to get up and make
such speches. I(wouldn't) hang him for hangin is much to good for
such fewles (fools) orer skin him alive or some other punishment for
hangin is most to easy deth for him. Well father we are expeck a very
big fight here now purty soon for the rebs is in twelve miles of us.
They is about on hundred thousand rebs and our little army is a bout

seventy five thousand to fight aginc (against) but we haf the advantage of the rebs if they attack us for we will fight them in our breastworks. Then I no it will tak five rebes to whip one of us. Father I told Frank to give you tenn dolares an if he has tell me in your next leter you right. Will you if you please. An also right an tell me how Sam got thought (through) the fight at Fredricksburg. if you get a letter from him any ways soon. I herd from him about a week ago and he was well. Then yours with respeck fully

right Soon

From joseph Cangundy
Well all I have to toast is my little enfiled rifle & regard goes (to) Genel Rosey Cran (Rosecrans).

Vangundy's letter is an example of how rumors and exaggerations of enemy forces were constantly plaguing the troops. In reality, Bragg's army was smaller than Rosecrans' Army of the Cumberland. It was Rosecrans who was planning the next offensive action. Chattanooga continued to be one of the most important strategic locations in the entire Confederacy and Rosecrans' primary objective. With such a great deal of emphasis on railroads due to their enhanced ability to transport everything from troops, supplies and equipment at previously unthinkable speed and quantities, Chattanooga was crucial to both sides. As the intersection of four main railroads, whoever controlled Chattanooga held a significant advantage in logistics. These lines were crucial not just to the armies but to the survival of the Confederacy itself. As this new campaign was about to begin Bragg and Rosecrans split control of one of those vital lines. Their armies lay across the Nashville & Chattanooga Railroad. Supplies for Rosecrans came south from Nashville and Bragg was supplied by cars running northwest out of Chattanooga. Just below Chattanooga at Stevenson, Alabama, the Nashville & Chattanooga line intersected with the Memphis & Charleston Railroad which brought important supplies east from Vicksburg. To the south the Western & Atlantic Railroad came up from Atlanta then continued northeasterly toward Richmond as the East Tennessee & Georgia Railroad. These lines carried a significant percentage of all materials the Confederacy needed to wage war and sustain its people. So important were these lines of communication that met near Chattanooga that President Lincoln himself believed that if Chattanooga could be taken and held by the Union the Confederacy would "dwindle and die."

Equally important was the need for Rosecrans to engage and occupy Bragg's army. He might be reinforced from other sectors presenting a more formidable obstacle. It might also be possible for Bragg to send part of his force to reinforce General John C. Pemberton who was defending Vicksburg. By June of 1863 Pemberton was besieged by Union General Ulysses S. Grant and reinforcements from Bragg might possibly swing the balance. It was crucial that Bragg's Army be held intact in Tennessee, if not destroyed. Washington had been imploring Rosecrans to move for months but he had demurred. In late June, Rosecrans finally began advancing towards Bragg's Army which stood between him and Chattanooga. The Army of Tennessee was still dug in along the Duck River in strong defenses with Bragg headquartered at Tullahoma approximately 18 miles to the southeast.

A few weeks before Rosecrans launched his campaign, Vangundy wrote to his brother. Rumors had reached him that his brother had become a Copperhead and prior to receiving his brother's recent letter he had not heard from him in six months. Hence he did not know what to believe

Tenn
Camp Near Murfreesboro
June 9th 1863
Mr T M Vangundy

Dear brother I take this opportunity to reply to yours of June 3rd received today and read with pleasure. I was very glad to hear that you were favored with good health. My health is good at this time and is my wish that these few lines may find you favored with fine health. I was also extremely glad to hear that you were so true to the Union. A report came to me that you had turned butternut or Copperhead as the traitors of the north are generally called and a very true comparison too, I think. I was also informed that it was your intentions *to resist the draft but I could not credit the report for I tell you truly borther I would rather give up my own life than see or know that you had turned traitor to your country. No, I could not harbor such a thought that you could become so demoralized. I think if we all pull together we can soon put down this infernal rebellion. Sooner or latter it must be destroyed and we should all as true patriots should do all we can to have it crushed out at once. The sooner the better. We are yet encamped at Murfreesboro but I have no idea at all how long we will remain here. Their was some fighting along our front last week but we were not called out for the rebs are getting very particular about bringing on a general engagement with this army and well they might be for they with inferior numbers and on ground of they own picking were defeated. You wanted to know how much money I had sent to you. I sent you $30 the first time and $30 the second time. You may give mother $10 dollars of it and let Alec Graves have the $50 dollars. Yes I should like very much to be with you at some of them shin digs. I think that we could put some of them girls through on the double quick or to a very good advantage. It is not often that you get to sea a girl here. Wenches are pretty plenty but then you know are poor picking even for souldiers but if you should sea more than you can attend to just tell them to hold their water for we will be back after a while and then we will try and accommodate few of them as we will be in good heet for our rations. I saw Julius Vangundy yesterday. He was Well. They are now encamped about a half mile from us. I will close for this time. Be shure to write soon again. This is the first letter I have received from you for about 6 months. I begain to think that you were not going to write anymore. Direct as before. Don't fail to write soon. Yours very respectfully. Joseph Vangundy. Fare well for this time.*

Between the Duck River line and the Union army in Murfreesboro ran a long ridge which contained 4 gaps suitable for passage: Guys Gap to the west, then successively to the east; Bellbuckle Gap; Liberty Gap and Hoover's Gap. Hoover's Gap ran through mountainous terrain assumed to be unsuitable for troop movements. Bragg positioned his troops to block the other three gaps. General Leonidas Polk commanded Bragg's largest corps which he positioned near Shelbyville to block Guys and Bellbuckle Gaps. Lieutenant General William J. Hardee was placed to the right of the line near Liberty Gap. Bragg sent General Nathan B. Forrest's cavalry far to the west to protect against any sweeping movement in that direction. Bragg was well prepared to receive Rosecrans' attack.

Rosecrans however refused a direct assault and instead developed an elaborate plan to flank Bragg out of his position by threatening his line of communications with Chattanooga.

There were several moving parts to Rosecrans' plan. On June 24th, in order to deceive Bragg, he sent Major General David S. Stanley's cavalry far to the west to convince Bragg that he was indeed avoiding the passes and trying to swing past Bragg's left. At the same time he sent Major General Gordon Granger's Reserve Corps through Bellbuckle pass toward Shelbyville in order to occupy Polk's attention. He also sent a single division far to the east toward the town of McMinnville beyond the Hoover Gap. Upon being notified of this small movement, Bragg thought that this lone division was a diversion and that the main attack would be launched against Shelbyville where he continued to focus his attention.

Rosecrans' plan was working perfectly. Instead of attacking Bragg's strength at Shelbyville he sent his main force to the east. The 14th Army Corps of General George Thomas came through the nearly impassable Hoover Gap. The lead element of that attack was Colonel John T Wilder's mounted infantry who charged through the Hoover Gap so quickly that the Confederates had no time to react and put up a fight. When Wilder's men reached the mouth of the pass they were almost 10 miles ahead of the rest of the infantry. This put them in great peril from the brigades of William B. Bates and Bushrod Johnson who now sought to counter attack and dislodge them. Fortunately, Wilder's troops were armed with Spencer repeating rifles. The tenacity of the troops and the firepower of the seven shot rifles enabled them to hold the gap for the balance of the day until Thomas could bring the rest of the corps through the gap to support them. The fighting finally died down as darkness fell. Wilder had suffered minimal casualties. 14 killed and 47 wounded. The toll taken by his men's Spencers was much higher. Bates lost 23 percent of his force. 146 men killed or wounded.

Confederate cavalry continued to report heavy Federal troop concentrations (Granger's Corps) on the road to Shelbyville, but Bragg had heard nothing from the passes on his right where Thomas and the 14th Corps had captured Hoover Gap. Likewise, Liberty Gap had been gained by Major General Alexander McCook's XX Corps. By the end of the 24th of June, Bragg had no concrete idea of what was happening.

On the 25th Bates and Johnson assaulted the Federals lodged in Hoover pass once more while Major General Patrick Cleburne attempted to regain Liberty Gap. Again the Confederates suffered more severe casualties than their counterparts while failing to dislodge them.

Finally, on the 26th, Bragg became convinced of the heavy fighting on his right and prepared to shift forces to that sector of the line but those movements did not materialize in time. By the close of the day he realized the true extent of the peril he was in after Thomas' corps, led again by Wilder's fast moving brigade, had broken through the rebel line at Hoover Gap and was headed south toward Manchester, a move that would threaten to cut Bragg off from Chattanooga.

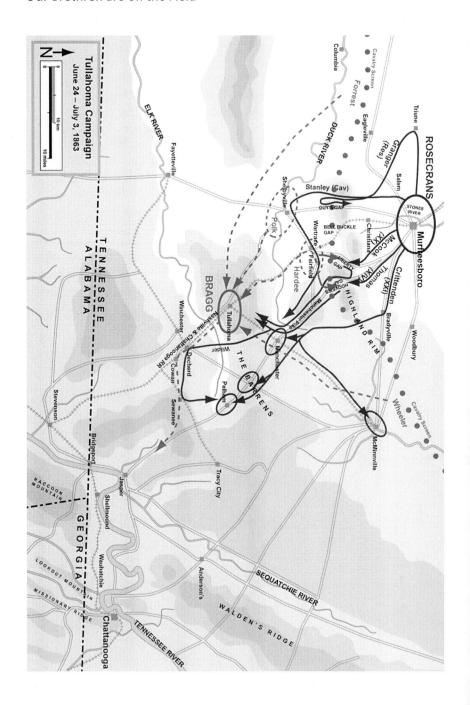

John Euclid Magee was a member of Stanford's Mississippi Battery, Stewart's-Strahl's Brigade, Cheatham's Division, Polk's Corp, Army of Tennessee. He was positioned near Shelbyville when Rosecrans commenced his advance. In his diary he recorded the following from June 22nd to June 26th.

Monday, June 22, 1863.   In camp, fine cool day.   Received two papers from Miss Nora Grant, which were like ministering spirits from some divine creature, to my soul. No news from Miss(issippi). Mrs. Coe and Mr. Ball paid us another visit today.

Tuesday, June 23, 1863. In camp, cloudy. Several rumors from Miss. Genl Grant has assaulted Vicksburg again, and been badly repulsed. The enemy driven out of East Tenn.

Wednesday, June 24, 1863. In camp. Fighting on our right and in front. Enemy supposed to be advancing. Nothing from Miss.

Thursday, June 25, 1863. In camp. Understood Genl Stewart had a fight with the enemy at Hoover's Gap, and was repulsed, the enemy getting possession of the gap. Also Lidell's Brigade were driven back from Liberty Gap. Some excitement, think we will have a battle before long. The enemy appears to be coming in heavy force. In evening were ordered out to front, say the enemy are coming on Guy's Gap. Went a few hundred yards and were turned back. Orders to cook two days rations and be ready to move at moment's notice.

Friday, June 26, 1863. In camp, orders to cook two days rations, cooked on hand. The enemy is advancing, have possession of Hoover's and Liberty Gap, very severe fighting.

Axel Reed, the orderly sergeant for Company K, 2nd Minnesota recorded the first three days of the campaign in his diary:

June 23. Orders were given at 5 a.m. to march at 7 a.m., with tents and baggage. Marched about 8 a.m. to near Harpeth creek where we took the road leading to the S. E. resting quite often through the day, arriving at the Murfreesboro and Eagleville Pike at sunset, where we bivouacked in a wheat field. Our whole division is along, viz: 1st brigade, Col Walker; 2nd brigade, Col. Steadman; 4rd brigade, Col. Van Diveer, and are about 7 miles from M.

24th; marched about 10 o'clock and reached the Shelbyville and M. Pike at 2 p.m. and marched past a body of troops, and our regiment relieved a regiment of skirmishers. Companies E, F and K were deployed and a sharp fire was opened on us from the rebels as soon as the deploying commenced. We exchanged shots with them for about three hours at about 200 yards. The rebels opened with a cannon. One shell burst about 15 feet over my head and I picked up a piece that fell close behind me. The rebels left about 6 p.m., and we were on the ground within ten minutes afterwards. We marched back at midnight and built fires. It rained all day long, hard, and during the skirmishing.

25th. Marched at 6 a.m. and struck the 'Pike' soon after and turned our course south, and soon came up to the balance of Gen. Thomas' corps. Gen. T. passed us on our route and it is the first time we have seen him since last _____. He is much liked. We formed in line of battle about noon at the right of the pike and were placed in support of some batteries on some high hills. Sharp cannonading was kept up for three hours and we could see the rebels moving back in line. The 18th regulars and 17th Ohio charged across a low piece of ground and drove upon the rebel battery and drove them back. The whole rebel line moved back and nearly the whole 14th Corps bivouacked for the night.

26th. Marched about 6 a.m. and soon struck Manchester Pike and, after marching about three miles in the gap (which is a range of hills or bluffs each side of the road), we waited some time for batteries and troops to get into position. While waiting Gen. Thomas passed us while we were resting, and the old fellow looks natural and in good health. AT 10 a.m. the division formed in line of battle at the right of the pike and marched forward to support the battery, which took a position on a high knoll in front of the 2nd Minnesota and on the left of the 9th Ohio, in the center, and the 87th Indiana on the right; the 35th Ohio in reserve. We then took position on the summit of the hill to the *left of the battery, where we could see the several batteries playing upon each other. The sight was grant to behold; not a man of the rebel army was visible, as they kept in the woods out of sight. We saw their cavalry retreating and our battery threw a few shells at them, but they burst before reaching them. It rained all the forenoon. We bivouacked on the flat between the hills...*

Bragg's position had become completely untenable. He ordered Polk and Hardee to fall back to Tullahoma immediately. Rain, which had been falling for 17 days, made the situation all the more treacherous and unmanageable. On the Federal side, Wilder and Thomas' XIVth Corp reached Manchester on the 27th in spite of the rain. The next day Wilder's mounted brigade sprinted south, reaching Decherd. There they destroyed a section of the Nashville and Chattanooga Railroad, temporarily cutting Bragg's communication.

The situation continued to deteriorate for the Confederates. By the evening of the 29th Bragg held a council of war with Hardee and Polk. Polk was in favor of retreating and Hardee wasn't sure what to do but leaned toward fighting. No decision was made.

On June 30th the three Federal corps of Thomas, McCook and Crittenden had all reached Manchester and started to close in on Bragg's rear from the northeast. The previous day Shelbyville had been taken by Granger's corps and Stanley's cavalry.

Reed's diary continued to describe the movement, engagements and conditions over this period of the campaign:

June 27th. Marched early and took the road at the right of the pike leading towards Tullahoma, until we reached a small town at Duck River, where we took the left-hand road and marched for Manchester, where we arrived at one o'clock at night, after wading considerable of a stream at midnight. Three brigades of rebels retreated ahead of us, but on the same road to Tullahoma on their retreat to Manchester, were cut off. Gen. Rosencranz established his headquarters here today and many troops are arriving. It rained again today.

June 28th. Laid in camp until about noon, occupying the time drawing rations, washing, etc. At noon marched six miles and camped on the road to Tullahoma. After marching about four miles the 9th Ohio was sent in advance to feel along for the enemy, and met them a mile further on, when skirmishing commenced and the enemy fell back. We could see the rebels on a hill a half mile in advance. They were mounted on mules and every conceivable thing that could carry a man. After remaining in line a short time we bivouacked and cooked supper. It rained in the forenoon quite hard. It appears that the enemy massed their forces at Liberty Gap, expecting us to come that way, consequently we got through Hoovers Gap so easy.

29th. We were ordered out at 8 a.m. and left our haversacks and blankets. Our brigade relieved another brigade about one and one half miles out. Companies I and B were deployed as skirmishers and our regiment took the advance of the brigade. We drove the rebel skirmishers back while a sharp fire was kept up and after driving them back three quarters of a mile, we fell back to our first position to await the arrival of Gen. Reynold's division to relieve us. It began to rain about noon and poured down, wetting us to the skin. The rebs followed us up after they found out we had dropped back. An escort of Gen. Wheeler's rode so near our lines that he was shot through the body and was brought back on a stretcher. He was taking orders to Col. Harrison from Gen. W. He tore up the dispatch, but it was found and read. His horse was captured. We again advanced on the enemy and drove them steadily back about a mile, where they held a strong position on a hill, with a field before us. They had a battery in position. One piece of ours came up and was put in position in the center of our regiment by the company dropping back, but Gen. Vandeveer had it moved to the road on our left. They fired two shots and limbered up when the rebel battery opened much nearer than was expected, the ball just passed our cannon and struck the horse of the doctor of the 35th Ohio, in the breast and passed through him lengthwise. We lay for an hour within 300 yards of their battery while our skirmishers were firing, as we did not wish to hold any more of the ground than we then held. It rained in torrents the most of the afternoon and we retried at dark, wet and hungry, and had to wade three creeks.

June 30th. Laid in camp all day. Occupied the time in washing up, inspection, etc. Troops are coming in very fast. Reynolds' division camped one half mile ahead of us. Rousseau's division camped nearby and General Sheridan's division camped at our right. All the surplus baggage is sent back, everything but a rubber blanket and a shelter tent to the man. We have been the whole time since we left Triune, with nothing but a rubber blanket, and it has rained every day since the 23rd, until today, and it has made the roads very bad, consequently it has retarded Gen. Rosencranz's movements. It is thought that we would have gotten into Tullahoma behind Bragg's army if it had not been for the bad roads. Weather pleasant today...

During these same few days Magee penned his thoughts in his diary from the opposing side:

Saturday, June 27, 1863. The revillie blown at 3 o'clock. Packed all camp equipage and moved out to the Pike. The general belief is retreat to Tullahoma. About 6, our brigade came along, and we moved on towards Shelbyville. Stopped and saw Miss Mollie Given, bid her good bye. The whole Army moving to the rear. We took the left hand road by Roseville to Tullahoma. Heard heavy cannonading in the rear. Travelled very slow – road awful bad – very long wagon trains – great many wagons broke down – came 8 miles from Shelbyville and camped. Reports from the rear say that early this morning the enemy advanced on the Murfreesboro Pike, drove our cavalry under Genl Martin back on Shelbyville – had some hard fighting. Our cavalry were repulsed and scattered in every direction. Genl Martin and Wheeler who was with him escaped by swimming the river, lost their horses, sabres, and everything. The enemy killed and captured over half the whole command with three pieces of Capt Wiggin's Battery. The enemy chase as far (as) Duck river Bridge, 3 miles from our camp tonight, and returned. They occupy Shelbyville tonight.

Sunday, June 28, 1863. Up at 3 and getting ready to march. Rained some during the night. Was detailed to help get Lieut Turner's baggage wagon out of mudhole. Started at daylight – travelled slow – roads very bad and miry – heard firing in the rear. Our cavalry in line of battle 1 mile in the rear. Got into Tullahoma at 5 o'clock. Cheatham's Division all camped together on the east side of town. Boys all very tired – every person and everything muddy. The enemy pressing our rear, and rumor of their flanking us. Mrs. McCall and Mrs. Coe came through in an ambulance. Weather very warm.

Monday, June 29, 1863. Bright beautiful morning, but very warm. Orders to keep two days cooked rations on hand. About 8 o'clock orders came to move immediately. Our brigade left everything, and double quicked nearly a mile – formed in line of battle ½ mile from town. The enemy at Dechards Station. 12(?) miles toward Chattanooga on the railroad. The whole army were soon in line by our fortifications, which consists of two large forts in the most commanding places – the timber cut down all in front of us. The enemy reported moving on us. Commenced raining about 10 o'clock and rained nearly all day. The whole army in line of battle, had left everything at camp unpacked, and all got wet. Laid in line of battle all night – awful times, the ground covered with water in many places. Not much sleeping done – did not rain but little during the night. The enemy were driven back from Dechard's by Walthall's Brigade, which was sent down on the cars. Every person expecting a battle in a few days. Buckner's Division from East Tenn. Came in during the night. We have 45,000 men here now. Can hear nothing from Miss or Virginia, all absorbed in passing events here.

Bragg feared he was about to be ensnared. That night, June 30th, he ordered the withdrawal from Tullahoma and fell back south of the Elk River where he thought he might make a stand. On July 1, after being in this position for only a matter of hours, convinced that Rosecrans was about to completely flank him he ordered a full retreat. Magee described that last day in the works and their withdrawal over night:

Tuesday, June 30th, 1863. Were stirring early – had cleared off. The ground was wet. The whole line of infantry throwing up breastworks. Our brigade building a parapet work for our guns. In afternoon the idea got out we were going to retreat – say the enemy are trying to flank us on our right, Genl Forrest fighting them in front. They are within a few miles, but do not appear to be advancing. About 4 o'clock orders came to cook 3 days rations, throw away all tents, reduce baggage, and be ready to move at a moment's warning. About dark commenced moving to the rear, came as far as town and waited till 1 o'clock. Troops moving all night – some went by railroad. Quartermasters and commissaries very busy shipping stores. We managed to get a lot of cracker and meat. We started for Alasonia at

1 – marched with our brigade over the worst of roads, marched all night.

Reed's diary continues with the occupation of Tullahoma and slow pursuit of Bragg's rear guard:

July 1st, 1863. We were ordered, at 10 o'clock a.m., to be ready to march immediately with two days' rations. Marched directly towards Tullahoma, marched through a dense grove of black oak on each side of a narrow road. Arrived in the town of Tullahoma about 2 o'clock p.m. and found enemy had gone. Our division was the first in town. One mile east of town we came to a line of breastworks hastily thrown up, with a half a mile of trees felled for an abattis. The works were much stronger to our right front. Gen. Alex. McCook came into town soon after we got there. After resting about two hours we took a position to bivouac. The town was nearly deserted, only a few women remaining. The enemy left a number of siege guns, entrenching tools, cornmeal, tents, etc. We did not destroy anything except the carriages of the guns. Squads of rebel prisoners are continually coming in, taken by our cavalry. They report Bragg's forces at from 35 to 45,000. Bragg's army worked on breastworks until 8 o'clock last night and at 2 o'clock a general retreat was ordered and the last left in sight of our column that first entered. Troops are passing continuously. Our boys are well supplied with tents and covers found about the houses. Weather fine and exceedingly warm toady. We learned that the rebel Gen., Stearns was killed, day before yesterday, in skirmishing with us.

2nd. Marched early this morning, took a road leading southeast, east of the railroad, while McCook's corps went to the right of the railroad. We passed a number of 'Secesh' wagons broken down and clothing strewn by the road-side, cornmeal was scattered all along the road. Cannonading commenced ahead of us about 10 o'clock. We had to move slow on account of the amount of troops moving on the road. Bigelow and Beard took, with two men of the 14th Ohio, eleven prisoners today. They got strayed from the regiment and came onto them. Buckner's division is said to be in front of us. We bivouacked at 4 o'clock, in the woods about 8 miles from Tullahoma. Weather hot.

July 3rd. We waited until noon for Rousseau's division to cross Elk river, which is much swollen by the recent rains. Our brigade moved down to the river about 12 o'clock. It was a novel sight to see the troops crossing the stream which was about six rods wide and four feet deep, with swift current. Two ropes were stretched across for men to hang onto to keep from going down stream. Some would strip naked, do their things in a rubber blanket and string it with their accoutrements on their bayonets, then they would make their way across, some by ropes and others hanging onto horses tails. I noticed Captain Roper (our division quartermaster) busy with his horse hauling the boys across and he would take nearly a dozen at a time. Someone remarked that it was too many hanging on to his horse's tail when Captain R. said, 'I'll pull them through if the tail don't pull out.' Some lost their haversacks, others their accoutrements, etc. One of the 10th Kentucky was drowned, and a number of Rousseau's division is said to have been drowned. Our brigade all got across about four o'clock and went into bivouack about three quarter of a mile from the ford. There was a heavy shower today from ten o'clock, until about noon. Vicksburg is reported taken and Lee's army whipped out by General Meade, who superseded Hooker. We have to move very slowly on account of the roads and streams and our transportation. is doubtful whether we come up with the enemy before they reach Chattanooga.

July 4th. We moved forward about a mile to a better camping ground. Rousseau's division moved forward from where we camped near Winchester and Deckard Pike. A salute of 35 guns was fired by the 4th regular battery.

5th. Have to live on mush with very little meat and salt. We never have been so short of rations before.

6th. Our teams, that have been back to Manchester, came up today, bringing our shelter tents, but no provisions.

7th. Rained nearly all night last night. Have stuck our tents in order today and signs of a stay here. Men started last night for provisions and succeeded in getting a few crackers. Got a pound of crackers to the man, meal all gone...

Over these same seven days, Magee's battery continued to struggle through the conditions and circumstances created by a full retreat on limited roads to get their guns to railcars to be taken to Chattanooga:

Wednesday, July 1st, 1863. On the road marching – got into Alasonia at 12 – very hot day – the enemy pressing our rear. Alasonia is on the railroad 8 miles from Tullahoma. There is a railroad bridge over the Elk river here the enemy have tried to burn. Several small redoubts and stockade forts defending it, ground very hilly. We put our guns in position on a hill pointing northward – say the enemy is coming, and expect to fight here. Streams are all very high – Elk river running high everywhere. In evening went about a mile to camp where our brigade was. No fight – expect to march again.

Thursday, July 2d, 1863. Up at 3 o'clock and ready to move. Forrest fought the enemy near Tullahoma last evening and was repulsed – lost the rest of Wiggins battery with the Captain and 25 or thirty of his men – some 8 or 10 killed – badly cut up. At sunup moved with brigade – had to haul 3 extra guns of another battery that were left to be sent on the cars. Boys complained, it was awful hard on me and horses both. Genl Anderson's Brigade bring up the rear. Went by way of Winchester to Cowan – heard cannonading in the rear – every person wondering where we are going to – all down on Bragg for leaving Tenn – some few Tennessee boys deserting. We got to Cowan at 5 o'clock after very hard work, winding about, and changing roads 5 or 6 times – weather awful hot – troops suffering. Loaded the extra guns we hauled on the cares. Rumors wild in regard to the enemy, reliable though, that they are pressing our rear. Camped near the railroad – shipping everything they can by railroad. Drew rations and cooked some.

Tuesday, July 7th, 1863. Cloudy morning. Reynolds and I went down town and got some coffee soda and tobacco – prices about as high here as they have been. About 9 o'clock the carriages came in – mounted guns and chests – rained very hard – all got wet – moved out to a small grove and went into camp to await orders where to go. Rained, very hard shower. In evening got orders to move out to Brigade camp about 3 miles and a half from town. Started and went about a mile to a creek that was so high we could not cross – went back a few hundred yards and camped on the side of the road. Rumored that Vicksburg has surrendered. News from Virginia quite flattering. Our army have captured Chambersburg, Carlisle, and have had a great battle at Gettysburg. Hooker has been superseded by Col Mead of McClellan's staff. We have captured 40 thousand prisoners.

Bragg's Army of Tennessee had drawn back across the Cumberland Mountains as well as the Tennessee River, taking up positions around Chattanooga on July 7th, 1863. Rosecrans' Tullahoma campaign had virtually pushed the Confederates out of Middle Tennessee in just 9 days and at a remarkably small cost to the Federal Army of the Cumberland of only 84 dead and 476 wounded.

On the 8th and 9th of July, Magee described their position and the depression that befell the entire Confederate army.

Wednesday, July 8th, 1863. Up early, and moved out to our Brigade right at the foot of a mountain. Rained a hard shower – everything wet. Camped in the woods – cleared off about noon. Boys drying clothes and washing up. everything dirty and wet.

Thursday, July 9th, 1863. In camp 3 ½ miles from Chattanooga. All Cheatham's and Withers' Division encamped hereabout. Report that Genl Hardee's corps is going to Loudon, East Tenn. Most every person bemoaning and cursing "Old Bragg" for leaving Middle Tenn. Some, however, wish to justify him, while others say it was ordered from the war department. Most of the army believe we could have whipped them at Tullahoma, and blame Bragg for retreating. From the best information I can get, we had a force including cavalry, at and about Tullahoma of 45 thousand men. This I believe to be so, and with the advantages we possessed over them, I do not see why we did not stay there, notwithstanding their stories about the enemy cutting off our supplies to the contrary. But I have nothing to do with plans, and know not why and what they abandoned Middle Tenn for! Tis bad enough – all confidence in Genl Bragg is lost, and I do not believe this army can win a victory under his superintendence. Hard upon the fiat of Tennessee comes the gloomy news of the surrender of the famished garrison of Vicksburg with over 20 thousand men on the 4th day of July. This news causes a depression of spirits in the whole army. Things are in a bad state in the Miss. Department. From Virginia the news is less cheering than at first – we do not claim a victory at Gettysburg, and our army is falling back rapidly. The fighting was desperate and our loss in general officers was very heavy. Northern papers seem to think Col Mead has whipped us badly. Fixing up clothes all day – warm and cloudy.

Joe O'Bryan, captain of Company B of the 1st Tennessee Volunteers, shared the same opinion as Magee, expressing the extent of demoralization and surprise by the decision to abandon strong positions without a fight and retreat before Rosecrans' advance. Upon arriving near Chattanooga he wrote to his sisters, disgusted by Bragg's handling of the situation:

Camp near Chattanooga Ten
Wednesday Evening July 9th 1863
My Own dear Sisters:

My last letter was from Martha & Just rec'd at while at Tullahoma the same day that I forwarded you a letter commenced at Shelby and finished at Tullahoma. It was written in quite a hurry and of course could not write much as you will in all probability only hear that our army is at Chattanooga without any explanations. I will write you somewhat in detail.

About the 25th of June Hoovers Gap on our right and in front of Manchester and also Liberty gap were taken by the enemy. It was considered a very great piece of carelessness on our part to leave such important points with so little protection. At the time it was thought that some one was very much to blame and as Bragg's at the head of affairs he (was) now censured for it until the fault was shown to be some where else which as yet has never been done. This loss gave the enemy great advantages so it was concluded to fall back on Tullahoma. We left Shelby the on Saturday the 27th and reached Tullahoma Sunday 28th. The mud was <u>miserable</u> and had a very bad trip of 18 miles. We remained at Tullahoma Sunday night, Monday night and commenced leaving Tuesday night. The place was very strongly fortified but we would have had great advantages had Rosecrans attacked us but he marched by our right flank within a few *miles of us and we were compelled to fall back towards Winchester. The movement commenced at dark and our Brigade left at 3 o'clock in the morning. We reached Allisonia on the south side of Ten River Wednesday Evening and camped there that night. When we left Tullahoma it was said that we were to attack the enemy wherever found and it was <u>not a retreat.</u> It having been said by the "slaves" of the high officers that we were to attack them it was expected that we would certainly have a fight that day near Allisonia. Col. Starnes was mortally wounded (and since died) in a few miles of Tullahoma. It was a very great loss and felt to be so by the entire Army. Thursday we left and camped at Cowans depot at the foot of the Mountain and next day ascended the Mountain and camped on the top and next day crossed the Tennessee River on a Pontoon Bridge at the Mouth of Battle Creek 4 miles above Bridgeport. Buckner's division crossed at Bridgeport and Hardees corps some 20 or 30 miles above. We halted one day at Shell Mound and reached here yesterday. The march was very orderly all the way. The army lost a large number who remained behind. I suppose the loss in that respect will be at 6,000. They were from the Tennessee Regts. Some went by homes to see their families & will be up shortly. Some remained behind to stay about home and Bushwhack – and some deserted. It is very mortifying that so many should have left and I think it is caused by the fact that the Army has no confidence in Bragg since Tullahoma giving up their homes without proper attempts to defend them. This is no more for them. ...Since the Murfreesboro fight Bragg has been very unpopular and did not have the confidence of the men although he and his friends have been attempting to get the men to like him. The Army thought Bragg was running from Rosecrans without sufficient cause and they, also thought that if a battle was fought Bragg was not competent to lead them. So you see that the Army has <u>no</u> confidence in Bragg and I think they have cause. I do hope some one else will be put in command. We are camped in the neighborhood of this place and not even a rumor of any movement. Mrs. Bailey came out to camp yesterday but I was absent and I am going to town this morning to see her.*

Tom Maney reached here several days since and is quite well. I have not time to write more now but will write again in a few days. I hope to get a letter from you this morning. Mr. Elliott is here & his family and they are well.

    Much love to Cousin Susan & Sister. I am very well having stood the "trip" fairly.

    With much love,

    Your own Brother,

    Joe

P.S. Tom Maney saw George at Meridian on the way to Woodville. He was very well.

In Rosecrans' camps, Axel Reed was infuriated by discovering that rations were being given to rebel prisoners and civilians while Union troops were forced to receive just half rations. He recorded the letter he wrote to the Nashville Union in response to this injustice:

Camp near Elk River, Tenn., July 10th, 1863.
To the Nashville Union.
"We, of the 2nd regiment, Minnesota, of Vandeveer's brigade, 14th Army Corps, have been marching night and day in mud and water nearly two weeks and have captured Tullahoma, and as our reward we have been put on half and three-fourths rations, while the balance is being fed out to rebel citizens and deserters. We think they ought to seek their grub where they do their rights, within the rebel lines, and by knowing if this is done by the order of Gen. Brannan, Gen. Thomas or Gen. Rosencranz would oblige.

MANY SOLDIERS."

    "The Nashville Union was distributed through camp the very next day and the boys that discovered the letter, hailed it with cheers of joy. The supply of lawful rations was at once made to the satisfaction of all except probably, Brannan, a new imported general from the eastern army, of the "McClelland type," who at once busied himself finding out who wrote the letter to the Nashville Union, asking "who was responsible," and he soon found out from the "Union's office," for the sergeant's own bunkmate did not know that his Orderly had written such a letter. In consequence of finding out who had violated the rules of war that had caused him censure, he issued an order worded nearly as follows:

Headquarters 3rd Division 14th Army Corps, July 20th, 1863.
To Colonel James George,
Commanding 2nd Minnesota Regiment
Place First Sergeant A. H. Reed, of Co. K, in close confinement and keep him until further orders.
(signed) J. M. Brannan
Brigadier General.

Outside of Chattanooga, John Magee continued posting in his diary routinely during this period as well. The down time between fighting and marching was spent repairing and maintaining the guns of their battery in preparation for some movement yet to be revealed. Also heavy on his mind are the events in Mississippi and Virginia, as he hears more news about Vicksburg and Gettysburg which continued to darken.

Friday, July 10, 1863. In camp – packed up some winter clothing to send off. Fixing up gun carriages and harness – artificers at work repairing wagons. News from Miss that Grant is marching on Jackson. Genl Lee's army is at Hagerstown Maryland. Weather warm-cloudy. Hardee's troops moving towards Knoxville. Great speculations about what move will be made, and where Polk's corps will go.

Saturday, July 11th, 1863. In camp – hot and showery – had inspection. Orders for artillery of our division to park together. In afternoon moved our camp one mile nearer Chattanooga where Turner's battery was and camped. No news from Miss. From Virginia – some skirmishing – another battle expected. Our loss at Gettysburg supposed to be between ten and 18 thousand. The enemy have attacked Charleston, S.C. again. Some Yankee cavalry reported across the river not far from Chattanooga.

Sunday, July 12th, 1863. In camp. I am twenty two years old today. No news except details of Virginia fighting and Vicksburg surrendering.

Monday, July 13th, 1863. In camp – all hands fixing up the battery. Many things out of order. Our inspector condemned all our carriages, but it will be a job to get new ones. Genl Grant approaching Jackson – skirmishing commenced with some little artillery firing – think Genl

Johnston will evacuate Jackson – his force is reported at 30 thousand and Grant's 65 thousand. Considerable fighting at Charleston – our loss so far 150 men – the enemy attacked with both infantry and gunboats. Nothing new from Virginia. Our cavalry fighting a little opposite Chatta. Weather warm.

Tuesday, July 14th, 1863. In camp. Meagre details keep coming from Virginia. It appears our loss was very heavy at Gettysburg – some 13 or 14 generals killed wounded and missing – aggregate loss estimated at over 20 thousand. Lee's army still at Hagerstown. No news from Charleston. Grant still threatening Jackson.

Wednesday, July 15th, 1863. In camp. Warm and cloudy – rained some. Lent a package of clothes to Dr. Ward. Virginia news about the same, and Miss. also. They have had a hard fight at Charleston, the enemy gaining possession of a portion of Morris Island. They charged Battery Wagner, but were repulsed. Warm weather.

Thursday, July 16, 1863. In camp – warm and cloudy. Nothing new from Virginia. Considerable fighting at Jackson Miss. Grant repulsed in two or three assaults – Breckinridge's troops highly complimented. Tis still thought Genl Johnston will fall back from Jackson. Tis said Rosencrans' army occupy Middle Tennessee, Tullahoma as their base, their cavalry scouting on this side of the mountain – do not think he will move on Chattanooga. Northern accounts say the people of Indiana are wild about John Morgan. He has turned up again, Micawber like, at Corydon Indiana – captured the town, and paroled the home guards. They think he is going to Camp Chase and liberate the prisoners. Every person wishing to know where John Morgan is.

Friday, July 17, 1863. In camp. Grant still pressing Jackson, Miss. Lee's army is falling back to south side of the Potomac. Weather warm and cloudy.

Saturday, July 18, 1863. In camp – warm and cloudy. Genl Johnston has evacuated Jackson and the enemy are in possession of it. Lee's army quiet on the south side of the Potomac. Rumor that some of Rosencrans' are about to make a raid in North Alabama. Every person wishing to hear news, but most of the people despondent. Wrote to

Dr. Ward for some flour and potatoes. Weather warm and signs of rain.

Sunday, July 19, 1863. In camp – warm and cloudy – no particular news.

Monday, July 20, 1863. In camp. Genl Johnston's army at Moxton, Miss. Weather warm.

Tuesday, July 21, 1863. In camp doing nothing – no news.

Wednesday, July 22, 1863. In camp – built arbors over guns. It appears our loss at Vicksburg is 30 thousand prisoners – no other news. Weather warm and pleasant.

On the 18th of July Joe O'Bryan followed up on his letter to his sisters with additional details including the reorganization of command and the happenings within the army, as well as updates on many of the people they knew either visiting or living in the area. He also expressed his feelings regarding his faith in the future and a Kind Providence.

Camp near Chattanooga Tenn
July 18th 1863
My Own dear Sisters
I have been here since the 7th and have written you but one letter since my arrival. I have been intending to write every day for the past week but have not done so. In the first place I have been very busy and then I have been "enjoying" a bad cold for some days past. Day before yesterday it was at its worst and hope soon to be entirely free from it. I have quit work only one day on account of it. I feel it very little today and hope tonight's sleep will make me "OK". Of course you are very much interested in the present state of our affairs and in no one place more than in this Army it being nearest your home. I gave you a short sketch of our move from Chattanooga to this point and told you that a large number of the troops had remained behind probably 5 or 6000. Since then I have ascertained more correctly and find the loss to be much less. The "Stragglers" or "deserters" (as they are called) of the entire army did not exceed 2500 from Shelbyville to this point. Many of those are now coming in only having gone by

home to tell all "goodbye". It is gratifying indeed to know such to be the true state of the thing. Cheatham's Division composed of Tennesseans had about 500 to remain behind. Many are coming in all ready. Several of the Regiments of the Division are stronger than when they left Shelbyville being reinforced by old absentees. This is the case with many other Regts. of the Army. Our Brigade lost more heavily than any other one brigade I have heard of. We have the 1st Tenn combined with regts. To consolidate with the 11th Tennesse & Maney's battalion. The 16th & 27th lost about 10, the 64th a few and the 11th 134. Battalions about ___. The 4th was raised in Bedford, Franklin, Coffee & adjoining counties also some companies parts of Co's between the Tunnel (beyond Stevenson) & there too five from Jackson Co. Ala. Maney's Battalion was raised in Humphreys Co. and has been deserting ever since it has been in the Brig. And no one is at all surprised at it. While at Shelbyville in camp they were deserting constantly. I think it was because they weren't settled & had nothing to do & under no discipline. I have written thus fully knowing that you will hear all sorts of rumors and would like to be posted upon the true state of things. There is very little if any difference in the number of men in the Army now & when it left Shelbyville. I mean of course all that part which now is middle Tennessee and have no reference to other troops which are here. You may rely upon the above as this is from good authorities. The army is in very good health but needing some clothing (some not suffering at all for the want of it.) A large number of shoes are needed (as many of the men are barefooted) and a lot is expected every day. All are so confident of success as ever although it looks rather dark just now. Everything is very quiet here and no probability of a move soon. The prospect is we will have another camp yet. We are building fortifications again but I hope it does not follow that they will share the same fate that those we built in Middle Tenn did.

Gen. Hardee & staff left Thursday to report to Joseph Johnston and D H Hill will take command of his corps. Gen'l Cheatham has a furlough for 15 days and has gone to Georgia to rest. Gen'l Maney being Senior Brig. is in command of the division & Col. Murray is 1st Regt in command of the Brig. I heard tonight that Gen. Withers had resigned but could hear no reasons. I was astonished that such should be the case as he is one of Gen. Bragg's few friends.

If it is true that he has resigned Patton Anderson will in all probability be made Maj. Gen'l. Anderson stands very high with the Army. He is now at Bridgeport with his Brigade. Tom Maney returned about the time we reached here. He found things doing very well on the plantation with a large grain crop but the Planters will get the benefit of it now. He left William Maney there to carry the negroes away should Vicksburg fall but I think it very doubtful whether he could come to any conclusion what to do before the enemy took possession. I have heard nothing from Betty since the letter I enclosed you. Hardy is in his old Cavalry Co in North Mississippi. Eliza is at Rome with John Bell. We have had rainy weather for nearly 3 months until Thursday this being about the only 3 dry days together since the commencement and it looks like rain every day now. The top of the crop in middle Tenn. was very great to us. It was large and fine quality. If we had not moved there till now in all probability we (would) have been there living on new flour instead of Corn Meal. I am rejoiced to hear of your good health & comfortable situation could gratify me more and my prayers that you may be as pleasantly situated during the war. I received two letters from George today.

Sunday Morning 19 July

I quit writing last night after finishing the last page to you as I was afraid the night air my effect my hand. I have not been in Chattanooga since Friday (last) but expect to go in today. Mr. Elliott has been staying with Judy Hook in town but left Friday to go to Macon Ga and expects to return in a day or so. He is thinking of opening a school at some point in Ga, probably Athens. Dick Leightner says he saw Frank Elliott in town yesterday and I will try to see him today. D. Bonner with his negroes is _____ in school 100 miles from here. I have learned nothing from Franklin since leaving Shelbyville. The evening after we left Shelbyville _____ Stricklers father came south of Duck River to see some of his friends and started home in the evening and upon reaching the river found our cavalry & the enemy fighting heavily and our cavalry put a wounded man in his buggy and made him carry him to Tullahoma and he could not get back to Shelbyville for

_____. He was very much troubled about it. I came by the command after our troops passed through and the family was very blue. Miss Mary & Laura were thus cleaning up. They were very kind & sent much love to you. Miss Mary promised to write to Aunt Martha as soon as the Federals came in possession and let her hear from us. The Ala. Lady wanted me to take some butter along with me but I had no way to take it.

The letters from you all are so kind and good that I sometimes think I was not deserving so much. You all manifest too much uneasiness about me; I do not want you to do so. I have been thus far blessed with the necessary for my comfort & happiness. I think peculiarly for I am thankful and shall ever be so for such kindness from Kind Providence. Let He decide for me in (the) future what joys or sorrows He may send. His will be done not mine. Let happen what may I know that "alls for the best" although it may not seem so to us at the time. The late letters I have received from yourselves George and Lou (if such could be the case) are more kind and affectionate than usual. I can not help asking myself is such the case? Let me and you my dear Sisters again not to feel so much uneasiness for me. If you do not hear from me regularly think that "all is well".

Probably communication between us may be interrupted and we are liable to leave at any time for any section of our country. The fall of Vicksburg is a severe blow but I suffered the loss a month or 2 ago as I was satisfied that it must sooner or later fall. I have every confidence in Jo Johnson and know he will do all in his power. Today we hear that he has given up Jackson and fallen back on Meridian. Such was expected & then herewith go still further back but when he gets his standing place which he himself only knows Grant will find himself in front of a General. He gives up his ground slowly and the enemy can not tell his intentions. He saw more than his generalship which I prophecy he will do: I never wanted him to attack Grant as our loss would have been heavy and we can not afford to loose as much. Our men are too valuable to be thrown away.

Miss Laura filled my canteen with her cistern water. Miss Mary would send me up a lunch. They were as kind as such and promised *assertions to do all in their power for me. They said I must let them hear from myself each opportunity offered which I will most dutifully do. I received a letter from Lou dated 20th June but suppose you have heard through her, so since that date. Lou and the children were very well but some of her father's family was quite unwell.*

Mr Armisted was here a few days ago and says that Charley Brigand is in very bad health and he does not think he will live long. I went to see Mrs. McBondey on the 10th and she was not very well having a headache. I will call on her again today probably.

I do not think its right to spend the Sabbath visiting but as I have been so much occupied the past week I have an opportunity of going soon so I find myself excusable. I have received just one letter from you since my arrival here but hope to get one today or tomorrow. It is nearly church time and no signs of preaching and I think its probable we will have none today. Why is it that there are so few ministers who preach to the Army regularly like they must to their congregations? The weather today is clear and pleasant.
My love to Cousin Susan.
My best love to you both.

Your own Bro.
Joe

On July 24th Adelbert Hannom wrote home to his father. The 104th Illinois was in camp near Decherd, Tennessee and Rosecrans was planning his next move against Bragg and Chattanooga. Hannom wistfully talks of fishing with his brother and apologizes for not sending home more money than he did after they were paid.

Decherd Staton
July 24 1863
Dear father I now sit down to write you a few lins. I am not very well at present. I cot cold and it has settled in my lungs but I am getting better. I hope that these few lins will find you enjoying good health. Well father I got 52 dollars day before yesterday.

I hav sent 33 dollars to you. hurm and hank and haling and mee sent our to gether and wee sent it to Charly Robison. I expect it will be thare by the time you get my letter. You can go and get it. Maby

98

(maybe) it will do you some good my dear father. Use it to the best advantage that you can for munny (money) is munny (in) these hard times. I only kept 10 dollars after I had paid my little debts. You must excuse this time and I will try not to spend so much munny another time. I want you to tell me all about the crops and you think about when the war will close. I think it will close this fall. I hope so any how. I hav ben tolerable well until know all the time. tell Thad not to run the gals to hard. Tell him that when I get home that wee will hav a good time once any how for wee will go a fishing and stay a weak. I think that I will get home a bout next spring about the write (right) time for giging fish. I hav no more to write at present only to tell you to answer my letter as soon as you get it. So good bye from your affectnate Son.

> *Adelbert H Hannom*
> *To my Dearest father G B Hannom*

Meanwhile, in Manchester, Tennessee, Maurice Williams was writing to his mother. Obviously home sick, he laments the lack of correspondence from home then explained what his unit, the 26th Indiana, had been doing of late: making 5,000 railroad ties that resulted in the rail lines being repaired and now bringing daily supplies to the front. He also thinks that the war can't last much longer and hopes to be home soon. Of particular import to soldiers and those at home, his regiment had just been paid.

Camp Manchester, Tennessee
July 24th 1863
Dear Mother

> *Once more I take up the pen for the purpose of writeing to you although I assure you I have poar enough encouragement for so doing for although I have written often I have receieved but two letters in the past two months and of them (one) of them contained your pitctures and the other was from uncle and it went to the 36th Ill. and was opened before I received it. It is very singular indeed that so few of your letters reach me. I have a bit of the Blues every time the Mail comes. It is to bad to be disappointed thus always but enough of this.*
>
> *I am as usal (usual) well and hearty. We are having very good times here although the weather is intolerable hot. Our Brigade has*

just finished their job of making five thousand railroad ties. It was a pretty hard job but Did not last long. The road is now in good order and trains arrive daily from McMinnville and Murfreesboro. Four companies were taken from our Reg't yesterday to guard the railroad between this place and McMinnville. Our Reg't was paid last Sunday. I sent forty five -45- dollars home by the Addams Express on the 22nfd. Be on the lookout for it. Well Mother I suppose you have had War pretty close to home. I presume you had some exciting times. We received the News of Morgan's Defeat at Blufton in due time and you can bet there was some rejoicing. I tell you Mother I begin to see signs of peace looming up in the Distance. For the past two months our arms have been crowned with success both by land and water. The Reble Soldiers are completely Discouraged and Numbers of them desert to our lines every Day and the Mountains are full of them awaiting their opportunity to escape to our lines. They are all in a very wretched condition. It is not possible for them to hold out much longer. Probaly (probably) the fall of Charleston May seal the fate of the Rebelion. Major General Palmer who commands while in conversation with a captain of the Sixth Ohio expressed his opinion that we would in 90 days be marching towards home. Of course, Generals can tell no more about it than we but still they have a better chance to know as they all hold correspondence with each other and with the authorities at Washington. Let it come when it will however it cannot come to soon for us. You can not imagine how we long to be at home once more. Two years is a long time to be absent from home and loved ones to say nothing of the hardships endured. But enough of this. It is past noon and I must quit. Please write soon and send me a paper occasionaly. Thomas Harris of Company F gets the Citizen pretty regular. Give my respects to all inquiring friends and I remain as ever your affectionate Son.

Maurice J. Williams

Co G 36th Ind Reg't
2 Division – 3 Brigade
21 Army Corps

Three days later Osso Quiggle, 14th Ohio, wrote to his father sharing the news that they too had been paid and he was sending much needed funds home. He also tells them of his band getting their Colonel a nice pair of spurs.

Camp Thomas Tenn July 27th/63

Dear Father,

We have been payed of(f) again and I hence sent $70.00 home to Lucy and Ma for presents to try and help buy a melodeon and sewing machine. I send Ma $40.00 I send Lucy $30.00. It will be sent to Columbus and there distributed to each county and you can draw it from the Treasury when they get it. I thought it would be better to send it in your name as could not send it in boath of there names and have you get it with out sum truble. I have sent home heretofore I think $120.00 and I think that will be enough to start me all I want after I get back. I have good luck. I drawed $48.00 so I have $18.00 left now. I think that will have to do me until we get pay again. Our band turned a number tonight. (We got) Colonel Costa a pair of spurs and presented them to him. They cost $10.00. they are real nice. He is going home today to recruit for the Regt. He made us since (a) little speech and set out the drinks but I did not take eny. I cannot drink whisky ever since I got sick. Well guess I will stop. Wrote to you yesterday just before we got payed.

From your son,

Osso Quiggle

The paymaster was obviously making the rounds during the last week of July. Although he hadn't reached the 74th Indiana near Winchester, Tennessee yet, John Bennett knew he would be there soon so that he could send some dollars home.

Camp Estill Near Winchester
Franklin Co. Tennessee July 30 1863
Dear Parents, sisters and Brother

I am once more seated to write you a few lines so that you may know that I am well and hopeing that this will find you all the very same, I received Ma's and Sams letter and should have answered it but we moved the next day after I got it and we have just got fairly settled *down again. We are within a mile of Winchester the rebel Capital of Tennessee, how long we shall stay here is more than I can tell. It is rumored that a part of the army is a going to the Potomac, I am in hopes that our division will be one to go if any. That is if we go by land on the cars or by water but if we go on foot I am not very particular about going, the place where we are camped now is a very nice place and as good a country as I ever saw in my life, Camp Estill takes its name from the Estill Springs not far from here, the same takes its name from one family of Estills who lived here nearly a Century ago. Three large monuments mark the spot where they are buried, there appears to be no other fruit here but black berries and we go in on our messes with them. The cars run up as far as Winchester now, and if the enemy is a going to advance it will do so before long, the old mountain tops look raged and saveage from here although they are eight miles off, I presume you wonder if we have enough to eat or not, there was a time since we left Triune that we was hard up for eatables but the Lord hath been wonderful unto us. He hath spread hardtack and sow bellie throughout the Army of the Cumberland once more, and green backs will be here in abundance in a day or two, part of the brigade has been paid off already, I am a going to send home $50 this time and I want Dady to buy me a mate to that colt of mine and he can do as he pleases with the rest, I heard that Co J of the 9th Mich. Cavelry had been taken prisoners. Was Ed a going to buy Doll of Pam and if so what was he a going to do with her. I understand the Flint Co. has been ordered out in defense of the state. I suppose that Morgan has done a great deal of damage since he entered Indiana and Ohio. I don't think they are very sharp if they let him get out of there. I saw Volony Carpenter not long ago. He belongs to the fourty second Illinois. John Morning has deserted. He belonged to the same regiment but I tell you (I) hate the matter. It is very warm and I am so lazy to write any more so good bye. Give my love to all inquiring friends. John G. Bennett*

By August 1st, the Army of the Cumberland was well rested and being freshly supplied daily. Denis Murphy wrote home to his brother, beseeching him to let him know if he'd received the $55 Denis had sent previously. He was also very concerned about rumors of the death of friends in the 53rd Illinois and wanted more reliable information.

Dechard Aug 1st 1863

Dear Brother I once more take the favorable opportunity of writing you these few lines hopeing to find you injoying that chief happenis that I am injoying which is good health. Dear Brother I am surprised that I do not get any letters from you. I know you do not neglect writing to me but there is something is the matter. I have not received but one letter from you since I left Murfreesboro. While I have wrote 4 or 5 to you and got no answer.

Dear Brother I have sent you $55 dollars and Tom sends for Janell 50 dollars and Barritt 50 for Joan. I want you to answer this. Let me know what the war news are in Ottawa. I hird that the 53d was in a fight at Jackson Cliffs. I hird that Mike Leahy was killed and several of the Ottawa boys was killed. One boy in our company had 3 brothers in it. One killed and 2 missing. Clancy and I sent you our pictures. You can give clancys 2 Pictures to Miss Hannah Burk, and that Pipe and that other picture is yours. Tell Miss Burk that he has had no letter since the first of July. Tell hir that he wants hir to write before she will get any more from him. Let me know if you got the money. And Pictures.

We are all in good health and have a nice camp. Every thing looks Good. Let me know how times is in Ottawa. Crops and so on I will say no more at present on this subject.

Tom Clancy Barrett Conners Dobbins and all join in sending you and all Michael Ryan Joan Jannell and all our best respects. Tom has had no letter since we came hear. Tell Joan Jinell to write to him.

Let me know how Father Mother Jim and Mary (are) getting a long.

So no more at present from your Beloved Brother

Denis J. Murphy

Direct your letter to me
Co A 104 Rgt Ill Vols
1st Brigade   2nd Division   14 Army Corps
Dechard Tenn

From the Confederate camp near Chattanooga B. F. Chapman wrote a longing letter to his wife Sarah on the same day. He too had heard rumors about action near the city but doesn't know what to believe or not. He asks several times in the letter for her to come to Chattanooga and visit with him. He spent a whole day at the depot hoping she would be on one of the trains but to no avail.

Camp near Chattanooga Tenn.
August 1 1863

Dear Wife,

I will drop you a few lines to let you know that I am well at the present. I hope that these few lines will come safe to hand and find you and the children all well. Sarah, I received your letter dated the 21st of July which gave me great satisfaction to hear from you and hear that you and the children was well. Sarah, I have nothing of much interest to write to you. I heard yesterday that the Yankees was at Bridgeport on the other side of the Tenn. River. The report was that the Yankees fired across the river at our train. they took a hoop or two and the Yankees mounted the breastworks as thick as blackbirds, but I don't know whether this is so or not for I hear so much and so many things that I don't know when to believe anything that I do hear. Sarah, you wrote you wanted to know whether I took that march barefooted or not. I had a pair of boots. I don't need any shoes at the present time.

Sarah, if I could see you I could tell you more than I ever expected to try to write you. Sarah, I want you to come to see me if you can fix it so you will be satisfied to leave home for I don't know when I will have the chance to go home to see you. Sarah I want to see you and the children worse than I ever did. You wrote that if you could get everything fixed up you might surprise me. Sarah I went down to the depot Thursday and stayed all day looking for you and father. Bennetts wife and Jos. O'Neal wife and Mrs. Lewis came in Thursday. Sarah if father or John Veatch comes out you and Ruth fix up and come out with them. if you all could come in a wagon you could all see more satisfaction. But you all can fix that up to suit yourselves. Sarah fetch your flour and bacon and I want you to fetch me some Irish potatoes and some onions and pickles and some apples and some fried chicken and butter if you can fetch it so the air can't get to it.

Sarah, I will come to a close for I have nothing of much importance to write at this present time. The health of the company is not as good as it has been. There are several of the boys that is complaining and Sarah I haven't heard anything from Pearson yet. Jackson Smith is dead. He died Thursday at Chattanooga. Peter Blankenship said he was going to try to get him sent home. Sarah, I will close I want you to write me as soon as you get these few lines.
Sarah, if you can come out I want you to write to me when you will come and how you will come.

Yours truly Husband

B.F. Chapman

Chapter Eight

Taking Chattanooga

To complete his triumph Rosecrans needed only to force Bragg out of Chattanooga and into Georgia. It wouldn't be until the 16th of August that Rosecrans would be pushed hard enough to resume his advance. Rosecrans had studied the topography of Chattanooga and the surrounding region. He determined to again move Bragg by threatening his communications. This time that meant the Western and Atlantic Railroad to the east and south of the town. Bragg, in his study of the situation, saw Rosecrans' easiest approach to Chattanooga as being a route over Walden's Ridge to the north of the town. This would lead directly to Chattanooga and easy access to the rail line to the east. It also meant that Rosecrans would have support from Major General Ambrose Burnside who was moving his Army of the Ohio toward Knoxville just 100 miles northeast of Chattanooga. This was Bragg's expectation.

Rosecrans, in another brilliant maneuver, chose instead to cross the Tennessee and approach Chattanooga from the southwest. As before, there were challenges to this movement. In order to cross the Lookout Mountain range there were but two difficult passes available and they were significantly distant from each other. The third route of approach was a combined rail and road which snaked along the Tennessee River. Using these approaches simultaneously was highly challenging and created a dangerous distance between the three columns as they advanced but offered significant benefits. One advantage of this strategy was that it kept the Union Army closer to its supply lines on the Nashville and Chattanooga railroad. The second advantage was that it placed Federal troops south of Chattanooga threatening to cut Bragg off from the Western and Atlantic railroad, his supply line. With any luck, Bragg would give up Chattanooga in order to protect his vital rail line and supply chain.

Axel Reed recorded the movement and experience of his group as they marched and crossed the Tennessee River during their initial advance toward Chattanooga. The meetings between Union and Confederate pickets along the river made for interesting entries.

Aug. 16th Received orders this morning to march immediately. Left camp about 10 a.m. Had not proceeded over half a mile when a terrific thunder shower came up. Bolts of lightning struck trees within a few rods of us and rain fell in torrents. Such peals of thunder I never heard exceeded. It seemed that we had invoked the wrath of the 'Almighty' by our military movement on a Sunday, as it is. It rained about one hour when we proceeded, passing Deckard station, and on the same road we marched on a year ago towards Pelham. The whole army appears to be moving towards Chattanooga.

18th. Ascended the steep and rugged sides of Cumberland Mountain. Found a good road on top along the ridge and camped, after marching about seven miles, at 'University Place,' where the rebel general Polk has laid the foundation for a university. It is a splendid site on the summit of the mountain, with a splendid spring near-by. A steep bluff, from which a splendid view of the valley below can be seen for miles.

21st. Marched at noon and struck Battle Creek some two miles east and followed down the right bank until we reached the Tennessee River. Camped about three miles above Bridgeport, Alabama, and the same distance from the Georgia line, due east. The rebels occupy the opposite bank of the river and shoot across at our men.

22nd. Have been down to the river and heard our boys talk with the rebels. They keep up a continuous conversation by mutual agreement, not a shot is fired.

23rd. John Barber, Charley Latham and myself have been to the top of the mountain today to take a spy-glass view of the opposite side of the river, and could see the Tennessee for four miles below and four miles above. Bridgeport, four miles below, was plainly seen, and the remains of the railroad bridge that the rebels had destroyed. No rebel camp is to be seen, although rebel pickets occupy the opposite side of the river. Three rebels came over yesterday and wish to stay. Have been in swimming today in the Tennessee River, and swam half way over to the rebel pickets. Had a long conversation with them. They promised to let me back if I would come over, but I dare not risk it.

25th. Three of our boys, one from Co. K (Bill Haskins) crossed the river today and had a long talk with the rebel pickets. They promised to let our boys come back if they would come over and kept their word. They shook hands like old acquaintances and wanted them to stay and take supper with them, but fearing that their officer of the day might come around they dare not.

26th. The rebel pickets refuse to receive our boys as visitors as their officers forbid it. Forty rebel deserters, it is said, came over today. We take a bath at the confluence of Battle creek.

27th. Two of our companies have been building rafts today, and it is said that a part of our force is to cross on them. More deserters came over today.

29th. Our pickets were put across the river about 4 p.m. on the rafts and canoes. A regiment of rebel cavalry was seen over the river this morning.

Sunday, Aug. 30th. Our brigade crossed the river today on rafts and canoes. Our regiment crossed near night and camped about half a mile from the river. Horses swam over beside the boats. The river is about four hundred yards wide at this point. The artillery is not yet over. Waiting for the artillery to cross. The boys find plenty of sweet Irish potatoes, which are a rarity to us.

To keep Bragg from suspecting his true plan, Rosecrans sent Brigadier General William B. Hazen with three infantry brigades and a contingent of cavalry on a feint to the north of Chattanooga over Walden's Ridge. The van of this force was once again Wilder's mounted infantry now known to all as the Lightning Brigade. In five days Wilder traversed the rugged mountainous region of Walden's Ridge sweeping up surprised Confederate outposts along the way and arriving on the northern bank of the Tennessee, opposite Chattanooga on August 21st. At 9:00 that morning his artillery battery, under the command of Eli Lilly, opened fire on the town across the river. Hazen's force remained in place on the north side of the river for nearly three weeks, continuing to harass the Confederates. They did all they could, day and night, to make the Confederates believe that a large force was gathering there.

Bragg's army had dwindled to approximately 30,000 men by this point and he desperately asked for reinforcements. He was promised 20,000 men, some from Joseph Johnston's Army of Mississippi but mostly by means of Major General James Longstreet's 1st Corps of the Army of Northern Virginia. Burnside was fast approaching Knoxville and the garrison there was no match for his 15,000 troops, so Bragg ordered those 2,500 men to reinforce Chattanooga as well. To face the perceived threat from the north, Bragg aligned Polk's Corps in the works of Chattanooga and Hardee's Corp, now under the command of Major General Daniel Harvey Hill, just northeast of the town to protect the East Tennessee & Georgia Railroad.

John Magee was despondent on August 31th. His diary entry is heart wrenching and he hopes for a battle soon to shake him from his melancholy. He would not have to wait long.

Monday, Aug 31, 1863. In camp – more cannonading. Rumor again that Knoxville is evacuated and Cumberland gap surrendered. Am not in good spirits – wrote to Mr. Haggard thanking him for the clothes. What beautiful days, and calm clear nights! The weather here is like fall even before the autumn months set in. They always bring back sad memories to me. I get the ennui very bad, and sometimes almost feel a feminine weakness. Oh for some one to converse with – some dear friend to pour out my inmost thoughts to and have an exchange of sentiments and sympathies. Alone! Alone! How sad and bitter the word. The very wind that howls around my weary and forsaken heart whispers to it in each passing breeze the dismal dreary word alone! I may try to read, and not remember one word I am reading – uneasy all the time, I cannot sit still anywhere – indifferent to most everything, I seem a nonentity. The few commonplace remarks of my messmates and fellow soldiers have no effect on me, and even my best friends, those who wish me well cannot draw me from my misanthropic mood. Gloomy sadness hangs like a pall over my weakened spirits, and my soul sinks low down in deep anguish. My heart yearns for something it cannot get. Oh, how often I think of my Mother, Sister and Brother, and my most beloved Grandmother. How many, many nights have I tossed about on my lowly bunk, praying for sleep to close my eyes and shut out such thoughts from my mind. To dream ah! Dream of home, and wake in a strange land among strangers alone! Alone! Alone!!

Hope brighter times may come. Oh how I wish for a battle, a move or anything to divert my thoughts, and bury them forever in Lethe.

From the 16th of August through the 7th of September Rosecrans was moving the bulk of his army toward the Lookout Mountain gaps south of Chattanooga. On August 31 Bragg was informed of a large Union force in the area of Stevenson, Alabama moving toward the mountains in the south. Now Bragg and his fellow officers really became confused about what the Yankees planned to do. For a week they vacillated back and forth between moving more troops to the south and maintaining a strong front to the north where the main blow might still be delivered. As more and more reports continued to come in over that time it finally became evident that Rosecrans had once again outfoxed his opponent and had a massive body of troops south of Chattanooga threatening to cut Bragg's line of communications with Atlanta. On September 7 Bragg evacuated Chattanooga heading south into Georgia. The town had fallen without a fight.

Axel Reed continued to journal throughout the march in the following words:

Tuesday, Sept. 1st. Moved camp forward to near Shell Mound. Only one team has got across the river. Camped at the foot of the mountain at the railroad. Some of our boys have been out rambling today. They found a New England family living on the mountain. One of them Professor Gillford.

Marched at 7 a.m. and some 5 miles out as the other brigades could not get up the mountain in time for us we proceeded to march back about a mile to near "Nick-a-Jack" cave, at the northeast corner of Georgia. The cave is a great natural curiosity, men having been in 11 miles. A salt-peter works are at its mouth, which has supplied the confederates with large amounts of saltpeter.

6th. Today we moved up to the top of Raccoon mountain, at Capt. Freighter's coal mine. We followed up a valley about five miles, where a railroad track is laid to the mines. The mountain is very steep and hazardous for teams and artillery. These coal mines have supplied Charleston, S.C. with coal. Are now in the state of Georgia.

7th. Marched nine miles today and camped about noon in a deep valley. Roads very dusty. Crittenden's corps camped near. Day very hot. Good springs near-by. Sixteen miles to Chattanooga.

8th. Laid in Lookout valley all day. General Van Cleve's division camped near us. Our band serenaded him tonight. Crittenden's whole corps is near.

Ninth - Chattanooga is reported evacuated.

Confederate artilleryman John Magee started September's diary entries with the same remorse and melancholy that closed his writing in August, but quickly things were changing and the "distraction" he had hoped for was beginning to materialize:

Tuesday, Sept 1st, 1863. In camp – beautiful weather. Rumor that the enemy are moving on us from Knoxville. Do not know what will turn up. We are getting a large army at this place and some think a move into Kentucky is intended. God grant it – anything to drive away these melancholy thoughts that hang like an incubus on my mind. How sadly mournful looks the grand old Lookout! How quaint the wind wounds coursing away among the trees down the valley? Everything in this poetic region has a tendency to make my spirits run very low. Such is life, full of trouble from the cradle to the grave.

Wednesday, Sept 2nd, 1863. In camp – still quiet and melancholy. Days roll by in beautiful weather and I still continue to chronicle passing events. Chattanooga is almost deserted. The enemy occasionally throw a few shell over into the place, but, as yet, have done no serious damage. No news of their movements – all quiet yet. Reading "No Name." Some diversion from my monotony – it cheers me and still keeps me sad too. It seems the result of life is the same, move in what circle you choose.

Thursday, Sept 3d, 1863. In camp – went over to see Maj. Palmer – was not at his quarters – had a spirited conversation with a young man of Semple's and one of Slocum's batteries who have been detailed as clerks for Col. Hollinquist and Oulisdousky – Mr. Bennet and Cenas.

Saturday, Sep 5, 1863. In camp – went early and saw Maj Palmer – told me (he) had been removed from command of our battalion and does not know where he will be sent – advised me to wait a while. Fine weather. No news of any movements.

Sunday, Sept 6, 1863. In camp – about 9 o'clock got orders to cook three days rations. Rondeau paid us a visit – said we go to Rome – that the enemy are advancing on Rome down the other side of the mountain. Our pickets on Lookout are skirmishing with them. Went up to Mr. Hopkins' and got some milk. A very fine family – Mrs. Hopkins much of a lady – her husband (is a) Maj. in conscript department. At 1- o'clock got orders to go to town and get iron guns from the fortifications and report to Genl Preston Smith on the Lookout mountain – came on a gallop – the dust awful, worse than ever I saw it. Go to the foot of the mountain and Genl Cheatham stopped us till further orders. Waited till dark, and then were ordered back to camp, ready to move at a moment's notice. Packed baggage – slept in open air – considerable fighting on the other side of the mountain today – the enemy going towards Rome.

Monday, Sept 7th, 1863. In camp till evening. Inspected baggage – some had to be left. Went up to Hopkins' – Mrs. Hopkins very uneasy, thinks the enemy will be here before she can get away. In evening got orders to start at sundown and report at McFarlane's one mile from camp – got there at dark, and laid all night alongside the road. Troops moving by all night – the whole army moving towards Rome – Hill's corps passed tonight. (In afternoon, before we left camp, the second piece was ordered to report to Genl Smith on the mountain – has not got back yet.) Dry and dusty.

The southern commander had withdrawn his forces from Chattanooga and moved southward, baiting Rosecrans to follow him into Georgia and hoping to catch him in an ambush. He had cleverly sent deserters into the Federal lines claiming that Bragg was in full retreat and that the Army of Tennessee was in disorder and demoralized. Quite to the contrary, Bragg was beginning to receive reinforcements and had reorganized his army into four corps, each consisting of two divisions. The corps commanders were now Polk, with a division under Thomas C. Hindman, just arrived from Arkansas; D. H. Hill relieving General Hardee; Buckner with his men from Knoxville and Major General William H. T. Walker who had just arrived with reinforcements from

Mississippi. The expanding Army of Tennessee was concentrating in the area of LaFayette, Georgia as Bragg plotted to entrap at least one of Rosecrans' corps, dismantle it, then finish off the rest of the Army of the Cumberland and retake Chattanooga as the result. Bragg's subordinates actually had a number of opportunities to fall upon individual corps of the Army of the Cumberland as it advanced in three columns separated by enough distance to prohibit each from readily supporting either of the others on quick notice. The first attempt was to catch Thomas' corps as it came out of Steven's Gap into McLemore's Cove.

Captain Silas S. Canfield described the 21st Ohio's advance from Decherd to McLemore's Cove in the regiment's official history as follows:

> *...On the 16th of August at nine o'clock in the morning, the regiment with its division marched from Decherd.*

> *We crossed the mountain on the 17th, and on the 19th reached Cave Spring, Alabama, and laid out a camp. The only thing worthy of note was the bad roads encountered. We remained at Cave Spring until late in the afternoon of the 1st of September, when we again moved forward, crossed the Tennessee on a pontoon bridge at Caperton's Ferry, at 11 p.m., and rested a few miles beyond the remainder of the night. The next day we marched to Moor's Spring, opposite Bridgeport. The morning of the 3d we began the ascent of Sand, or Raccoon Mountain. Nearly all day the 3d brigade, except Captain Alban's Company F, of the 21st O, was engaged assisting teams up the mountain. The train up, we moved forward toward evening to Warron's sawmill, where we found Captain Alban engaged in taking down the upper part of the mill, to build a bridge across a deep narrow chasm, now the bed of a dry stream, in which the mill was situated' there being no eligible crossing either above or below. The lower part of the mill was to serve as part of the bridge. In the work he was relieved by the 78th Pa., who completed the bridge, over which the train and artillery passed safely.*

> *The next day we descended to Will's Valley.*

Leaving knapsacks, early in the morning of the 5th, the 21st O and the 78th Pa. regiments, with a section of Battery G, 1st O. artillery, started up the valley on a reconnaissance. We were absent two nights without meeting the enemy. The 21st took possession of a mill, ground the grain on hand for our use, returned on the morning of the 7th for knapsacks, and marched to the foot of Lookout Mountain.

After a hastily prepared and hastily eaten breakfast, early in the morning of the 8th, the 3d brigade was deployed up the mountain, to again assist the teams. Without a complaint the men labored faithfully at this until noon of the 9th, when the teams being all up we crossed the mountain, and descended to McLeMore's Cove, in the valley of the Chickamauga, at Steven's Gap.

General Thomas having been ordered to march rapidly to Lafayette, Georgia, General Negley's division moved early the next morning, the 21st in advance, and Captain Alban's Company F as skirmishers.

At Bailey's cross roads they came upon an outpost of the enemy. A spirited skirmish ensued, but the rebels, though resisting stubbornly, were steadily pushed back and driven into Dug Gap, a deep narrow pass through Pigeon Mountain. Arriving at the entrance to the gap, the command was halted, and the regiment deployed to watch the enemy. At evening we were relieved, permitted to get supper, and assigned a position for the night. The next morning at three o'clock we were moved about a half mile to the rear, to guard against a surprise. Early in the morning the enemy came through the gap, and engaged our skirmishers without gaining any advantage.

On arrival at the gap, and learning that Bragg had concentrated his army at Lafayette, General Negley sent back for assistance, and shortly after three o'clock on the morning of the 11th, General Baird with his division marched to his support. From information received, Generals Negley and Baird were convinced the enemy intended to attack with a superior force, and they thought it prudent to retire to Steven's Gap.

The train pulled quietly out, the 21st O. took a position near Widow Davis', with Company K thrown out to watch the approach from the south. After informing the men that the enemy was near, and ordering them to watch, and be ready every moment for action, on visiting the skirmish line I found one man with both shoes and socks off paring his toe nails. This called forth pretty strong language. The troops past, the bugle sounded the recall just in time to allow us to escape from the enemy, who were moving to the attack. Joining the regiment, we hastened back over the Little Chickamauga creek, and past the next position chosen for defense, and where a brigade of General Baird's division was posted; a part of it behind a stone fence. As the rebels approached, a well-directed fire from the brigade and a battery made them recoil.

The battle was short but decisive. A gentleman I met in Chattanooga in 1881, informed me that he saw this battle at Bailey's cross roads, and that the rebels lost forty killed. He said he saw them buried next day.

At some distance to the rear from where this fight occurred, the 21st took another position, and when the troops were all past, deployed and marched back to the gap, closely pursued by the enemy, where we arrived after dark.

In this affair, the 1st division lost three killed and several severely wounded.[1]

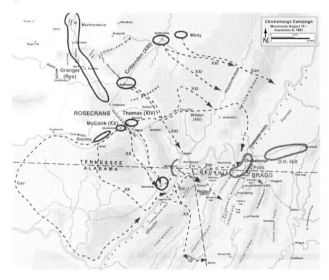

Axel Reed's diary continues to give a fascinating description of their ongoing movement over Lookout Mountain. On the 13th he writes of hearing of Nagley's fight with Confederates at McLemore's Cove. By his posted observations it is clear that the Union troops still thought Bragg was retreating toward Atlanta at that point.

10th. Marched early this morning; course south, down Lookout Valley. Lookout mountain close to our left and Raccoon to our right. Valley about three-quarters of a mile wide. Came onto the 'Wells Valley Railroad' 3 miles north of Trenton. Marched about 15 miles. Came up to Reynolds' division and had to stop for the night. The bed of the railroad bears along our track, but no further than Trenton.

Sept. 11th. Marched at 8 a.m.' crossed a creek and keeping close to Lookout mountain. Had to halt about noon for other troops to cross the mountain. We halted near a high point of Lookout mountain where it breaks off from a south course and bears east, then a south and west course, forming a cove or basin. At the foot of this point a furnace is standing for manufacturing pig-iron, as ore is plenty. Laid until dark when we took two days' rations and left the teams. Marched until 10 at night, when we halted upon a rise of ground in the center of a large cove, surrounded on nearly every side by a high range of mountains. Orders to stop two hours and we laid down without tents or blankets to cover us, as we expected to move soon. Lights could be seen moving along up the mountain side as high as the top. Bands were playing as they ascended and troops were moving the whole night long. We lay until morning of the 12th...

(12th)... when we moved up the mountain in a zig-zag course until reaching the top. The side is very steep, nearly 45 degrees. Half way up the mountain there is a level spot where a family of four children and a woman were in a starving condition. They were so weak that they were unable to be out of bed. Our boys gave them their rations and money, some four hundred dollars it was said. We arrived over the mountain 6 miles about noon and camped at the foot of the mountain (Lookout). Troops all march (with)out light.

SUNDAY, Sept. 13th (1863). Laid in camp here all day; nothing important; plenty of camp rumors rife. A fight occurred here yesterday, the eleventh, in which the 11th Michigan, 19th Illinois and 18th regulars were engaged, as they occupied the outposts about four miles at the crossroad, where the mountain road intersects with the valley road from Chattanooga to Rome. Our forces (one division under Gen. Nagle) by a force estimated at from ten to fifteen thousand, were driven back. It was necessary to fall back to protect the train. Our side lost about 100 killed, wounded and missing. The rebel loss was estimated at two or three hundred. Our men remained unburied on the field yesterday, partly devoured by dogs. The rebel object was probably only to drive us back from the road so that their trains could pass on towards Atlanta, as this corps of the enemy had been cut off by our coming over the mountain at this unexpected point, but not in sufficient force to stop the enemy from passing. It was impossible to get our batteries over the mountains in time to resist their passing on. Gen. Thomas was present and hurried up reinforcements. The enemy was gone next morning, which we ascertained when we moved out. The 11th Michigan and one company of the 19th Illinois had to throw away their knapsacks, it is reported. The rebels stripped them of their contents, changing their clothes, leaving their own ragged clothes in place.

John Magee's transcript over this same period gives a sense of how one of Bragg's commands was placed in one position then repositioned as he determined how he might strike one or another of the Union corps as they continued to advance. The Union high command was still unaware at this point that he had stopped his retreat and was looking for an opportunity to attack.

Tuesday, Sept 8th, 1863. Were stirring early – troops still passing. Hindman's division passing this morning. On detail after hay – went back to our camp – saw Mrs. Hopkins, she is moving. Everybody in and around Chattanooga ordered to leave. More cannonading at town. About 10 the second piece returned from picket – they fired about 20 rounds, doing some damage to the enemy – Genl Smith complimented the boys highly. About 12 o'clock our Brigade started, we marched in the center – marched slow, often stopping – roads very dusty and weather warm. Went to Chickamauga creek, 12 miles from Chattanooga and camped at 9 o'clock at night. Slept without blankets in an old field.

Wednesday, Sept 9th, 1863. Up at sunup – no orders to march. Changed our camp to get in the shade. In camp all day. Gov. Harris made a short speech to the Tennessee troops, telling them the coming battle would decide the fate of their state, and he expected to see them whip the enemy. He said the enemy were crossing over the mountain 12 miles in front of us, and was certain the battle was not 4 days off – that, for the first time in the war we outnumbered the enemy, and we must and we would regain the good old state in six weeks! Every person jubilant in expectation of the coming fight. Got some corn in evening – drew rations. No orders, nor news from the enemy.

Thursday, Sept 10, 1863. Up early – no orders. Rumors of a skirmish at or near McFarlanes. Orders to go on picket – the enemy supposed to be advancing from Chattanooga. We moved 1 ½ miles to the left and laid all day in line of battle. No firing. Several rumors about the enemy – one, that 12 thousand have gone down to Ringgold from Chattanooga; another, that Generals Thomas and McCook have crossed the mountain, and are now between us and Rome in the valley. In evening got orders to march – went back to where we camped yesterday, and waited till 12 o'clock. The army all on the move toward Rome, we bringing up the rear as usual. We traveled slow – went 6 miles, and had to wait for Buckner's corps to cross our road – they say he is going in the rear of Thomas and McCook to cut them off from the mountain pass. Slept some on the roadside – very dusty.

Friday, Sept 11, 1863. Moved on at sunup – travelled 7 miles to Lafayette, through the worst dust I ever saw. It has not rained for near six weeks, and the dust is suffocating – good many give out. Got into camp, in the edge of town at sundown. Made the acquaintance of some young ladies by the name of Bice. Spent a pleasant evening in their company.

Saturday, Sept 12, 1863, Up early – no orders. We are camped within 50 yards of Mr. Bice's. Went over and staid a few hours with the young ladies – Miss Fannie A and Mollie S. Bice – drank some wine – very nice and refined young ladies – an excellent family. A great many sick, and some wounded, soldiers in a hospital near our camp, under *the care of Mrs. Bice. Understood Genl Buckner failed on account of some mismanagement of Genl Hindman. Buckner's troops came in this morning. Heard Breckinridge had a fight with some of Thomas' troops yesterday 5 miles from here – only a few killed and wounded. The whole army is now at this place – Lafayette. It is a small village, 40 miles from Rome and 26 from Chattanooga. A general battle is expected near this place in a few days. Genl Crittenden's corps reported at Lee and Gordon's Mills on Chickamauga Creek. Every person seems eager for a fight. About 10 o'clock orders came to march. Went back towards Chattanooga 5 miles to Rock Spring Church. The belief is we are going to fight Crittenden. Only Cheatham and Walkers Divisions came out – formed a line of battle, our Brigade on the right, in front of Genl Wilder's Lightning Brigade – expect some fun in morning – Wilder says our cavalry are not worth one cent, and Genl Cheatham put our Brigade before him to see if he will run over it – laid very quiet without any fire all night – the enemy ½ mile off only. Still as dusty as ever and no signs of rain. Dr. Montgomery returned yesterday evening. When leaving Lafayette, I bid good bye to the Misses Bices – presented Miss Fannie with a book.*

On September 11th, William E. Stillwell of the 53rd Georgia wrote to his wife that they were being transferred from Virginia to Tennessee. As part of Longstreet's corps, the 53rd would be part of the crucial reinforcement of Bragg's army just as it went into battle once again with Rosecrans. He was pained by the thought of passing so close to home without seeing her but was excited about the powerful blow they were about to deliver in the western theatre of the war.

Headquarter Bryan's Brigade, Camp Hanover Junction,
20 Miles above Richmond, Virginia – Sept. 11th, 1863
Dear and loving Molly:

I wrote you on the 7th and stated that everything was still and quiet, but that evening orders came to cook three days rations and to march the next morning at daylight. We marched to this place and have stopped for the present; that is our brigade has. The rest of our division is gone on – shall I say where? They are gone to Tennessee somewhere. We will follow in a few days. we are left here for the present but will come on in two or three days. I have no doubt but what I will pass through Atlanta, Georgia in two or three weeks and it may be in less than a week. Oh, how shall I come as close to you as Atlanta and not get to see you but if I do pass through there, I shall cast a look toward you and thank God that I have got so near you as that. If ever I get on Georgia soil again I shall feel like Columbus when he discovered America. I shall feel like kneeling down and kissing the earth. Molly, there is one of the greatest movements now going on that ever has been. I don't know but I understand it to be about thus.

Ewell is gone by way of Lynchburg and Bristol, Tennessee and from Bristol he will attack old Burnsides in the rear. His corps is already gone. Longstreet's corps will go by way of Richmond, Augusta, and Atlanta, Georgia and on to some point in Tennessee and wipeout Burnside and then unite Longstreet and Ewell together and in conjunction with Bragg will attack Rosecrans and drive them out of Tennessee. I think it will be one of the greatest movements ever undertaken and if it can be accomplished will make the Yankees howl. God grant that it may be done. Oh, God for the sake of Jesus Christ bless us.

Molly, I shall have to close as we leave for Richmond in a few hours, we will take the cars there. I think perhaps I may be in Georgia before this letter reaches you. I am in good health, give my love to all and kiss the babies. Don't write any more until you hear from me unless you send it by hand. I must close. Goodbye my dear Molly. Colonel Bryan has been appointed brigadier general. I will write again soon, I am your Billie forever.

W. R. Stilwell

Following the missed opportunity at McLemore's Cove, Bragg attempted to isolate and destroy in detail Wood's division or Crittenden's corps. In directly following Bragg's line of retreat south of Chattanooga while heading straight for Lafayette, Crittenden had sent Wood's division ahead to a place called Lee and Gordon's Mill. In so doing, Wood held a position much closer to Polk's Corp than to his own two fellow divisions following him. Bragg ordered Polk to turn on Wood and destroy him, then move against the remaining two divisions of Crittenden's corps. Unfortunately for the Confederates, Bragg's instructions sent Polk to the wrong location in order to attack Wood and by the time the error was corrected it was too late. Crittenden's remaining divisions had joined Wood and Polk feared that he was outnumbered and thus did nothing.

Magee described the movement and limited action of the missed opportunities. Upon returning to LaFayette he learned that Longstreet's corps was about to join them from Virginia.

Sunday, Sept 13, 1863. _Were early stirring – the lightning Brigade had gone. Lidell's Brigade came up and took our place, and we were ordered to the left, and Walker's had taken his place. Orders were read from Genl Polk that, we are about to engage the enemy. Cheatham occupied the left Walker the right and centre with his sub-corps, and Hindman's division in reserve and he expected us to drive the enemy. About 10 o'clock Genl Strahl was ordered forward with his Brigade to reconnoiter and try and draw the enemy out. We went forward towards Lee and Gordon's Mills about 8 miles, accompanied by Genl Armstrong's Brigade of cavalry, and found the enemy. Our brigade drew up in line of battle, and sent out skirmishers. The second section of our Battery was posted in front, and the first section 14 hundred in the rear on another small hill. About 12 o'clock firing commenced and soon grew pretty warm – the enemy commenced advancing on us. The second section fired a few rounds to which the Yankees replied with a Napoleon and rifle battery – firing now got pretty warm, and our Brigade fell back on line with the first section of our battery. The firing still kept up, the enemy advancing. The second section drew up on line with the first, and when the enemy got within 12 hundred yards, we opened on them with three guns – fired about 50 rounds, the enemy replying hotly, and firing very accurate. In a few minutes, we again fell back ½ mile. The firing now became slower, and soon ceased. The enemy stopped advancing, nor could we draw them any farther – no more firing during the day except an occasional sharpshooter. We had one man wounded slightly – our Brigade none hurt. The cavalry had one man badly wounded. We now laid in position till evening, and then fell back in the rear of our line of battle and camped. Cold night – expect to fight the battle tomorrow. Cool night._

Monday, Sept 14, 1863. *Were stirring early – no firing in front nor orders to move. Waited in suspense till 9 o'clock, and then were ordered back to Lafayette. It is reported the enemy in our front have fallen back, and gone round to form a junction with Thomas and McCook. No fight this time – all the troops moved back to Lafayette – got into camp at 4 o'clock – dusty as ever. Wild rumors going the rounds of reinforcements coming from Virginia – Longstreet's corps is on the road – great cheering in consequence. Genl Breckinridge and Cleburne had a fight between here and Rome yesterday which resulted in the enemy falling back. In evening made a call on the Miss Bices with Mr. Chatham – enjoyed ourselves very well – our Brigade band serenaded them – very fine music and accomplished ladies. Dry and dusty.*

With each of these opportunities not executed upon, the Confederates lost a real chance to destroy a significant portion of Rosecrans' army. Now Rosecrans was fully convinced that the Army of Tennessee was not in confused retreat, but concentrated as reported near LaFayette. He moved urgently to concentrate his own Army in order to meet and defeat the threat. Thomas was ordered to move to his left and concentrate around Pond Spring in close proximity to Crittenden. McCook who had marched far to the south was ordered to return and join the other two corps. This resulted in an exhausting 57 mile march back over the mountains to arrive at Steven's Gap where Thomas had entered McLemore's Cove. The grueling march took 4 days and all the while Bragg did nothing. By the 17th of September the Army of the Cumberland was safely reunited around Lee and Gordon's Mill.

Without knowing details, Magee reflected on Bragg's indecision and his subordinates' failure to move aggressively enough during this period as Rosecrans was concentrating his army.

Tuesday, Sept 15, 1863. *In camp – no orders to move – was on detail after corn – artificers at work shrinking tires. News confirmed in regard to Longstreet's coming. All Polk's baggage and commissary wagons sent to Osyha (?) to haul their baggage to this point. Great speculation about moving, think we will move for Kentucky. Tis said Loring's Division from Miss. is coming here. Sam Ebbert returned yesterday evening. Made a call at Mr. Bice's in evening. Weather cool and signs of rain which we need very much.*

<u>Wednesday, Sept 16, 1863.</u> In camp –fine day – on guard – got some washing done. In afternoon got orders to move our camp. Wrote some verses for Miss Mollie and Fannie Bice. No news of any fighting. Do not know anything of the enemy's movements – all expect a fight soon and are perfectly willing. In evening went 1 ½ miles from town, and camped on Chattanooga creek. I stopped at Mr. Bice's - had a long talk with Miss Mollie, made her a present of a book and some verses – Mr. Chatham is rather smitten with Mollie, and was uneasy – she is a very fine young lady. I started for camp at 10 o'clock but could not find it – staid all night with some boys who were guarding cattle. Heard we had orders to move at 8 in the morning. Cloudy and signs of rain.

<u>Thursday, Sept 17, 1863.</u> In camp – orders countermanded – in camp all day – troops moving toward Rock Spring church all day. Heard our cavalry had a fight with the enemy. Orders came in evening to move out – started at 5 o'clock – travelled slow – came 6 miles and camped at 12 o'clock with(in) 2 miles where our Brigade had the skirmish last Sunday. Cool and pleasant night – slept very well.

Captain George Dobson of the 10th Mississippi took a moment to write home to his wife on the 16th. He reflected on the missed opportunities of the last few days with her, but knowing the numbers of the Army of Tennessee were stronger than ever before, he excitedly awaited the chance to bag Rosecrans and his troops.

Camp Near Lafayette, Georgia
September 16, 1863
(To Jane)

I may find a chance to send you this and write while I have time. My last was from near Chattanooga. We have had a stirring time since then – have been marching ever since hunting up Rosecrans, but he gives the slip every time. We thought twice we had him hemmed up but he got away. We have a larger army now than we have ever had here and we will shortly make clean work of it. Our next move will I expect be into Kentucky which will have the effect of relieving you or your detested Yankees.

As Rosecrans concentrated his forces and Bragg continued to receive reinforcements, Axel Reed expressed the same anticipation for the battle to come as the opposite side's diarist, John Magee. The 14th through the 17th included marches and countermarches as commands continued to consolidate and position themselves for the fight to come.

Near Pigeon Gap, Ga., Sept. 14th, 1863. I was released from confinement yesterday, to return to my company, but still under arrest. I am in hopes to have a trial before long. I have now suffered many indignities for which I shall long remember their authors. I have been a subject of the guard-house in close confinement 51 days. I am nearly sick, caused by being kept inactive. Are laying in McLamores Gap or Cove by Pigeon mountain branching off from Lookout mountain, which is two thousand feet high, extending East.

15th. Moved E. S. east five miles to near Pigeon and Hagger's Gap, near where the fight commenced on the 11th. We occupy a ridge near Pigeon mountain, where the enemy is said to be in force.

16th Laid in camp and polished up. 'Lee's mill (Lee and Gordon's mill) is on Mill creek close to our rear. Bald Headed mountain to our front. The enemy's pickets are only a mile distant. We can hear their drums and see their camp smoke plainly.

Sept 17. Received orders about 7 a.m. to move immediately. Everything ready at 8 and moved E. northeast about six miles to where the enemy had attacked Gen. Reynolds and driven in his pickets. Halted about an hour when we were ordered back to the creek, about two miles, when we unslung knapsacks, left them and hurried on to bring up the train, as it was reported that the enemy had attacked it. Marched back to Big Spring, within half mile of our old camp. Two companies of rebels had just left as we got there. They had robbed the 38th Ohio Sutler, as he was behind, and that was all the damage they did. We could see the dust rise as the enemy moved along the foot of the mountain, 2 miles distant. Five of our boys came near being taken prisoners as they went out foraging. They went within 80 rods of their pickets and talked with some of them.

There seems to be a great battle pending with near a hundred thousand men on each side. Our side commanded by General Rosencrans and the rebels by Ge. Bragg. Our army consists of three corps, the 14th, 20th and 21st, commanded respectively by Generals Thomas, McCook and Crittenden.

Bragg was now ready to engage Rosecrans and John Magee recorded Bragg's orders to the troops on the 18th of September in his diary. Positioning and skirmishing occurred all day but the general engagement would wait one more day.

Friday, Sept 18, 1863. Up and moving at sunup – went out to where we camped last Sunday night and waited a while – watered horses. Weather cool – tried to rain last night – it is still as dusty as ever. An order from Genl Bragg was read to us, stating "we are to fight the enemy this time sure, that we have offered him battle twice and he would not fight, that we have thwarted all his attempted flank movements, and we are now going to force him to fight or run." The line of battle was now formed, and we moved forward at 9 o'clock. Canonading commenced about 10 in front and some musketry. Our line is 5 miles long, Buckner on our right, Polk the centre and Hill on the left. Some firing was kept up till night – no general engagement – some very heavy cannonading. We moved on to within 1 ½ of Chicamauga Creek and camped. Understood Buckner was across the creek on the right. We expect a general engagement tomorrow. Firing ceased at dark – could not hear the result of todays fighting – weather cool and pleasant.

Captain Canfield wrote of the orders from Rosecrans to consolidate the army to meet Bragg's threat and what that looked like on the right of the line as it was formed.

General Rosecrans was not aware of Bragg's strength and intentions until the 12th, when he made haste to concentrate his army.

On the 13th, at midnight, General McCook received orders to join General Thomas at Stevens' Gap. Leaving a division to guard his train, with the rest of his corps they started back. There being no road up the mountain, he was obliged to return by way of Will's Valley, and cross the mountain where the 14th Corps crossed, and he did not reach Stevens' Gap until the 17th.

The morning of the 12th found us strongly posted in front of the gap. We remained here guarding our positon until arrival of General McCook's corps, when we marched to Owen's Ford, where we remained until 3:30 p.m. of the 18th. At that time we moved to the left to relieve General Palmer's division.

He not having had marching orders, delay occurred to find what disposition would be made of us. One brigade was ordered to Crawfish Spring; this was changed to an order to encamp the whole division; then two brigades were ordered to return and relieve General Palmer. The distance and the hindrance to our progress, by crowded condition of the road, filled with troops and transportation moving to the left, or north, prevented us getting in position until about daylight.

John Ellis of the 16th Louisiana wrote in his memoirs of the two days leading to the battle and how flush with confidence Bragg's army was for the fight to come.

From LaFayette we began to move slowly back towards Chattanooga, upon which point Rosecrans was cautiously moving by the left flank. On the night of the 17th we lay in a deep gorge of the mountains guarding the entrance to a cove. That night came to the camp fire W. H. Wheat and others who had been away on furlough. Stewart also returned with them. They brought us letters from home and by the flickering and uncertain light of the bivouac fires we sat to read the messages of affection from fond hearts. Young Bailey of the Washington Artillery took supper with Lt. Kent and myself that night. He was so full of life and hope and predicted for our arms a brilliant victory before the setting of a few suns. Before two more had set he was torn to atoms by a shell while standing at his gun.

On the 18th we slowly moved onward and on the same night the brigade guarded a ford. Rumors were rife that a portion of the army of V. had reached Dalton. Now it was known beyond doubt that at least two divisions of Gen. Longstreet's gallant corps were near at hand.

The troops cheered loudly and seemed in the highest spirits at this intelligence. These heroes of McLaws & Hood had never moved but to victory; the little army of Bragg was stronger than ever and we would meet Rosecrans this time with double the numbers we had at Murfreesboro while he could not be much stronger than then. The banners of the armies of Lee and Bragg would wave together for the first time. Victory could not be doubtful. The army of the south must triumph. There could be no other result. When soldiers feel and reason thus, it is not easy to defeat them.

George Foster of the 51st Illinois wrote what he suspected might be his last letter home on September 17th. As part of Sheridan's division of McCook's corps they had spent that day struggling to get across the mountains and close up on Thomas's command as quickly as possible.

Blew Bird Gap Georgy

September the 17 1863 Dear Father & Mother,

I seat myself this morning to drop you a few lines to let you now how I am and how I am well. To commence I have bin very unwell for a long time. But not so bad but what I have staid with the company all the fine days. I got sow bad I could not keep up. I am now beter but not well. I haven't had very good health ever since we left Murfreesboro. I got cold on that march laying on the wet ground. George Peterson & George Johnson is well now. Well dad I will have to give you a little history of Georgy and of my soldiering when I was on the first six months. I thought I new something great a bout it but it was usually the first degree. The next six months I found out more about it and this six months I have heard something more. This is one of the mountainous Country I ever saw. We marched hard all day yesterday and only got six miles. We started yesterday morning soon as we could see. it took us till now to make too miles. We come up a very large mountain and went down it yesterday. I am that sore that I cant scarcley move. we are stoped in Blew Bird gap but I guess we will move farther to the left this afternoon. We are expecting to fight a battle soon. Thare is cannonading to our left about five miles distance. We are on three sides of the rebels. But they have a good position. It is a goin to be a hard mater to rout them. I fere thare will be a good deal of blood shed and a good many lives lost-----------they say thare is 75 thousand of them. That seems pretty scary. (I) tell you I wish the war would end sow I could come home as cep well. I didn't mind to soldering, but it is a drag to me of late. Father I would like to be at home to have some of your cooking about now. Mother I wish you had what coffee I have on hand up a company savings. I guess I have got prety near a bushel. I have shared since I have bin on this march. We got plenty to eat such as it is. Crackers bacon beef coffee a hog. When in camp we git more, we git rice peas beans some times potatos ------------

Father & Mother I write no mor and I will close and that is this. We all expect to be in this expected battle and I may never be permited to write a nother letter to you all. Thou I am in hopes I will. Mother thare is one thing that is a grate consulation to me and that is this. I now I have a praying for mother at home. Thank God for it. I (k)now to thar has bin a many prairs went up before the throne for yur son. That he mite be spair to return home once mor. thank god for a prayer mother. mother it is my daily prair that I may live to see your face once more. Dear cousens sisters and brothers if I could be permited to meat you hear on earth, may we meat in haven where parting will be no more. Well I must close hoping to here from you soon. the order has just come to have 100 hundred rounds of cartrages with us sow I will have to tend to it.

Sow good by George W. Foster

Direct to Co. F 51st Regt Ill. Vol.
 Murfreesboro Tenn.
To follow the regt.

Chapter Nine

Chickamauga

On September 18, Braxton Bragg ordered an attack on Crittenden who held the right flank of the Federal army. His objective was to turn Crittenden's flank and ultimately pin Rosecrans' entire army in McLemore's Cove with no route of retreat to Chattanooga. With no chance for escape, this would enable him to destroy the Army of the Cumberland.

Everything went wrong that could have that day. Movements by his forces were delayed and confused commanders did not act aggressively. Opportunities to cross Chickamauga creek and hit the enemy with a devastating blow were lost that day partly due to timing and partly due to the tremendous fight put up by Federal Cavalry units and Wilder's Lightning Brigade at both Reed's Bridge and Alexander's Bridge. By the end of the day only a small portion of Bragg's army had crossed the Chickamauga but they continued to move across throughout the night. By morning almost three quarters of the Army of Tennessee was on the same side of the creek as the Army of the Cumberland.

Lieutenant Otis Baker of the 10th Mississippi wrote of his unit's approach to the battle from LaFayette as part of General Hindman's Division over the 17th and 18th. He could not know of Bragg's frustration with the slowness of his commanders to get their men into assigned positions on the 18th, but he does describe the miserable conditions for moving an army over roads that have experienced a recent draught.

LaFayette, Sept 17th – Still in camp. Nothing has occurred to disturb the monotony excepting the orders rec'd last night to be ready to move at daylight this morning. But they have since been countermanded. We now await further orders. - Took up the march about 6 P.M. the other divisions of the army having preceded us. Continued the march until 3 A.M. having made a distance of eight (8) miles in the direction of Lee & Gordon's Mills. This was a very tedious march owing very much to the extreme slowness of the gait & in the early part of the night to the dust. When it is come in mind that there has been no rain in this section for two or three months, one can easily imagine how the parched earth has become powdered thoroughly to a considerable depth by the passage & repassage of the army & its trains. Upon a great portion of the roads in this vicinity, the dust is four or more inches in depth, flies so dense one cannot distinguish a man fifteen or twenty yards distant.

Sept 18th At 8 ½ we resumed the march. About 10 A.M. formed line of battle a couple of miles from Lee's Mills. Our division being in the second line. An artillery duel commenced a short time previous, still continuing. The weather which had changed during the night was uncomfortably cool. 12 M moved about a mile further to the right in the woods where we were permitted to build fires. The day closed with a skirmish between Gen'l Strahl's Brigade & the enemy, the former striving to obtain possession of a certain spring, an undertaking in which they succeeded. Desultory cannonading during entire day.

Meanwhile, Rosecrans had been concerned about a possible flanking move on his left so he had ordered Thomas to move to Crittenden's left extending the line. By the morning of the 18th two of Thomas's divisions under Brigadier Generals John M. Brannan and Absalom Baird were in position to block Bragg's attempt to move around the Federal left. Instead of the Federal left still being in the vicinity of Lee and Gordon's Mill as Bragg had assumed, it was now three and a half miles to the north. Instead of coming in on Rosecrans' flank Bragg's line was overlapped by Thomas' two divisions.

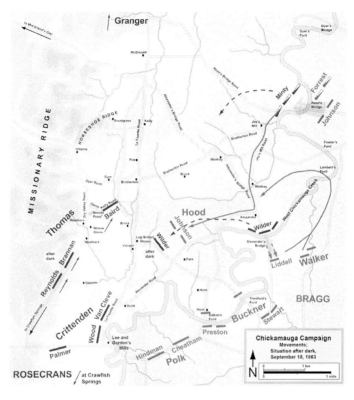

Rosecrans for his part had no idea that the majority of Bragg's army was on his side of the creek. Early on the morning of the 19th Thomas was informed that a rebel brigade had crossed the creek. Thomas in turn ordered Brannan to attack and capture the "lone" brigade. Brannan ordered a brigade under Colonel John T. Croxton toward the bridge to investigate. Running into Confederate General Nathan Bedford Forrest's cavalry, Croxton skirmished and drove Forrest back toward the creek before he came into contact with a full division of Confederate General Walker's corps under the command of Brigadier General State's Rights Gist. Completely overwhelmed yet showing his sense of humor, Croxton sent a courier back to Thomas requesting just which of the several enemy brigades to his front he was supposed to capture. The battle was on in earnest from that moment.

Brannan immediately sent the rest of his division into the fray to support Croxton. Gist's Division was quickly pushing through

131

Brannan's forces when Thomas ordered Baird and his division to advance and support Brannan. Walker responded by sending a division commanded by Brigadier General St. John Liddell into the fight just as it was beginning to turn in favor for the Federals. The shock of Liddell's added troops succeeded in driving Both Brannan and Baird back to their starting points.

Thomas, feeling the desperation of the situation without his two still detached divisions of Negley and Reynolds, pleaded for reinforcements from Rosecrans. Rosecrans sent General Richard Johnson's division from Alexander McCook's corps. These fresh troops quickly turned the tide against the Confederates in this constantly seesawing struggle for control of the ground on the Federal left.

As Walker now retreated he called for reinforcements and soon Major General Benjamin F. Cheatham's division came to his aid. The battle again swayed the other direction as the intensity of the fighting continued to escalate and expand to the south as more and more units were committed on both sides.

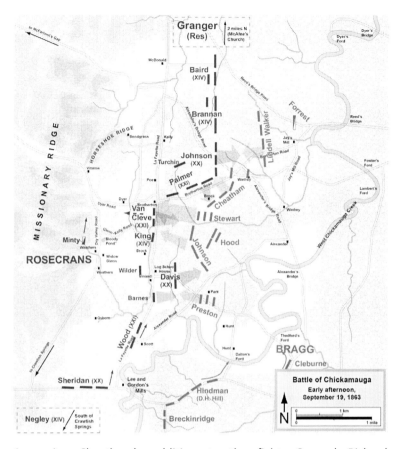

Answering Cheatham's addition to the fight, General Richard Johnson's division counterattacked threatening to break the Confederate line. His attack was in turn answered by Bragg sending Major General Alexander P. Stewart's Division to support Cheatham. Stewart came onto line on Cheatham's left around 2:30 in the afternoon and drove into Brigadier General Horatio P. Van Cleve's division, pushing him back past the Brotherton farm house, but at a terrible cost. One of his brigades lost a third of its men in a matter of minutes.

At this time Reynolds and Negley, Thomas' missing divisions, were arriving behind Van Cleve and Reynolds and immediately pitched in to the fight. This timely reinforcement saved the day for the Union. Stewart had broken the Federal line and gained the LaFayette road which was the main line of communication between Thomas on the left and Crittenden to his right. Further advance would have enabled the Confederates to gain the Dry Valley Road, totally cutting off Rosecrans' headquarters from a line of retreat to Chattanooga. Reynolds, forming a line with Van Cleve's remaining troops, poured a deadly fire into Stewart's advancing Confederates stopping them in their tracks.

Major General John Bell Hood of Longstreet's Corp had arrived earlier in the day with the advance units of his division. On his own initiative, Hood, having tired of listening to the sound of battle all day yet receiving no orders, took action. He led the divisions of Evander Law and Bushrod Johnson to an assault on the Federal right striking the division of Brigadier General Jefferson C. Davis.

Rosecrans had been constantly shifting troops throughout the afternoon and Davis' flanks were exposed. Hood and Law crashed into two of Davis' brigades and it seemed for a moment that the deciding moment of the battle had arrived. The assault threatened to overrun Rosecrans' headquarters. At this moment of crisis, Brigadier General Thomas J. Wood threw his division in on Davis' right threatening Hood's flank. Eli Lilly's artillery battery unlimbered and fired into Johnson's left flank. Wilder's Lightning Brigade, moving from Thomas' right, added the firepower of their Spencers into the fray. The slaughter was more than the Confederates could endure and still continue their advance.

The day had been a brutal and confused melee from one end of the line to the other. The wooded area where the fighting occurred made it difficult to coordinate attacks and understand the entire circumstances at any moment by either high command. The term "fog of war" was amplified in these conditions. It had truly been a soldier's fight where the actions and ferocity of small units determined the fight in each sector.

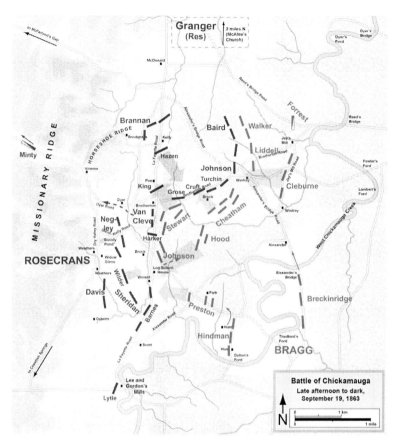

John Magee, as part of Cheatham's division, wrote of his battery's experience in the action of the 19th:

Saturday, Sept 19th, 1863. *Up and stirring early. Heavy skirmishing commenced about sunup. Our Division moved forward and got across the creek by 8 o'clock, and formed in an old field. Firing was now pretty heavy – brisk cannonading on the left, which grew gradually more rapid and extended towards the right. Longstreet's men, says Hoods and McLaws' Divisions are here on the field, and will occupy our left. About 9 o'clock the engagement commenced in our front – our division moved forward, our Brigade in the rear – passed by Hood's division. Firing now became very hot – the battle began in earnest – shell and shot flying in every direction – "double quick, march!" was the order for about one mile through a rough, unbroken, wooded country, and we came up in the rear of Smith's and Maney's Brigades. Here I ascertained that Walker had been repulsed, but being speedily reinforced by Smith's and Maney's Brigades of our division, and succeeded in driving them back, and capturing 6 pieces of artillery and 200 prisoners. Firing very heavy now in front and on our left – engagement general. Our Brigade was now ordered forward to support Genl Smith's, the battery to stay with the Brigade – moved up within 6 hundred yards of Smith's lines and laid in line. Canon shot and shell flew pretty thick among us – two of the 19th Tenn were killed within a few yards of me. The battle appeared to be very hotly contested – the enemy giving way very stubbornly, and sometimes making us give way. The battle raged in its wildest fury – Genl Cheatham, the glorious old hero could be seen galloping along the line, encouraging the troops, and giving his orders with coolness. At 12 we were ordered to relieve Genl Smith and hold the position. Genl Strahl led his boys bravely, the battery following closely – crossed an old field, and the battery halted under the crest of a small hill, the Brigade moving on. They moved upon the line, the enemy not firing on them, and then marched by the right flank to close an open space between them and Maney's Brigade. The enemy were ambushed, and opened a destructive enfilade fire on our brave boys, and nobly they stood it. I witnessed it all, I never saw so many men fall on so small a space of ground. The 19th and 33d suffered the worst. The battery did not fire a shot – could get no position, nor did our Brigade fire but very few shots. The enemy had a very strong position and outnumbered us, flanked us on right and left, and we had to fall back. The deafening roar of musketry was sublime, and booming of canon was terrific, Wright's Brigade gave way on our left, and Maney on our right, and in 20 minutes the whole line was driven back ¼ of a mile. The carnage was fearful – saw Capt Carnes – his battery captured and nearly all his men. Many officers in the division killed. Our brigade lost in 15 minutes 186 killed and wounded and 45 missing. We had 3 men wounded in the battery, John McNeil, Robert Bart and Cicero Chatam. The enemy did not advance on us and the firing became slower and soon almost stopped in front. Over on the left we could hear rapid discharges of canon, and one continuous roll of musketry. The battle raged with unabated fury, at times all along the line till evening. We moved our battery up and fired a few rounds at long range. At dark the firing had nearly ceased. Genl Cheatham boiling over rage and stung to the quick, to see his Division driven back for the first time in the war, got permission to make a night attack on their strong position in front. His division with part of Cleburne's attacked them furiously a little after dark. I never did hear a more deafening roar in my life – but little cannonading. We drove the enemy from the place, but at an awful cost of life. Genl Smith was killed and several other field officers. Our men held the field. We encamped a few hundred yards in rear of our Brigade. The firing ceased altogether about 8 o'clock. Our men have suffered awful today and gained nothing. We have captured about one thousand prisoners. Polk's and Walker's corps done most of the fighting today. We expect to fight the hardest battle tomorrow ever witnessed on this continent. Cold Chilly night.*

Canfield's history of the 21st Ohio recorded their mid-day movement from Crawfish Springs to become briefly engaged against Hood's troops as their momentum was being broken. Their day concluded as skirmishers opposing the Confederate pickets across the fields of the Brotherton Farm bordering the LaFayette Road.

We remained here (Crawfish Springs), in hearing of heavy fighting at intervals, until 3:30 p.m. (Sept 19th), when General McCook's corps having passed, leaving us the extreme right of the line, we were ordered to the left. Passing General Rosecrans' headquarters, General Negley discovered the enemy coming through a gap in the line, threatening General Thomas' rear, and he was ordered to drive them back. We engaged them about three-fourths of a mile a little north and east of the Widow Glenn's, drove them a quarter of a mile or more, and took position on the east side of a strip of woods, about 500 yards west of the Lafayette road; the 2d and 3d brigades took position in line, and the first brigade was placed in reserve. Company K was ordered to hold the skirmish line in front of the regiment, and was deployed and moved about two hundred yards to the front, and occupied a ridge about three hundred yards from the Lafayette road, on the west side of which were the enemy's skirmishers. Though they were so near they were heard to cough and stamp their feet, to keep them warm, there was no firing in our front during the night, the regiment being allowed to gain the rest they so much needed. Nothing disturbed the stillness of the night save the groans of the helplessly wounded, and the moving of the enemy's artillery to the left, which began about 1 o'clock in the morning. Permission was asked to bring in the wounded, but it was denied, for fear of drawing the fire of the enemy. Lieutenant Mahony crawled out and gave a couple of them water, and covered them, for the night was very chilly, the ground in the morning being covered with a heavy frost.

Otis Baker's 10th Mississippi had been active moving during the day but not engaged in the fight.

Sept. 19th. – Skirmishing resumed soon after daylight, and occasional cannonading along the lines, somewhat later. Between 8 or 9 A.M. engagement opened on the right & continued heavy during the day. At midday we moved from the left to the center but were not engaged that day. After dark, the weather being still cool we were carried a short distance to this place. Allowed to light small fires, by which we comfortably reposed until 4 A.M. We had for our couches, ground which had resounded to the tread of troops formed during that day & got protection from the cold dead trees that had humanely obstructed missiles which were intended to deprive fellow beings & brothers of the precious boon – life. Nothing seems to have been gained by either party by this day's work.

John Ellis and his 16th Louisiana, along with Breckinridge's Division, were positioned on the far left of Bragg's line, south of the main fighting of the 19th. Starting their day near Crawfish Springs, they moved parallel to Canfield's 21st Ohio as both divisions moved toward the sound of the guns.

On the morning of the 19th the brigade moved before daylight and took up a positon in line of battle. Only the western fork of the Chickamauga Creek separated us from the army of the enemy. The sun rose in a cloudless sky and a light wind stirred the foliage dressed in regal dyes of Autumn.

Suddenly a half a mile to our right burst a cannon shot upon our ears, followed by the howl of the shell and its explosion over towards the enemy. Then came another and another in rapid succession. A dozen guns perhaps had sent their hurling missives towards the enemy's line when their silence was broken and an answering gun sent a shell towards our batteries which exploded far short of its mark. A loud yell along the entire brigade front answered this first hostile demonstration of the enemy, but the guns of Cobb's and Slocumb's batteries returned far more effective answer. Then for an hour the duel raged. Twice the Yankee artillerists shifted their position under the fire of our guns. Finally Major Graves, advancing his guns by section, charged across the creek, supported only by the 2nd Ky. Infantry, drove the Yankee batteries from the field and retired to his original position. In this duel our batteries suffered severely. Lieut. Blair and 30 of Slocumbs company (including my friend Bailey) were killed and wounded. Cobb lost four or five men. But none of their guns and but few horses were injured.

In the meantime a severe fight was raging seven or eight miles away to our right. The bellowing of the artillery was incessant and now and then the long unmistakable roll of musketry was plainly audible.

At 11 o'clock A.M. we began to move slowly towards the firing. The enemy were also moving in the same direction. Skirmishers were thrown out to guard against surprise and moved parallel with our line of march. At 5 P.M. the firing had not ceased and we began to move more rapidly. At sundown we were three miles from the scene of action and "double quick" was ordered. About that time Gen. Cleburne, with the brigades of Polk, Deshler and Wood, advanced to the support of Walker who, with his own division and the brigades of Walthall and Liddell, both under the command of the latter, had for nine mortal hours held his ground with varying fortunes against the attacks of the enemy. He had suffered fearfully and it was a welcome sight to him, the long line and bayonets glittering in the last rays of that September sun, of Cleburne's advancing battalions. Passing over Walker's line, the gallant Irishman advanced directly upon the enemy. He drove them with fearful loss over a mile and a half, capturing 1800 prisoners and 16 pieces of artillery, including the celebrated 1st Michigan battery of parrott guns. In the meantime our division was moving rapidly to his support. I could hear the intense and steady roll of musketry and breaking through like the burst of thunder through the roar of the storm, came the hoarse braying of artillery. Now there was only a dropping fire of musketry as if of skirmishes warmly engaged. Then suddenly it increased and grew stronger and denser until it seemed one consolidated roar, the individuality – if I may use the term – of each musket shot being sunk into the volume of terrific sound. It continued ten, fifteen minutes, the artillery fire guns rapid and with its "hip, hip, huzza", but a genuine rebel yell, the yell of men moved to do or die and fast closing with the foe. Suddenly the roll of musketry is hushed, then the silence is broken by two or three cannon shots, then all is still again, except the yells which grow louder and are prolonged. We knew then that the Yankee battery had been captured for it took no very experienced ear to interpret the meaning of those fearful sounds.

The fighting ceased about an hour after night and our division bivouacked for the night, which was cold and frosty. Very soon however, huge fires blazed along the line and by their cheerful light the hungry and tired troops lay down to sleep. We had had no rations for two days and yet our men were cheerful and confident. But there was very little merriment around the camp fires that night and soon all was still, except the tramp of the sentinel, the neigh of a horse or the distant jolting roll of an ambulance or artillery wheel.

Axel Reed and the 2nd Minnesota had been in the thick of the fighting on Rosecrans' left flank early in the day. He described the action as such:

Saturday, Sept. 19. Received orders to march at 4 p.m. yesterday and marched all night, about N. E., as fast as the blockaded condition of the road would permit. Halted at 8 o'clock this morning for breakfast, but did not have time to cook any; got coffee partly cooked and had to go on. Kept on the road leading northeast towards Ringold, and about 13 miles from Chattanooga turned off from the main road to the right toward Chickamauga Creek, where we saw our troops in position, expecting the enemy. Skirmishing commenced at about 9 a.m. and at 9:30 the 2nd brigade was hotly engaged. Our brigade took position on their left on the point of the ridge, sloping to the south, east and north. The 2nd Minnesota took position on the extreme left. Smith's Co. I, 4th Regular Battery close to our right. At ten o'clock the rebels advanced on us. Hard firing lasted about an hour, when the enemy fell back. A number of our men were carried back wounded. I had no gun when I went in, as I was under arrest, and deprived of gun and accoutrements, but one that belonged to the first man that was wounded, and that he had been using, belonged to Co. C. I got it and made the best use of it I could. One or two companies on our right were ordered to swing back so that the cannon could use grape and canister as the rebels were close onto us. The whole line, seeing the right falling back, commenced with some confusion, but were soon quiet, laid down, and kept up a withering fire. The fire of the enemy ceased about 11 a.m., when we found the enemy was flanking us on the left. We marched by the left flank and filed left and formed front to the east. They opened on us before we got into position, killing Sergt. Holdship, of Co. D, and mortally wounding James A. Bigelow, of my Co. K. Another heavy fire was opened on the enemy, which was kept up until 11:30 o'clock a.m., when the enemy disappeared, but soon appeared before our front facing south. The Regular brigade of Rousseau's old division, 1st Div. 14th Army C., consisting of the 15th, 16th, 18th and 19th Regular Infantry had advanced in the direction we had changed from and again fronting south. The firing had hardly commenced when back came our own men enmasse, the regular brigade in utter confusion, some of them running through our ranks, without guns or hats. We succeeded in stopping some of them but the most ignominiously fled to the rear. As soon as they were past, we opened on the enemy, who were following closely on a charge, having captured Loomis's battery of 7 pieces. They were soon driven back, the 9th Ohio following them on a charge, recapturing the battery. Some of the regular brigade was rallied by Gen. Brannan and pushed forward, he telling them that his men had retaken their lost battery and for them to go and haul it off. We found ourselves being flanked again on our left when we quickly changed front to the east, when the enemy came on us with a rush, but every man stuck to his post and they failed to get up to us, but kept pressing towards our left (then extending north), when we made a left backward wheel and formed front north just opposite of our first front and near the same ground. Robert McClellan was mortally wounded while fronting east (of Co. K). The enemy was again repulsed, leaving us in full possession of the field. Wm. Evans, of my Co., visited the ground over which we had fought and counted 143 dead rebels killed opposite our last front. The fight ended on our part of the field about noon (19), when firing commenced about a half mile to our right. Our brigade was relieved and moved a short distance to the rear for a support. Towards night we were taken toward the right a mile and a half, to where General Van Cleve's division had fallen back. Some of his troops behaved badly. About sunset we took position on an elevated ridge sloping to the east, where we laid during the night. Heavy firing continued until long after dark. General Nagle's division being engaged.

Unaware that the battle had already passed one bloody but undetermined day, W. R. Stillwell's 53rd Georgia was still moving toward the field on September 19th. He took a moment to write to his wife from Atlanta.

Atlanta Georgia, September 19, 1863

> *My dear Molly:*
>
> *You may be somewhat astonished to receive a letter from me here though I suppose you will hear of it before you get this. We got here yesterday or last night at twelve o'clock. I tried to get a furlough and go home today but could not, there was so many that runaway and went, that they would not give any. General Bryan tried to get me off but could not. I have not much time to write as all the couriers are gone but me. I am well and doing well. I think we will leave for Dalton or Rome tomorrow. There will be a big fight up there if the Yankees don't run off. I got the ambrotype and drawers and two pairs of socks that you sent me by Lieutenant Farrar. I can see that Tom favors himself a little but not much, the baby looks fat and pretty but you don't favor (each other) or (you) don't look like you did when I left. If it looks like you you have broke very fast. I fear that you are not cheerful enough, you must not grow old and get ugly before I do come home.*
>
> *Molly, I seen Uncle John McKibbin today and all of Sloan's Company from Henry (County). Uncle John is going home tomorrow or next day. Molly, I will enclose a letter that I wrote before I left Virginia. I want some of you to come and see me if I get stationed soon, but I will write again soon and let you know where I am. I am very glad to get back to Georgia. Give my love to all the friends. I have not got time to write longer. You need not write to me until I write again. I am yours always till death.*

W. R. Stilwell

As the fighting on the 19th died down, General Thomas, commanding the left wing of the Union Army ordered his men to begin fortifying their positions. While he assumed the fighting was over for the day due to growing darkness, he also reminded them to be ever diligent and keep a high level of preparedness.

As described in some of the Confederate diaries and letters, Southern General Patrick Cleburne's men had started the day to the south near Lee and Gordon's Mill. They had moved toward the center of action all day and fording the stream as the sun was setting, advanced on Thomas' men. Another bloody and confused fight ensued until the darkness was so complete that men could not see. In the hazy darkening evening, soldiers on both sides aimed their weapons based on sound and muzzle flashes, sometimes firing into friendly units. When the fighting had ended, Cleburne's final charge of the day had pushed the left of the Federal line back another mile, capturing some artillery and a number of prisoners.

The night of the 19th and 20th was miserable for all on the field. The temperatures dropped dramatically. Most soldiers had no blankets and orders on both sides were given not to build fires. As the all-consuming sound of combat died into the darkness, the cries for help and anguished moans of the thousands of wounded made it a nightmare. The wounded lay intermingled between the combatants. No one on either side could risk going forward to assist them and bring them to safety, so the horrid sounds kept up through the entire night.

One could also hear the sound of axes and the construction of breastworks out of felled trees. The ground was too rocky and hard to dig trenches so the Union soldiers of Thomas's command used everything they could to strengthen their position and prepare for the morning. The sound of wheels from supply wagons, ambulances and artillery were constant as both armies repositioned their troops to improve their positions. Sleep was at a minimum if at all.

Rosecrans had determined to make a defensive stand on the 20th and continued to shift troops to strengthen his left wing under Thomas. For his part, Bragg informed his commanders that he was reorganizing the army again. This was a very unorthodox decision in the middle of a huge battle. The right wing would be commanded by General Polk made up of Polk's, Hill's and Walker's corps. The left including Hood, and Buckner would be commanded by Longstreet who had arrived overnight along with the balance of his corps. Bragg's plan for the 20th was the same as the 19th. He wanted to flank the Federal left cutting them off from Chattanooga and push them into McLemore's Cove where he felt he could isolate and destroy the Army of the Cumberland. At dawn the division on his far right would launch first, and the others would join in echelon, meaning that they would enter the fight successively from that point to the left.

The complicated reorganization of the right and left wings of Bragg's army required significant shifting of troops in order to be ready for the morning's attack. D. H. Hill never received the order until the time the first attack was to have commenced. He notified Polk that he would take at least an hour to prepare his troops and Polk waited to hear that he was ready. The delay of a number of hours incensed Bragg who ordered the attack be executed immediately. It was 9:45 a.m. before the attack was launched.

Breckenridge's Division was the first to engage and two of his brigades were able to get around the Federal left flank. Union General Negley's troops were just arriving in that area, deploying against Breckenridge's assault. For a moment Breckenridge's men captured the road to Chattanooga but could not hold it. The fighting was as intense as any of the first day. Confederate General Benjamin Hardin Helm, Lincoln's brother-in-law, was mortally wounded in this attack. Both sides struggled to hold on.

The next Confederate division under Patrick Cleburne marched directly into a line of log breastworks the Union soldiers had erected overnight. They were stopped cold by powerful volleys from muskets and artillery canister from behind the protective barrier. Next in succession came Walker and Cheatham. They met a similar fate charging against the Yankees behind their breastworks.

John Ellis and the 16th Louisiana were part of Breckinridge's initiating attack on the Union left that morning. He provided a highly detailed and opinionated description of the morning's action:

The morning of the 20th of September, 1863 broke bright and beautifully over the opposing armies. Before daylight we were in motion and advancing over the scene of the battle of the previous day. The field was thickly wooded with a growth of pine, oak and birch. The trees were scarred with bullet marks. The wounded had all been removed but dead men and horses lay all over the woods. The leaves were on fire and the air was filled with the fumes of burning flesh. While moving amid such scenes, the wagon overtook us with rations. Very soon they were issued and the troops tasted food for the first time in 60 hours.

By a little after sunrise we were in position on the extreme right of the army. Austin's battalion with its 32nd Ala. Infantry was deployed on the skirmish line.

Never before had I seen a lovelier day. It was Sunday and the calm of that solemn sunshine seemed fitter for chiming bells and church going people, than for scene of strife and blood and suffering.

For three hours the opposing armies stood motionless as if loath to disturb the calm of that holy day. Not even the sound of a picket's gun had been heard up to 9 o'clock. A light breeze stirred the crimson leaves of the forest, yet so light it came that the folds of the battle flag hardly heeded its invitation to play.

Gen. Hill (D.H.) Breckenridge and Adams rode along the lines but the troops were forbidden to cheer. Hill was not a remarkable man in appearance. He stooped in the saddle and there was an air of general negligence about his whole bearing. He appeared, however, entirely at his ease. Breckenridge looked all himself and glanced with evident pride along the ranks of those who had followed him so long. His broad, open brow bore no traces of care, his large eyes were full of light and confidence and a bland smile rested upon his face and slightly raised his inimitable mustache. Breckenridge had the finest mustache in the army.

At 9 ½ A.M. we were ordered to advance and the whole line went steadily forward with but little opposition while Austin drove the skirmishes of the enemy far in our front. A brigade of Yankees were soon dispersed and four pieces of artillery and 150 prisoners captured. This was mainly the work of Austin's battalion, 32nd Ala. and 13th La.

Very soon we crossed the Chattanooga road and became exposed to the fire of a battery of artillery, which had position lower down on the road to our left. Gen. Adams then changed front to the left and advanced his line to the cover afforded by the valley of two small but abrupt hillocks. Here we remained a few minutes while the shells and grape of the enemy flew harmlessly over our heads. Soon came the order "forward double quick"! "March!" and away went the line over the open space into a skirt of woods where the line was dressed and then moved forward.

We had advanced two hundred yards when the Yankees opened upon the 19th La. on our left, then upon us and then on to the 13th. The troops answered with a cheer and pressed forward. Their first fire killed one of my men, Tom Bridges, and mortally wounded Tom Deltis. They fell together almost at my feet. Our line still advanced, firing as it went. The Yankees began to give way. The artillerists left their guns and their infantry was in great confusion. Then a mistake was made, somewhere, by someone, which altered the whole face of affairs, and prevented the rout of the enemy at that hour which occurred a few hours after and forced us to retire. Brig. Gen. Adams had fallen severely wounded and the command devolved on Col. Gibson who ordered the lines to halt. The troops amid the din and uproar of battle could not hear the order, but Col. Gober spurring through the line rode along the front of the regiment amid a perfect tempest of bullets, waiving his sword and ordering the halt. Why, in the very moment of victory when the troops with resistless valor and the wildest enthusiasm were moving on and the enemy wavering and in confusion, a halt should be ordered, neither Col. Gober nor the troops could tell. But the order had been given and alas! was obeyed. The enemy rallied and reinforced their swaying line, poured in volley after volley and then came the alarm from the right "We have gone too far, we are flanked." Order was lost and a precipitate retreat began. The troops fell back two or three hundred yards and were rallied without trouble.

They were not panic stricken or demoralized, but angry, for they saw they had been sacrificed and defeated through the incompetency of someone high in command. In this retreat I received a fall from a fence which at the time I did not feel, but which a few hours afterwards welled up my right knee, incapacitated me for further service during that day and almost prevented me from walking for three weeks afterwards. The enemy attempted a pursuit but the Napoleon guns of the Washington artillery drove them back in confusion. They then opened upon Slocumb with artillery and in this fight the gallant and chivalric Graves (Breckinridge's chief of artillery) received a mortal wound. In half an hour our brigade and battery withdrew to the woods across the Chattanooga road and rested until 4 P.M.

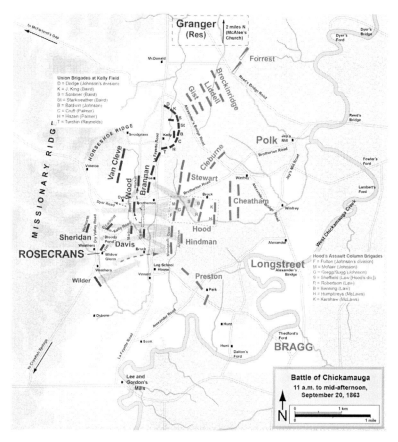

Thomas was continually calling for reinforcements to buoy his pressed line. During one of those requests, a staff officer of Thomas' informed General Rosecrans that, as he had passed the center of the line, he had seen a gap where it appeared a division that had been sent to Thomas' aid had moved but not been replaced. Rosecrans urgently ordered General Wood to move immediately to the left and close up on General Reynold's right in order to fill that gap.

Wood knew that there was no gap between his division and Reynolds. However he had been berated earlier by Rosecrans in front of his men for not following a preemptive order. Not wishing to feel the commanding General's wrath again he began moving his men behind the division "in the gap" in order to support Reynolds' right flank. Jefferson C. Davis was ordered to move his division into Wood's place from the reserve in the rear. General Sheridan was ordered to send two of his brigades to reinforce Thomas at the same time. This put two Federal divisions in motion to the left creating a quarter of a mile gap in the center of the line where no gap had existed.

Quite by chance on the Southern side, General Longstreet had ordered the three divisions of Hood, Johnson and Kershaw to attack directly into the gap the Federals had just created. The effect was instant and shocking. The Confederates rushed into the gap and overwhelmed the forces on either side. Union General Davis' division offered little resistance before giving way. In minutes, most of General McCook's entire corps was in disorderly retreat. Brigadier general William H. Lytle attempted to break the Confederate attack by ordering his outnumbered force directly into the Confederate assault. The effort was short lived as was Lytle. As he lay dying his men broke to the rear.

In short order the entire right of the Army of the Cumberland was fleeing the onslaught, including General Rosecrans whose headquarters was about to be overrun, causing him to join the retreating troops flooding through McFarland's Gap toward Rossville, Chattanooga and safety. Bragg's plan had been to push the Federal army to the left toward McLemore's Cove, but this changed everything. The right of the Army of the Cumberland had collapsed while its left was holding fast. The opportunity now depended on the Confederate's ability to crush Thomas from his right.

After a short time reforming the lines of his assaulting force, Longstreet wheeled his men to the right advancing on an elevation known as Snodgrass Hill or Horseshoe Ridge. Gaining this eminence would put him on Thomas' right and rear flank enabling him to roll up Thomas' entire line while Polk's forces continued to hold the Union left in check by the bloody stalemate that continued in that sector.

Defending the crest of Snodgrass Hill at the horseshoe were the brigade of Brigadier General William B. Hazen and a portion of Brigadier General John M. Brannan's division, along with remnants of other units that had been collected from the retreating right wing. Brannon was on the right flank of what remained of the Union army with Hazen to his left adjoining the balance of Thomas' pressured line.

Against these forces, Longstreet threw four divisions under the command of Brigadier General Joseph B. Kershaw, Major Generals Thomas C. Hindman, Bushrod Johnson and Brigadier General William Preston.

Kershaw's assault hit the full force of Hazen's and Brannan's men at the crest. The intense fire of the Union troops halted his attack a mere forty yards from their lines. Kershaw reformed and attacked several times until his troops were literally out of breath and too exhausted to push forward again.

Bushrod Johnson and Hindman attempted to assault the hill on Brannon's far right and rear. Requesting reinforcements, Brannan received the 21st Ohio from Negley's division. The 21st had entered the battle as one of the largest regiments in the army of the Cumberland, numbering 539 officers and men. Additionally, eight of the regiment's ten companies were equipped with Colt Revolving rifles. These five shot weapons gave this regiment amazing fire power in battle. Deploying on Brannan's right, the 21st took the brunt of the initial flanking attacks but held their ground and pushed Longstreet's shock troops back down the slope. After the battle, Longstreet commented that during the time the 21st Ohio was holding the flank he thought he was up against a division.

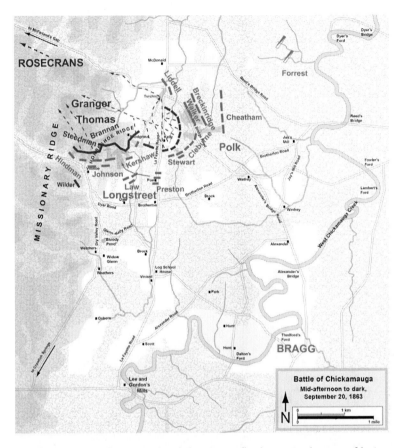

Battle of Chickamauga
Mid-afternoon to dark,
September 20, 1863

The fighting was desperate and the Union flank was in danger of being turned when Major General Gordon Granger arrived with Brigadier General James Steedman's division of reserves. Frustrated with being held in Rossville as reserves and not receiving orders to join the fight, Granger took initiative at 11:00 that morning and marched Steedman's troops to the relief of Thomas. No sooner had they arrived when they were rushed to the right flank of the 21st Ohio in time to thwart Hindman's assault that would have surely turned the flank and gained Thomas' rear, cutting off his line of retreat through McFarland's gap.

Otis Baker and his 16th Louisiana fought as part of Anderson's Brigade this day. His diary entry for the day talked of the quick success of the initial attack but the inability to drive the Federal troops from Horseshoe Ridge:

Sept. 20th - The morning opened very smoky, so much so that the engagement was not resumed until near 9 o'clock A.M. An hour and a half later the centre (Hindman's Division) moved forward to the charge. In one hour we had driven the enemy three miles. Our brigade (Anderson's) captured twelf pieces of artillery & our regiment three pieces. The brigade was engaged during the remainder of the day with a reserve Division of the army. They charged us once but were repulsed with heavy slaughter. They occupied a high ridge we stormed three times but were unsuccessful not being well supported on the flanks. It is astonishing how small our loss was, compared with that of the enemy. Providence in its goodness seemed to turn aside the deadly missiles.

By late afternoon, every unit of Thomas' force had been heavily engaged, receiving heavy casualties. Ammunition was perilously low, especially for the 21st Ohio on Horseshoe ridge. Their colt revolving rifles required .56 caliber rounds while the most common Enfield and Springfield muskets fired .577 caliber bullets. Going into the battle the regiment's ordinance officer had made sure that each man had at least 90 rounds of the precious ammunition. Pockets and haversacks had held all the extra rounds each man could acquire. But now they were down to a few rounds per man, having searched each wounded and dead comrade for every round they could salvage.

About 5:30 p.m. Thomas ordered his units to begin retiring from the field and head through McFarland's gap to safety. He ordered Reynolds' division, furthest to the south of the line, to march behind those still in line. Then the next division in line was to follow until his right wing of the army was safely disengaged and off the field. One last charge was made toward this departing line as Reynolds began to move out. General St. John Liddell's men hit Reynolds men as they began their withdrawal. Thomas ordered General John Turchin's brigade to break Liddell's assault. As Turchin beat back Liddell's attack the balance of the army commenced its retreat.

On Horseshoe Ridge, Granger's men, after two hours of fighting and having sustained 44% casualties, had pulled back from the line, exposing the right of the 21st Ohio once again. Ordered to hold the flank as the balance of troops withdrew from the line they, along with the 89th Ohio and 22nd Michigan, were left alone in the gathering darkness with empty rifles and fixed bayonets. All three regiments were surrounded and captured by the Confederates. The combined casualties of these three regiments alone were 322 killed and wounded with 563 captured.[1]

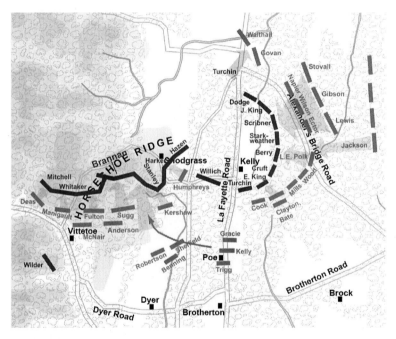

John Magee's battery was on the right of the Confederate line as part of Cheatham's Division. His diary tells this of his experience that day:

Sunday, Sept 20, 1863. *Up early – very foggy – no firing on any part of the lines. Very cold – frost. Moved our battery up to the Brigade. Understand Genl Polk's corps will act as reserve today. About 8 o'clock firing commenced in front, which soon grew very hot. Cannonading commenced at 9 very heavy in front, and soon grew general along the line. By ten o'clock the battle had commenced in earnest all along the right and centre the deafening roar of musketry and the loud reports of canon made the earth tremble. D. H. Hill made the attack with Breckinridge and Cleburne's divisions, supported by Buckner's corps and Walker's Sub-corps. Soon the booming of canon told of the attack on our left making by Longstreet. The battle now raged again, sometimes the enemy wavered, and sometimes our men. Louder and heavier grew the reports of canon as the day advanced, while the musketry was unceasing, at some place all the time. About 12 o'clock the firing grew a little slower; up to this time we had not gained much – understand Longstreet has drove them on the left. The fighting is desperate – thousands wounded and killed. About 2 o'clock our men fell back four hundred yards that they had succeeded in driving the enemy, to replenish ammunition, and there was comparatively little firing till 4 o'clock any more. Our Division, Cheatham's, was moved to the right in support of Breckinridge – we were not engaged yet. About 4 a part of Walker's Sub-corps, Lidell's and Walthall's Brigades made an attack on the extreme right, and were repulsed running in great confusion – they lost 3 pieces of Sweat's Battery and two of Fowler's. They were, however, immediately retaken by Echol's Georgia Brigade. No more firing till near sundown, except some cannonading. As the last streaks of the sun tinged the sky, a general attack was made all along the whole line. The enemy fought stubbornly for over an hour. The roar of the battle was terrible. Hill's, Buckner's, Walker's, and Longstreet's corps with a part of Cheatham's division were engaged. Charge after charge was made – shell, shot and bullets shrieked and whizzed in every direction, while louder and deeper grew the terrific roar of musketry. A little after dark our boys made a grand charge, and the enemy gave way, and fled. The deafening cheer was now given – the victory of the day was ours, but bloodily won. Our Brigade was not engaged the entire day. I did not get a chance to go over the field – we camped in front line expecting to renew the fight in morning. Our losses are very heavy – Maj Genl Hood mortally wounded, and Brigadiers Deshler Adams and Helm killed. I saw some of Cobb's battery of Breckinridge's division – they say it is badly cut up.*

Axel Reed and the 2nd Minnesota began the day near the center of the Federal line near the Kelly house representing the left of Brannan's division. As the day progressed they moved to Horse Shoe Ridge and participated in the later fighting for that ground. His diary tells their story of the 20th of September.

We were up early Sunday morning (20th). The sun rose red and fiery. The smoke was dense in our front. No firing at 7 and some thought that the enemy would not attack but about 7:30 skirmishing commenced. Our brigade formed in double column and moved a half mile for support, the left (north) and formed line of battle, then changed to the east. Heavy artillery firing commenced about 8 a.m., which soon brought on heavy musketry. Cannon balls nearly all passed over our heads, some striking close to us. We moved forward towards the firing through the woods with much underbrush and into an open field where a block house stood (the Kelly house), a battery stood in position pointing south. We formed on the right of the battery, but had hardly got laid down when orders came to change front to the left and had hardly got into position when the enemy fired from the woods on us. The 9th Ohio, which was in our front, while the balls whizzed over our heads like hail, not a man could remain unhit had he been standing up, in a few minutes they came back in a rush and laid down behind us, when we opened a withering fire on the rebels. Our men were firing over breastworks two hundred yards to our right.

The sound of cannon and musketry was terrific. Shell and shot were flying through the air in all directions, with all the hideous sounds imaginable. In about half an hour the enemy's fire slackened, when the 9th Ohio rallied, fixed bayonets and moved forward on a charge, closely followed by the 2nd Minnesota. After gaining the day at the woods we laid down by column by regiment, 35th, 9th Ohio and 2nd Minnesota, the 87th Indiana being on our left. Two rebel guns played on us with grape and canister from the left oblique. Our cannon fired over us at the rebel battery from 300 yards behind us and diagonally across us. The enemy was re-enforced and pressed hard. The 35th Ohio was ordered back to form in our rear, also the 9th Ohio in a few minutes, then we took our turn at firing. Forming again behind the other two, and they behind us again after exhausting their ammunition. At this juncture the troops on our left commenced giving way. I cast my eyes to the left and saw our men running back, but still we kept up a steady fire to the left oblique. The enemy passed around

that way. The fire was terrible on us, many shots taking effect.
Sergeant Pomeroy of my company laid about six feet from me. I saw
him just as a ball struck him in the top of his head. He raised his head
a little, gave a groan and his face dropped upon the ground as he lay
quivering. I could see that he still breathed. A cannon ball struck
Francis F. Sulterious, of Co. G, about one rod to my right and took off
his arm and tearing his leg. He lived but a short time. John A. Cutting
was shot through the head and hardly moved afterwards. Corporal
Alex. Metzger was also shot through the head and laid close by
Cutting's right side and but a few feet from me. Pomeroy, Cutting and
Metzger belonged to my company. Wm. Hamilton and John C. Smith
were helped back badly wounded. The groans of our own and rebel
dying and wounded lying in close proximity was terrible. I lay just in
front of a large pine tree and a grape shot struck in it just over my
head. All the rest of the troops had fallen back across the field to the
battery leaving us without any support and alone with no troops on
our left flank. When our Colonel saw this he ordered us back which
was made in tolerable good order, forming again behind the battery,
in its old position. We were ordered to leave our knapsacks if we
wished. The rebels passed on up towards the left (between us and
Chattanooga) as we could hear the rattling of musketry as they moved
forward. All our field and staff officers had their horses shot. Major
Davis being slightly wounded in the head, Col. George had a ball pass
through his boot. This fight lasted one hour by the watch.

Col. Bishop requested me to go down over the ground we had charged
over and look for his horse and get his pistol which was left in the
holster, where he fell. I failed to find them, but found a horse that I
thought was his but had been stripped of saddle and bridle. I was soon
on the ground where we had fought. It was a horrible sight to look at
the men of my own regiment, lying in line just as they were shot, on
their faces. Sergt. Pomeroy, Corporal Metzger and little Johnny
Cutting, who had long been my mess mate lay there within ten feet of
each other, just as though they were sleeping. Sergt. Pomeroy was still
breathing. A deep feeling came over me that I cannot express, but still
I felt not like shedding a tear for they had died gloriously, fighting the
battle of a righteous cause. I hurried back to my regiment, found them
lying down, waiting the approach of the enemy, as the rattling of

musketry could be plainly heard. Our brigade was cut off from the rest of our division, and from the main army. A rebel battery soon fired on us from a southerly direction and a severe artillery duel progressed for half an hour. We moved off by the right flank, nearly west, towards where the fighting continued. Soon came into a large corn field, a narrow ridge running along on our left, where our forces were stationed, the enemy being on the opposite side. Granger's men were just coming from the right of us. We were taken up along the side of the Ridge, and stationed along its summit to the right of a house, used for a hospital. This was about 2:00 o'clock p.m. The 21st Ohio was occupying a line in front of us with five shooting rifles, which we relieved as they were out of ammunition. The 9th Ohio and 87th Indiana were on our left, the 35th Ohio placed on our right. The enemy soon came up to take the hill but were repulsed. We occupied the place of the 21st Ohio, when they became short of ammunition and they moved to the rear.

From this time until dark the rebels made several charges, coming on in full force, with the determination of taking the position, regardless of loss. Once they succeeded in planting their flag on a slight breast work our forces had laid up, but the color bearer was shot down, their colors captured and the rebels hurled back. The 9th Ohio made one charge over the hill and lost many men in the fool-hardy act. Darkness came on leaving us victors and in possession of the Ridge (Snodgrass) but the enemy held most of the battle ground of the two days' fighting. The hill was still ours and that was the key to our safe retreat. The enemy ceased to assault and indications showed that they had withdrawn, for a rebel came up into our lines who had been after water, who was much surprised to find himself among Yankees. He said that when he started after the water his regiment (rebels) lay just at the foot of the ridge and when he returned they were gone and he supposed they had taken the hill. We confiscated his seven canteens of water which was a great luxury at the time.

The groans of the rebel wounded in our front was awful and that must have been the greatest slaughter pen of the whole field. Rebel general Buckner had massed twenty thousand men there for the express purpose of taking that Ridge but failed.

Captain Canfield of the 21st Ohio, wrote a detailed account of the regiment's action on Horseshoe Ridge in defense of Thomas's right flank after Longstreet had broken the center of the Union line and the entire right wing of the army was in pell-mell retreat. Not knowing what the regiment would face that day, but anticipating a severe struggle, Ordnance Sergeant Bolton had taken every precaution to make sure the regiment's colt revolving rifles would be able to maximize their fire power. His determination that the men not run out of ammunition was to play an important part in the contest for Horse Shoe Ridge.

...Early in the morning of the 20th, Company K, who had been now two nights without sleep, was relieved by Company E. The enemy's skirmishers advanced to the attack, but they were soon driven back. Ordnance Sergeant Bolton says he was ordered to, and brought forward ammunition, and supplied enough to each man to make him up 95 rounds. Of the amount each was furnished, I only know we urged the men to take all they could carry, and some was put in pockets, some in haversacks, and some in knapsacks...

Canfield described the scene of the breakthrough and movement of the 21st Ohio to their position on Horseshoe Ridge where they made their gallant stand.

The 21st's heroic actions followed Longstreet's breakthrough. Sometime between 9:00 and 10:00 that morning, General Negley was ordered to move his division to Thomas's far left as they were being pressured strongly by the initial Confederate attack. Negley's reserve division moved immediately as it wasn't in line at that time. It was the first to reach Thomas's left flank. The second and third brigades, including Sirwell's brigade, to which the 21st Ohio belonged, were soon relieved by General Wood's division and proceeded to the top of "the ridge", that being Horseshoe Ridge and Snodgrass Hill. It was some time after that when Wood was ordered to move to his left to support General Reynolds by closing a gap that didn't exist. That movement created the actual gap which was exploited by Longstreet's assault. Brannon, requesting reinforcements on Snodgrass Hill, was sent the 21st Ohio from Sirwell's brigade.

... Regiments, brigades and divisions were involved in the movement until all to the right of General Brannan, nearly all of Generals McCook and Crittenden's corps were in a disorderly retreat, carrying with them the two corps commanders and the department commander.

Bushrod Johnson thus describes the situation from a rebel standpoint: "The scene was unspeakably grand. The resolute and impetuous charge, the rush of our heavy columns sweeping out from the shadow and gloom of the forest into the open fields flooded with sunlight, the glitter of arms, the onward dash of artillery and mounted men, the retreat of the foe, the shout of the hosts of our army, the dust, the smoke, the noise of fire-arms, of whistling balls and grape shot, and bursting shells – made up a battle scene of unsurpassed grandeur." But if it was sport to the rebels it was death to the Federals, for a more appalling spectacle can hardly be conceived than an army in full and disorderly retreat. To stop this "rush of heavy columns" and "onward dash of artillery and mounted men" the 21st Ohio was turned over to General Brannan. We remained in position behind "the log and rails breastwork" but a short time (not over fifteen or twenty minutes), when we moved by the right flank, south and west, about one-fourth or three –eighths of a mile. Our progress to this point was very much hindered by retreating masses of infantry and artillery, passing north, making it necessary for the regiment to halt several times, until the way was cleared. At the base of the hill, where we were soon exposed to a scattering fire from the enemy, several moves were made, and feeling anxious to avoid a panic, the writer said to Lieutenant-Colonel Stoughton, "I am afraid if we attempt to maneuver these men much longer under fire we will lose control of them." We shortly fell back, or north, two thirds or three fourths of the distance to the crest of the ridge and formed line, facing nearly south. Here we were charged by the enemy with great vigor and determination, but they were soon compelled to retire before the rapid fire of our repeating rifles.

This attack on Snodgrass Hill was evidently made by Benjamin G. Humphrey's brigade, consisting of the 13th, 17th, 18th and 21st Mississippi regiments...

...by sharpshooters and a feint or two, we were not allowed to forget the enemy were in our front.

It is my recollection that, during the interval between the first attack and the renewal of the conflict in the afternoon, Lieutenant-Colonel Stoughton was wounded. Having on a cloak made him conspicuous, and it soon became evident he was the target at which they were aiming. Several shots struck or passed near him, and once he asked me to see if his horse was hit, remarking, "The d—n cuss is firing at me." On being cautioned to keep moving to prevent them getting a fair shot, he said, "I guess they won't hurt anybody."

Presently some one to the left called out that he saw where the shot came from. Surrendering his hose, he stepped that way to see if he could see the one who fired at him, using his glass.

Just as he was through looking, another shot was fired, hitting his arm. I went back with him, and assisted in examining his wound. The ball had passed through his left arm, about two inches from the shoulder join. Said he, "I think this will use me up." On my saying, I hope not, he answered, "These joint wounds are dangerous." He cautioned me not to say anything to the men about it; told me to take his horse and assist the major in command of the regiment, and said, "I want you to see that the men do their duty, for they have a hard fight before them."

The position now occupied by the regiment, it continued to hold until out of ammunition, except, that later in the day Captain Alban sent a messenger to Major McMahan, suggesting a change in the right. To this the Major replied, directing him to use his own discretion; and the right wing of the regiment was refused, or swung back to secure a more advantageous position, and conform the line more to the trend of the ridge. There was not much to be obtained with which to construct defensive works or shelter, and though the men took advantage of everything at hand, most of the regiment was without protection during the battle.

Meanwhile Longstreet was preparing for the mighty struggle, upon the result of which so largely depended the fate of the Confederacy (Rebel General Hill says in a letter written since the war, that the Southern soldiers were too intelligent, not to know that the loss of Chattanooga meant death to all their hopes.) by concentrating the victorious left wing of the Rebel army, with which to assault the last stronghold of the Federal army. General Brannan says in his report, "My entire force during the day and afternoon on this ridge, could not have been over 2,500 men, including the stragglers of various regiments and divisions, besides my own immediate command."

Against this force, Longstreet was preparing to hurl six divisions, comprising seventeen brigades.

Inasmuch as the troops on the ridge fought almost entirely on the defensive, and it is impossible to designate the particular commands that assailed the 21st Ohio, I shall treat of the regiment as a part of the force defending the ridge, and by extracts from Rebel reports, show the means resorted to, and the efforts made, to drive the Union force from its position. By this I hope to give the reader a better idea of what we had to contend with, than by any description I could give of the battle.

The time of the second attack on the ridge is clearly established by the letter of G. E. Dolton, already referred to. He says: "As we went in, we were fired on by about 100 men, Union or Rebels, on the crest of the hill where the 89th Ohio was latterly. (As the 21st Ohio was formed quite a distance down the slope, south of the crest of the ridge, this force of the enemy must have been past the right of the regiment at the time.) The infantry marching on each side of my battery, formed line at once, and started up the ridge on a charge. General Steedman came back from the head of the column on a gallop, yelling "halt," with all his might. By taking their flag he succeeded in halting them, and marched us along to the right. ****
This was about 12:30, not later."

General Granger says, "AS rapidly as possible, I formed General Whitaker and Colonel Mitchell's brigades, to hurl them against the threatening force of the enemy. With loud cheers they rushed upon the foe, and after a terrific conflict, lasting but twenty minutes, drove them from their ground, and occupied the ridge and gorge."

This was the beginning of a conflict that was to terminate only with the light of day. As often as the enemy were repulsed, they reformed and returned to the charge, or procured fresh troops with which to renew the conflict. Such was the obstinacy of the resistance, and the effect of the fire of the Federal troops, that the enemy fancied *the Union line was entrenched, behind barricades, or continually being reinforced. It is related by some members of Company C., that in one charge the enemy approached to within a few yards of the regiment, when they retreated in great disorder. One man threw up his hands and came in. Looking around and seeing only a single line, he asked in great astonishment, "Where are your men?" "Here they are," was the answer. "My G-d!" said he, "I thought you had a whole division here."*

Toward night it was reported to me that the men were getting out of ammunition. I rode back and ordered the adjutant, who was posted some distance in the rear of the regiment, to send for more immediately. He informed me we could not get any we could use in our guns.

Starting to go to the right of the regiment, I had not gone far before a ball struck the Lieutenant-Colonel's horse in the left lower side of the neck, not far from the shoulder. Dismounting as quickly as possible, and getting on his side opposite the enemy, I took off saddle, bridle and holsters, and laid them down by a tree.

I then proceeded to notify company commanders, where to have their men rendezvous when out of ammunition. All that could be found was taken from the dead and wounded.

About this time two regiments arrived behind the 21st and lie in wait to support them when their ammunition was gone. This was somewhere about 2:30 in the afternoon. Canfield remembered the time based on remembering this incident which occurred approximately at that point.

... A boy apparently not more than 16 years of age, was standing by a tree, back of the regiment, which was lying down, on our left, and after passing him several times, I said, "give them a shot, my little man:" whereupon he went to work with a will. I recollect passing and speaking to him several times, and admiring his fearlessness and energy. Forgetting his cove, he was intent only on his work. A few moments before the horse was shot, I met him going to the rear (he was 30 or 40 yards to the east of me). He had been shot through the cheeks, but he still had his gun, and looked as animated and determined as ever. I supposed he belonged to the regiment lying in reserve, but W. H. Bayliss, of the 2d Minnesota, wrote me, he helped

him up after he was shot, and that he did not belong to their regiment. The men retired singly, or as their ammunition was exhausted, and when the line became about like a skirmish line, I ordered in the two regiments lying in reserve, which I afterward learned, were the 35th Ohio on the right, and 2d Minnesota on the left. I then went to where I thought I left the saddle and holsters, for the purpose of taking the latter to Lieutenant-Colonel Stoughton; they contained a fine pair of pistols. (I mention the wounding of the horse and searching for the holsters, to show why, or by what means, I remember, but a short time elapsed between the regiment being relieved, and marching to the right.) Not finding them where I expected, I spent a little time searching for them, and when I came to the regiment it was about ready to march; having received an order, Major McMahan said, to "occupy a position on the extreme right, from which a part of our line had just been driven." Equalizing the ammunition, which amounted to about one round to the man, of those present, the regiment fixed bayonets, moved as ordered, charged the enemy, pushed them back, and occupied the position; the enemy retiring out of sight. It was said the bayonet was used in this charge. Just what time the regiment was relieved by the 35th Ohio and 2d Minnesota, I am unable to say. It was about sunset. Firing ceased soon after we left, and the smoke of the battle settling down among the trees, and the lateness of the hour, gave it the appearance of twilight.

Canfield went on to quote first sergeant George W. Hathaway of Company K, 21st Ohio regarding the final charge made by the 21st Ohio that day.

"The last charge that was made that day, while I was on the ground, was about 5 o'clock. During this charge I was wounded in the left thigh. I got back to a tree, where I remained some time, then, taking an extra gun for a crutch, I went to the rear. As I got to the top of the ridge, the sun was just going down out of sight, and the regiment was then on the line holding its position. In this last charge, I used my last round of ammunition – 150 rounds that day."

. G. S. Robinson wrote: *"I was a member of the 115th Illinois (of Granger's command), and after my brigade had been withdrawn, I returned to the battlefield to find a wounded comrade. It must have been nearly sunset, as I passed along the ridge from east to west, going through the ranks of the 22nd Michigan and 89th Ohio, formed across the ridge, facing west or southwest until I reached the skirmish line. After a few minutes on that line, I was wounded, and rendered nearly helpless.*

While lying on the ground just as twilight was coming on, between the lines, I suddenly saw a line of blue from our rear coming on the charge. It seemed to me I never saw a steadier or better line on review or dress parade. As it reached me, files dropped out to avoid treading on me, then the gap was filled and the line went on. A few moments, and a fragment of that line came back, such men as had ammunition left, stopping occasionally to fire. One of these men, H. H. Van Camp, of company C, as I now know, helped me for a short distance to the rear, at the risk of his life, and disappeared. It was the only time I ever saw that regiment, which I soon after learned was the 21st Ohio; but I shall remember it as long as memory lasts. That charge was, as I believe, the last charge made at that battle. It was made against overwhelming numbers, and hopeless from the first, but it was made with remarkable coolness and bravery.

Having pushed back the enemy as above described and fallen back to the position designated to be held, the regiment waited in suspense with fixed bayonets and empty guns. After an indefinite period of intense anxiety, troops were heard approaching. Some thought reinforcements were at hand, and some thought they were the enemy. A messenger sent to ascertain who they were, was taken in by them; another sent, was not permitted to return, and when they were but a few yards distant, being still unable to decide whether they were friends or foes, Captain Alban went to ask and was greeted with, "All right, come in here, we are Virginians." Finding ourselves surrounded, or nearly so, surrender was a necessity. During the time the enemy were approaching, a number of the men went quietly away, and as we were being marched off the field, some troops fired a volley at the rebels and us, at which the rebels scattered, and a large number broke for liberty. But few of these were recaptured.

The capture of the regiment is thus described by rebel Colonel Trigg: "When near the base of this ridge, I learned from Colonel Kelly *the precise locality of the enemy, and immediately determined with him to attempt the capture of that part of the force in my front. *** I immediately wheeled my brigade to the right, which brought me in the rear of the enemy, and moved rapidly up the hill, to within twenty paces of his line. This movement surprised him, and resulted in the capture of the 22d Michigan, the 89th Ohio and a part of the 21st Ohio regiment, and five stands of colors. *** Darkness having fallen ** no further movement was made." Hindman says, "between 7:30 and 8 p.m., the enemy was driven from his position, surrendering to gallant Preston, 600 or 700 prisoners, with five standards." Of the time of the capture Preston says, "it was now moonlight."*

Thus ended the fighting at Chickamauga. Thomas had been able to disengage and withdraw his troops, but the 21st Ohio, 22nd Michigan and 89th Ohio were sacrificed in the process. Major McMahon had taken command of the regiment upon the wounding of Lt. Col. Stoughton. He was captured at this point with the others. Upon his return as a prisoner of war, Major McMahan reported the following casualties from the 21st Ohio Volunteer Infantry at the battle of Chickamauga.

Killed and died of wounds ....1 officer, 47 Enlisted Men,   48
Wounded...3   "   98   "   "   101
Prisoners...12   "   104   "
Total...   265
Rounds of Ammunition Expended 43,550
We moved into action with 22 officers and 517 men with rifles.[2]

The 21st Ohio had suffered over fifty percent casualties in their defense of the Union right flank. Overall, the two days of fighting at Chickamauga had cost Bragg 18,454 killed wounded and captured. Rosecrans had lost 16,179. The bloodiest two days of the war.[3]

Confederate Troops Advance at Chickamauga – sketch by Alfred Waud

Major General James Longstreet   Major General John Breckinridge
(Breckinridge served as the 14th Vice President of the United States)
Confederate States of America

(all images courtesy of the Library of Congress)

Major General James S Negley   Major General Jefferson C. Davis

Major General Gordon Granger   Major General James B. Steedman

United States of America

(all images courtesy of the Library of Congress)

Chapter Ten

Aftermath of the Battle and Confederate Advance

Overnight, the remnants of the Army of the Cumberland trudged through the darkness toward Rossville. The escape of Thomas' command was nearly miraculous. Engaged on three sides by a superior force of the enemy, he skillfully disengaged and removed his troops without the Confederates realizing he had escaped until it was too late to stop them in the darkness. After taking a position at Rossville for a day as he anticipated another attack, Thomas continued his withdrawal arriving in Chattanooga on the 22nd.

Axel Reed recorded the retreat to Chattanooga in his diary.

Monday, Sept. 21st. At 7 P.M. last evening we were ordered to withdraw from that bloody scene and to keep as quiet as possible we being the last brigade that left the field. The balance had safely retreated towards Chattanooga. Arrived within four miles of C. (Rossville) about 12 o'clock. I helped Henry C. Roberts back of my company who was badly wounded in the shoulder. I made him a comfortable bed of straw and my shelter tent - built up a fire and rested with him the balance of the night. No surgeon or hospital attendant could be found to aid the wounded a particle who lay thickly around the fires – suffering from the cold night added to the pain of their wounds. They bore all patiently like martyrs. I found the regiment nearby. In the morning what boys there were left were in good cheer and just receiving rations for the first time in three days. My company fell in and counted off – numbering six files (12 men) with a little fellow by the name of Frank Tovy, belonging to the 16th regulars who had fought bravely in our company ever since his regt. retreated through our ranks on the 19th. We lay there in an open field in line by brigades merely talking over events of the past two days until noon when our pickets were fired upon when we were marched to the top of the hill (Mission Ridge) where we lay until dark.

This was near Rossville, between two mountains, four miles (from) Chattanooga. It was reported through the day that the enemy withdrew from the battle field when we did and left it unoccupied.

Tuesday, Sept 22 we marched back towards Chattanooga. What was to be done? was thought by many. It was reported that the teams and troops were crossing the river (Tennessee). Were we to abandon Chattanooga and give back all we had gained? I never knew what it was to be faint-hearted before until then when signs showed that we were going to evacuate Chattanooga. I was really heart sick at the idea. If any one could have assured me that we would make a stand a great load would have been taken from my mind. On we marched, neared town and halted, made coffee and rested until about 8 a.m., when we moved up to a frail line of works that had been constructed by the rebels, took our positions, stacked arms and went to throwing up breastworks just at the left of a partly finished fort. (Fort Nagley.)

Bragg had made no immediate attempt to pursue Thomas and Rosecrans as he felt his battered army was in no condition for further action and lacked the horses necessary to move artillery and supplies.

John Magee (Sanford's Battery) recorded both pride and frustration in his diary on September 21st. He is joyous with the complete victory but complains about Bragg moving too slowly and allowing Rosecrans to escape after the loss.

<u>Monday, Sept 21, 1863.</u> Up and stirring early. Our Brigade moved forward 600 yards to the right and front, and took a position in an old field. Genl Polk ordered our heavy skirmishers, who soon brought the news that there was nothing in our front for over 3 miles. We laid in position nearly all day. I went over on the left, where the hard fighting was yesterday, and looked over the field; hundreds of dead strewed the ground, and the canon shot and minie balls had riddled the timber. The fighting here was long and desperate – positions and batteries were taken and retaken several times; but the invincible will of the Southerners, fighting for all mankind holds dear, could not be withstood by the hirelings of a tyrant however well trained, and yesterday's work has taught them a lesson they will not soon forget. They had been told the "rebels" were nothing but a rabble, utterly demoralized and disheartened, and would run at the first fire, but they have found out the contrary to their own dear cost. The victory is glorious, but dearly bought, and why the enemy have been allowed to get away so easily I am at a loss to know. That they are not in front is

positive, and that they should be allowed to quietly withdraw at night is a shame to our arms. As yet I have heard no estimate of ours or the enemy's loss. Our numerical strength on the field was 75 thousand or more, and from all the information I can get the enemy had not a man over 50 thousand – Burnside failed to reinforce Rosecrans. There is something mysterious about this fight that remains to be solved. About 4 o'clock orders to move towards Chattanooga. We marched about 10 miles, to the right of Chattanooga near Byrd's mills on Chickamauga creek. Heard firing near McFarlans. Do not know what this move means – the general belief is the enemy are retreating. We arrived at camp about 12 o'clock at night and camped, we are now nearly due east of Chattanooga on Tennessee soil again. Polk's whole Crops came in during the night. Very cold night, and no blankets.

W H Reynolds wrote to his sister on September 22nd to let her know that he was alive but that his regiment, the 5th Georgia, had been in the thick of the fighting and suffered tremendously.

W. H. Reynolds to Mrs. W. J. (Anna M.) Dickey – Sept 22, 1863
Chickamauga Tenn
Sept 22nd 1863
Dear Sister

I expect you have heard of the battle fought near this place and the result. It was one of the most terrific battle of the war – and resulted in a complete victory for us. Our Regiment suffered immensely – being in the thickest of the fight on both days. We went into action with two hundred men and lost one hundred and thirty in killed and wounded. Our company went in with twenty men and came out with five, I was one of the lucky five. I had a ball shot through my coat and pants and struck my knife in my right pocket which saved me from a severe wound. My blanket was struck twice.

Col. Young lost his right arm, amputated above the elbow, Col. Mitchell is severely wounded in the shoulder, Black Jones is killed. This is all the paper I can get and cant write but one letter – please let the rest of the family know that I am well.

Rosencrans is crossing the Tennessee River today. I expect we will follow him into Kentucky. We have had frost enough to kill vegetation, Give my love to Tom.

Your affectionate Brother

W. H. Reynolds

Otis Baker continued with his diary documenting the movement of the 10th Mississippi to within two miles of Chattanooga, describing their slow and cautious approach before taking a position at the base of Missionary Ridge. In reading captured letters and newspapers he feels the Union soldiers are being deceived.

Sept. 21 – The enemy retreated to Chattanooga during the night. Rested that night & the following day upon the field until 2 P.M. when having buried nearly if not quite all of our dead & sent all of or & nearly all of the enemy's wounded to the hospitals we took a circuitous route to Chattanooga. Marched about eight or nine miles & bivouacked at 11 P.M. six miles from the town.

Sept. 22d – Remained here the following day and night.

Sept. 23d – At daylight started again at 9 o'clock A.M. arrived & formed line of battle at northern base of Missionary Ridge, two miles from the town. Found the enemy occupying the fortifications built by us & throwing up more rifle-pits & breastworks. The line was altered several times during the day. Finally got into position built fires & bivouacked for the night.

Sept. 24th – At mid-day the lines were withdrawn from their position. The first was drawn up at the foot, the second half way up & the third at the summit of the ridge. Bivouacked for the night in this position.

Sept. 25th – There was heavy skirmishing at mid-night last night.

Many letters & papers were captured in the late engagements. It is strange that if the hopes of that nation are enlisted in favor of this crusade, there are so few of the better chaps found in the ranks. The letters are about on a par with those taken in former battles. They moderate the class from whence the army has been raised. Few discuss the object policy of the war. Those what do, show they have been deceived by their papers, which characterize the war as one for their "rights" etc.

The editorials as well as the published sermons & speeches abound in appeals intended to excite the most bitter prejudices & passions of their readers against our people. Quotations are made from the speeches of some of our former literary speakers, but who were men generally of little influence. Sentences of better men here are garbled as to answer the same end.

A Union soldier, Denis Murphy, 104th Illinois, wrote to his sister to let her know he had survived and asking to tell others of his and a few friends' wellbeing. He has seen as much fighting as he wants to but doesn't know how much longer this campaign will go or its outcome.

Chatanooga, Sept 23 (1863)

Dear Sister,

Much fateiged and worn out I set down to write this letter for I know the ancious harts a waiting to hear from me. We have been fighting for 2 weaks of(f) and on but last Thursday Friday and Saturday Sunday Munday we got all we wanted of it. Our Brigade was badly cut up. Our redgment can only muster 150 men. We lost eleven out of our company killed and wounded on Sunday. Patt Dobbins is killed. Mike Conners wounded through the bowels. Our Captain is wounded through the sholder. More thru the legs and arms. We were drove back 20 miles.

We are now at Chatanooga all busy intrenching and the enemy only three miles off. I will not say any more until the battle is over. We have come out all right so far. Thank God, that locket I got from Tim Cunningham in town when I was working at Tom. He owed some money to me and I took that for payment. So it don't belong to any boddy but you for I gave it to you. Tell Jon Tinel that Tom and Bill is all right. I don't know as I have any more to say at present. You get the papers and you can see how the fight is going on. Give my kind love to all inquring friends. Give my love to Father Mother Jaima and Mary and have them to pray for me.

So no more from your beloved brother,

Denis J. Murphy.

That same day, L B Wort, a 21st Ohio survivor of the carnage on Horse Shoe Ridge, wrote gratefully to his wife. His letter vacillates between the horrors of the battle and joy to hear from her and be able to write to her.

Camp at Chattanooga Tenn.   Sept. the 23rd 63

Dear and beloved wife,

It is with the greatest of pleasure that I again pen a few lines to you to inform you that I am well at this time. Our line of battle is formed at this place and whilst I right this our men are a skirmishing with the enemy and I think their will be a great battle faught at this place. we had a battle with them last Sunday and it was a very hard one. all of our regiment was killed or wounded or taken prisoner except one hundred and eighty. Smith was killed dead and John Kauffman is wounded in the arm. there is but one captain left in our regt. and five lieutenants. our colonel is badly wounded our regt got out of ammunition and they made three bayonet charges after all of their ammunition was all gone and drove the rebs and then they had to surrender but some of the men would not stand it and they cut their way out and ran away. I think Dunifin (Isaac) is taken prisoner. There is only 15 men in our company I tell you it makes me cry to think of it. Well I got Seven letters day before yesterday. One from George one from john Aimsworth and the rest from you and sis. one of yours had 4 stamps in (it). I was glad to hear from you. I tell you for it was the first time in this month. We have not had a chance to right or receive any letters. I rote you one I think about the 16 of this month but do not know wether it went out or not but hope it did. I tell you I am as anctious to right letters to you as I am to get them for I know that you are anctious to here from me as I am from you. I tell you this battle beets Stone River. this was the hardest fighting ever known and it is not over yet. The rebels thrown shells in our camp yesterday but they done no damage. The rebels have a much larger force then we have. The prisoners say they have one hundred and fifteen thousand. apart of their Richmond army is here. threw the providence of god I am still spaired and I hop he will still continue his goodness to me. this is a peace of my old letter that you sent me. my paper is in my knapsack and that is on the colonels wagon. I will right as often as I can get a chance. The battle lasted two days Saturday and sonday. we was forced to fall back and leave the field so we did not get a chance to berry the ded and a great many of our wounded fell in to the hands of the rebs. It is heart rendering to behold a battle scene. Well I hav ritten all that I can think of at theis time. Will Yeagly is safe yet. I saw him since the fight. Briton is here and Wayne miller and Jake Dowell. Well good by loved one for this time.

L.B. Wort to S.G. Wort

Following their safe arrival in Chattanooga, Alfred Searles, as another of the surviving soldiers of the 21st Ohio, wrote to his parents to let them know that he and his brother were still alive. He also talks of the defensive works they now have between Chattanooga and the enemy expressing his confidence in Rosecrans.

Sept. 24, 1863
Chattanooga, Tenn.
Dear Parents,
*   I suppose you have all looked with ancious eyes and have awaited patiently for news from us, but it has not been in my power to write the past month. But through the mercies of god I am sparred and I take this unocupied moment to try to let you know a small part of what we have passed through. Since the eavening of the first of Sept. we have been upon the go all the time since, and have been a fighting them the rebs since the 10th of the present month and are a still doing so. Sunday our regt. was in the fight from 10 in the morning till after dark. We went into the fight with 575 men, came out with 152, a part of them are prisoners, but the most are killed and wounded. Our Luten. Col was wounded. Our majar is prisoner, our agutent wounded, sarjent majar is killed. All the comishined officers they is with us is one Capt., four lutenants. Our Col. Is at home in Findlay, Ohio.*
*   I cannot give you but a very slight thing of the thing, but the generals say it was the hardest fought battel ever fought upon this continent. The enimy cut our supplies, so we could not get eny amuntition. Our regt. made 3 charges and drive them without a*

carridg (cartridge), nothing but the cold steel. The enemy massed their whole force upon our center, but I think they suferd the worst with killed and I think wee took the most prisoners but I can't tell. You will see by the official reports in the papers.

Addison and myself are yet unhurt. I had 2 or 3 balls scrape me, but did not brake the hide. But we are both of us nearly sick and God onley knows when we shall see a settled time again. This is the 25 day since we brock up camp and last night was the first night that I have had to sleep for six days and nights. The whole army is a laying in battle line with their acotrments on all the time and non are allowed to go away from their lines. We have got this place prity well fortified and we have dug miles of breast works, and they are of the best kind. The rebs are a trying to cross the river and get in our rear, but I think that Old Rosy will be sharp anough and will keep them from getting across.

But I shall have to close for this time. Give our respects to all. Excuse poor writing and I am dirtier than eny of your hogs and very raged. I have tore my close all to pieces a skirmishing through the thick woods and brush. Give my respects to all friends and except our best wishes and kind love and believe us to be your, sons A. and A.D. Searls.

Write soon. Direct to Chattanooga, Tenn. 21st Regt. OVI care Capt Caton   We will write soon as we get a chance.

(Alfred Searles)

The postal service was swamped by letters from soldiers to their loved ones trying to console them with news that they were still among the living. Charley Caley of the 105th Ohio of Reynold's division was one of those Union soldiers that flooded the mail with a letter home on the 24th.

Chattanooga Sept.24th 63

My dear wife it is with much pleasure I sit down to rite a fu lines to you. it has ben so long since I have had a chance to rite to you. I received yours of the 13th yesterday and was very glad to hear from you and the rest of the folks at home but sory you had such a hard time in Cleveland as well as being disappointed in not having Sarah to go with you. I hope you enjoyed your viset at Mareys but am

174

afraid you can not as you are not very wel acquainted with her and the rest of them

I am wel but it is not wel with all of us. Last Thursday our regiment was sent out on picket on the right wing of our lines to support the pickets which was having some trouble with the enemy. We stayed until Friday noon when we were relieved and went a back to the plaice we had ben for two or three days. Stayed their until darck and started for the extreme left of our lines whair the rebs was concentrating their forces intending to brake through to Chattanooga. We marched all night and the next day until about nine oclock halted in the road until about eleven oclock when the enemay and Wilders men began to commence a quarrel. they had it rather hot for a spel and was driving our forces back and we was ordered into the field a bout one. we got at it and kept up a brisk firing until about four. the rebs began to drive our right wing three regiments on our right and comensed a cross fire on us. we was ordered to fall back. as we started on our retreat it incouraged them on and the bulets thinned our ranks so fast that we had to brake and run as the rest had done.

We had a great many wounded but not but a fu killed. those in our co was E. Crawford severly in the ankle and will probably have to have his leg taken off, O Dimmick co. f wounded in hand. Corp King in the leg and H. F. March also in the leg and R.B. Barlas Woodard was wounded but I don't know whare. the rest of us got off all right. a small shot hit my shoe just above the sole and went through just enough to make a mark on my foot. We retreated back about two miles stayed until about darck and went back to or near the plaice we had fought. it being my turn I went out on picket and stayed until the next morning and was relieved by some of the other boys ho took our plaices. they had not ben their long before Som Sharp Shooters began to fire on them and they had to fall back to our brigade for support. the rebels following them as far as the edge of the timber when our batteryes opened on them. they kept up heavy firing for about three hours when the enemy tried to charge on our bateryes but was driven back by the 68th, 101st, and 75th ind Regiments several times with very heavy loss. they wer behind some breast works and suffered but very litel. the enemy then tried to flank them. our regiment was held back as reserve and lay behind them on the ground and the shot shel and bulets went over us as thick as hail. when the rebs came round on our right we were ordered to charge. having our bayonets fixed we rose and swung round to the right and went forward with a yel which scard the rebs. we let them have a voley killing men and horses with great slaughter. we drove them about a mile to another line that they had and they turned and tried to flank us but we turned and swung on their flanking party and drove them then as before. we then turned and swung on their right and drove them a third time but charging to far we got through their lines and they tried to close in on us but as we had cut through of course we could cut our way out again and did.

So loading and fireing all the time through the charge our loss was very small losing but ten men in the charge. Co. F loss was C. R. Brown and George Martin. I suppose they were wounded and fel in the hands of the enemy as we of course had to leave the field. The wounded of the day before was at a house and some of them fel in the hands of the Rebels. I am sorey for the boys. I should like to see emery and all the rest of them. Since the battel we have fel back into Chattanooga and are fortifying very strongly. worked nearly all night last night. I nearly forgot to say that we took a brigade of General Adams killed a Capt. And two Lutenan and wounded a Majer and took twenty six prisiners. It is said to be one of the hardest bayonet charges ever made and that the 105th is all that saved the fourth division this time

I must draw a close but I have lots more to rite if I had time. So no more this time

From your husband in love

Charley

John Magee wrote daily notes in his diary about the movement to Chattanooga, the attitude of the troops over the slow advance which enabled Rosecrans to fortify the city, and the rumors about where the army would head next.

Tuesday, Sept 22, 1863. Were stirring early – feel very bad, did not sleep any so cold. About sunup moved towards Chattanooga – the whole corps in motion, our Division in lead. Moved slow. Found the enemy's pickets on Missionary ridge – Maney's and Smith's Brigades had considerable fighting with them. One section of our battery went forward – fired a few rounds. Reported that the enemy are still in Chattanooga. About sundown heard heavy cannonading on our right and left and considerable musketry. It appears the whole army are advancing in line of battle, as much as possible. We got over the ridge about dark, and our Division formed a line of battle along on the same ground they were camped on before leaving Chattanooga. We are now within 3 ½ miles of town and the enemy reported before us. Wild speculations as to the future – some think the enemy are going to leave, and others that we will have a fight. Camped in line of battle. I am unwell.

Wednesday, Sept 23, 1863. Up early – weather has moderated – signs of rain but it seems it never will rain again. No orders to move. About 9 o'clock heard some firing in front. The enemy are certainly at Chattanooga, and fortifying they say. Troops coming in all day and taking position in line of battle. Cannonading at times all day. About 4 o'clock Cheatham's Division moved 1 mile to the right and camped. Hear the enemy have thrown up heavy fortifications, and have planted siege pieces in them. The general opinion prevails that we are going to attack them tomorrow. We have now been without blankets for over a month, and some very cold nights. Tis remarkable how well we stand it without more getting sick. The nerve of the army is steady and firm, eager to fight again if necessary, and censorious of our Generals for moving so slow, and allowing the enemy to fortify.

Thursday, Sept 24, 1863. In camp 3 ½ miles from Chattanooga in line of battle. Our army is now stretched from the foot of Lookout mountain to the Missionary ridge, thence along it for 3 miles, and then to the Tennessee river 6 miles above town. Our Division occupies the right wing of the army. The enemy still in Chattanooga, and have thrown up rifle pits 1 ½ miles this side – the belief is they are going to stay there. Some skirmishing going on all day and some cannonading. In afternoon the enemy threw some shells over among us. At sundown we moved our camp back ½ mile, to the foot of the ridge and encamped. The weather is fine – bright moonlight nights. Do not know what movements are going on. Some say Bragg is trying to cut off the enemy's supplies. About 9 o'clock at night heavy musket firing in front and some cannonading. All up and ready for action – could see the flash of the enemy's canon – thought they were advancing. In *about an hour the firing all ceased and we went to bed again. First good sleep for some time.*

Friday, Sept 25, 1863. Camped in line of battle. Moved our guns up on a hill to the right. Some cannonading and skirmishing in forenoon. Beautiful weather – rations very scarce, have to bring them ten miles over the ridge, and the whole thing badly mixed up – some get more than they are entitled to, and some get hardly any. Could see the enemy's camp fires very plain from our positon. No firing during the night. It seems we are not going to attack the enemy – the time has passed – they are too well fortified now. Do not know what movements are going on.

Saturday, Sept. 26, 1863. In camp on the hill – some little cannonading today. In afternoon built parapet works around our guns with logs and stone. Several wild rumors about ours and the enemy's movements. One thing certain he is still in Chattanooga, nor can we drive him out now he is so well fortified. Can see their campfires very plain at night.

Sunday, Sept 27, 1863. In camp. Lieut, C.L. Reynolds and Lieut C.H. McCormick, two of my old schoolmates paid me a visit – was very glad to see them; they seem like relatives being the only persons of my childhood's acquaintance. We had a long talk over old times we once enjoyed in the old state of Ohio – sadly is she fallen. They are my only friends in the South who know my family, and can sympathize with me in my troubles. Clear and nice weather – beautiful nights. Some musketry during the night.

Monday, Sept 28, 1863. In camp – wild rumors afloat about both armies – none reliable. It is believed however we will soon start for Kentucky. No firing today. Army still remains encircling Chattanooga. Fine weather but no rain.

Tuesday, Sept 29, 1863. In camp. Charley Reynolds came over to see me. Our knapsacks were brought out – put on clean clothes once more. Several more rumors – Maj. McSwain (?) says all the negro's are to be sent home, and 4 men detailed to cook for each hundred men. Our wagons are to be taken away, and we must carry our baggage. It appears we are going somewhere certain. Longstreet's' artillery arriving from Virginia.

Wednesday, Sept 30, 1863. *In camp – Reynolds came over to see me. Heard Genl Polk and Forrest were under arrest. The wrangling has commenced. Old Bragg wants to vent his spite on some one. Wrote letters to _____ and Mollie and Nannie Bice. Commenced raining in evening.*

William Stilwell of the 53rd Georgia wrote to Molly on the 28th wishing he could get a leave to come home in order to secure a new horse. As a courier for the brigade, he had lost his at Chickamauga and needed to secure one on his own. He mentioned little of the battle but wanted his father to come and bring him some new pants.

> *September 28th, 1863*
> *Dear Molly,*
> *I am writing you a few lines but don't know when I will get to send it off. I would have wrote before now but could not as I had left my knapsack behind. I have been sick ever since I left Atlanta with (a) cold. I am some better now. I have had a very hard time as both the other couriers have been gone but they have come now. If I thought I could get me a horse cheaper by coming home I think I could get a furlough for a few days but I am afraid that they are harder to get there than they are here. If Father or Uncle knows of any horse that I could get by coming home let me know as soon as you can and if not, I want Father to come and see me and bring me some pants. I learn that the bridges that were burned will be built by Tuesday so he can come, if we stay where we are now, (or within) a few miles of us. If he comes tell him to inquire for Longstreet's corps, McLaws' Division and then for Bryan's Brigade and he will find me here. Molly, I would like for you to come too, but under the circumstances I don't think it best now, there is nowhere for you to stay. If I get sick or wounded, why you can come then.*
>
> *I have had some very narrow escapes from shells but not hurt yet. You must continue to pray for me. The Yankees still hold the city but it is reported that we have their supplies cut off, but I don't know. We whipped them very bad last Saturday and Sunday. I think they will leave in a short time. Molly, if Father comes to see me, send me a pair of pants and a towel and send me that little testament that I sent home. I had the misfortune to have my bible thrown out of the car.*

Give my love and respect to all the friends. Write to me soon. Kiss the children for me. I am as ever your affectionate husband until Death.

William R. Stilwell

Dalton, GA.

P. S. Direct your letter to McLaws Division in care of General Bryan.

On the second of October, Addison Searles, the brother and mess mate of Alford in the 21st Ohio, wrote to their father reiterating details of the losses the regiment suffered during the battle of Chickamauga. He had been through two major fights and wanted nothing more of war and to come home.

Chattanooga, Tenn.

October 2, 1863

Dear Father,

Once more I will try to pen you a few lines to let you know that we are still in the land of the living. Alford is about as yourself, but my helth is not very good. I have bin un well for a month and a half, but I hope to get to rest and recup up again. I suppose you hav had all of the particulars of the late battel.

We suffered a great deal in this fight. Our old regiment is cut all up. We went into the fight the morning of the 20th and fought all day until after dark. We had 585 men when we went into the fight and came with 150 men. So you can judg whether we had eny thing to do or not. Our company had 49 forty-nine kild ded. Our captain was taken prisoner and the balance of our company. Our Second Lieut was wounded and died yesterday. Our Liuet. Colonel was badly wounded and sent to Nashville. Our majar and adjutant was taken prisoners. Most all of our wounded was taken prisoners and parold. Then we sent out a flag of truce and brought them in. They are sending them north as fast as they can. We have but one captain left in the regiment and we have five Liuets that came out of the fight. Our first Liuet is in command of our company and company C has not got an officer higher than seventh corpril.

Well, I cannot write all today and I do not know whether this will reach you or not. But when the male gets to coming through strate I will try to write again. That is if my life is spared. I have bin through two hard battels and bin spard. But I hope that I never will have to witness (another).

We was on the march for a long time and skirmishing with the rebs for some time. Wat I hope that our regiment will be kep in the rear for the balance of our time. We have done our share. But God only knows who will live to see home. But if ever there was a boy that want to see home, I am one of them. I feel more anxious than I ever hav before to see home.

Well, father if this reaches you please write soon and, let us know how things are a going at home. Tell me where you think of moving to and whether George has got home yet or not. There is little cannonading in the front today, but do not know whether it will bring on an ingagement or not. Well, I will have to bring my letter to a close for this time. Please write soon.

This from your son Addison Searles to his father Mr. E.G. Searles.

Direct to Chattanooga, Tenn. 21st Regt. CO. H in care of Capt. Caton no more at present. So goodby. Give my best wishes to all.

Nearly two weeks after the battle, soldiers were still trying to communicate with loved ones at home, sharing the result of their unit's fight in the thick of it. Harrison Dewater of the 13th Michigan shared the following with his sister on October 3rd.

October 3rd 1863
Camp of 13th Mich. Infty.
At Chattanooga Tennessee

Wal Sister Ann your letter of the 16th was received yesterday & I was glad to hear from you to know that all of you was alive & that mother has got well & all of the rest of them that was sick for as you said health was the best thing that was to be had in this world. I tell you I wated very patient to hear from you for the last that I heard from home as far as that was mother was sick. Wall I suppose you would like to hear how the army is situated. Wal as I said in them few line that I wrote to Alise we are so close to them that we talk to them & exchange papers. you will hear the paticulars in the papers about the fight but as luck would have it I got out alive we –lost ½ of our co. in the battle. we have only 100 guns in our regiment. what they will do we don't no for they cant call us a regiment but I suppose they will keep us in the front. the rebs held the field & took the ambulances & brought them out. some of the wounded laid on the field for 4 days so some of them say it was very could. they suffered. the first night that we laid on the field you could heard them scream 2 miles in but they are in a place that they will be taken care of but not as good care as they ought to have but the damed rebs have not got them. We have heard of all of our co but 2. our Lieutenant Perley & Corpoel Germond. them we cant hear nothing of but think thy must be taken prisoner. Well about Unkle Joseph he is at Chattanooga but I have not seen him. About the men that was wounded an laid on the field & suffered you may think that they could have bin took care of but they was between our line & their so if we went to pick them up they would shoot at us but we got up the most of them but the next day they took the hospital & the wounded fell in their hands. Wal about some thing else you said you wanted I should send you my picture. Wal Ann I will send it to you if I can get (one) & if you & Alice get your(s) send them to me. Wal Ann I am very sory to hear the news of Aunt Judy death but so the world gos. I have written to Unkle Orville 3 or 4 times but have received no answer. When you write tell me the directions & also Aunt mandy so I must close so good by. this from Harrison Dewater.

Not every soldier was able to write home with good news, having survived the battle. The hardest duty of every officer is to write to the parents and loved ones of the death of their soldier. The sheer volume of those generated by Chickamauga made it a seemingly endless task for the company commanders closest to those who numbered with the slain. John Baker was one of those commanders.

Camp 96 Illinois Infantry
Near Chattanooga, Oct 2nd 1863
Mr. Truman A. Bennett
Brookfield Iowa
Sir,

It becomes my painful duty to inform you that your son Truman F. Bennett was killed in a charge in the battle of Chickamauga, Sunday Sept. 20th. Ever faithful in the discharge of his duty he fell in the foremost rank, shot through the head, dying instantly. We were compelled to fall back and his body was left on the field. He was a good soldier and his comrades join me in tendering our sympathies with yourself and family in your bereavement. As soon as our company books come up I will make out and transmit (to) the War Department the necessary papers to enable you to draw his bounty and back pay and will at the same time send you a statement of same. Any information you may desire will be promptly given by myself or either of the lieutenants. As near as I can learn from his mess mates he had nothing but a blanket (except what he had with him) and that was burned by the rebel while on the train between here and Bridgeport.

Yours Truly,

John Barker

Our Brethren are on the Field

Part Four

Chapter Eleven

Siege of Chattanooga

Rosecrans was distraught over the loss at Chickamauga. His clear and well thought out reasoning seemed to escape him. Three days after the battle he had the last brigade called down from Lookout Mountain and back into the defenses of the city. In so doing he opened the commanding position of the mountain to Bragg who immediately seized on the opportunity and positioned artillery and infantry in position on Lookout Mountain's prominence, blocking the Tennessee River and cutting Rosecrans' line of communication to Nashville. Missionary Ridge was likewise occupied above the town, commanding any approach from Knoxville via rail or the river.

Otis Baker's regiment took position at the base of Lookout Mountain. His diary talks of their station and duties in establishing the siege, but he continues to focus on political issues and deep thoughts regarding the lack of knowledge and understanding of the Constitution and education in general. By the adoption of his ideas by those in power, he feels it would lead to the betterment of the state and the nation itself, possibly ending or at least preventing another such conflict.

Sunday Sept 27th – Two miles from Chattanooga – On picket last twenty-four hours ending 9 A.M. Nothing has occurred excepting during our absence. The army erected breast-works along the foot of Missionary Ridge. Longstreet adds artillery to the Army.

Sept. 29th – Same positions as yesterday. Twas the intention of Gen'l Longstreet to shell the enemy's camps with two siege guns which he has mounted upon Lookout but for some reason it was not done, commonly believed to be that the enemy ambulances which had come into our lines for some of their wounded had not returned. Nothing of interest today.

We think it would have been far better for the country, had the rights of secession been admitted years ago. Would not the prospect of dissolution of the Union which might at any moment take place should our rights & privileges as separate communities be interfered with, have arrayed the masses which to the last cherished a love for the Union, against any intermeddling which might lead to such an unhoped for result? Would not the admission of this right then, have produced a more studied observance of the rights of each State by its sisters, than we have ever noticed? When States are united as ours are under one government, especially when spread over such a wide extent of country, causing thereby a wide diversity of interests, habits & employments, is such remedy or rather preventative issues cursory to ensure the stability of the general government & hence the welfare of each and every one.

Sept 30 – In the same position. As we have observed in some of our previous notes, we believe that a wide diffusion of knowledge is all that is requisite to ensure the success of our system of government and this is absolutely a prerequisite. By our association with men from all sections thrown in contact with them, as we have been by the operations of war, we have discovered an amount of ignorance of which we have been astonished. We think it the duty of our State government & have the help of others than our own to consider how by legislation this great evil may be diminished.

The question should meet with the same attention of every well-wisher of his country.

Free schools, the orphan of the lost soldier, is a good one to follow ought if possible to be established in every county in the states. One college ought to be founded and supported by the State. The principals or number of visitors of each county school should select each 4 years several of the most studious & deserving of their scholars, who are anxious to have a complete collegiate education but who have not the means to enable to do so and these young men should receive their education at the expense of the State. Mississippi would in a few years take a higher position among her sisters for to long for intelligence. A more liberal sentiment & prominence of reasoning & thinking would exist among the masses. The State would soon occupy a place in the affections of her sons which she has never before enjoyed & etc.

Thursday Oct 1st – In the same position. Rain set in about dark last night & has continued with but slight intermissions all day. The first rain for two or three months. It was much needed.

Oct. 2nd – Ordered on picket again. Rain ceased about mid-night. The morning opened clear & cool.

Oct 3d. – Returned to our position in line. I think it can scarcely be denied that whatever were the original objects of the Federal government in prosecuting the war, the principal one now is the abolition of slavery, it is now declared by the fruitful examples that they will stop short of nothing less than the attainment of that end.

This settles the question, whether they are fighting for the Constitution as it is or that instrument & the laws based upon it not only permitted and protected the institution. If the end of this war then will doubtless be a remodeling of the US really & the south be subjugated.

Thus, the Army of the Cumberland was trapped inside the confines of its Chattanooga defenses. The original rail line from Bridgeport, Alabama to Chattanooga was a distance of about 30 miles. Now, with that line cut off, it took anywhere from 8 to 20 days to bring limited supplies over Walden Ridge on very questionable trails. Heavy rains made the conditions nearly impossible. The situation was bleak. Bragg felt it was only a matter of time before he would starve the Federal Army into surrender and recapture the prize.

John Ellis described the early days of the siege in late September and early October as days of tedium and drill. In recalling the aftermath of the battle of Chickamauga he talked about visiting one of his wounded soldiers in the hospital who subsequently died.

Life was dreary on Missionary ridge. On the night of the 23rd (September) a portion of my regiment, Austin's battalion and a Kentucky regiment (the 16th) displayed as skirmishers, drove the federal skirmishers into their works, killing, capturing and wounding about 30 Yankees. This affair occasioned a pretty heavy fire of musketry and artillery from the works but not a single "rebel" was wounded. The Federal army next day duly notified his government that *"Bragg had made a night assault and had been repulsed with terrible slaughter". Bragg's object was to ascertain the character of a report brought him by a citizen that the Yankees were evacuating Chattanooga. They were formed in full force and our line of skirmishers withdrew.*

Our time on the ridge was passed in drilling and picket duty. For three weeks I was too lame to do any duty and I passed the time listlessly in camp. Then I succeeded in borrowing a horse and went out to the field hospital to see Ellis Evans. I had sent Stewart to him to remain as long as he needed attention. I could not have sent a more faithful nurse, a better attendant. My first visit found the poor boy with his limb amputated above the knee. But the surgeon, Dr. Childs, 32nd Ala. a kind hearted human Christian gentleman, as well as a skillful surgeon thought he was doing very well. Yet, when I particularly questioned him, his head shook and his face was grave, as he said in a low voice, "He may recover. It is extremely doubtful and the chances are against him." Yet the little sufferer was cheerful. But at times his eye was restless and of unnatural size and brilliancy. His mouth was parched and dry and a low fever was slowly but alas! Too surely burning the little frame, exhausting and scorching the blood destroying the fountain of life. I stayed only a few hours for my time was short. Then I went to his bed and he said "You are going and it will be so long before I see you again. Do come closer." I told him he must soon get well and go home and that I would come again and give him letters to carry to mother and father. "yes, if I go," was the reply. "I will take them. But I fear it will be long before I am able." He pressed my hand long and earnestly, said "Goodbye." I turned from the tent and never saw him again. In three or four days I heard of his death. This blow, though expected, fell heavy. In a week afterward I again went to the hospital and found Stewart very sick. I visited the grave of my little friend and Stewart put in my hand the letters which he had written before the battle and at the time of his wound and delivered his last words.

Not long after we had become settled at the ridge we were moved some two or three miles to the left. We then built chimneys to our tents and prepared good quarters for the winter when we were again moved to the left over a mile and this time out of the division of

General Breckenridge. The Kentuckians were sent to Bates, who was now Majr. General; the Floridians to the same division, while the Louisianians were transferred to the division of Gen. A. P. Stewart. We all regretted the disintegration of the old division and no one more heartily than he who had so long commanded it.

Our battery (Slocumb's 5th Company Batt. Washington Artillery) was sent off also to a strange division. "This was the unkindest cut of all". It was at this last camp that Lieut. Jas. McArthur, a gallant young Scotchman, returned after a long illness to the regiment and was assigned to my company. Sergt. W. C. Kent of Co. A. old 16th regiment was here promoted and assigned also to my company as 2nd Lieut.

Charles Roberts was reassigned as the clerk to the quartermaster for Strahl's Brigade following Chickamauga. His battery was posted on Missionary Ridge as the army approached Chattanooga, and while the early days of the siege were relatively quiet, his duties were keeping him extremely busy. He found time on October 3rd and 4th to write to his beloved wife.

Headquarters Quartermaster Dept Strahl's Brigade
Near Chattanooga Tenn. Oct 3rd 1863
My darling wife,

I have an opportunity of sending a letter by Mr. Humphreys who is going direct to Oxford and I am anxious to send a few lines by him, for I have not yet heard whether you have received any of the letters I have written you since my return to the army. I wrote you the early part of the week, stating that I had safely passed through the firey ordeal of the battle of Chickamauga and that since the fight I have been detailed as clerk to Maj. McQuerrie, Brigade Quartermaster. I am now busily engaged in making up monthly and quarterly returns and in addition to this have to attend to considerable outside work for major McQuirrie is sick and gone to Marietta and consequently I have to perform his duties as well as my own. I am very well pleased with my position for which it is a much pleasanter position than I have occupied heretofore. I feel that I can every day accomplish a days work for the government.

Everything is quiet in front. The Yankees are still busy in strengthening their fortifications and we are daily humping more artillery to the front from preparations that were making a short time since it looked very much as if we were getting ready for a long march, but the probability of such a movement has died away for the present and we have no idea what is to be the program and I don't suppose any one except Genl Bragg himself knows what our next move is to be. I was out at the Battery day before yesterday, the boys were all well. I could plainly see the Yankees walking on their fortifications. It looks singular to see two such large armies so close together and yet every thing as quiet as if you were on a plantation. You can very distinctly hear their bands play and when "Yankee Doodle" is played they raise a shout which is more than equaled by the shout which meets the air when our bands strike up "Dixie".

(Sunday morning.) I was not able to finish my letter to you yesterday but will endeavor to do so today although what at home would be a day of leisure is with me a busy day for I am receiving and piecing clothing to the Brigade. Mr. Doyle received a letter today from home, which is the second he has received since my last from you. I carefully look over the bundle of letters which is brought to me every morning for the Brigade but have not yet been cheered by recognizing your hand writing. It know it is not your fault dearest but I can assure you I feel disappointed when I find a letter for anyone from Oxford and none for me. I hope however mine will be along soon for I am very inpatient to hear from the "dear ones" at home. When I do not hear from you regularly I am always afraid something is amiss and all anxiety until a letter arrives. My darling wife, I pray earnestly that you and the dear children may be spared to me in health for you are so closely entwined around my heart, that I feel as if life would be robbed of all its pleasures if anything was to happen to you. Take good care of yourself my dear during the coming cold and wet weather and use every precaution with the little ones against catching cold.

When you write me give me all particulars as to what you are doing for your winter supplies and any other particulars as to your domestic arrangements. I am constantly pondering over in my mind what you will do for different articles which appear to be absolutely necessary. Be sure my dear and get a supply of wood before wet weather comes and watch what kind of load they bring you for these times although many say Confederate money is not worth anything they are mighty anxious to obtain all they can for as little "value received" as possible. Take good care of what little sugar you have for it will be almost impossible for you to obtain any more and if you or the children should be sick you will find it of great use to you.

I have just been conversing with an officer that has lately visited the battlefield of Chickamauga. He says our dead have been all buried but the Yankees still remain unburied. They are lying about in all directions, black, putrefying and swollen. There's an arrangement being made to cover them with dirt. They are too much decomposition to remove. For miles around you can occasionally find them where they had dragged themselves off out of range of the missiles and died. Many of our own men and of the enemys were burned to death after they were wounded by the undergrowth and leaves catching fire from the explosions of shells.

Considering the exposure and hardship our army has undergone, they are in excellent condition and there is a cool quiet spirit of determination in the army which Rosencranz with all his leashed reinforcements will find difficult to overcome. I think we shall go into Middle Tennessee this fall without a fight if Rozy falls back and with a fight if he does not for it looks to me that it will be absolutely necessary for us to do so in order to forage and feed our army.

I see Mr. Doyle's letter was mailed for Oxford so I will send mine direct by mail for I have not been able to get it ready for Mr. Humphreys.

Kiss my darling children forheads. My love to sister Mammie. Kind regards to the Doctor.

My love to you my own sweet darling wife. I love you with my whole heart dearest and long for the time when our country can once more allow her soldiers to return to their homes and then my dear Maggie I will devote myself to making you comfortable and happy.

God Bless you all
Yours devotedly,
Chas Roberts

The first ten days of October were a mixture of business and leisure for John Magee. The battery received new guns to replace their old tubes which required them to move the old pieces back to the depot, returning with the new artillery and preparing the caisson and limbers for the new ammunition. In between he spent some time with a pair of sisters he'd met recently.

Thursday, Oct 1ˢᵗ, 1863. *In camp – rained all night last night, and all day today – it seems to be making up for the past dry weather. No news – everything wet – not much sleep tonight.*

Friday, Oct. 2ⁿᵈ, 1863. *In camp. Sun rose clear and beautiful, not a cloud in the horizon. Went over and saw Lieut Reynolds – took a walk around the line – saw some of Longstreet's men. All the troops have got heavy breastworks but Cheatham's division. Came back to camp. Charley wrote a letter to his wife. Fine clear day.*

Saturday, Oct 3d, 1863. *In camp – fine sunshiny day. Our new guns have come, and the Capt. Gone back after the caissons. In afternoon moved 1 mile to the right and in rear of Maney's Brigade. No news of any movements. The enemy in Chattanooga – all quiet.*

Sunday, Oct. 4ᵗʰ, 1863. *In camp – went back to the wagon camp – formed a new mess. Troops arriving from Mississippi – Vicksburg prisoners exchanged. In evening went over and saw some young ladies by the name of Witt. No news of army movements. Fine weather – some cloudy.*

Monday, Oct. 5ᵗʰ, 1863. *In camp – fixing up my clothing. Heavy firing from our batteries on Lookout. The enemy replies. No other news – signs of rain.*

Tuesday, Oct 6 1863. *In camp – went over and saw the Miss Witts. In afternoon Lieut. Reynolds came over to see me. Orders came for us to go after our new guns at Chickamauga. No cannonading today. Rumor that Wheeler has 17 thousand cavalry in the rear of the enemy. Cloudy.*

Wednesday, Oct 7, 1863. *Up early – raining – hitched up and started after our guns. Had some trouble getting up the ridge. Stopped raining at 6 o'clock – got to Chickamauga at 11. Turned over our old guns and all the ammunition. Our new caissons have not come yet – will have to keep the old ones until they arrive. The guns went back to the front in the evening, the caissons remaining to be fixed for the new ammunition. I stopped with them.*

Thursday, Oct. 8th, 1863. In camp fixing chests. Heard some cannonading at front. No other news. Beautiful fall weather. Today is the anniversary of the bloody battle of Perryville – long, long will Cheatham's division remember the glory they achieved on the 8th of Oct. 1862. The shrieks and moans of the dying and wounded still ring in my ear.

Friday, Oct 9th, 1863. Up and stirring early. Caisson chests being all fixed, we hitched up and went over to the depot and commenced loading ammunition. Got loaded about 2 o'clock and came on back, stopped at wagon camp a few minutes. Got into camp at front at 5 o'clock. We have now got the new battery ready for active operations – new guns and some new harness, and will get new caissons and more harness. The enemy continue to fire a little.

Saturday, Oct 10th, 1863. Up at ½ after 3 – packed baggage and hitched up horses. Some say the enemy are advancing. As usual, every conceivable kind of a rumor on foot. No noise nor no firing. About 10 o'clock the President Jefferson Davis passed along the lines cheered by the soldiers – this accounts for our being up so early. No firing today. Went over to see the Witt girls – had a long talk with them.

William Stilwell wrote to his wife on October 2nd. He was still desperate to hear from her and begging for new pants to get to him some way or the other. He describes the establishment of the artillery along the Confederate line and how he and a friend traversed much of that line finding friends they had not seen in quite some time. It was clear that he was frustrated by being so close to home yet unable to connect with her or his family.

Headquarters Bryan's Brigade, Army of Tennessee, Camp
Before Chattanooga, October 2nd, 1863
My dear beloved and loving Molly:
*   I wrote you a letter a few days ago which I hope you have received. I was very unwell at that time but I am better now. I have*

not had a letter from you in a long time but have heard from you by several persons who went home from Atlanta. There was 22 of my company that went home but they all went without leave. I couldn't do that, it would not do me any good to go home that way. If I live I think I will get a furlough this winter and if I knew that I could get me a horse by coming home I think I could get home soon. I have still got the money that was sent me but our regiment has not yet been paid off, it is going on eight months since we have been paid off. Molly, I am needing a pair of pants very bad, I want you to send me a pair of pants as soon as you can. I was in hopes that Father or Uncle William could come to see me. They can come within six miles of me on the railroad and if they was to bring anything they could not carry, they could leave it with Major Davis of our brigade who is at the railroad who would take good care of it. I am still in hopes that they will come and see me and bring me something good. Molly, I want you to send me a towel. I wrote in my last letter how for Father to find me but for fear you did (not) get it, I will write it again. Inquire for Longstreet's corps, McLaw's Division, Bryan's Brigade and there he will find me. If he don't come and can see any one that is coming if you will send me my things it can be left with Major Davis at the depot and I can get it from there most any day.

Molly, I little thought this fall two years ago when we was together in Chattanooga – so happy together, that today I would be so near there under the circumstances that I am under. I am (with) in two miles of the room where we stayed. I can't help but love the spot, and not only the spot, but all other spots wherever I have seen and enjoyed your company.

But I must tell you, the other day I and James Speer concluded that we would go down our line of battle and hunt up Dick Turner, your cousin. He is Lieutenant Colonel of the 19th Louisiana Regiment. We did not get to see him as his regiment was on picket. He is well. Strolling about, I found Charley Crenshaw, Bob Shurard's son-in-law. I did not know him at first, he has never been home, can't hear from his family. He tells me that old man Shurard and the Dr. and one of the others are dead. Jones Lloyd is dead also. It has been so long since he has heard from home that he could not tell me much. He says Miss Malissa is not married yet.

A little further down, I found the 30th Georgia and found Van McKileline lying in the ashes eating parched corn. He is a Lieutenant now and is well and hearty. I found many more of my good friends, all tired of the war and want to get home and all think they have seen the hardest service, but I know what I have seen and history will say so too. The truth is, I have seen so much hard service that I am used to it and feel like I would not be satisfied anywhere else. I assure you dear Molly that I am faring as well as anybody can in service and all of my regiment is astonished to see how some get along and have good friends but the great secret is I do my duty and do it well. I am always at my post though it is sometimes very dangerous. The other day the shells flew thick and fast but I trust in God and fear them that is able to kill both body and soul. I think that we will shell the city in a day or two; perhaps tomorrow; we are planting artillery today. I long to see the Confederate flag wave over Chattanooga. I think I will see (it) before long. We whipped them very bad the other day. Our brigade did not get there in time to get a chance (to fight). If we can rout old Rosecrans, I think I can capture me a horse. Molly, I don't like to write with a pencil but I haven't got any ink or pen that is any account, if it rubs out you must let me know and I will try and get ink.

Now Molly, because I said I thought I would get a furlough this winter don't you expect too much. Perhaps I ought not to have told you for if I don't get it you will be disappointed. You need not expect much although I intend to try to get one if there is any chance. Give my love to Grandma, Uncle Em (William) and (aunt) P. B., and Father, Mother, Sister and all the negroes and friends. A letter from Brother John the other day informed (me) that himself and Darnell was in good health. Oh do kiss the babies all over for me. Oh, how I want to see them but I want to see you more than they. I am yours until death. Goodby.

William R. Stilwell

P.S. Direct your letters Dalton, GA. Longtreet's corps, McLaw's Division, care of General Bryan.

Another Georgian, George Burns wrote a brief note to his wife on the 4th. His regiment was posted at Chickamauga Station behind Bragg's line.

Chickamauga Oct the 4th, 1863

Dear wife, I am well and hope this will find you all well, though I fear it won't. I am uneasy about the baby. I want you to write as quick as you get this and let me know how she is. I got to my command last night before dark. We are stationed hear. General Cummings thinks we will stay hear several days. We are 12 miles from Chattanooga on this railroad. Bragg's army is between us and there. I can't find out much from there but it is the opinion of men that ought to know that there will be no fight hear soon. I will write again if anything strange occurs. Captain Jackson is hear. He has been further down. He don't think they will fight at Chattanooga. They have them completely surround on the side, our cavalry are on the other side. Direct your letters to Chickamauga post office. Write quick. I will close for the present. Your loving husband.

G H Burns

To Nancy Burns

To J. L Burns, I saw H.P. Burns about that receipt. He said he sent the form of it to his father to sign up. If you would send a form of it hear he will sign it up in his name or his father's either.

The surgeon of the 6th South Carolina was Dr. G. L. Strait. On the 27th of September he determined to begin a diary with the intent to forward it at some point to his sweetheart, Miss Bettie Baskin. What remains of the diary contains the entries for the 27th through the 3rd of October. Strait's entries are a mixture of pleasantries with occasional comments related to the soldiers that were his patients, and the death and destruction wrought by the war. For the most part his focus was on trying to keep an upbeat and spirited presence for his sweetheart's benefit and that of the troops.

In line of Battle of Chattanooga, Sept. 27, 1863

My Dearest Bettie – You may perhaps think somewhat strange of the manner in which I propose entertaining you, but my object is to interest my little Angel as much as may be and have thought that making a sort of diary that that end could be attained perhaps best. Nevertheless I shall adapt that plan for the present, and I leave your good taste and discriminating judgement the result of my efforts.

From sunrise to sunrise will comprise the labors and events of each day, since early in the morning is the most favorable period for writing. The letter I sent yesterday having embraced a portion of the first 24 hours. I consequently have only from 12 o'clock of the 26th to sunrise of the 27th to note which can be done in a few words. Quiet prevailed during the period mentioned hence I lay quietly around and finished "The Cavaliers" which terminated as most love tales do in the consummation of the ends and hence the happiness of Bernard and Lucy. Of course they passed through the fiery ordeals of trial and hair-breadth escapes before they reached the happy goal. But what of that so they became happy in each other's happiness? So may we some day. Don't you say Amen? The sun rose as usual with a hazy sky so rendered by the dust, upon a still parched earth. My sleep was quite pleasant last night. I sleep between Humphreys and Dr. Davis, both pretty warm fellows and consequently don't fear any danger of freezing. From present appearances we are promised another day of quiet. Hoping to have additional items for tomorrow – au revoir. God bless you.

Monday 28th. The sun rises on another quiet, beautiful scene, but his brilliancy is considerably obscured by the dusty element. Our slumbers were suddenly disturbed about 11 o'clock last night, by quite heavy picket firing. We thought for a while a fight was imminent, but it soon passed away and we slept beautifully and comfortably til morning. Yesterday was passed rather dully. However I whiled away the weary hours by reading "The Pioneer's Daughter", an Indian novelette, love entering largely into the "spirit of the dreams" of the principle characters. Edward Allen and his most dear Lucy Danforth, after running the gauntlet of savage captivity and at other almost countless more than hair breadth, ay, miraculous trials and escapes, they too become exceedingly happy. The last we see of our hero and heroine is the former with silvered locks sitting by a winter's fire, surrounded by bright, sparkling eyes and sweet little faces listening with breathless interest to Papa's thrilling narrative while Mama is absorbed in her exquisite happiness. I have heard so much about the picturesque beauty of the scene presented by the lines of battle of the two hostile armies, in and around Chattanooga, as seen from the mountain knobs, for which this country is so famous. I have determined to go observation making today and should I meet with success, my tomorrow's note may be quite interesting. I hope so at any rate. Heaven bless my Bettie. More anon.

Tuesday morning, 29th. The last 24 hours has been an almost unbreakable silence. From rumors – called by the boys "Grape Vine and Spring Telegraph" – the next 24 hours will be entirely the contrary. Preparations are being made to open upon the enemy, if we may judge from the movement of the artillery during the night. However, as each day's record answers for itself, I shall not occupy space with futile surmises; but return to my task proper. I spent the day reading various spicy tales, love , romance etc, etc. In the afternoon as rather late in the evening I took a pleasant ride solus, on my favorite "Billy Wilson". I shall take Billy home, if he lives, for Bettie to ride. Had it not been for the dust, the ride must have been extremely pleasant. The sun arose, as on yesterday, with the exception that the sky is more murky and has somewhat the appearance of rain. I have, in all of my notes forgotten to tell you that our Genl. Jenkins, was slightly wounded Wednesday evening, the first of arrival here. A piece of shell struck across the root of the nose, on a line with both eyes, the latter being suffused or bloodshotten therefrom. It merely broke the skin, which slightly affects the General's beauty, and made it altogether quite a narrow escapee. I had one man accidentally shot in the hand and will loose one or perhaps two fingers. I had quite a pleasant sleep last night, had it not been for the extreme hardness of my couch. The nights are getting quite cool. The same Telegraph before mentioned, puts us enroute, in a few days, for Knoxville. I only hope it may turn out true, since this is the most complete wilderness and completely – cut off – from civilization place – that I ever saw. I hope to be able to continue tomorrow morning. I forgot to say that I visited the Catawbas yesterday. I was pleased to find the boys getting along finely. Gus was rather unwell, but seemed very glad to see me. Jim rather shy I thought. Farewell, God bless my Bettie.

September 30th, 1863. Good morning my Bettie. I hope you are in a gay mood. I hail this but by no means with joy, as my birthday. Were I at home we might get up something that would be worthy of the 29th anniversary of a man's existence, as it is, the day must need be passed unnoticed, save by a sigh. The sun is completely obscured this morning *and we have good prospects of early rain. All quiet as on yesterday, and our many conjectures and rumors leave us equally as ignorant of our General's plans. I spent the day reading some and visiting my friends in the sixth. Thomas Wylie is looking quite badly – is not in good health. The Catawbas were quite gay and I spent a very pleasant few moments with them. By the way, I have succeeded in getting a change of clothing. Hence I feel very much better. Had a pleasant night, but rather strange dreams – You had a part in them but they seemed disconnected, so much so that I cannot shape one of them intelligibly. We have a tent, hence we will hereafter do much better in the sleeping line. Goodbye – God bless sweet Bettie.*

Thursday October 1st. Rain, rain. It commenced sprinkling about noon yesterday and about 10:00 o'clock last night the rain began in earnest and poured incessantly all night. There is a slight abatement this morning; but I fear we'll be almost as anxious for sunshine, as we were for the dust to be settled. I wish it would clear so that I could go upon the mountain to see the magnificent scenery so much lauded by those who have the pleasure of beholding it. The utmost quiet obtains. Indeed the pickets of the belligerents have become quite intimate. They use water out of the same creek, exchange papers, and converse at leisure. I heard that Genl. Jenkins had issued stringent orders forbidding any communication whatever. We are as much at a loss as ever in regards to military operations. A hundred and one reports, rumors, surmises, etc., etc. go the rounds of the lines respecting movements, General's plans & c. Indeed it is interesting and amusing to hear the men talk and foreshadow our prospects. When I get tired reading and sitting around in our won regiment, I go to the sixth, where I am certain to be regaled with the "camp talk". The old Catawbas are pretty good for news, and no better than their Captain, who always has a pleasant and spicy budget in store. I rode over to my old company yesterday. You perceive I go over pretty frequently and was very much pleased to meet my old friend Sam Lewis. He is sergeant of ordinance in Claiborne's division. He is looking as well as ever I saw him and in fact, is the same Sam Lewis he was when he left Chester. Thomas McCullough is quite well and seemed to be getting on finely and in good spirits. We are informed and doubtless correctly, that there is much dissatisfaction in the three other Brigades, composing our division, in respect to the division commander, Jenkins being Senior Brigadier is, of course, in command, while those brigades desire Law to be their Commander. We also understand that the officers of those brigades have petitioned the President to promote Law to the ranks of Major General, and assign him to the command of this division until General Hood returns. The belief is that Jenkins will be "out-generaled" in which event I think he will about "go up the spout". More anon. Heaven bless my Bettie.

Friday 2nd Oct. What a delightful morning; -- forth with all his glory, the skies being clear of the faintest shadow of yesterday's cloud. The rain poured almost incessantly yesterday notwithstanding, I thought it the most fitting opportunity to visit Capt. Roddy, and struck out about 11 o'clock for Gist's Brigade. After a ride between 4 or 5 miles, over the worst country I ever traveled, I reached Roddey's bivouac, considerably wet. I found Lyle quite well but low in spirits. He wants to get home. I was so extremely cheerful and light hearted that all were rather surprised. I told them that I merely reflected the spirit of the old soldiers generally. Lyle said, "I know the reason why you are so gay. You've been living high and having a delicious time while at home." I think my visit will be of benefit to him, because I don't think he had seen a cheerful countenance in a "coon's" age before. He was slightly wounded on shoulder – contusion by a piece of shell – but is entirely recovered. About 4 o'clock I started for home, the rain almost pouring; but back to the Sharp Shooters I must get and the idea of being caught in the wilderness in the dark and perhaps rain too, I could not stand. So back I bent Billy Wilson's weary steps and plodded our way through mud and mire, over hill and dale through brush and swollen ravine, the rain pouring nearly the whole time. You can very readily imagine my plight when I reached my own tent, wet, wet to all intents and purposes. Instead of meeting the pleasant smile of a sweet face, a warm fie, and smoking coffee, slippers &c, &c. what do you suppose met me? "Alas, how do you like Gist's brigade?" "Pleasant trip over there?" "When you going back?" "You take Gist's in yours," and a hundred other like expressions. Poor comfort don't you think? However John came to my aid with dry clothes and soon made a cheerful fire in front of the tent and soon had me prepared for a pleasant night's rest. Everything is still this morning save an occasional shot either on the picket line or at some unfortunate squirrel. I have not received any communication from home since my arrival or which is more desirable, anything from your own dear self, but am patiently waiting and anticipating the pleasure I shall realize on the receipt of a much coveted letter. Goodbye – dear Bettie.

Sat. Morn Oct 3rd. The sun is again completely obscured. It is not only cloudy, but a very thick fog o'erhangs the valley, so dense indeed that you cannot distinguish a man a hundred yds. I fear more rain. A most perfect silence has reigned along our entire line for last 24 hours. Professional duty called me from my notes, for about an hour or more, and on resuming, the sun has broken through the cloud of fog and today promises another cloudless sky. Yesterday morning accompanied by my friends, Capt. Garvin and Lt. Wilkes, the latter being the rare specimen of humanity, the former the very eccentric Capt. You've heard me speak of. I ascended Lookout Mountain to avail myself of the grand "sightseeing" of which I spoke, in a former note. Lookout Mountain is one of considerable note, being the highest range in this portion of Tennessee, besides its being a place of resort, for the gay, the beautiful, the lovers of romance, poetry, of lovers and sweethearts, the invalid, the adventurous and pleasure seekers ad infinitems, during the summer months. The range is about 70 miles in length, and has many points of natural interest, besides historical and traditional renown. There is an immense cave, which is said to have been explored 15 miles; still leaving the adventurous explorer in utter darkness, as to its full extent. A great many women and children took refuge in it during the belligerent demonstrations, in and around this place. One of the unfortunate mothers died in this luckless place, leaving two poor miserable, almost famished, little children who made their way out to some of the houses for succor. The entrance to the cave is between ours and the enemies' lines, so that it was impossible for us to give to the unfortunate occupants any assistance. The savage and inhuman foe, whose, guns commanded the entrance, tis said, not only shot at every male who attempted to go to the cave, but even at the women and children whenever they attempted to leave it. One of the wretched little children whose mother died, was wounded in the hand, by one of their shots. I also heard it asserted positively by both soldiers and citizens without contradiction, that they shot at a woman who was going to a spring nearby and killed her child in her arms. Oh; too hard to think of! There is also a niter mine on this mountain from which is obtained a good deal of salt petre. This has been developed I think since the war commenced. There are a good many precipices and majestic rocks mounting up to a perpendicular of twenty and thirty or perhaps in some instances, fifty feet. Of its history and tradition I must confess ignorance, further than we are informed that this mountain was the resort and hiding place of the notorious John A. Murell and his devil-may-care followers during a part of his time serving career. It was also a place of considerable note and pleasant little villa called Summerville with an extensive hotel and apartments for the accommodation of the many pleasure seekers before mentioned. The scenery presented to the eye from the summit, or rather from a point called "Lookout Point" is enchanting. Beneath we behold on the east and south, the beautiful Chattanooga valley rendered more beautiful and magnificent by the immense camps, bivouacs, entrenchments, forts batteries and lines of battle of the two hostile forces. For miles may be seen these vast preparations which may turn at any moment this beautiful place into a charnel house of death and tinge the waters of the meandering Chattanooga Creek and the innumerable other sparkling streams with the life's blood of hapless men. Even the limpid and majestic Tennessee might have cause to complain bitterly of the unnatural intermingling. Immediately beneath your point of observation winds the remarkable old river, remarkable if for nothing else but its crookedness. It is about 500 yds in width at this point and extremely shallow at this season; but during the winter, boats run up here. Immediately at the foot of the mountains, the river makes a most interesting bend. -------------- (rest of diary missing)

To strengthen his siege on Chattanooga and further disrupt the weak Federal supply line, Bragg sent the cavalry command of Joseph Wheeler to further harass the Union supply line. On October 1st Wheeler crossed the Tennessee and soon fell upon two wagon trains which were captured and destroyed, further diminishing the Federal ability to supply Rosecrans' hungry troops. Over the next six days, clashes with Federal Cavalry forced Wheeler to move southward toward the river. By the end of his raid Wheeler had burned a number of railroad bridges, destroyed over 500 wagons and killed over a thousand mules. The mules were a most precious and shrinking commodity between the Confederate raids and the tortuous terrain that had already claimed many a mule's life. 10,000 draught animals died trying to supply the besieged troops in Chattanooga that fall.

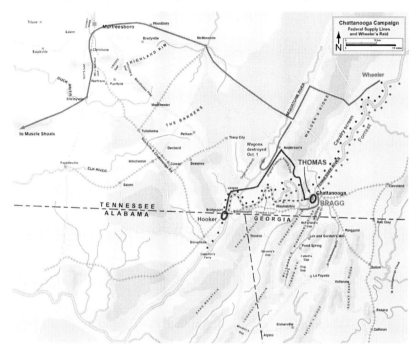

In the Union camp Axel Reed continued his missive while besieged in Chattanooga. His entries for the first half of the month shared hardships but remained very positive when looking to the future and his belief in the success of the army.

Thursday, Oct. 1st. The new month commences cloudy and the afternoon rainy. Last night was a sad one for us, as the night was rainy and our new constructed 'bunks' did not shed water and we took the full benefit of all the rain, and in the morning we were completely saturated. The trenches are ankle deep in mud and the continual tramp of soldiers mixes it well up.

Oct. 2nd. Report has come in that the rebels (Wheeler's Cavalry) have burned the train of our army corps. They were coming from Bridgeport, loaded with rations, clothing and ammunition. Over three hundred wagons were destroyed. The teamsters got away with most of the mules.

Oct. 5th. About 9 a.m. a rebel signal flag was observed on the summit of Lookout mountain. Soon after a few guns were fired along the rebel lines at our works, when nearly a dozen guns from the side of Lookout opened and kept up a brisk fire all the afternoon, while a 32 pound siege gun kept playing upon us from two and one half miles distant to our front. The balls passed over our lines to our rear and just over the left of our brigade. The guns from Lookout mountain threw a number of shells into our camp, but succeeded in wounding only two men and killing one horse. I noticed Gen. Thomas, standing on the fort, while the shell and shot came close to him.

Oct, 8th. One year ago today the battle of Perryville took place. The Union armies have achieved much the past year. One year more will probably crush secession.

Oct, 9th. Commissioners Dean and Stone, from Minnesota, arrived here yesterday and today proceeded to take the vote of the regiment. Everything passed off quietly. Hardly a Democratic (or Copperhead) vote was cast. Col. George went the straight Union ticket, uncontaminated by a mixture of Copperheads.

Saturday, Oct. 12th. I visited our wounded boys in hospital today, and found them all in good spirits. McClellan and Roberts, of my company, Sergt. Keen, of Co. H, Jones of E, Sylvester of E, Fitch and work of Co. A, Reynolds of A, and Sergt. Cavocizel of F, all getting along well. Keen had his right arm amputated, but in good spirits; Jones has his right arm amputated near the shoulder. Flags of truce have been corresponding between the rebels and us today.

Given Campbell had been a resident of St. Louis when he left to fight for the South. The love of his life was a young woman named Sue Bettie Woods. St. Louis was a town controlled by the Union from the start of the war. Mail was nearly impossible to get from Campbell in the Confederate ranks to her in St. Louis. As an officer in Nathan

Bedford Forest's cavalry, he was in Courtland, Alabama in route to disrupt Union lines of communication when he tried once more to get a letter to her.

Courtland, Ala. Oct 18th, 1863
Miss Sue Bettie Woods
St. Louis, Mo.
I have written so often & as yet have had no indication that my letters reached their destination, that it seems almost useless to write again but I have written & intend to write as often as a chance presents itself. I have great hopes that this will reach you & that you may be enabled to answer it also. It seems an age since I saw you and that I have not seen you since is by no means my fault, for I have applied for leave of absence several times & from the exigencies of the service my application was refused. I have got another one up through all the generals up to Bragg & have that yet to hear from. It is the dictator of honor & duty which prevent me from going to see you anyhow.

I think more often with sad delight of you & past happiness than ever and it is the ultimate aim of my hopes to meet you again & that not far off in the scale of time. If ever a human heart was true in its allegiance, mine is, & ever has been to you my own darling Bettie. I suppose you may have been uneasy about my safety not knowing if I was engaged in the fights preceding and subsequent to the Battle of Chickamauga which was fought on the 19, 20th & 21st of last month. I was in it all. For five days prior to the battle Forests Cav. To which I belong was fighting almost constantly, and during that bloody battle we shared our part of it. The enemy were disastrously defeated and their loss was very heavy, losing about 12,000 prisoners beside great numbers killed. Our loss was heavy in killed & wounded, especially in officers.

In these different fights I never had any apprehension, though death blew his breath in my face as he passed on. In the last fight we were in which was about 10 days ago, I lost one third of my men in killed & wounded. I do not know that any of your friends or acquaintances were hurt in battle. I have no news to tell about except that our troops are in fine spirits & equal to all emergencies. We are & have been bivouacking for over a month, no huts or shelters of any kind & no wagons so you see we must be leading a hard sort of a life. The hardships of the war have come upon us so gradually that I have not felt their weight so sensibly. This war makes men grow old very fast & though I do not notice it on myself but when I see my friends after an absence of some time they look so much older, the wrinkles begin to gather around the eyes and a gray hair now & then shines among the black locks of youth. If I do not get a leave of absence I will either be taken captive or killed before many months more for life with such a protracted absence from you is unendurable and relief can only be had by daring all dangers.

I have no news at all to impart and will close this letter my darling with an assurance of my everlasting love & devotion. I know but one love & will never know another. Good bye. If this letter reaches you it will tell you on an accompanying note with how to write to me.

Believe me. As ever your own most affectionately,

GC

Conditions continued to deteriorate in Chattanooga for both the soldiers of the Army of the Cumberland and the citizenry. While the army received some aid from the resupply attempts, the citizens were on their own. The town became destitute and even homes were demolished in order to provide fire wood for the troops. Rosecrans had no comprehensive plan to change the situation. While ordering repairs to rail lines and attempting to improve the supply line, there was no concerted effort. It was as if Chickamauga had broken the man and left him confused and unable to divine the plan needed to break the siege.

Toward the end of September, Benjamin Mason of the 137th New York Infantry wrote home that they were preparing to move. He assumed it would be toward Fredericksburg. A few weeks later he added the note that they had been ordered to prepare five days rations and be ready to march. However the destination was not Fredericksburg. His corps and another from the Army of the Potomac were headed to Rosecrans' relief in Chattanooga.

September 28th 1863

Aquia Landing VA
Dear Mother

I Write a few lines and let yo know that I am well and hoping these few lines will find you the same. We have just got our pay and I shall send the check home in this leter. We drawd four month pay. You wished me to let yo know if I got the box and ten dolars. I did. For the last two days it has ben quite rainy but to day it is quite pleasant and I hope it will be for we are under marching orders and have ben for the last too weaks. They Boys (say) that the quartermaster orders to be redy to march Monday morning. Where to I don't know but I presume that we will go to Fredricksburg and make a strike there. It is said that our cavalry has the sides at Fredricksburg. If that is trew I presume that we will haft to go there and the boys all hope that we will and I for one hope so.

I can't think of much more at presant. This is from your son B F Mason to Mrs Mary Mason

A few weeks later: *…We are know (now) picketing along the river. The rebes (rebs) fire on us when we show our head. We are expecting a move every minute. We have eight days ration on hand five in our knapsacks and three in haversack(s). there was to (two) men shot ought (out) of our corps for desertion. I send the chek*

B. J. Mason   To Mary Mason

At the end of September Major General Henry W. Slocum's XII Corps and Major General Oliver O. Howard's XI Corps were ordered west from the Army of the Potomac to reinforce Rosecrans' 35,000 men. Major General Joseph Hooker, former commander of that army, was to be in overall command of this force. They moved by rail as far as Bridgeport, Alabama in early October. With the route to Chattanooga still not open for significant supply they could advance no further without putting themselves in the same position of not being able to be supplied. The stalemate continued.

During this period Otis Baker found time to wax philosophically in his diary. One such subject was the right of secession as he saw it and another was the justification of slavery as a natural condition. He finished this series of entries on the 16th by comparing the behavior of soldiers in "captivity" to their duty with that of slaves.

October 5th Shelling commenced at about ___. As the old Union had its conception & foundation in the "consent" of the people, and as it was expressly declared that "governments derive their expressed powers form the governed" it seems astounding that such intelligent men as Crittenden and Everett & others should be betrayed into such a gross infraction of the foundation principles of their loved Union, as to make war upon a people, who felt that they could not in justice to themselves or posterity, longer consent "to be subject to their government". Bombardment was continued at long intervals by ten or twelve guns, throughout the day, but with what effect is not generally known. A frost today.

Oct. 6th – quite cold. Bombardment was not resumed.

Oct. 8th – President Davis accompanied by Gen'l Bragg & others rode along the lines this morning passing a point of our position about 11 A.M.

Sunday Oct. 11th - All quiet.

Huber the naturalist mentions a strange fact of natural history to me, that slavery exists among the ant creation. He testifies of an instance in which he noticed the battle between two races of ants in which the conquered were born off by the conquestors and used as slaves. This fact is said to be confirmed by Latneilie & others. In Harpers Family Library Vol. VIII pp 12.

Oct. 12th – Brigade went on picket. Began to rain about 12 P.M. Continued to do so throughout the night & following day (13th) & night.

Oct. 14th – Relieved by Deas' Brigade. Rained until about 11 A.M. Continued cloudy. Continued raining at dark & continued during the night.

Oct. 15th – More rain. We have been without tents since the evacuation of Shelbyville, June 25th. Had a few while at Chattanooga, but were deprived even there by Gen. Anderson while at Lafayette. The only shelter the men have is such they can obtain by stretching blankets. (one) of as disagreeable things in the world the life of a soldier under these circumstances is therefore unpleasant – "The proper study of mankind is man." Hence the use of philosophies has been truly said that "we cannot always judge the characters & motives of men from their public transactions."

Oct. 16 - The soldiers life brings to the sun the faces of many qualities of human nature. The white man, under the authority & subject to the control of another exhibits the same dispositions as the negro slave. He shifts his duty upon his fellow that he can avoid (and) leaves that unperformed (that) he will not be held responsible; forgets the rules of courtesy & politeness, seldom or never anticipates the wants of another, in fact is apt to be extremely selfish. He disbelieves in all goodness. He gives few credit for pureness of motive for their deeds especially if they are favored for a superior. Human nature is such that (self interest) gives one a dominant influence over the minds of most persons. It excites a kind of respectful give aire and with it there is also created some assurance & audacity, the former is immense. The last with the weal minds meet with more admiration than does ____ producing the appearance of inferiority they _____ captivate them. We submit to many rules however unjust to others, while they operate to our advantage, but rebel against them in the converse.

G H Burns wrote home to his wife on the 11th from his camp near Chickamauga Station. He expected some sort of movement for the 34th Georgia and could see signs that something was up, but could only guess as to where and when they might go.

Chickamauga Tennessee
Oct the 11th 1863
    My Dear wife, I can inform you that I am well and hope this will find you all well. I rec'd your kind letter yesterday. You don't know how glad I was to hear that my little babe was well. I had suffered much uneasiness about it. Oh the cries the little thing give after me when I left you at the creek. It haunts me yet, but I must bear it. I have nothing new from the front, only Rosencrans is being largely

reinforced. 3 corps of meads army are on their way to join him. Wheeler captured 5 hundred wagons loaded with commissary stores on the other side of the river. We are receiving reinforcements also. We had orders yesterday morning to keep one days rations cooked ahead. We think there is some move up but we can't tell what it is nor where. Some think we will move up towards Cleveland when we do move. I understand we will be put in Longstreets corps (that is, our division). They are shelling some at Chattanooga occasionaly. I think the yank's supplies are very slim. We are having pontoon bridges built. I expect part of our forces will cross the river and make some flank movement on them.

I saw Harrison Davis hear. He is camped in a half mile of us. He belongs to a company of sappers and miners.

We still have preaching every day and night. I can set hear and hear two and three preachers preaching at once. They want John to come and preach very bad. Tell John when he gets time to come and stay a few days and see some of the army doings. It all goes up in life any how. Tell him not to think hard of me for not shaking hands with him when I left him. I intended to get on the car and then shake hands with him, but they crowded me so I could not get to him. Tell him I wear my comfort (in) these cool times in memory of his kindness towards me.

My dear wife, I hope you will be as cheerful as you can under all the circumstances, bearing in mind that God does all things well. I hope He will permit us to meet again, if not I will chearish your kindness so long as I live. I will have the pleasure to know that I died a loving and beloved man. I must close. I send my parole. Keep it to show what I have suffered, when I am no more.

G H Burns

To Nancy Burns.

William Talley wrote of this time during the siege in his memoirs, sharing a few stories that paint a clear picture of what the

Confederate troops faced during this time as they battled not just the Yankees but the elements.

The army was soon occupying a line of battle around Chattanooga. On account of the scarcity of water on Missionary Ridge we had a heavy line of pickets at the foot of the Ridge and the troops were camped on the east of the Ridge on down the Chickamauga valley. Our battery was camped near the road from Chattanooga to Chickamauga station which was on the W & A RR. The road crossed the Missionary Ridge through a small gap in the ridge. Gen. Bragg had his headquarters in a little white house on top of the Ridge south of the road.

The rains began to fall and we had a long wet spell. You could hardly go anywhere without bogging down. Chickamauga station was the depot for supplies for the army and the road became so boggy teams could not haul supplies for the army and food became so scarce that we boys suffered with hunger. We would go where the horses were fed and pick up the grains of corn they had dropped and wash and parch it and it did eat good. One day we had peas issued for rations and the peas were so full of weevils that every pea had two and more holes. We cooked and ate them and they were the best peas I ever ate. The infantry was detailed to cut and split the oak trees and place them in the road so about four of the five mile to Chickamauga Station were laid of these logs. While in camp there, Major Robertson found out that the Yanks had a camp of instruction for fresh troops across the Tennessee River opposite the mouth of the Chickamauga River and went to Gen. Bragg to get permission to take his battalion of artillery up there and shell the enemy's camp. Gen. Bragg very reluctantly gave his consent but ordered Major R. that if the enemy replied with artillery to limber up and return at once. We left camp after sundown and went to the top of the Ridge and a road ran on top to near the Tennessee River. As dark came on I saw the most beautiful sight of camp fires. Our little line of fires along the foot of the Ridge looked so insignificant while toward Chattanooga, all over the plains were fires of the enemy, line after line and as far as we could see were lines of fires. We crossed the W & A RR and soon struck a field it looked at night to be about 100 acres or less. When we got near the River there was a high rise and on top of the rise it was level for 30 or 40 ft. and then down a high bank was the Tennessee River. We could see the water through the bushes. We unlimbered our guns and put them in position for firing, then lay down and went to sleep. Just before day we were awakened and ordered to our posts around our guns. Just at daylight we were ordered to fire at will. And we made music from the 16 guns of our battalion but as our gun fired its 8th shot the enemy shot a three inch sell just over our heads and then five other guns shot. The order was given "Limber to the rear, by piece double quick march". We didn't' wait for the 2nd order. We struck out, the horses in a gallop and we cannoneers on foot right across that field, and the Yanks firing almost down our line of "get away". I ran till my tongue almost hung out of my mouth and I said to myself I am going to walk if it kills me. I walked about 20 steps when "boom" from the Yanks' gun and a three inch shell came over my head about twenty feet high saying "wich wich" and boom about 40 yds. Ahead of me it bursted. I said I can't stand this and started in a run again but soon I said again I'll walk if it kills me, so I walked about ten steps and here it came again. Boom from the gun and "wich wich" and (it) bursted just ahead of me. I then noticed that I was running almost in a direct line the shells were going and as this gun was the farthest to the east and if I would turn to my left I'd soon be out of range of the gun. I ran to my left and was soon out of range so I walked the balance of the way.

That field seemed to be two miles across while we were going back. Some of the boys ran to the right as the timber was nearer but the Yanks' guns were playing there more than anywhere else. Two of our boys were going through the timber when a three inch sell exploded behind them and the butt of the shell struck one of them on this right side under his arm and tore his ribs out and made hole to his insides. The boys got him to a safe place and left him. We went back to camp and sent an ambulance for him. They got back with him about 3 o'clock and I went and looked at him. He is the only man I ever saw inside of. The tissues around the heart were not broken but I could see the beats of his heart. He was started for the hospital but died at Chickamauga Station.

We camped at the foot of Missionary Ridge some time. Rations for men and horses were very scarce on account of the roads to Chickamauga Station were almost impassable with a team and wagon. There was corn on the other side of Lookout Mt. along the Tennessee

River, but wagons could not go over there. The only road across the Mr. was on the side over the Tennessee River. The River at the bottom, some 100 ft. above the river the N & C RR ran along a ledge of the Mt. some one or two hundred feet above the river, then for two hundred ft. perpendicular was the road on a ledge but most of the way was on the slope of the Mt. and thick and the road could not be seen from across the river at the Moccasin Point which was fortified by the Yanks right where the river made a bend, Moccasin Bend as it is known. Some times or places, it was straight down for over 100 ft. to the RR and 200 or more straight up. Opposite the Yankee fort for about 20 yds. the road was in plain view of the guns across the river. The road had been dug out of the Mt. and a large rock was left 3 ft. from this overhanging rock down then across the road and way down you could see the RR and on down below the River. To get corn from over the Mt. men were sent on horseback with a sack apiece and they would bring the sack of corn in front of their saddles. I was detailed one day to go after corn with a lot of others. Just before we got to the overhanging rock we stopped in the bushes and dismounted and one man would lead his horse and go across for fear the Yanks would shoot at them. We got across and got our sacks of corn and got to the place of the overhanging rock. The man ahead of me was riding a mule and said he was going to ride across, so I gave him time to get across and started. As I came out in the open there was that fellow. His mule had shied at the open fall to the RR and had jammed his sack of corn against the rock and the sack had caught his leg against the saddle and he could neither go forward or backward and I was scared to death nearly. Up was hundreds of feet perpendicular, down was the same and across the river I looked into the mouths of the guns. I looked every second to see the puff of smoke but they didn't shoot and then the man behind me came out and there was three of us. About that time I saw No.1 get his leg out and he hit the ground running and I was right behind him. I was detailed to go after corn the next day but a boy who was on guard wanted to go and offered to swap places with me and I needed no one to advise me so I swapped and stood guard all day & night, on two hours and off four hours. That P.M. when my man got to that overhanging rock the Yanks shot a shell at him but it struck about ten feet above him. He was not hurt.

W R Stilwell found a horse he thought would work out as quite a deal and wrote to his wife to let her know. He still needed pants and a towel, but now added a request for a shirt. Conditions were very difficult for the troops with limited supplies and shelter.

Headquarters Bryan's Brigade, Camp near Chattanooga, Oct.16, 1863

My dear Molly:

I have just received your letters of the 9th. You can imagine how glad I was to get it. it is the first I have got since I left Virginia nearly five weeks (ago). I have been looking for Father but no word of him. Now if he has not started tell him not to start now. The bridges between here and Atlanta are well washed away and General Bragg will not allow any citizen to come up. He had better wait some two weeks before he comes. I want him to bring me something good to eat and please send me a pair of pants and a shirt. I had a shirt stolen from me a few days ago, also please send me a towel. I am in good health. I have got me a Yankee horse. he was wounded in the fight in the foot. I think I can cure him. He won't cost me but very little. I told the man that I got him from if I cured him I would pay him twenty-five dollars. He is a young horse four years old and, (if) I get him well, will be worth eight hundred or a thousand dollars. Ain't I smart, I think you ought to brag on me, I am smart enough to get me a horse from old Eric.

Molly, General Bragg has just issued an order that no furloughs will be granted for the present. I don't think I will get home before winter, if then, but I will try very hard to come this winter. Molly, if my horse gets well, I shall send some money home soon. I want to send that that I borrowed and perhaps a little more though I shall have to buy a saddle and bridle and they are so high. I don't think I can spare any but that which was borrowed if he (the horse) gets well. I shall send that.

No sign of a fight here now. General Wheeler captured twelve hundred wagons the other day. Write soon. Oh, do write. No more at present but I remain yours always until death. Goodby, (Kiss).

W. R. Stilwell

P.S. Direct your letters to Chattanooga Tennessee in care of General Bryan, McLaw's Division, Longstreet's corps.

The 34th Georgia was being repositioned to the east (right) of the Confederate line near Charleston, Tennessee and G H Burns wrote home to let his wife know about it and when she may visit him in camp.

Tyner's Station, Tenn. Oct 18th, 1863

Dear wife, I am well and hope this will find you well. I have just rec'd your letter and was glad to hear that you were all well and doing well. We are on our way to Charleston, Tennessee. We will go up tomorrow. Barton's Brigade goes up tonight. You wanted to know if we had tents, we have none. We are taking this wet weather like beasts. Don't send me any money. If I kneed any I will write for it. I will write when for you to come to see me if we get to a place where we expect to stay. I will write and you can come, as you are a married woman. Save your money you get for Kit for a rainy day. Kiss Tennesse Jane for me. I will write as quick as we get up there. I must close as I am in a hurry. I will send this to Dalton by Mr. Mitchel. My love to you all. Your affectionate husband.

G H Burns

To Nancy Burns
All our Division are going up.

Bragg continued to have organizational troubles during this period. Key subordinates had turned on him after Chickamauga. Generals Longstreet, Daniel Harvey Hill and Buckner led the dissent and called for Bragg's removal. Bragg had already relieved Generals Polk and Hindman for their parts in not securing a complete victory at Chickamauga as well as the lost opportunity the previous week in McLemore's Cove. President Jefferson Davis personally made the trip to Bragg's headquarters in mid-October to resolve the dispute and address the insubordination.

By the time Davis left, a number of changes and demotions had been implemented in the Army of Tennessee. General Polk, who Bragg refused to reinstate, was transferred to Mississippi under Joseph Johnston's command. General Hardee was sent to Bragg's command from Mississippi in return. Simon Buckner was reduced from corps to division command. Daniel Harvey Hill was suspended and sent home. He was replaced as corps commander by Major General John C. Breckinridge. Hindman was reinstated under Breckinridge's command.

The conflict within Bragg's command was not a secret among the troops. John Magee mentioned the infighting and rumors of resolutions in his diary entries. By the twenty-first rumors were abounding that his division would be moving, but to where nobody knew.

Sunday, Oct 11th, 1863. In camp – went over to see Lieut. Reynolds. No news of importance.

Monday, Oct. 12th, 1863. Incamp. Rained all night last night; and is showering off and on today. Went over to Witt's and got some hominy made. Very mean weather.

Tuesday, Oct 13, 1863. Rained again all night, and still pouring down. Everything very wet. Creeks and rivers all up and still rising. Understand the President left it to the Generals whether they should serve under Bragg or not, and they voted him out – also Pemberton as corps commander and Hindman as division commander. They are having a time of it about the battle of Chickamauga – Polk is removed, and Hill relieved – Forrest resigned and general dissatisfaction everywhere.

Wednesday, Oct 14th 1863. In camp – still raining – awful muddy – all our clothes and bedding wet – no tents – the army suffering very much, while the generals are squabbling about who is to blame.

Thursday, Oct 15th, 1863. In camp – still it seems it is never going to stop. Every person out of humor, and some getting sick. Heard the bridge over Chickamauga creek has washed away, and we will get no rations tonight. Ceased raining in evening, but still cloudy.

Friday, Oct 16th, 1863. In camp – no rain today. Went out to an old mill to get some wheat ground – could not. No army news.

Saturday, Oct 17th, 1863. Charley Reynolds came over to see me. No news.

Sunday, Oct 18, 1863. In camp. Heard they have had another fight in Virginia – Lee victorious. Cleared off, and cool wind today.

Monday, Oct 19th, 1863. In camp. The second section went back to wash. I saw Maj. Cromwell – tried to swap some wheat for flour – could not. Pleasant weather but very muddy.

Tuesday, Oct. 20th, 1863. In camp. The first section went back to wash. Wrote a letter to Mr. Haggard in answer to one received. Rumor that our Brigade will go to Mobile.

Wednesday, Oct 21st, 1863.   In camp – fine day. Rumors of our moving somewhere – do not know where.

Thursday, Oct 22, 1863. In camp all day. In evening the enemy threw some shells into our lines creating great confusion – killed 1 man and wounded 2 others in Jackson's Brigade. In evening about 9 o'clock orders came "to get ready" to move. The whole division under orders. The infantry moved out immediately. The Batteries started at 6 o'clock – roads very bad – commenced raining about 11 and rained all night. Awful times crossing missionary ridge – all night at work – mud knee deep – horses baulking, and guns miring, and the rain still pouring down, while every half hour the flash of the enemy's guns at Ft. Cheatham could be seen, and soon a shrieking messenger would fall near or among us, as the weary and benumbed soldiers pushed at the muddy wheels of the guns. All night long we worked in mud and rain, and morning found us with but half the battery up the mountain.

What remained for Bragg to resolve was what to do about Longstreet. As one of the most popular and successful generals in the Confederacy he couldn't be cashiered. He also couldn't remain under Bragg's command. Neither he nor Bragg would stand for that. Longstreet's command was reduced to the original two divisions he brought with him from Virginia for starters. Davis then suggested to Bragg that Longstreet be given the independent command he so desired then send him to wrest Knoxville from Union General Ambrose Burnside. Bragg took the advice but waited to follow through with the order.

On the 20th of October, G H Burns wrote home that the division was preparing to move on Knoxville and Burnside. This was one of the false starts and reconfigurations of the Army of Tennessee that seemed endless throughout the fall.

Charleston, Tenn   Oct 20th, 1863

My Dear wife, with pleasure I this morning seat my self to pen you a few lines to let you know that I am well, and hope this will find you all well. We arrived hear last knight about 10 o'clock. I saw Robert Carson's folks standing in the door. I threw off a letter to them. It was after knight. I don't know whether they saw me or not. I saw William in Cleveland. I wanted to stay all knight with him but they would not let me. George and Camel Johnson were there. They will be up hear this morning. We are ordered to cook 4 days rations and cross the river today. We are going in the direction of Knoxville from (what we) hear. We are after Burnside. Our cavalry are on ahead. Now my Dear wife, I fear we are going to be a while again that we can't write to each other. Oh how I wish you could have got to a come to me before we got away, but it can't be helped. It would have been a great pleasure to me to have seen you in our camp, knowing it would have been so much pleasure to you to have seen me, and then it would have given you some idea of our camp life. I would have sent for you at Chickamauga but the weather was so bad and we had no tents, and there was no chance for a house. Don't think that I don't want to see you in camp. Nothing would please me so well as to have you pay me a visit, for you are so kind to me and so good to me that your presence is like the visit of an angel to me. What do I care to live for now but you and little Tenny & my folks. I don't know where for you to write. Ther is no mail runs up hear. You will have to just write to this place and risk it coming to me. You wanted to know if I had any drum. I have a brand new one. I will take your advice and stay out of a fight if I can. You wanted to know if we got plenty to eat. We don't. We get some bacon, some beef, flour and corn meal, but not full rations. I will close. Do the best you can. I will do the same. Give my love to all my folks. I remain your loving husband till death.

G H Burns

On the same day W R. Stilwell wrote to his Georgia wife. He continues to work on healing his horse but misses her very much as demonstrated by the poem he wrote and enclosed along with this letter.

Headquarters Bryan's Brigade, October 20, 1863,
Camp near Chattanooga, Tenn.
> *My dear Molly:*
> *Your very short letter of the 17th inst. was received on the evening of the 19th making the trip in two days. It reached me in due time and found me in the enjoyment of good health and spirits. I was very sorry that Father could not come to see me and also that I could not get those good things that you had prepared for your ever faithful Billie, but I hope that I may yet get them or some others as good. I have had great misfortune in getting things from home. I think that Father can come before long. I think that he can come in a week or two. Molly, you need not send me my bible. I have got one that was captured at Gettysburg, Pennsylvania. I have wrote to you to send me a shirt, pair of pants and a towel and any other things that you may have and want to send. That is all that I need at present. I have all my baggage hauled and can take care of my things very well. Molly, my horse is getting well fast. I wish you see him and the rider too. I imagine if you could see me rein up my fine steed and dash into the battle once, you would say it was not me. I think he will be able to ride by the time we have to march, he is worth all of eight hundred dollars and he will only cost me 200 dollars. I shall have to buy a saddle unless we could have another fight and then I think I could get one. I was sitting in the tent the other day reading a newspaper and T. M. Polk tapped me on the shoulder. I had not thought of him in a long time. You will not know anything about him, but the rest will. He is well. I have been trying to find Cousin John Rea (?) but have not yet found him. If Uncle Washington told what regiment he belongs to I would be glad if you would let me know. I wrote long ago to Aunt P. B. to know what regiment cousin Margaret Glass' two sons belonged to, but have never yet received an answer from her about it. I think it is a mistake about Brother John and Darnell being up here. I think they are still at Charleston, S. C. If they have had come here I should have known it ear (before) this. Molly, the longer I have been in my position, the better I*

am pleased with it. I would not, as much as I admire office, give it for a lieutenant's position in a company. There is plenty of them that would gladly exchange with me. It is better to be born lucky than rich and with all my bad luck thank God I have some good. I have no doubt it is (He) that has guided me through.

I have received many letters of late. Uncle John's well-written and sympathetic letters are good. He admires my courage very much and says he is proud of me. Bob McDonald is another good friend of mine. Letters from W. N. and R(ichard) M. Everitt have been received. I am going to write to Granma Stilwell this evening. I have never wrote her a letter since I been gone, the reason is I did not know who she could get to read them or write letters but Marshal Polk says aunt Clevet can write. Give my love to Granma, and Uncle William and Aunt P. B. Tell them all howdy for me. Tell Pa to come when he can and to bring me a goose quill for a toothpick. Howdy to Mother and Mag. Kiss the children, God bless their little souls. I want to see them and enclosed you will find a piece of poetry written last night by moonlight. I am as ever.

W R Stilwell   Goodbye, oh for one kiss, oh how sweet

Evening Moonlight by W. R. S.

1 – This world is very lonely now since I'm so far from home, I have not a friend with me to bow before my father's throne.

2 – Long and lonely have been the days since I have seen my wife. The moon is dark it hath rays and not much pleasure in my life.

3- I am setting now in the broad moonlight and thinking of the past that awful and that solemn night you held me to your bosom fast.

4 – Our little boy was fast asleep, I thought he would not miss and while I stood by his bed to weep upon his cheek I placed a kiss.

5 – I am going now where I've often gone to appear before the throne and pray the Father. Oh, how long before I shall see my home, home, sweet home.

6 – The Lord has been very good to me. In all the conflicts past he has promised that a friend he'll be and guide me safe to the last.

> *7 – Molly, you have my heart and life and if on the battlefield I die, you are my darling and my wife. My only request is by your side to lie.*
>
> *William R. Stilwell*

> *Molly, there were several other verses but having to write it by moonlight and with a pencil I can not read them. This morning I have composed many such. Since I have been from home and as I walked past my post at night this will show you that not withstanding my long absence from home and have seen so much murder, I still have the same tender feelings that I once had. Nothing was said in my poetry about Jinney (Virginia) but nothing is known, I know she lives but that is all. I love it because I love you. I will give her a feast some time.*

> *W. R. Stilwell*

Around this same time Major General Ulysses S. Grant had been summoned to leave his command in Vicksburg to meet with Secretary of War, Edwin Stanton. They "coincidently" met on October 17th while boarding the same train in Indianapolis, a stop on Grant's roundabout path to the meeting. From there they rode together to Louisville, Kentucky. During the ride Grant was given command of the new Military Division of Mississippi which included all three major Federal Armies; the Armies of the Cumberland, the Ohio and the Tennessee. Materially, Grant was now in command of the western theatre of the war. He immediately relieved Rosecrans of command of the Army of the Cumberland and replaced him with General George H. Thomas, the "Rock of Chickamauga." Thomas was issued orders to hold Chattanooga at all costs. Grant then set out for Chattanooga.

Leaving the rail line at Bridgeport, Grant traveled the exasperating route over Walden Ridge that served as the current supply line to Chattanooga. It was strewn with broken wagons and thousands of dead mules and horses. The seriousness of the situation was quite pronounced in his mind. Upon reaching Chattanooga on October 23rd, Grant was thrilled to hear that Thomas and his chief engineer, Brigadier General William F. Smith, had put together a plan to break the siege and open a new supply line to Chattanooga.

This plan would open an overland route of only eight miles from Kelley's Ferry which could be reached by steamboats from Bridgeport. The land route from there to the city traveled over existing roads on a peninsula formed by the river called Moccasin Point. This new route would be out of range of Confederate artillery on Lookout Mountain. In order to open the route, they would have to dislodge the Confederate troops guarding Brown's Ferry, the only enemy position that could block the suggested route. On the 27th of October a combined force of infantry moved on Brown's Ferry. One was floating down the river as the other marched along the bank. William B. Hazen commanded those on the pontoons on the water while Brigadier General John B. Turchin led the 3,500 men on shore.

Hazen's men caught the Confederate pickets at Brown's Ferry by surprise and easily grabbed a bridgehead. Turchin's men used the pontoons to row across the river and join Hazen in securing their position on the enemy's side of the river. A spirited fight was joined, but by midafternoon, the pontoon bridge had been completed and breastworks were being built by the Union soldiers.

Stilwell wrote home to his wife on the 27th and mentioned hearing the sound of fighting to the left which would have been this engagement. Clearly homesick and desperate for the clothing items he has asked for continuously, he nearly begs that his father comes by rail to visit and deliver them before they have to move again.

Headquarters Bryan's Brigade, October 27, 1863
Camp near Chattanooga, Tennessee
       My dear Molly:

No letter has been received from you in some time, the reason is not known. I hope I will get one this evening. I am well and doing well. Some fighting yesterday here and (they) are fighting on the left now about two miles from me. I don't know whether we will have a general engagement or not, everything is ready for a fight as far as I know. I think our division will move camp this evening. So much rain that our camp is almost a pond of water. I don't think we will move for I am in hope we will go nearer the railroad. I would be glad if Pa could come now for fear after this fight is over we may not stay here long and he can come on the railroad now. Buck Lemmond come up a day or two ago. He says anybody can come now that wants to. I think the sooner that he (Pa) comes the better and if we have a fight I would be glad if he could be here.

I just returned last night from a trip of three days up in Walker County, Georgia after corn. I could not find any corn to buy and had to press some. I pressed it from a lady whose husband is gone to the Yankees. It was very hard to do so and she crying and begging but I could not help it, my orders was to get corn and I was obliged to get it. I don't want to go anymore. I had much rather fight Yankees than take corn from women and children. I had a good time otherwise, eating butter and milk and potatoes and other vegetables but it did not last long, but like the hog I had to return to my wallering in the clay and vomit again.

I received a letter from Brother last evening, he is doing well and has and has good health and thinks many will be the days before Charleston will be tread upon by Yankee invaders. God grant that it may be. Chick Speer is here, got here last night from home. He looks well, better I think than any of the boys, but I fear from what I notice that he will go like the rest of the boys.

The bridges that was washed away between Atlanta and Chattanooga have been rebuilt and the cars run through the Chickamauga station. If Pa comes he can leave any thing that he may bring with Mr. Ben Straten at the railroad until he finds me. I can get them most any day from the road. I would be very glad to see him. Molly, them long letters that use to come to me in Virgina have played out, I don't hardly ever get none at all and when I do they are very short. Come, you must do better than that. Molly, I want this war to close, I want to see you and the children but I have been trying to stop it for a long time and I don't see that the end is any nearer now than when I begin, but I don't think it will last always and if it ever does and I am still alive I shall be very glad. Write soon and often and lengthy.

My love and respects to all the friends. Kiss the children and God grant that we may all live to meet again. I am yours always until death.

William R. Stilwell
Mrs. Mary F. Stilwell Goodbye   Kiss me.

Coordinating his movement with Hazen and Turchin's action of the 27th, General Hooker had begun marching his reinforcements toward Chattanooga from Bridgeport and by the evening of the 28th, General Oliver O. Howard's XI Corps was within a mile of Brown's Ferry. Brigadier General John W. Geary had the lead division of Slocum's XII Corps three miles further to the south in Wauhatchie.

Confederate General Longstreet had been slow to respond to the attack at Brown's Ferry. In delaying his response by a day he created the opportunity that had allowed Hooker's force to advance unmolested through the valley to this position. Bragg was furious when he learned about what was happening on the western side of Lookout Mountain. He ordered Longstreet to use his entire corps to blunt the Federal effort and recapture the Ferry. Instead, Longstreet determined to attack Geary's division at Wauhatchie with a single division and do it that night.

One of the few night fights of the Civil War, the battle of Wauhatchie was fought under a bright moon, commencing shortly after midnight on the morning of October 29th. The fighting was intense and confused. Reinforcements sent by Hooker from Brown's Ferry engaged a Confederate force under Brigadier General Evander M. Law, positioned to hinder just such an attempt. This left Geary to fight it out alone against Micah Jenkins' division. By 3:00 A.M. the two sides had fought themselves out, with the Confederates withdrawing and leaving the field to the Union forces. Longstreet's withdrawal from the Lookout Valley opened the proposed supply line, known hence forth as the "Cracker Line". Grant immediately sent reinforcements to assure that the line would remain open. Now it was only a matter of time before Bragg's grip on Chattanooga was loosed.

Another Confederate on the eastern side of the mountain wrote to his sister, including his understanding of the night battle that Longstreet had fought in the dark morning hours of the 29th.

W.H. Reynolds to Anna M. Dickey – Oct 29, 1863

Near Chattanooga

Oct 29th 1863

Dear Sister

It is impossible for a soldier to write letters whenever he feels like it; or I would have written to you long ago. Since the battle of Chickamauga and the retreat of the enemy to Chattanooga, My brigade has been immediately in front of the enemy. Doing very heavy picket duty or building fortifications.

We are now about four miles from Chattanooga on the reserve line and have a better opportunity to procure writing material etc. It has rained a great deal lately and this whole valley is covered with water. The roads are so bad that we have great difficulty in moving either troops or Wagons. A portion of our forces had a fight last night – with several thousand of the enemy – who had crossed the Tennessee eight miles below here, and were marching towards Lookout Mountain. Our forces were repulsed, but the enemy afterwards retreated across the river.

Our Regiment is greatly reduced by sickness, there are only four men in my company present for duty. Everything is quiet today but we expect stirring times in a few days. Give my love to Bro William and the children.

Address me at Chickamauga Tenn.

Your affectionate brother

W. H. Reynolds

Axel Reed's diary reflected the removal of Rosecrans, the arrival of Grant and shelling and drilling that occurred during this period. Most significantly, he mentioned the opening of the cracker line on October 31st.

Oct. 28th. Gen. Rosencranz has been relieved from the command of this army and Gen. Thomas assumes command.

Oct. 31st. A steamboat went down the river yesterday morning for Bridgeport after rations. Boats can come up within six miles of here now and we will have plenty of rations soon. Visited town today and assisted George H. Wiley, of my company, to the hospital. The town is barren of anything worth buying. The rebels fired a few shots at our camp this afternoon from the top of Lookout mountain, but none of them reached us.

Nov. 2. Considerable cannonading has taken place between the rebel batteries on Lookout mountain and our batteries, one on the other side of the river at Moccasin Point, close at the foot of Lookout and from Fort Nagle. The rebels fired three shots about noon at our Pontoon party at the river, the shell passing over our camp, two lighting in town and one bursting high in air over our hospitals.

Nov. 3rd. The rebels threw more shells at us. One shell weighing 24 pounds passed down through the roof of one of the hospitals, a short distance back of us, passing down through every floor and into the ground without bursting and passed just at the foot of a sick man's bed. Some shells burst high in the air above us. Drew two days' rations from the 4th to the morning of the 6th, drew 1 pound of crackers per man, a little coffee and bacon is all we get, but we are bound to stand it rather than give up Chattanooga to the villians that would destroy this nation.

Tuesday, Nov. 10th. I have made out three muster rolls today. Paymaster is around it is rumored. The boys will welcome him this time if ever for they have been out of the needful for a long time. Received notice of the death of John W. Shontz, who was wounded at Chickamauga, towards the close of the fight Sunday afternoon. A rebel bullet lodged in his bowels, and he was sent to Stevenson hospital. He was a good soldier and well liked by all.

11th. George W. Wiley, of Co. K, died and was buried yesterday. Poor fellow he has been with the company until a few days ago. Chronic diarrhea. No friends to mourn.

Nov. 13th. We have been paid four months' pay, until Oct. 31st, by paymaster Rhoads. The boys hail pay day with a good heart, although a number do not draw 1-8th their pay this time, as they have money due them. 'Chuckaluck'will be resumed now until a few get all the money there is, when it will stop until next pay day.

Monday, Nov. 16th. Generals Grant, Thomas, Brannan and Beard ride through our camp occasionally, looking after the welfare of the army.

Gen. Beard (commanding division) comes around and drills our camp guard quite often. He undertook to instruct a sentinel of the 9th Ohio who was guarding the colors in the manual of arms when the 9th boy protested and said: 'Dat's not de way we drill by a damn site.' Gen. Beard left the 9th boy to do his own kind of drill.

Charley Caley of the 105th Ohio began a letter home on the 30th of October but finished it on the 7th of November due to heavy rain and fatigue duty. Compared to Confederate troops begging for clothes from home, he boasted of a seemingly unlimited supply of clothing, but the Cracker Line had yet to restore full rations for the army. Although it had been more than a month since the Battle of Chickamauga, Charley's description of artillery damage to trees and losses in his company were yet reminders of that fight.

Oct 30th 1863

Ever remembered parents brothers and sisters. I was sitting here in my little tent and the thought occurred to me that I might write a few lines to let you know that I am well and hoping that this will find you all the same, there is nothing of importance to write that I can think of at present. There has been some pretty hard fighting done the last two and three days. The rebels occupy lookout mountain and have got a battery planted on top of it so that we cannot run the cars in yet on account of their shelling them but they will have to get off there if it takes all the forces in Chattanooga to do it as we cannot get supplies in to the town. Nov 7th - I had to quit writing on the 30th as it rained as hard that it beat through the tent and wet my paper so and have not had time till to day to finish it and it was all for the best as I got a letter that you wrote on the 22nd. Since that the stamps was all right and came just in time I have 7 on hand now and think that they will do me till I can get some.

We get 2 crackers a day now and quarter a pound of meat. coffee three times a day. to day we got 2 spoonfulls of sugar. think that we will draw full rations to day. If we can not get rations we will certainly have to evacuate the place.

One of the boys has brought in a shell that has been throwed in here by the rebs it weighs 34 pounds it did not burst you had better believe it is a pretty good chunk of iron. Hello another mail call and every man jumps and runs to see if he is to get a letter well I go with the rest and lo to behold I get your kind letter dated the 17 it has been delayed on the road some where. I tell you it does me some good to hear from home. tell Nel when you write her again that I wish she would write oftener and tell Laura that I have wrote to her While I was in Chicago and have not got a letter yet. I like first rate if we would get enough to eat. have clothes a plenty can draw anything we want once a month. I have sent in for a overcoat and then I will be riged for winter We have drawers undershirts in fact everything we want in the clothes line is being furnished by Uncle Sam. we expect to be mounted this winter and armed with spencers 8 shooters and then git out of the way boys. I will send you my likeness as soon as I can get it taken if it costs five dollars and I want the family likeness sent to me that I can see you all again. tell Molly that if she was down here she would see some fellers coming along zip zip and strike a tree and cut it of(f) quicker than lighting. there was a shell on the battle field that struck a pine tree 2 foot through and cut it of(f) clean so that the tree flew ten foot killing (and) wounding several. we had 28 men in our company of which 15 got out alive we lost just half of our regiment in killed and wounded. if you could get an oyster can and fill it with honey and send it through it would not go bad. however I must draw to a close thanking you for your past kindness and begging that you may all think of me and write often. from your affectionate son Charlie

Things are very high her(e). butter .50 cents a lbs coffee $5.00 a lbs. sugar 50 cents and every thing else in proportion

Tell Arthur and Willie to be good boys and I may live to see them again.

A few weeks following the battle of Wauhatchie, Union private George Smith of the 111th Pennsylvania Volunteers wrote to his mother to let her know that he had survived the battle and was "enjoying himself" in Tennessee.

Camp Six miles from Chattanooga Nov 15, 1863

Dear Mother
It is with much pleasure that I inform you about I am well and enjoying myself way down in Tennessee. I hope when this reaches you it will

find you enjoying the same at home. I suppose you have heard before this of our corps going from Va and joining the Army of the Cumberland. It was a pleasant Journey as we came by railroad. I must tell you I have been in one battle and came out all right while 20 of my Co. were killed and wounded. It was on the night of Oct 28 about midnight that the enemy attacked us and the fight lasted nearly three hours but the rebels finely withdrew leaving some of their dead and wounded in the field. It was a very hot battle while it lasted.

When you write please tell me you got the money I sent you. It was one hundred & fifty dollars. I wish you would send me a few postage stamps paper and envelops if it is convenient for there is no chance to get them here where I am. as I have no more news to write I will close by asking you to write soon. Direct to Cn. 111 Regt. P. V. 12 A. C. Nashville Tenn

From your affectionate son
> *George Smith.*

While the opening of this segment of the Cracker Line enabled Union supplies to more easily reach Chattanooga, it was still insufficient to build a stock pile and furnish all that was needed to sustain the reinforced Army and prepare it for offensive action. Thousands of horses and mules that had been lost during the siege had to be replaced and over 180 destroyed bridges and 100 miles of torn up tracks from Louisville to Bridgeport had to be repaired in order to open a second rail line from Nashville to accommodate the rebuilding of an army. All of this was accomplished within 40 days.

Samuel Withrow served in the 22nd Indiana. On November 10th he wrote a long letter to his mother, sharing the good fortune of his regiment during the battle of Chickamauga and his esteem for General Rosecrans as a general officer. He exudes confidence in the Army of the Cumberland and hopes that Rosecrans will be restored to command.

Chattanooga Tenn.
Nov. 10th 63
Dear Mother,
> *As I have not received any letters from you for some time and*

as I am deeply interested in your well fare I take the present opportunity of writing you a few lines to let you know that I am well and getting along as well as could be expected under the present surrounding circumstances.

We have been here at Chattanooga ever since the 22nd day of September which was directly after the Battle of Chickamauga. We cross(ed) over 3 ranges of Mountains, big Cumberland, Tennessee and Lookout was the last one we cross and went into Georgia on the 18th of Sept. and on the 19th the Battle of Chickamauga commenced. This battle derives its name from the creek on which it was fought. The battle commenced near Rosseville and the Chattanooga & Atlanta Rail Road and continued all day of the 19th ,entailed great slaughter on both sides but with little assurance of victory on either sides , and the 20th we were over powered by greatly superior forces by the combined forces of Longstreet, Bragg, Johnson. Our army was about forty five thousand strong with the forces of the rebels according to their own statements at seventy thousand. There was great slaughter upon both sides our loss was estimated at sixteen thousands, the rebels acknowledge a loss of seventeen thousand. The carnage was awful. Our regt was to the battle detailed as rear guard of General McCook corps consequently we were not to get (in) the battle until late. We were not engaged in the two days of the hardest fighting. We reached Chattanooga the 22nd of Sept after being largely cut off from our main army two different times. We lost in the whole regiment since we left Winchester onely 8 men killed wounded & missing and onely one killed in our company. We had to fall back about twenty miles to reach this place which is now and in past the greatest purpose of this armys movements since we left Murfreesboro.

I consider we gained a victory although we were forced to retire a short distance as the intention absent were to occupy Chattanooga with our whole entire army which could not be done without a battle in order to concentrate our army to this place. We have fortified this place since we come here so that the whole combined southern confederacy cannot assault us and drive us out. We have been pretty short of rations since we came here part of the time and not more than one quarter rations but we are doing better now and the future prospects looks bright for provisions as we have communications by the river now to within a few miles of this place &

boats are running daily between Bridgeport and here and we will have tolerable plenty of rations. We have put up tolerable winter quarters and are tolerably well fixed to spend the winter here as I presume we will as we are closely (watched) by the rebel Army who are lying all around us. in the north and south their camps are within (a) mile at any time. our pickets and their(s) stand out more than a hundred yards in part. (I)n some places they are constantly shelling at us but with little or no affect as their shells fall short. The rebels still occupy Lookout Mt. & Missionary Ridge. from the former Mt. is where they have their many batteries stationed. The Mt. is about two and a half miles from town. The boys are all well, health is generaly good throughout the army. The army of the Cumberland. Gen. Roscrans (is) greatly respected by the whole army but we still live in the hopes that he will be restored in a short time and again command of this army and be our leader and guide through the balance of our term. he is the right man in the right place and was highly esteemed by both officers and men in the whole army. Some but what spoke well of Old Rosey as we called him under whom this army has done such more service the best wishes of the Army of the Cumberland is with him and if we had too enough men we would have whipped the rebs as we had here if not worse than at Stones River. General Grant is in Command now who all seem satisfied but without Grant more or else would have suited at all. We hold Rosy as the best General in the United States. Grand is excepted . I will have to quit writing and have prolonged my letter so far. I want you to write to me as soon as you can. this and let me know how you are getting along and be shure and let me know whether you got that money which I sent you. I am afraid it has been lost. If I have not heard from you since I expressed it to you for the 10th of September. expressed you a hundred and fifeteen (115.00) dollars from Stevenson Alabama. I sent it at Moores Hill. I also wrote you a letter stating that I had sent it. probably the letter was lost. If you have not recieved any notice of it yet you had better go to Moores Hill at the earlist time and see if it is not there, probably it might have been stopped at Arura

> *I remain yours as ever and hope this may find you all well*
> *Write Soon*

> > > *Samuel G. Withrow*

On November 3rd Grant ordered Sherman to advance his troops from western Tennessee to Chattanooga. Sherman arrived in Bridgeport with the van of his forces on November 13th. Grant now had the forces he needed to take the initiative, but he still needed the supplies to support them. Bragg was unintentionally about to enhance Grant's odds of success with his next move.

John Magee was just settling in to a new camp site with adequate food and comfort at the end of the month when his brigade was ordered to return to Missionary Ridge. While he had been sure they would move north into Tennessee, Bragg's plans didn't include his battery.

Saturday, Oct 31, 1863. *In camp on the Widow Johnson's land – cleared off, fine day – will stay here some time it is thought. Our forces are in possession of Loudon on the Tennessee River 12 miles from here. Rumors of fighting at Chattanooga. The cars will be running in a few days.*

Sunday, Nov. 1st, 1863. *In camp – fine clear day. George Sledge and I went over in Pond creek valley and got our dinner with a Col Ramsay – very nice and clever man. We stopped at several houses and found the finest kind of people – intelligent and refined, nearly every family having a library. Saw some young ladies. Heard of horrible atrocities the enemy committed on some ladies.*

Monday, Nov. 2nd, 1863. *Moved our camp to another woods nearer town. Heard our ordnance wagons were coming up. Got a letter from Mollie. The cars came in the evening, weather clear and fine – am very unwell. Wrote to Dr. Ward.*

Tuesday, Nov. 3d, *In camp – plenty of forage coming in – will fatten our horses. Hear they have had a fight at Chattanooga, and Longstreet was repulsed.*

Wednesday, Nov. 4th, 1863. *In camp – wrote letters to Mr. Haggard and Mollie. About 10 o'clock orders came to move back to Missionary ridge. Oh how we hate it – just got here in a fine country plenty to eat, and have to turn back to starvation – it is bad, very bad. Started at 12 and went 5 miles and camped. Am very unwell.*

Thursday, Nov. 5th, 1863. *Up early and moving – showered a little and soon got to raining steadily. Passed through Athens at 1 and got to Riceville at 5 and camped. Raining all the time. I rode on the caisson all the way – was so unwell. Went over to Mr. McKinney's and staid all night. Very clever people and fine young ladies. Stopped raining in the night.*

Friday, Nov. 6th, 1863. *Got up at sunup – slept well – feather bed a luxury to a soldier. Found all the batteries gone – left before daylight – contented myself by waiting for the cars. In the society of Miss McKinney's the hours unconsciously slipped away and noon was soon past. I enjoyed myself very much – wrote some poetry in their albums. Got excellent meals and some fine brandy which done me good – also apples. In afternoon, found no train coming yet I came on down to Charleston, and found the batteries camped ½ mile from town, only 6 miles after such an early start.*

John Euclid Magee
Nov. 6th, 1863
(These were the final entries remaining from Magee's diary)

By the first of November W. R. Stilwell's depression over the continuation of the war and absence from home was worsening, and to add to his pain he had discovered that the horse he had put so much effort into healing wasn't a Yankee horse but belonged to a fellow Confederate and must be returned. Still he looked for those much needed pants and clothing.

Headquarters Brigade Camp near Chattanooga Tennessee
November 2, 1863
My dear Molly,
        Your letter of the 30th October was received last evening. I was sorry to hear that the baby was sick but hope it is better before now. I am in enjoyment of good health but am troubled some about other matters. The war seems to have no end and I am tired of living without my family. I don't know what is to become with me and mine. Sometimes it looks like I will go deranged and perhaps it would be best for me. I am tired of the war. I have not had any meat for some time and don't know when I will.

I lost my horse this morning. It turned out that he was not a Yankey horse but belonged to one of our own men. I gave him up this morning. I shall have to buy one as I am obliged to have one and it will pay more to have a horse. I get most out of heart some time but when I remember how much I have been blessed above my fellow soldiers, I don't think I have any right to complain at my lot. I think if I can get a horse by next year I can save some money for you. I am afraid you will need money now but if I buy a horse it is impossible for me to furnish any but I will try and save some by next year. Everything is so high that the soldier can't save much.

I was up on top of Lookout Mountain and took a grand view of everything for many miles around. Our present camp is near the foot of the mountain. Molly, I will try and come home this winter and some time I think if they don't let me go I will go anyhow, but my honor would be injured and I may had as well be dead as to lose my honor. There is but one thing that ever will cause me to desert my post. I need not say what that is for you know.

If you get any chance to send my pants and shirt, do so and let me know when and by whom you sent them. I think I shall write for a furlough soon as Mr. Morris gets his furlough. He is a son of Richard Morris of Henry County; lives six miles from McDonough. Pa will know where he is (lives). He is one of our couriers and one of my mess and will bring anything for me that Pa will take to his Father's. He has made application for leave of absence for ten days. If he gets it I will let you know. I may keep this letter a few days and see if it comes.

My love to all of the folks, tell them all howdy. I want to see them very bad. Write soon. I am yours until death.

William R. Stilwell

Back behind the Union works, L. B. Wort wrote to his wife from the 21st Ohio camp. A large sum of money had been sent with their colonel to a number of soldier's families and he hoped she would receive it before she got this letter. He also spoke of Rosecrans being replaced. It is clear from the letters of the soldiers that while higher powers were finished with Rosecrans, his men still held him in high esteem.

Chattanooga, Tenn.
Nov. 12th 63

 Dearest of all on this earth to me. I once more take my pen in hand to pen a fiew lines to you to let you know that I am well as usual except my eyes and they are no better. I hav tried that eye watter that I made at home but it wont do any good and I hav tried three other kinds an all to no purpos but I think they will take a turn soon for the better. Well we hav been paid off and I sent you eighty dollars. We sent all of us hicksville, (Ohio) boys in a package to Edgerton (Ohio) by express to John Ainsworth. Your uncke Fin (Sgt. Finlay Britton) sent sixty dollars. I can bet him every time and I get 12 and he gets 17.

 Well I got a letter from you today of the 10 and one from Sis and was pleased to here from you again but sorry to here that your health is so poor. You said if I did not like you(r) letter that I must tell you in my answer. Well I like your letter, all of them. You said that one of my letters had no stamp on. Then some body must have taken it off for I hav not sent any letter without a stamp. You said that the news there is that Rosecrans (General William S. Rosecrans) is turned out and some other man is in his place. That is so. he is relieved of his command here and General grant commands here at this time. I do not know the reason of this but think it some of their abolition meanness. You said that you hurd that our supplies is cut off and that we would bee likely to starve. This is not so. We hav more to eat now than we did some time ago. I think that provisions will bee plenty Pretty soon. The reason of the seecresy is that they hav to hall them in wagons so far and the route is very bad, but the steam boats up the river now within ten miles and they will fetch a plenty. Tell Sis I think hur dress is very nice. She said she sent a piece of lattas and it was green but I guess she furgot to put the grean in. I think you will get your money by the time you get this letter. I sent the money last Monday by our colonel. He went home. You can see that my eyes is poor by wrighting. Our regt. was on picket yesterday and their was seventy rebs came to the line and gave them selves up and they say they are a starving for something to eat. Some of those are from South Carolina. Well my eyes hurts me so I guess I will have to quit for this time. Hopeing to here from you soon

 I remain as ever your affectionate husband till deth.
 L.B. Wort to S.G. wort

tell sis I will answer hurs in a fiew days. So good by loved one for this time

Over in the camp of the 75th Indiana, Edward Hutsell wrote to his parents that they were beginning to see more rations and he was feeling better than he had. He was also sending money home as soon as it was practical.

November the 16th/63
Father and mother
I with pleasure embrace the present opportunity of writing you a fiew lines to let you now I am well. I hope this finds you the same. I have not heared from you since the battel. I cant think whats the resen without your letters have been miss carried. I have written twise since that. I suppose Sean is thar by this time. I hear from him yesterday I heard he was at Si Thorns. We are getting along vary well here now tho we don't get quite as mutch is to eat as we would like to have Tho we can get along. I guess it will not be many days until we well get plenty. The cars will soon be ready to run here. Then we will get what ever we want. The rebbs camp ar in site of us. We trade the rebel pickets crackers for tobacco. They are vary friendly with us. they like to get to talk with us when we are on picket. We are not allowed to shoot at one another. They say they want the war to end. they are tird of it. Thare is a good many of them disserts. We are getting this place well fortified. Well pap we was payed of(f) yesterday I would like to send some money home but I guess I well (wait). it is vary uncertain the road it has to travel about whether it would get through. I thought I would lend it here so I guess I can send a hundred dollars next payday. Pap I will send a half dollar in this letter for you to get me some stamps with. I cant get any thing of that kind here. Thar is no post office here yet . Will I guess I have written all that I have to write at present. Well mother I am the stoutest now that I have ben for three months. I have just got to feel like myself a gan. I was not vary well for a long time that I have got well now. I guess half rations dident agree with me. if you have any socks you want to send to me by Si I will not refuse them for they are so mutch better than we get here. so good evening answer soon

Yours Edward Hutsell

Speaking of socks, on the 19th the commander of the 5th Georgia Regiment sent a thankyou note to a school teacher who's students had acquired and sent 38 pairs of socks to the colonel to disburse to his men.

Headquarters, 5th Ga. Regiment
Lookout Mountain, Nov. 19th, 1863
Mrs. H. E. Morrow
Respected Lady – I have the honor to acknowledge the receipt of your note of the 18th inst., also thirty eight pair of elegant socks to the men of my command, who are destitute of these articles, and distant from home, from the pupils under your charge.

They were distributed as you requested, and a timely gift. Permit me, kind lady, in their behalf to tender you and the pupils of the two schools, our sincere thanks, and rest assured that the pupils of College and Morrow's Classical Schools, together with their noble representative, will ever be held in grateful remembrance by the members of the 5th Georgia Regiment.

A people can never be conquered upheld at home by the sentiment which these tokens represent in the rising generation of our blood stained country. I have the honor, with much respect, to be, your obedient servant,   E.P Daniel, Col. Comd'g.

Once again from behind the Union lines, Jonas Hollem of the 74th Illinois reported to his brother the circumstances of the army. Again affirming that they were not starving and lamenting the loss of Rosecrans as their commnander.

Chattanooga Tenn Nov 20th
1863
Dear Brother!!!
*   Yours of the 1st first is at hand. I am glad to hear that you are all well at home. I can say for myself that I am now enjoying first rate health, that prisoner "John's assertion" that a dose of starvation is better than any dose of medicine. I don't mean to say that we have actually been starving but I will say (in contradiction of*

all the newspapers that have reported the Army of the Cumberland to be on full rations) that we have been on <u>half rations,</u> the large & part of the time since we took possession of this place and it has been, and is yet impossible to buy anything to eat, at any price. Well that's all right. We can't spend so much money, as we would were it otherwise, and besides we don't realy need it now as we get along very well on the rations that we draw and it will not be long before we have an abundens of every thing. Perhaps before you get this. So <u>don't' you</u> be all anxcious for me. I have stated the simple facts just as they are not by way of complaining about our hardships and privations. Far be it from my intention to harass your feelings in that way, but I thought you might hear worse <u>rumors</u> than <u>facts</u> so I thought that by stating the simple truth you would be spared from many painful conjectures. Things did look dark hear one spell, we were almost surrounded by the infernal Rebs, then they destroyed a <u>large</u> train of our supplies. <u>That</u> was a severe blow, and for a long time they were constantly bothering our supplies, our communications are now free from such annoyenses and although we have lost our beloved leader <u>Gen. Rosey,</u> we have another in place who I think is fully competent, to handle this Army. Gen Grant has already commenced to renew the aquaintence, he formed with the Rebs at <u>Vicksburg.</u>

It was neither religion nor opinion that caused the removal of <u>Old Rosey.</u> You know it has got to be a custom in this Army to supercede any Gen who fails to win the <u>battle field.</u> Well Rosey came here to take Chattanooga, and <u>he did take it.</u> But could not hold the <u>field</u> because the reinforcement he called for <u>did not get here in time.</u> Look at the consequence. Well I hope Grant can do better, that's all I can say. The reason why I speak of Grant instead of Thomas as taking the place of Rosecrans is because Grant is now in command of <u>this</u> Army.

I send you ten dollars in a letter to morrow I will send you ten more in this one and now I will be sending my best respects to and kindest wishes to <u>all</u> of you.

Ever your effectionate Brother, J. S. H.

Back in September, Major General Ambrose Burnside had ceased Knoxville and garrisoned it with approximately 12,000 infantry and 8,500 Cavalry. Still angry with Longstreet for his delayed response to Hooker's movements in the Lookout Valley, Bragg determined to exercise President Davis' suggestion to send Longstreet to retake Knoxville and open the rail lines from eastern Tennessee to Virginia. Bragg now ordered Longstreet to move north to Knoxville and secure it for the Confederacy.

Longstreet's two divisions numbered about 10,000 infantry. He was also given around 5,000 cavalry under Joseph Wheeler. Longstreet correctly reasoned that he would be outnumbered while attempting an offensive and diluting the Army of Tennessee in the face of a strengthening northern force before it was not a wise strategy. Bragg ordered Longstreet to proceed with his orders and by November 5, Longstreet and his men no longer supported Bragg's army which now held an even thinner siege line around Chattanooga.

Burnside was secure in Knoxville and supported by the local populace of Unionists. Yet supply limitations reduced his ability to aid Rosecrans during his trial under siege. Lincoln had urged him to support Rosecrans prior to Chickamauga and early in the siege, but now felt it best for him to stay in Knoxville and defend against a Southern attempt to retake the town.

Longstreet's approach to Knoxville was fraught with issues of transportation and supply. It took him eight days to make the first 60 miles. He continued to move slowly toward his objective, pushing his troops forward each day. On the 13th of November a Confederate cavalry force of three brigades was sent forward with orders to take the heights on the south bank of the Holston River, commanding the town. When they arrived they found those heights to be heavily fortified and had no choice but to return to Longstreet.

In an attempt to slow Longstreet's advance, Burnside had taken 5,000 men south to meet him and delay his progress. On the 15th, as Longstreet was crossing the Tennessee River he was informed that Burnside had a force within five miles. Longstreet attempted to cross the river and gain a point on Burnside's line of retreat that would certainly lead to his destruction, but Burnside moved too quickly and the opportunity was lost.

There was another opportunity for Longstreet as both forces approached Knoxville. Fifteen miles south of the city the roads merged into a single road heading to town at Campbell's Station. Longstreet had been informed of a shortcut that was lightly used and undefended and moved to again cut Burnside off. The night of the 16th was a rainy affair and both armies slogged through the mud and mire toward the pinch point. At one point the Confederates, moving parallel to Burnside's column, brushed against his right flank. Thus alerted, Burnside pressed on with added vigor in order to reach the crossroads ahead of Longstreet.

His exhausted troops gained Campbell's Station fifteen minutes before Longstreet's van engaged them. Longstreet outnumbered Burnside and could easily drive him but didn't want to push him toward Knoxville and the safety of his fortifications. Trying to flank the Union forces and yet cut off their line of retreat, Longstreet sent 2 brigades around the Federal left to get in Burnside's rear and force him away from Knoxville. Burnside observed the movement and was able to defend against the attempt and hold the crossroads and keep the path to Knoxville open. By noon of the 17th, Burnside was safe within his Knoxville works and Longstreet had been frustrated in each of his attempts.

Chapter Twelve

The Union Breakout

In Chattanooga, things were about to take another turn for the worse for Bragg. Upon the securing of his line of communication through the Cracker Line route, Grant began plotting a way to take the initiative and go on the offensive. He now had three commands to work with. Sherman, his favorite, had arrived with the Army of the Tennessee. Not only did he have the utmost faith in his friend "Cump" Sherman, the Army of the Tennessee was his previous command that had performed so well during the Vicksburg command. George Thomas had the Army of the Cumberland entrenched in Chattanooga and was rebuilding their morale following the debacle of Chickamauga. Grant was not sure if they were ready to take the offensive against an enemy entrenched on high ground; particularly the army that had thrashed them so soundly during the previous battle. On the right, Grant had Joseph Hooker with the XI and XII corps. They had come west from the Army of the Potomac to add weight to the Union effort there, but Grant was sure that Meade hadn't released two of his top corps. Both corps had not performed well at Gettysburg or previous battles for that matter.

Axel Reed's diary entries of the 20th and 22nd portended the upcoming fight to drive Bragg from his heights around the city. He espoused the hopes of fellow soldiers of the Army of the Cumberland to have the chance to avenge their defeat at Chickamauga and conquer those who had beaten them so soundly.

Friday, Nov. 20th, '63. General Sherman is said to have reached this place and is going to take his command to our left. It appears that preparations are being made to drive Bragg's rebel army from their stronghold, occupying Lookout mountain south of us, Missionary ridge, forming a semi-circle out three mile from the city, to the Tennessee river above. We have been besieged here ever since the 22nd of September, on one-half and three-quarter rations, but the rank and file of the army have good heart and all we ask is the privilege of fighting our enemy and driving them from their stronghold. The Tennessee river forms an "ox-bow" and the main part of the city of Chattanooga is in the 'apex' where our army lies, hemmed in on three sides, south, west and north, leaving us but one way out by a wagon road to the southwest over the Cumberland mountains. General Hooker has brought the 11th and 12th Corps from the east, camped in Lookout valley, near the base of Lookout mountain; Gen. Sherman brought a portion of the army of the Tennessee from Vicksburg, secreted them behind Waldron's ridge on the north and west side of the river, while 'Pap Thomas' holds the army of the Cumberland in hand ready to strike a heavy blow when Gen. U. S. Grant says the word.

Sunday, Nov. 22. Our company with the brass band turned out this afternoon and accompanied their deceased comrade, Gilbert Jackson to his long resting place. It is the last act of respect that we shall ever have to show to the departed comrade. He has gone from this world of trouble, where wars and conflicts rage, to one of peace and quietude. While our band was playing a solemn dirge over his grave, our cannon were booming from Fort Wood, throwing missiles of death and destruction into the enemy's camp. In another part of the camp, unprincipled squads of men are gathered together gambling, by a game called 'chuck-a-luck,' common in the army. Tonight brings us a renewal of orders to march in the morning with 100 rounds of cartridges, with two days' rations. A fight is expected, for we cannot move far without having one. God grant that we may be victorious. Whose lot it is to fall no one knows but Him that directs all. We have the consolation to know that we fall in a noble cause.

Grant determined to rely on Sherman's army to execute the critical maneuver. Sherman would march from Bridgeport to Brown's Ferry where the Confederates would certainly see him cross to the north side of the Tennessee River. He was to then march north of the city, disappearing behind the hills to confuse the enemy. Ultimately he would make a night crossing of the Tennessee east of Missionary Ridge and move on Bragg's supply hub at Chickamauga Station. To further conceal this movement, after Sherman had taken position behind the hills north of the town, the XI Corps, under Howard, moved forward from behind those same hills, crossing the Tennessee to take positon behind Thomas. Grant's hoped for enemy confusion was accomplished.

Bragg was uncertain of where Sherman was headed but decided in the end that he was headed north to Knoxville to reinforce Burnside. On November 22, Bragg, in turn, ordered Simon Buckner's and Patrick Cleburne's divisions north to reinforce Longstreet. That evening, a Confederate deserter informed Grant that Bragg was withdrawing from Missionary Ridge. If true, there was an opportunity to strike immediately. Sherman was not yet ready to advance, so Grant ordered Thomas to make a recognizance in force into the Chattanooga Valley to see if the Confederates had indeed withdrawn. The valley lay between the heights of Missionary Ridge and Lookout Mountain and the Federal works of the city. A wooded hill named Orchard Knob was central to the valley and Thomas was told to advance and if practicable take the hill.

On the 23rd, Thomas Wood's division marched forward on the left and to his right was the division of Philip Sheridan. Both had fled the field at Chickamauga after Wood's movement created the gap in the army's center which was used to such great effect by Longstreet's assault. Both divisions were eager to prove their fighting worth as a consequence.

Both divisions marched smartly and quickly toward Orchard Knob. A fierce battle ensued for a brief time, but before long Orchard Knob was in Federal hands. Thomas ordered Wood to hold the ground while he sent support to advance the line. The Army of the Cumberland had gained a mile's advance position from where they had started. That evening they fortified their ground.

In addition to bettering his starting point for an assault by a mile, Grant also learned that Bragg was still in place and intended to stay. Bragg realized that Grant was looking to take the initiative and recalled Cleburne's division from Chickamauga Station where they were about to board trains to reinforce Longstreet.

That same day, Sherman had moved his army to a hidden point eight and a half miles northeast of Chattanooga and had pontoons hidden on North Chickamauga Creek, waiting to cross the Tennessee River.

Shortly after midnight on November 24th, Sherman began moving the pontoons into position and ferrying men across the River to the east side at the foot of Missionary Ridge. By noon the next day, the pontoon bridge was complete and both his men and three divisions of General Howard, who had been assigned to support Sherman, began crossing in earnest. As the lead elements ascended the hill they faced no opposition. When they reached the crest, Confederate artillery opened on them as they hauled their own artillery to the top by pulling them manually with ropes.

Sherman reached the crest and looked around. It had been raining and misty throughout the day. When he had viewed Missionary Ridge two days earlier it had looked like the ridge was continuous to the point where he had launched his attack. Now that he was there he realized that a deep ravine separated his current position from the true objective looming to his right and front. The movement had been smooth and faced little resistance for good reason. It was the wrong hill. All hope of surprise had been lost as well as a valuable day's effort.

On the far right of the Union position on the morning of the 24th, Joseph Hooker had positioned three divisions with instructions to attack Lookout Mountain. His ultimate goal was to get around the base of the mountain and into the valley that separated Lookout from Missionary Ridge in order to threaten Bragg's left and rear while Sherman was rolling up his right.

He ordered a two pronged attack. Geary's division waded across Lookout Creek and assaulted the base of the mountain from the west and further to the south. When he reached a ledge beneath a sheer cliff he moved to his left and proceeded toward the north end of the mountain.

One and a half miles north of Geary's approach, Brigadier General Peter J. Osterhaus moved his division over a bridge capturing the Confederate Pickets in his front. It was a very foggy morning and the Confederates on the slopes above couldn't see what was going on beneath them. While a respectable force of 7,000 Confederates defended the mountain they were spread out across its front and could not concentrate to defend against the Federal assault on the plateau beneath the cliffs.

By 10:00 A.M. Geary's force had reached the shoulder of the mountain at the site of the Cravens farm and was joined by Osterhaus to form a line across the entire plateau ledge. They drove into Brigadier General Edward C. Walthall defenders who were only 1,500 strong. They faced 10,000 Union troops motivated to take the prize. Worse for the Rebels, the guns atop Lookout Mountain couldn't be depressed enough to fire upon the assault just beneath them.

Walthall's men fought desperately but reinforcements became lost in the fog and arrived too late to afford relief for this position. Walthall was driven four hundred yards to the rear to a second line of defense, as his reinforcements under General John C. Moore arrived to lend a hand. The fighting was hand to hand in the trenches.

At 1:30 P.M. a fresh brigade of Confederates under Brigadier General Edmund W. Pettus arrived from above to try to hold the line. Walthall's Brigade was all but demolished at this point. As Pettus' men entered the works, Walthall pulled back his tattered remnants to reform and replenish ammunition.

The Confederate line held in this position as darkness, hastened by the heavy fog, finally brought the fighting to a close.

That night Bragg decided to evacuate the troops on Lookout Mountain. Fearing Hooker's men might gain Rossville Gap and cut them off while reaching his own rear, he felt the need to preserve the troops positioned on the mountain and attempt to strengthen his left flank that had become vulnerable.

The morning of the 25th found Old Glory floating in the breeze on the crest of the mountain. For all the drama and duration of the fight, the casualties involved were light. Hooker lost a total of 480 men. The Confederates lost 1,251. Over 1,000 of those were captured and missing.

Years after the battle J.P. Smartt, the assistant historian for the Chickamauga and Chattanooga Military Park, reported on General Walthall's memory of the fight to the "Confederate Veteran" in the following excerpt.

Gen E. C. Walthall on the Battle of Lookout Mtn.

From his dedication of the Chickamauga and Chattanooga Military Park as reported by J. P. Smartt, assistant historian of the park:

Battle of Lookout Mountain wasn't much of a battle "above the clouds". Nov 24th: The result of the combat was the capture of Lookout Mountain by the Federals under Major General J. Hooker. The fight itself was not much of an affair. Walthall's Brigade was posted on the "bench", a ledge part way up the mountain that extended from the eastern face of the mountain around the northern tip then back south on the western side of Lookout. Beneath it the ground was rugged and steep. Above it was sheer cliff. It was wide enough, according to Walthall "with enough open space for a garden and a small field west of Craven's house." Craven house was on the northern tip of the ledge and visible from the Union artillery positions opposite on Moccasin Point.

Confederate batteries on Lookout Mountain controlled Brown's Ferry which was the key access point for any supply line via rail or river into Chattanooga. Until the Union Army captured the hills covering Brown's Ferry on October 27th. This opened the "cracker line" providing uninterrupted supply from Stevenson and Bridgeport and effectively breaking the siege.

With Longstreet's withdrawal to eastern Tennessee in early November, Bragg's lines were critically thinned, particularly on his left, including Lookout Mountain.

Walthall's Brigade was detailed to picket a line about a mile up from Lookout Creek to the cliff and then west and north on the "bench" to the Craven house on the northern tip. Union batteries controlled any approach that reinforcements might attempt in order to assist him. Hooker had nine thousand men committed to the effort. Walthall had a brigade of fourteen hundred and eighty nine effectives for the defense of the mountain access. Heavy columns of Union troops crossed over Lookout Creek on the morning of the 24th where Walthall had 2 regiments to contest their assault. Others moved quickly up the rugged slope of the mountain so that Walthall's greatly outnumbered men faced an enemy assaulting them on two sides. Despite the odds, Walthall's men fought courageously and as Gen'l Thomas report said,

"the resistance was obstinate,". *Bragg in his report called it*
"desperate". (pge 563)

Ultimately a large part of the command was captured but their tenacity combined with the rugged terrain made it tough going for the attacking Union troops. Any support from the top of the mountain was meaningless as a dense fog made visibility from above and below impossible. As Walthall's troops withdrew towards and past Craven House they were supported by Gen. Pettus who came to his aid with 3 regiments. Reforming at a narrow point on the eastern side of the mountain and out of the range of the Union batteries on Moccasin Point they held this position until nightfall.

Overnight, Bragg withdrew his forces on Lookout to the east, repositioning them on Missionary Ridge. Consequently, Hooker advanced to the top of the mountain, securing the crucial position for the Union.

Some 180 miles to the south, John Hagan of the 29th Georgia was recovering in the hospital following Chickamauga. He wrote to his wife Amanda telling her he would soon be returning to Chickamauga. Of course he had no idea of the fighting of the 24th or what was to befall the Army of Tennessee on the 25th.

Lagrange Ga Nov 25th 1863

My Dear Amanda, I jest receved yours of the 20th & the letters enclosed from Harriet. I was proud to hear you got home Safe & found all well, but Sorry your father had Such truble about the trunk. I have no news to write you times are as usual here. I am yet at Mrs. Hoffs but do not expect (to) stay here long. I am still improving. I am so lonesome it Seams like I know not what to do, but I know I shal go to Chickamauga as soon as I get the box if I continue to mend. Amanda I did not Say as much as I should have Said to you in regard to renting the land to Mr. Thomas. If he rents the place he will want to plant some cotton & if he plants cotton he must pay the 4th of it when picked out, it matter not how small a patch he plants & he must pay the third of everything elce such as corn fodder sugar cane & potatoes you know he got the rest of the pease at the house for nothing. This you must look to that if you should rent it to him. You know I told you to sell the place at 1700 dollars & if you have not bargained the place away at that price before you get (this) letter you had better put 300 dollars more on and ask two thousand as & if any one wants it bad enough to give that price you can sell & if not you can rent it as we want to rent it a nother year anyhow. So asking 2000 will do no harm as we are not anxious to Sell, til a nother crop is made. You must not forget to ask enough for both the mule & hogs for pork is agrate object now but be shure to sell it on its feet if you can. I would not sell the corn if I could move it for it will raiz you a nother bunch of hogs for a nother year, etc. I understand times is very warm about Chattanooga now. We espect a big fight soon. I entend going to the command as soon as I think I can stand the cold. We are having a cold time here now. I will close as I have nothing to write. You may deredt the next letters to me at Chickamauga, Tenn or I will enclose you an Envelope. Give my love to all.

I am as ever your truly
John W. Hagan
P.S. you never said anything about Reubin in your letter you must not foget him when you write.

Back at the far left of the Federal Line, Sherman had spent the night of the 24th preparing to attack the correct hill on the 25th. There he had 25,000 men in six divisions ready to advance at day break. Cleburne's Confederate division had been reinforced by troops from Lookout Mountain overnight and together they totaled 10,000. They were well entrenched on the top of Tunnel Hill. Sherman's force would have to move down from the hill they occupied, cross the valley floor under fire, then attack well entrenched troops at the top of a steep ascent.

At 10:00 A.M. on the 25th, Sherman ordered the advance and three divisions moved toward the Confederates on the opposite hilltop. Confederate artillery blasted holes in their lines as they moved across the valley floor before they became protected by the base of Tunnel Hill. When they reappeared on a ridge less than 100 yards from Cleburne's line, he ordered his infantry to open fire. For over two hours the lines swayed back and forth, charging and retreating in close combat. Both commanders of the opposing brigades at the point of the attack were badly wounded in this melee.

Further to the right of Sherman's line, the assaulters of Loomis' Brigade fought belligerently against two Georgia Regiments. The Georgian's gave ground slowly, but ultimately Loomis was stalled by their relentless resistance and artillery canister that took a heavy toll. Loomis called for reinforcements and troops under Brigadier Charles L. Matthias climbed through the fire and up the hill to join Loomis' left. The entire crest was ablaze with fire and remained so until around 3:00 P.M. when two groups of Confederates, two regiments under Brigadier General Alfred Cumming and Smith's Texas Brigade under Cleburne's direct command, made bayonet charges on Matthias. The union center was beaten back by this vicious attack and the right under Loomis withdrew down the hill as well. Sherman was getting nowhere.

Grant wanted one of Bragg's flanks turned in order to complete his plan. By 10:00 A.M., with Sherman's efforts off to a slow and questionable start, he ordered Hooker to advance on Rossville Gap and take it. Hooker moved as quickly as he could but had to repair a burned bridge over swollen Chattanooga Creek. He arrived at the gap around 3:00 and immediately engaged an Alabama brigade under Brigadier General Henry D. Clayton. With Cruft in the Federal van, Hooker drove two of Clayton's regiments from the gap and held a foothold on the southern slope of Missionary Ridge. Breckinridge had arrived on the scene as Clayton's regiments were falling back from the gap in order to take direct command, but Hooker's three divisions were too much for him. All he could do was carry out a fighting retreat as Osterhaus' division poured through Rossville Gap into the Confederate rear.

With Bragg's left flank gained, Grant now ordered Thomas to advance the Army of the Cumberland on the Confederate center to take pressure off of the struggling Sherman. Thomas' orders were to only take the rifle pits at the base of the ridge and await instructions.

Thomas' assault included some 20,000 men with Absalom Baird's division on the left, then Thomas Wood's, Philip Sheridan's and Richard Johnson's on the right. As this strong line approached the rifle pits at the base of the ridge, the Confederates opened with a tremendous volley that ripped holes in the attacker's formation. But the Union troops of the Army of the Cumberland would not be stopped and continued their advance. The Confederates in the rifle pits immediately turned and retreated up the slope behind them. The Union troops were encouraged by their flight and pushed onward. The Confederate troops on the crest above were dismayed at seeing their front line dissolve so quickly. The effect was demoralizing. None of those on the top of the ridge were aware that earlier in the fight, Bragg had ordered the troops in the rifle pits to fire one volley then withdraw if attacked; an order that would prove to be disastrous.

The Federal artillery stopped firing at this point so as not to inflict casualties on their own men. The Confederates above started firing down upon them and creating a situation that would be untenable if they remained. Grant, Thomas and Granger were watching from Orchard Knob as suddenly the blue troops began moving up the ridge. Grant demanded to know who had ordered them forward. The answer was, "No one." With their blood up and bound to make the day successful, some men in Willich's brigade began to move up the hill. Soon more were moving up and quickly after that the entire line swarmed toward the crest of the ridge.

The Army of the Cumberland fought its way toward the crest through terrible terrain including brush, trees, boulders and steep inclines. It was arduous and draining but the Union troops' adrenalin was pumping and on they came. As they came nearer the top, the Confederate defenders were again the victims of Bragg's initial order and poor planning on the part of their defensive engineers. Many of the defenders couldn't fire on the advancing enemy due to Bragg's order. Their friends, who were still making their way to the main line after abandoning the rifle pits below, were in their line of fire and they refused to risk shooting their own men. The chief engineer of the Army of Tennessee had laid out the defenses for the Confederate line on the true crest of the ridge instead of the military crest. The military crest is several yards below the crest, creating a clear line of sight for firing on an advancing enemy. With works on the true crest of the hill, their line of sight was blocked by the edge of the ridge, so that advancing troops were under cover until they crested the ridge itself. This meant far fewer casualties for the assaulting force as they advanced as well as a shorter distance to the works once they did come under fire.   While this wasn't the case along the entire Confederate line, it created enough opportunity for the Union troops to gain the crest at crucial spots despite heavy fire from properly positioned Rebel soldiers.

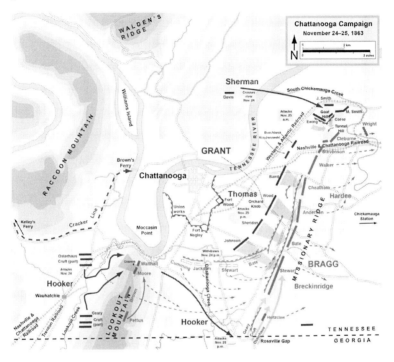

As more and more soldiers of the Army of the Cumberland breached the Confederate positions on top of the ridge, the Army of Tennessee seemed to lose its will to fight.   It was clear that the Union soldiers they had defeated at Chickamauga could not be stopped.   Slowly at first, then suddenly the entire line dissolved and every man fled with only the thought of saving himself.   Bragg and Breckinridge tried desperately to stop the stampeding retreat but to no avail.   The two commanders barely escaped capture themselves.

Almost the entire Army of Tennessee was fleeing in disorder with the exception of Patrick Cleburne's division which had held Sherman's attackers at bay and beaten them back.   When informed by General Hardee of the disaster to his left, Cleburne reluctantly pulled his men off of Tunnel Hill and formed the rear guard for the defeated and retreating Confederates.

Brigadier General John Turchin's brigade was the first to reach the summit of Missionary Ridge during Thomas's assault. He completed this after action report on his brigade's action on Missionary Ridge. The impetuous assault of his brigade was generated by its impossible position in the rifle pits and rebel works at the base of the ridge once they'd gained them as originally ordered.

Hdqrs. First Brig., Third Div., 14th Army Corps

Chattanooga, Tenn., November 30, 1863

SIR: On the 23rd of November, I received orders from the general commanding the division to move my brigade, consisting of the Eleventh, Seventeenth, Thirty-first, Thirty-sixth, Eighty-ninth, and Ninety-second Ohio and Eighty-second Indiana Volunteer Infantry, and take position in front of the fortifications in two lines, the right resting on the Rossville road, the whole division forming an oblique line with the Fourth Army Corps, then advancing on our left toward Mission Ridge. Our pickets drove in the pickets of the enemy, and during that day and the 24th we remained in the same position.

On the 25th, the division was ordered to the left, and at 1 p.m. took position on the left of the Fourth Army Corps, my brigade being on the left of Beatty's brigade, Wood's division. As was afterward ascertained, the order was that, at the signal of six guns fired in succession, the whole line of the center, including our division, would advance and storm the enemy's position on Mission Ridge, but the order was brought to our division after the guns were fired, and some troops of General Sheridan's division on the extreme right were storming the ridge when we commenced to advance, which was a little after 3 p. m.

I had the first line (Eleventh, Thirty-sixth, and Ninety-second Ohio) deployed, and the second line (Seventeenth, Thirty-first and Eighty-ninth Ohio and Eighty-second Indiana) in double column at half distance. The last two, being small regiments were formed in one column. Thick underbrush, Citico Creek, and the rebel rifle-pits impeded considerably the movement of my first line, so that when it had passed through the woods to the edge of the clearing between the woods and the foot of the ridge, other brigades on my right and left were already crossing the clearing, advancing toward the ridge. I halted my brigade for a moment, and saw at once that the space between the woods and the ridge was under a cross-fire of powerful rebel batteries on the ridge, on the right and left, and the rebel skirmishers, partly in rifle-pits at the foot of the ridge and partly on the slope of the hill on our front. I saw General Beatty's brigade on my right and Colonel Van Derveer's brigade on my left, reaching the rebel rifle-pits at the foot of the ridge and dropping down along the ditches, and I decided to cross the clearing at the double-quick.

Both lines moved on a run with a cheer, passed the clearing, reached the rebel rifle-pits at the foot of the ridge, and wavered for a moment, some men dropping down to escape the murderous fire from the enemy's artillery and musketry. Knowing that men dropping down under fire are very slow to get up and start again, I urged my regiments on, and they again rushed forward and commenced to climb the hill, some of the flank regiments running over the heads of General Beatty's and Colonel Van Derveer's men lying in the rifle-pits on my right and left.

It was impossible to require regularity in the movement up the hill. The bravest and the strongest men grouped around the regimental colors, advancing steadily, the balance following irregularly, the head of the column being very narrow and the tail spreading right and left widely. Three regimental flags of my brigade waved to the breeze almost on the top of the ridge, while the brigades on my right and left were yet lying in the rifle-pits at the foot of the ridge.

Three regiments, the Eleventh, Thirty-first and Thirty-sixth Ohio, reaching the rebel breastworks on the point A* of the ridge, stormed them, driving the enemy partly down the hill, but mostly along the ridge to the left toward the house B, to which the rebels drove two cannon from the point A, and where there was already one cannon planted, working along the ravine in its front. This last cannon *was captured, but the other two continued to drive down along the ravine.*

At the same time, the Ninety-second Ohio and Eighty-second Indiana, with a detachment of the Eighty-ninth Ohio, working their way along the ravine to the left, reached the point C, where two more cannon were captured.

The Seventeenth Ohio having been directed by me in the first place to the right of the point A, drove the rebels from the ridge, charged them down to the woods, and turning to the left to join the other regiments of the brigade struck at the Point M, down in the hollow, the two cannon before mentioned, which had passed the house B and were trying to escape down the ravine. Our men fired at them, and the rebel artillerymen cut the traces and ran away with the horses, leaving the cannon. These two pieces, with the limbers, were brought on the ridge to the point A, a little before dark, by some men of the Thirty-sixth Ohio sent be me for that purpose, and were left there to the men and officers of Beatty's brigade, Wood's division.

When the point C was taken, our fire obliged the rebels to abandon two pieces of artillery which had been planted at D to fire along the ravine to their front.

The bravest men rushed up the next knob to the left to the point E, and charged on three cannon planted there and supported by rebel infantry. In the first charge they captured the cannon, but the rebels rallying, drove our men back. At this time the men of the Second Brigade of our division climbed the hill. Another charge was made and my men, supported by men of the Second Brigade, took those guns and drove the rebels more to the left.

At this time the Third Brigade reached the top of the hill, and our division took the ridge to the point F, where the fighting continued some time after dark, and where our men built in the night some breastworks.

During the assault and fighting on the ridge my brigade captured alone 7 cannon, and with the Second Brigade captured 3 more. Most of them were smooth-bore 6 pounders and Napoleons; 1 or 2 rifled 10 pounders. Some of the cannon, as the prisoners stated belonged to Scott's Arkansas (Tennessee) battery.

Besides the cannon, 2 rebel flags were captured – 1 regimental flag by the Thirty-first Ohio and 1 battle-flag by the Eleventh Ohio. These flags were subsequently sent, with a separate report, to the general commanding the division.

The fighting continuing on the left, and the regiments being somewhat disorganized, my whole attention was paid to organizing the regiments. It soon became dark. I was ordered to bivouac at the point G on the east slope of the ridge, and soon afterward I received orders to leave the ridge, move backward on the western slope and occupy a position at the foot of the ridge, facing north, to prevent a surprise from the enemy, who still occupied the ground between our division and Sherman's troops at the tunnel.

After leaving the ridge, I do not know what became of the cannon captured by my brigade, but as Beatty's brigade, Wood's division, occupied the hill which we stormed and most of the ground to the left of it, I presume the guns were taken by the regiments of General Beatty's command, and perhaps some by the Second Brigade of our division.

The fact was that, reaching the top of the hill, we had more serious work to perform than to count and guard cannon. The enemy was in strong force on our left, and until the Second and Third Brigades climbed the hills assigned to them, all our energies were directed to fighting the enemy, and not to grouping and displaying systematically the captured cannon.

The enemy's fire on our right, and with it all danger there, had ceased for a long time, while my brigade was still fighting alone with a powerful enemy on our left. I moved my brigade down the ridge to the position assigned to it, and bivouacked there during the night.

At 7:30 a. m. of the 26th, the brigade was ordered on the ridge again, and at 9:30 a.m. made a reconnaissance to the front to the bridge across Chickamauga River on the road to Chickamauga Station, *the general commanding the division being present. Some 20 prisoners were captured.*

At 12 m. the brigade was ordered to move on to the ridge by the Chickamauga Station road. There we joined the other two brigades, and the division moved on the Ringgold road, bivouacking for the night 6 miles from Ringgold.

On the morning of the 27th, the brigade moved to Ringgold, and was placed in position in the reserve of the division. We remained there during the 28th, and on the 29th returned to Chattanooga.

The gallantry of the officers and men of my brigade, during the assault on Mission Ridge, cannot be surpassed. They showed a nerve and bravery that can dare any danger.

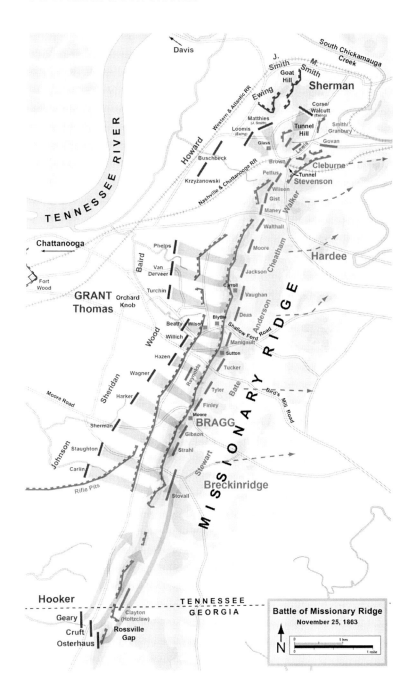

Axel Reed participated in Thomas's assault of Missionary Ridge. His diary tells his personal story of the 2nd Minnesota from the 23rd of November through the 25th. His description of the fighting on the 25th had to wait to be recorded until February.

Monday, Nov. 23. Fell in line at 4 o'clock and stacked arms and remained ready to move, but was not called upon until about 3 o'clock, when we marched to the front, outside of our breastworks and in front of Fort Nagle. The 11th Corps came over the river last night and laid during the day at the right of Fort Wood. Our forces advanced on the rebels on the left and heavy cannonading and musketry took place. The object is thought to be to turn the enemy's right and get possession of Missionary Ridge.

Tuesday, Nov. 24th, 1863. Bivouacked last night in line of battle about half a mile in front of Fort Nagle (east). All quiet along our front, but considerable firing occurred away to our left where it is said that our men have possession of Missionary ridge. About 8 a.m. we heard a skirmish fire of Hooker's men, over the point of Lookout mountain, and by spells until about 11 o'clock, when it appeared closer, and steadier, it became evident that our men were driving the rebels and gaining the mountain. Our batteries opened heavily and we could plainly see the shells burst far up the side of the mountain near the point. At 12 the firing became heavier and we saw the rebels come running over the ridge in haste, followed closely by our men. Every man along our line cheered lustily for the success of our boys. The rebels retreated across the field and over their own line of works, to the edge of the woods, where they still resisted the advance of our forces as our victorious column rushed across at double quick. The side of the mountain being steep and rocky the rebels had the advantage in ground, as they could fight behind rocks. The heavy firing ceased about 2 p.m., and only desultory firing until 4 o'clock, when the rebels were reinforced and advanced to drive our men back, and at this writing the batteries are raging hotly. Our batteries have moved down to Chattanooga creek, and are keeping up a brisk fire on the rebels. A thick fog has settled over the side of the mountain and shut out the exciting scene from our view.

I returned to camp (in Chattanooga) about 4 o'clock to draw a day's ration for the men and take out to them. Rainy and signs of a bad night. The last sentence written with right hand.

Feb. 18, 1864. My journal was cut short on November 24th, and has remained unwritten for reasons of an accident which occurred to me November 25th at the storming of Missionary Ridge, which resulted in the loss of my right arm. After returning from camp with rations, to my regiment, we lay in line of battle all night near the picket line. It was a very cold night and we suffered greatly. The fight was kept up by Hooker's men and the enemy on the mountain until 11 o'clock at night and we could distinguish the two lines by the flash of their guns, the rebels leaving the mountain during the night. In the absence of any commissioned officer, the command of the company fell on me. During the forenoon of the 25th, we marched towards our left to the support of Gen. Sherman, but turned back about noon and marched back to the front a little to the left of Fort Wood, and about four o'clock we were ordered to charge the rebel works at the Ridge, without firing a gun – the 2nd Minnesota being deployed in front of the Brigade. The line of works was taken without serious loss. The impetuosity of some of the troops led them over the works and up the Ridge after the enemy. Gen. Grant seeing this, ordered the whole line and support forward; and the whole Ridge in front was swept as if by a 'hurricane' and about fifty pieces of cannon fell into our hands. I reached the top of the Ridge and fired two shots into the retreating and confused rebels, and then in company with more disorganized troops, followed them up every man for himself. After following them some distance I came suddenly near them where they were rallying for a stand around a new Confederate flag. I fired at a rebel that had just mounted a horse to ride off with a piece of artillery, and before I got loaded again a Minnie ball struck my right arm, shattering the bone for eight inches above the elbow. I had to lie for some time between the fire or our men and the rebels, before our men succeeded in driving the rebels, which was a happy moment to me. I succeeded in getting off my coat with the help of a wounded comrade, and tearing the strap from my haversack, and tying it above my wound, partially stopping the blood. I walked down to the foot of the Ridge, (meeting our victorious legions rushing onward to victory) about dark, just in time to find a wagon drawn by six mules, going to Chattanooga (3 miles distant) which carried me direct to the 3d Division, 14th Army Corps Hospital, where my arm was amputated about 9 o'clock p.m, Nov. 25th, 1863.

Charley Caley's 105th Ohio also participated in the successful assault of Missionary Ridge. He began to write home on the 23rd but was interrupted by orders to advance and remain in line ready for action. He was finally able to finish his letter on the 27th with good news for his family.

Chattanooga Tenn Nov 23rd 163

Ever dear ones at home it is with pleasure that I now seat myself to pen you a few lines to let you know that I am will and I sincerely hope that this will find you all enjoying that necessary blessing. I have answered all the letters that I have received from home and have waited anxiously every day but have received no answer yet. therefore as I expect to be in a battle before long I could not forbear writing to you as it may be the last time. we got marching orders last night every man to have a hundred rounds of catdriges and full rations and be ready to march by four o Clock in the morning but from some cause or other the order was postponed for a while and I snatch this opportunity of writing to you. Yesterday they throwed about 30 shells over into the rebels camp from our fort but could not get any reply. to morrow or next day we will have some hot work with them for they have got to git out of there

Nov. 27th Well now I will write a few more lines I received your kind letter written the 16 of nov. I got it on the 24 but had to read it on the battle field where we have been every since the 23. But I must give you some more of the particklars of the late battle on mission ridge. it was this way, I was writing in the tent when the bugle sounded fall in. then the officers gave orders for every man to have 60 rounds of catdridges. we attacked the rebels that afternoon and drove them to the foot of mission ridge which was about two miles. stop that night and built breastworks all night and the next day rested. that night slept about 2 hours. the next morning (25th) went on picquet at 8 o,clock. while we was out there the bugle sounded to advance the *lines. every man of us took his arms at a trail and then went creeping through the bushes as though he was hunting deer. Well we went on about half a mile that way when bang-bang came all along the rebels picquet lines. however we routed them and drove them into camp where we was ordered to halt and hold our position which we did. we was then relieved and went back to the reserve lines rested about to hours had our catdridges boxes replenished and then the whole army moved forward to take mission ridge. they had all gone to the top of the mount. well we advanced through the timber without any difficulty but when we emerged into the open field no pen can describe with what swiftness they poured in their shot – shell grape cannister and every other deadly missle you could think of. still we advanced right up the hill. it was when we got about 2 thirds of the way up the hill that my pardner was (shot) through the thigh and the lieutenant was shot in the breast killing him instantly. the 49 Ohio got within stone throw of their fort when they stoped to fixed bayonets and then charged on the works. never before did men fight with such fury as the rebels did to hold their fort. they even shook their flags in each other faces but it was of no use for they had to give back. our brigade captured two thousand and 1000 stand of small arms. I would write more if I had room write as soon as you get this from your affectionate son CC to M.S.C*

Captain John Ellis, 16th Louisiana recounted his experience from the 15th to the 25th in his memoirs explaining how his regiment held its position on Missionary Ridge quite handsomely until they were flanked and attacked in both the left and rear with no support.

About the 15th of November Stewart came to camp and I determined to send him home. Through this instrumentality a breach was healed which was made in my boyhood, between myself and one for whom I should and for a long time did cherish the warmest feelings of friendship.

On the 23rd of November I rode some 6 miles to defend before the court martial of Hardees corps an Irishman of the 13th, named Patrick Mooney. He was tried for mutinous and seditious conduct, but was acquitted. The verdict was most righteous, but the Lieut. who appeared against him should have been cashiered.

On my return soon after crossing the ridge I noticed that the firing of artillery was more constant and rapid than usual for there had been every day more or less cannonading. In the camps I saw much bustle and confusion. I stopped and listened. Soon I heard away out towards the picket line the sound of musketry. I rode rapidly on for half a mile and again I listened and this time I could not be mistaken. The picket lines were hotly engaged and occasionally a volley could be heard which told me that the reserves also were fighting. I hastened on to camp and found the regiment in the trenches. However, at night the firing ceased and we withdrew to our tents and cooked three days rations. That night I gave Stewart a pass, money and letters and directed him to go next morning to Chickamauga station, take the cars and go home.

At daylight (November 24th) we were in line and moved forward to the picket station. The day was dark and gloomy and the rain fell incessantly. From our position with glass we could see the fighting which was going on at the base of Lookout Mountain. We could plainly hear the musketry. Towards evening we sent to camp details to pack up the baggage and load the wagons. A little after midnight I went back also and saw the wagons loaded. The firing had gone steadily up the mountain and had not ceased. Our troops had been driven back. Upon the dark mountain side there was incessant flashing as of thousands of fire flies and the smothered dull report of the guns were quite distinct. Browns gun brigade came down off the mountain and passed through our old camp.

That night I saw the last time a valued friend, Capt. Sam B. Wilson 45th Tenn. He was killed some months afterwards in Georgia while gallantly facing the invaders of his country.

At daylight (November 25th) the brigade moved back and when the sun was rising, it moved up the ridge and took up a position, built fires and made ourselves as comfortable as possible. I lay down and slept an hour or two and then was awakened to move further to the right. All day long we were moving from left to right then back again to the left. From the top of the ridge we could see the Yankees in countless numbers swarming the valley below. About three o'clock dense masses of infantry were moving towards our right where Gen. Hardee was posted. At 4 we were placed in position and drawn out in a single rank. The men were from four to six feet apart so as to cover as much ground as possible. And now we saw three lines of battle emerge from the woods and advance toward our position. Our batteries opened on them and shell after shell burst over and in their ranks, but they pressed steadily forward. When within two hundred yards our skirmishers opened and after firing a few moments retired up the ridge. Still the Yankee lines came on and began to climb the ridge which was so steep that our artillery was of no use, for guns could not be depressed sufficiently to bear upon them. They came on slowly to within 100 yards when our Col. as cool as if on review ordered us to fire. There was a spurt of flame a thousand jets of smoke and roar which shook the hill and when we could again see through the drifting war cloud, the Yankee line broke and in disorder was retreating down the hill. The second line came on, again we opened and again it was hurled back. The third fared no better and in turn was compelled to retreat. At the base of the ridge another line was formed and advanced up the ridge. At a distance of 150 yards, the enemy lay down behind rocks, trees and stumps and began desultory and scattering fire up the hill. They seemed to make no effort to come further and our men by order of the Col. almost ceased firing. He was in high spirits and affable to all. He reminded me of MaCauley's remark about William III at the battle of the Boyne. Writes the historian "Danger acted on the spirit of William like wine upon other men. It rendered him affable and gentle and took away all the constraint of his saturnine nature." (I quote from memory). This is eminently the case with Gooer. That evening he was unusually gay and good humored. His last words to me were, "Save your ammunition. This fight may last for hours and there is but little now to shoot at. Let you men fire only when they have a good shot. If your ammunition gives out fix bayonets and remain at your post. We can hold this place with rocks." He passed on and I communicated his instructions to the company. But there were no troops on our left and a division of the enemy moved up the ridge without opposition and came down on our left and rear. The left began to give way but I could as yet see no cause for it. Soon a Yankee came running along parallel with our line, but 30 yards in rear of it Lieut. McArthur thought him one of our own men, for they some times, out of sheer necessity, dress *in Yankee uniform, and running towards him with uplifted sword, ordered him back to the line. The Yankee raised his gun, it almost touched McArthur's face, and fired. The brains of the gallant Scotchman were spattered over the ground and he fell dead without a groan. Lieut. J. F. Kent rushed forward and snapped his pistol in the Yankee's face. It failed to fire and the Yankee sprang behind a tree. Then a whole platoon of the enemy discharged their guns at Kent. They were not over twenty yards distant and how he escaped I cannot divine.*

Now for the first time I saw the extent of my danger. I could see myriads of Yankees in our rear and I started to retreat. But it was too late. Arriving at the top of the ridge I saw that we were totally surrounded and all hope of escape cut off. A Yankee captain demanded my surrender. I threw my sword down the ridge and with very bad grace, submitted. I was a prisoner. Lieuts. J. P. & W. C. Kent were also captured and indeed my whole company, with the exception of two or three men. We were immediately marched down the ridge where a crowd of prisoners was collecting. As I passed down the ridge my only satisfaction was the sight of many dead Yankees. They were lying thick all along the course which their lines had occupied. Our regiment lost about 60 men and officers captured & 1st Lieut. Eastman, Ganter and McArthur. Not one of my company was wounded, except a little fellow whom a brute who wore "shoulder straps" shot with a pistol after he had surrendered. Only a slight wound, however, in the hand was the result of this brutal and cowardly act. Just at dark we entered Chattanooga and were turned over to the provost marshal of Maj. Gen. Gordon Granger's corps. He was a very gentlemanly man and in fact with one or two exceptions I was treated as a gentleman by all the officers of the Army of the Cumberland. But the provost Marshal, Cpt. Kaldenbaugh, was especially kind to me. I had not been totally disarmed and still wore a pistol and knife under my overcoat. I gave them (belt and all) to Capt. Kaldenbaugh. He furnished me with pens, paper etc. to write and promised to have the letters mailed which he doubtless did. He was from New York originally but was a Captain (before his staff appointment) in the 50th Ohio Infantry. For a long time we were kept out in the cold, for the night was frosty and then we were separated, the privates sent I don't know where, and the officers, 135 in number were placed in a room 20 by 30 ft. We lay down after a time and went to sleep. There was scarcely room for us on the floor and some of us were compelled to lie upon the feet and across the legs of our fellow captain. Thus passed away my first night of prison life.

Bragg's army collected itself at Chickamauga Station before retreating further south into Georgia that night. When the battles for Chattanooga were over, the casualties for both sides had been relatively light compared to the enormity of the victory for the Union. The Confederates lost 6,700 men. 4,100 of those were prisoners. Grant's armies had lost 5,800 men, killed wounded and captured.

William Talley described the escape of the 14th Georgia artillery as follows.

...Not long afterwards the Yanks began to advance. We were ordered on top of the ridge and the plains were alive with moving Yanks. Bragg thought the Yanks were concentrating on his right and moved most of his army to the right. The troops passed us nearly all day. About night we got orders to go to the Chickamauga River near the station and lay down but a courier came with orders to go back to the place we had left where the road crossed the River near Bragg's headquarters. The Florida brigade supported us and they were deployed one man eight feet apart. At Bragg's HQ the 5th Co. of Washington Artillery from N. O. was stationed and the brigade who was to support them failed to get there and the Yanks charged with three lines of battle but the Florida boys, even if they were only one man every eight feet apart, held the line till the Yanks got to the place where we did not have a man and came on the flank on the Washington Artillery and captured every one of their guns. Our lines broke just north of us and the Yanks turned down our line from there and Bragg's HQ and had the Fla. Brigade and our battery between three fires and we were ordered to retreat and we <u>got.</u> Bragg wanted to make a stand on the next ridge and our battery was ordered to go up that ridge. We got about half way and 'twas so steep and rugged we had to turn back. One wheel horse fell as the place was so steep and ran the wheel behind a tree so orders were given to cut loose and leave the gun, so we lost it. When we got to the little narrow valley, the Yanks with three lines of battle

were coming down Missionary Ridge far enough apart so that they could shoot over the heads of those in front. We struck the little road and made for the gap where the road went to Chickamauga Station, in full view of those three lines of battle and all three lines shot at us all they could but strange to say they did not hit a man or horse so we got out and made for Chickamauga River & Station. The next day we started the retreat for Dalton, where we arrived in safety, and went into Winter Quarters.

George Thorn of the 13th Ohio was happy to write home on the 27th that he had survived the battle and was among the land of the living.

Nov 27th 1863
Chattanooga Tenn
Dear Parents

It is with the greatest of pleasure that I write you a few lines to inform you that I am still in the land & among the living after another hard desperate battle which I have been in which commenced on the 24th & lasted until the present time & whitch we have gained one of the greatest victories of the war. We have taken Lookout Mountain & also Missionary Ridge capturing 64 pieces of artillery & from 12,000 to 15,000 thousand prisoners & the rebs flying in evry direction leavin all of their stores & way on trains of about three thousands wagon whitch they had to burn (to) keep from falling in our hands. Theire is some forty thousand of our Cavalry & mounted infantry after the flying foe just cutting them all to pieces.

My health is very good only I have caut a badd cold on the acount of having to lay out on the battle field with out our blankets for we did not want to bother of caring them so we left them in camp last night but are under marching orders. That is our division. I thought we will go to knoxvill to help Burnsides out of a snap that he has got in to. I can not tell you any particulars about the battle now for it would be long & tedious. You will see in the papers for your selves. Perhaps before this reaches you. I hope the time is not long before I will be home if my life is spared & then I can tell all of what I witnessed & took a part in.

Father I now inclose a recipt of the state agent of Ohio for forty five dollars which I payed over to him for you to draw for me to be payed through the State & county treasure of Ohio & I want you to go to Newark & draw the same so I shall close by sayin good by till you hear from me again.

My love & respects to all of our friends. Your Son with Respect

George F. Thorn

Direct to Chattanooga Tenn
Co H 13th Regt 3rd Division 3rd Brigade
4th Army Corps

Not all soldiers were able to send good news home. Alfred Searles had been detached as a guard for a wagon train during the fighting that would secure Chattanooga for the Union. Upon his return to a mostly joyful Chattanooga, he received surprising news regarding his brother who had been sick, but not hospitalized, when he departed.

Chattanooga, Tenn.
Nov. 27, 1863
To my dear parents, brothers and sisters,

This also will bring sad news to you, but the painful truth I am now like any others forced to tell and that is my dear brother is dead and buried. Oh, it seems hard dear parents, but Jesus heals all wounds, they say. It may seem strange to you that I have not written but I will tell you I have been away with a supply train. I left camp the 24th of Oct. and returned yesterday. When I left Addison was no worse when I left then he has been for a month. Oh, little did I think it was the last time that I should ever see him, but he was taken worse rite off and sent to the hospital and our lieutenant applied for his discharge and got it fur him about two weeks before he died. But he was too weak to move, and all this time I was only 40 miles away and never was notified by him or any one else of his sickness. He died and was buried the Day before I got back.

Oh, none but God can tell how I felt when my comrades told me Ad was dead. Oh, it rings in my ears yet, and I am all most crazy to day fur I am not well nor never expect to be again. It is a lung disease. The doctor said one of Addisons lungs was all gone. I have learned that the Lieu.(Lieutenant) Has wrote to you fur to come after Addison. If you have not started befur this reaches you, perhaps you had better wait a few days till you hear from me again, fur it is a matter of doubt weather I shall find his grave.

Alfred Searles

Henry Robison took the responsibility to write the letter informing Adelbert Hannom's father that his son had died from a wound suffered during the assault on Missionary Ridge.

Chattanooga Tenn Nov 30th 1863

Friend George. It is with pain that I inform you of the Death of Adelbert. He was shot in the bowels in making the charge on Mission Ridge on the afternoon of Nov. 25th and died sometime in the night of Nov. 26th. After the fight was over myself Herman and 2 of the other boys went back to the ambulance station to see how he was and if he was well taken care of. We found him in good hands but he complained of his wound hurting him at times. he would get up by himself and set up awlrite but could not lay down with out help. I thought at the time he would not get well as he did not bleed any that we could see (although the ball had passed through him) the doctor came there before we left and he said he was filling up with blood inside and said he might live a day or two but could not get well. We staid with him as long as we Dare to and the Doctor said he would take him to the Hospital wich he did. He gave Herman his pocket book and told him to send it home. Herm will send it home by Express in a few days. There is also 2 lettrs here for him wich he will send to you. George this is a hard letter for me to write and perhaps before this letter reches you in all probability his Death may be published in some of the Northern Papers and you will see the account of it. But at the same time I thought it my duty to write to you and let you know how it was. I have endeavored to do so to the best of my ability

George it is hardly worth while for me to attempt to tell you all that we accomplished on this expedition as you will get a better acount of it in the papers than I can give you but I think by the way the Rebs Deserted over to us when we was fighting them and the Cannon guns and clothing they threw away that the Rebelion was about played out in these parts anyhow. At least I hope so any how. George we got back in camp after Dark last night. I am tired and sleepy and am not very well just at this time. The rest of the boys is about like myself and that is very tired as these Tennesee and Georgia hills does not rest one very much. I will now close this short letter hoping that it will find you and your family all well. My best respects to all and a share for yourselfs I remain your friend and well wishes.

Henry Robison

Some two weeks after the battle, sergeant C. H. Williams wrote another sad letter to Mrs. Mary Mason, describing the death of her son Benjamin of the 137th New York during the taking of Lookout Mountain by Hooker's corps.

Wauhatchie Valley Tenn.
December 8th/63
Mrs. Mary Mason, Dear Friend

It becomes me to break to you the painful news of the death of your son Benjamin F. Mason. He fell with many of his comrads while Charging Lookout Mountain the 24th day of November. He was hit with a Rifle Ball. It entered the left side and come out of his back. He lived about ten minutes when his spirit took its flight I trust to a world where trials and troubles never come. Benjamin was a good soldier ever willing to do his duty when called upon. We feel to mourn his loss with you. You have lost a dear son. We have lost a comrade. He is buried on the North side of Lookout Mountain. There is a board at the head of his grave bearing his name and date of his death.
You have our consolation "that is this" he fell at his post & in the discharge of his duties. May god Comfort his weeping mother while I remain your friend.

Sergt. C. H. Williams
Co "B" 13th Regt NYV   Nashville Tenn.

Summit of Lookout Mountain 1864

Signal Corps Station

(all images courtesy of Library of Congress)

Major General Ulysses S. Grant   Major General William T. Sherman
(Sherman was Grant's most trusted general. Sherman was also
Grant's closest confidant and supporter.)

Major General Joseph Hooker   Brigadier General John B.Turchin

United States of America
(all images courtesy of Library of Congress)

271

Major General Patrick Cleburne   Major General Benjamin Cheatham
Confederate States of America

Action at Missionary Ridge Tennessee Nov. 25 1863 between Troops
under General Corse and confederate troops under General Cleburne.
Pencil drawing Possible Alfred Waud Library of Congress

(all images courtesy of Library of Congress)

Chapter Thirteen

Longstreet 's Failure at Knoxville

At the time of the assaults on Lookout Mountain and Missionary Ridge, Longstreet had pushed on to the outskirts of Knoxville. Upon arriving, he and his staff surveyed the Federal defenses and spent some time determining where an assault would best stand a chance of success. By the 23th of November they had determined to attack Union Fort Sanders on the northwest corner of the Federal defensive line. All was ready for the attack on the 24th when a courier told Longstreet that 2,600 reinforcements were on their way to him from Bragg. Longstreet decided to wait for them.

On the 26th, Bragg's chief engineer, Brigadier General Danville Leadbetter, who had built the original Knoxville defenses, arrived in order to provide his advice regarding the best place to attack. Another day's delay was made. Later that day, Longstreet was observing the Federal position at Fort Sanders one more time when he noticed a soldier walk across the ditch in front of the fort. Having no idea how deep the ditch was that stood at the base of the eight foot walls, this observation made Longstreet confident that the assault would be successful at this point and rescheduled the attack for the 28th. It rained all day on the 28th and the assault was again delayed.

The original battle plan called for a heavy bombardment of the fort preceding the infantry assault, but late on the evening of the 29th Longstreet opted for a dawn assault and surprise instead. In advance of the assault he ordered sharpshooters to take the enemy rifle pits in front of the fort prior to the attack. This was done at 2:00 A.M., but the capturing of the rifle pits alerted the fort's defenders of an impending attack. The element of surprise was lost and when dawn came the defenders were ready.

Part of the reason for selecting this point for the attack was that a wide creek bed that afforded stealth and cover allowed the attacking troops to get within 120 yards of the Federal works. What had been unobserved was that the Union troops had wound telegraph wire around stumps that had been cleared for a field of fire creating a maze of wire that tripped up the attackers and slowed their advance. The waiting defenders threw a massive amount of canister and rifle rounds at them as they stumbled their way to toward the ditch at the foot of the fort's walls. When they reached the ditch another surprise was waiting for them. Longstreet had observed a soldier walking across the ditch 3 days before. What he failed to observe was that the soldier was walking across a plank. The ditch was eight feet deep. The assault troops descended into the ditch but couldn't get up the sixteen foot walls that faced them. It was like shooting fish in a barrel.

A few of the attackers made the top of the parapet only to be slain or captured. Within 20 minutes the assault had become a massacre and completely blunted. Longstreet called off the attack. He had lost 813 men and the defenders in the fort had lost eight dead and five wounded. It was another unmitigated disaster for the Confederates.

South of Chattanooga, Grant had ordered the pursuit of Bragg's troops on the 26th. Hooker followed Bragg and fought a spirited but short fight with Cleburne at Ringgold, Georgia on the 27th. On the 28th Grant ordered the pursuit to cease. He was concerned about the low amount of supplies available to sustain a further advance as well as Burnside's situation in Knoxville. On the 29th, the day of Longstreet's failed assault, Grant ordered Sherman to take his Army and Granger's Reserve Corps to relieve Burnside. By the time Sherman arrived in Knoxville on the 3rd of December Longstreet had abandoned his siege, having failed his attack and knowing that Sherman was in route with a large force. He found sanctuary in the mountains of Eastern Tennessee for the balance of the winter and would return to the Army of Northern Virginia in the spring and serve out the rest of the war under Robert E. Lee.

After their long march from Chattanooga to Burnside's aid, Thomas Maroney, 89th Illinois Volunteers, expressed his disappointment in not catching Longstreet before he broke off the siege and abandoned his attempt on Knoxville. He also shared his sadness for their captain who had been wounded during the attacks on Missionary Ridge and died in the hospital. This loss left his company and the entire regiment very saddened.

Camp near Strawbery Plains Tenn
Dec 21 1863

Dear Father, parents
*   I received your very kind letter that arriving after cumming up from picket and was very glad to hear that you were all well as this leaves me at present. Last night was the first mail we got since we left Chattanooga. It took us nine days to march from Chattanooga to Knoxville about a week when we marched to this place it is 13 miles north east of Knoxville. We did expect a fight here but Longstreet ran away. So we did not march any futher nor I didn't think we will. It is reported around that we will go back to Knoxville or Chattanooga and go into winter quarters, but I don't know how true it is. We all felt very sory when we hear of the death of our Captain. We did not hear of it until yesterday. I don't think we will get another mutch better a man for Captain. He was the best man in the whole regiment. We don't draw government ration any more. They give us flour and corn meal and mutton. Salt pork is played out. We make our flour and meal up into flap jacks. When I come home I will show you how to make jake cakes. When you write again let me know if you heard from Mr. O'brien. We would like to know if he is in our lines yet or not. We don't hear any thing here from the boys taken prisoner only what we hear from home. I am very glad that Thomas is hear, and is well*
*   now close for this time. Ned Whalen sends his best wishes to you all no more at present from your loving son*

Thomas Maroney

Direct
Thomas Maroney Co. C 89th Regt Ill. Vol.
1st Brigade, 3rd Division 4th Army Corps
Department of the Cumberland Knoxville via Nashville Tenn

Our Brethren are on the Field

Part Five

Chapter Fourteen

Winter of 1863-1864

As December settled in, the Confederate and Federal armies found themselves squared off on either side of Rocky Face Ridge which ran east to west just north of Dalton, Georgia. The south would never recover from the events that led to the securing of Chattanooga by the Union. Bragg had resigned on the 30th of November and his demoralized army wintered near Dalton.

There the Army of Tennessee's new commander, General Joseph E. Johnston, began to evaluate his army's condition and rebuild morale.

Benjamin Chapman wrote to his wife Sarah early in the month to let her know that he was well. He described the losses in his company of the 19th Alabama and expressed how forlorn the troops felt. His level of depression is such that he tells her he will come home anyway if he doesn't get a furlough.

In Camps near Dalton Ga.
December 8th, 1863
Dear Wife,
I thank god that I have the pleasure of informing you that I am yet on the land among the living well and hardy. I do hope that these few lines may come safe to hand and find you and the children enjoying the same blessing. Sarah, I have nothing of much interest to write to you at the present. Sarah I wrote you a few days ago but not knowing whether you got it or not. I will give you the number of our boys that we lost in the fight at Missionary Ridge. We lost 15 of our boys, not knowing whether they was taken prisoners or killed. I will give you the names of our lost. Lt Crowley, Sgt. Strong, Sgt. Jackson, and Angle, W. H. Busbin, Gilham and Downy and Godfeys two boys. Wm. Mason, James Smith, Whit Vandiver and Wm. Nichols, E.M. Richardson. We don't know whether those boys was killed or taken prisoners. Benjamin Howard was killed dead in the breastworks. Sarah, the Yankees came on us three lines deep. They crawled up the mountains to our breastworks. There was some of our boys knocked

them back with rocks as they came up on us. The rest of the boys is all well and hearty at the present time, but are all out of heart about the war. I don't think that this war can last much long(er). I think that we are all good but the shouting.

You wrote you had all your corn shucked and measured up, you had 57 bushels of corn, Sarah I wrote to David H. to have my corn hauled down home or sell it and buy down there. I thought it would be better to haul it and buy close to home if he could do that. I wrote to him to get my lather to Mr. Rice to make them for you and the children could get your winter shoes made. Sarah I sold Whit two of the sows hogs for $80.00. John Veatch will pay you for them. You can take up that note Whit has got on me. I will come to a close Sarah. I sent my clothing home by John. I sent two pair of pants, two pair drawers and my short coat and pair of pants was William Busbin and a cap he sent John B. Busbin and I sent one to Isaac Newton. If I could see you I could tell you more than I can write in a week.

Sarah if they don't give me a furlough before long I intent to come home anyhow. Write as soon as you can and I will do the same. I would be glad to see you and the children.

Yours truly husband until death
Benjamin F. Chapman
to Sarah A Chapman

In the Union Camps, men were preparing winter quarters and looking to refit their units and increase the supplies needed to sustain them through the winter while preparing for the offensive campaign that would certainly begin next spring. In mid-December, Charlie Gano of the 21st Ohio wrote to his brother after receiving a letter from him for the first time in a number of months. His brother's missive had apparently provided an adequate excuse for the long delay since he had answered a letter from Charlie.

Chattanooga Tenn,
Dec. 14th 1863
Dear Brother,

I once more seat my self to answer your kind and welcomed letter that came to hand yesterday. it found me in poor health but glad to hear from you and glad to hear that you was all well but

278

mother. I was very sorey to hear that she was sick. Tell her that she must write to me. I am always glad to hear from her. I hope that these few lines may find you all well and so doing you said that you had been away on a viset. I thought it very straing that you did not write to me as I wroat several letters to you that I had not herd from and I had maid up my mind that they was not welcomb aney more an I had better quit writing but your being absent accounts for it. and then you also said that you had taken you a wife and that accounts for it all. I wish you much joy a long and happy life. there is comfort to be taken in a married life if there is nothing raised to make disturbance in the family. I hope that there will be nothing to mar your peace or prosperity. You said that you would like to hav my stove if I would sell it and that I should set a price on it. I could not do it as I know not what it is worth now, but you can have the youse of it if you want and if I should be spared to git home it will not be hard to settle and if I should not you will please give to the suport of Mary the valu off it and it will be all right. You may please write to me and tell me if father had sold jentel. I heard he had sold her. I would not take forty dollars for her. I was offered forty five for her. I was offered thirty five for her in cash when I was at Nashville.

I have wroate several times to you to know about that place and about the pens around it but I have received (no) satesfaction a bout it. I have wroat a bout the last battle that was fit hear. So I will not say aney thing bout it. Presedential Linkien sent his thanks to the army off the Mississippi for what it had dun and gave us prase. I must close for this time. I send my best wishes to you and all hoping to hear from you soon. I have but little time to write so good by.

I remain as ever your brother
    C. M. Gano
    to W.W. Hill
    Direct as befor

Another Ohioan from the 89th Volunteers of that state wrote to his parents to let them know that he was well and settled into his camp. What supplies and rations they had were good but still not plentiful at that point.

December 16 1863

Dear parents,

It is with great pleasure that I write you a few lines to let you know that I am well and hope that you are as I write you a few lines will find you the same condition. We are still in our old camp in good health but not much to eat. But still as good as could be expected.

We have prety good what we have but not much of it. The army is in the best health that (it) ever know. I suppose that you have got some letters from me since the battle. I have wrote you all the past news of the great battle of look out and mission ridge. Deserters still coming in with reports Braggs army is demorilized and will not stand a fight. There is one after another, great many wounded rebs in the hospital and some of them is sick of the war, and there (was) one came to me and was talking and he laid his hand on my shoulder and said that if he could get well and get home he would never take up arms against the old flag. But he thinks that he will never get well. He is shot in the head and he is in a bad fix. There is some of the noblist kind of rebs here out of a few the most of them is as clever as any bodey there was. Some of them gave me crackers and I was glad of that. we have a nice time here. Nothing to do but eat and drink. We have not got our haversacks yet. But the teams have gone after them and we would have them soon. I have not a letter for 10 days and I am tired of writing. I want you to write often. I want you to send me some stamps and paper small sheets and some yellow envelopes for we can not get them here. I did not send any money home for rations is scarce and we can get bread once in a while and I have that you do not want to starve. I will save all the money that I can with out suffering my self for I know it is at home & I want to buy a home

Your son Samuel

Charley Caley of the 105th Ohio wrote to his wife on Christmas telling her about the winter quarters he and his mess had constructed out of tents and wood. Half way through the letter he remembers that it is Christmas.

Chattanooga
Dec. 25th 1863

My Dear Juliaett, I hope you wil excuse me for not riting sooner after getting your leter of the 13th which I reseived last

Thursday but come to think that was but yesterday. wel yesterday I was very busey and also for two or three days before we have ben fixen up our tents for winter quarters and I think we have got very comfortable tents to live in now. we put up four shelter tents for the roof then got some boards and built up the sides and ends and have a good fire place and chimney and have two beds inn a tent for four of us. I like them very much beter than I did the large sibley tents that we stayed inn last winter. My tent is warm as a house and I think much nicer. I had almost forgotten that to day was Christmas and I now wish you a merry Christmas. how I wish I was home with you. Wel I suppose you would like to know what I have ben doing this morning. I went to the slaughter yard to see if I could get a beefs head to eat but thare was no one butchering. I then came back to camp and don my washing then made a door for my tent and by the time that was don it was noon and I guess you cant guess what I had for my diner. I had just one thin slice of pork about three inches square. We got but one cracker for to day and I was so hungrey that (I) eat mine for breakfast and should of liked one or two more to put with it. Last evening was (a) very mery one inn camps all round here. the boys got out and fired off their guns and oald anvels and hallowed round until ten o'clock. it make me think of some of the scirmishers that I have ben inn.

I am glad that my box is on the road but I am afraid it wil be a long time before I get it as it is about all that can be got through now is about quarter rations for the men. dos Wars folks hear anything from Hiram yet. it is time for them to hear from him if he is a prisoner at Richmond. I have not had a leter from Bil Thomas for a long time. neather have I hear from Marey. I don't see why they don't rite oftener. It has ben very coald here for four or five days and the ground is frozen quite hard. ice is about two inshes thick on the small ponds but I have not seen a snowflake this winter.

I wil now bid you a good by and rite soon again. rite often to you husband　　　　　　　　　　　　　　*Charley*
　　　　　　　　　　　　　　　　　　　to Juliaett

As the Army of Tennessee settled into winter quarters, Wesley Connor's diary recorded the despair the army felt after the retreat from Missionary Ridge and establishing winter quarters.

Friday Nov. 27, 1863 – Received orders to build stables for the horses. Indications are that we will winter here, though we will be governed entirely by Grant's movements.

Wednesday Dec. 23, 1863 – Nearly all the boys have built themselves winter quarters. Some have received supplies from home, and all are getting on remarkably well, but this state of things cannot last long. 'Twould not be compatible with military laws to let a private or privates see any more enjoyment than they could possibly help.

Friday Dec. 25, 1863 – Christmas has again rolled around and finds the Confederacy still stocked with soldiers. How long, Oh how long shall this curse rest upon us? How long shall our men be butchered up by the vandal hands of Yankeedom?

On New Year's Day, 1864 Connor wrote a few lines expressing his continued commitment to the southern cause.

Camp near Dalton
Friday January 1ˢᵗ 1864
The new year opened without anything of special interest. January 1ˢᵗ 1863, I believed the war would be closed ere another year has passed, and the strife still continues. Everything now has a gloomy aspect. The soldiers are disheartened, and deserting in large numbers. Some course should be adopted to encourage the army. Genl. Johnston having taken command of the Army, will in a great measure restore that confidence which is necessary to the success of an army. I have never been discouraged. Believing that we were engaged in a righteous cause, I have ever felt that, whether the war continued three years or ten years, it would end in the independence of the Southern States. Another year will probably decide the contest.

John Ellis spent his winter on Johnson's Island in Lake Erie. He had been captured along with his company of the 16ᵗʰ Louisiana during the assault on Missionary Ridge. Sometime after his arrival at Johnson Island Prison Camp for officers he penned this experience detailing his journey from Chattanooga to that camp as a prisoner of war.

I woke up early next morning and went down with a sentinel to the Tennessee River to wash my face and get some water. On the street *were four or five negroes, two of whom were dressed in the livery of "Massa Abe's Boys" (i.e.) in Yankee uniform. As I approached they retired out of my way and to my "how 'dye boys", they returned a respectful "Mornin Master" at the same time touching their hats. The negro <u>never</u> loses the instinctive respect which he feels for the Southern man. He may forget his inferiority to the Northern man, but no amount of contact or association will lesson his sense of inferiority and subordination to the Southerner.*

We remained four or five days in Chattanooga. Our mess was composed of Capt. Stagg, Lieuts. J. F. & W. C. Kent, John H. Prater and myself of the 16th La. Lieuts. Oliver 13th La. And Lt. C. F. McCarty, Austin's battalion, together with Maj Jas. Wilson, A.A.G. to Maj. Gen. Breckenridge and Joseph Cabell Breckenridge 1st Lieut. to A.D.C. to his father; Lieut. Robert Rollins, 2nd Ky. also belonged to the crowd. We were very kindly treated by the Yankees generally and had plenty of beef and "hard tack" to eat. We were guarded by the 10th Ohio Infantry and they allowed us many privileges.

We started on the evening of the 30th November for Kelley's ford, eleven miles below Chattanooga. Remained all night and took the boat next day for Bridgeport. Arrived there at three P.M. and remained till eleven that night, when we took the train for Nashville. We moved very slowly and it was dark on the evening of the 2nd of December before we reached that city. After two hours delay at the office of the Provost Marshal, we were marched to the Golicopper building where we found a place to sleep. The next morning we were again marched to the Provost Marshal's office and remained standing in the streets for three hours. Many ladies assembled on the opposite side and I knew by the glances which they cast towards us that they were patriot ladies. Glancing over the columns of a morning paper I found it filled with enormous lies. At the head of the telegraphic column was the startling announcement in tremendous capitals, "Rebels totally routed, 1500 prisoners, and 20 cannons captured." I wrote on a piece of paper a short and concise statement of the results of the battle for the Yankee officers at Chattanooga, were honest in their statements of their own as well as our losses and frankly avowed the defeat which they had sustained at Ringgold, as well as Sherman's repulse by Hardee on our right in the battle of the ridge. In my note I *wrote that the Yankee loss in killed and wounded was greater than our total loss, that only a portion of our army was engaged, that they were severely repulsed on our right and had received since the fight a bloody check at Ringgold. That they had captured only 3500 prisoners and that the people of the Confederate States were as far from being conquered as at the firing of the first gun at Sumter. Wrapping the note around a pebble I caught the eye of a lady (for they were not permitted to approach or speak to us) and when the sentinel's back was turned I threw it towards her. If fell at her feet, was eagerly seized and passed rapidly through the entire assemblage of ladies. I thought I could perceive a lightening of features, as if a load was taken from hearts weighed down by suspense and fear.*

After a time we were marched back to our quarters. About 3 o'clock a Yankee officer came into the prison and inquired for "Capt. Ellis of La." I answered and he simply told me that I was wanted at the office of assistant provost marshal and bade me follow him, which I did conjecturing the probable cause of my being called away from my fellow prisoners. Perhaps I would be paroled, or specially exchanged, or perchance I was to be placed in close confinement and held as a hostage for some "Rebel barbarity". I followed my shoulder strapped guide across a street, up two flights of steps and into a room which was occupied with beautiful and richly dressed ladies. There I also found Lieut. Breckenridge. My reception was most cordial. I was introduced to about thirty ladies. Some of their names I have forgotten, but others I will never forget. My wants were eagerly inquired for, money clothing was offered me – I accepted a pair of shoes, a blanket a towel, soap and comb. One lady <u>forced</u> me to take a little money. They left me with blankets, shoes, socks, etc. to carry to my fellow prisoners. They were much needed and I tried in distributing them to aid the most necessitous. God bless Nashville and its ladies. May the hour soon come when the invader shall be driven from the soil of Tennessee. Then these ladies who for so long have borne the insults of the Yankee, who have assisted in alleviating the distress of so many thousands of their wounded and captive countrymen, who have hoped and prayed and trusted, who have remained firm and steadfast in devotion to their native land through storm and sunshine, win their reward. May that day be not far away in the future.

From Nashville we went to Louisville where we found a most miserable and dirty prison. We remained a day and night. Had a splendid dinner with Lieut. Breckenridge, sent him by Mrs. G.R.P. crossed the Ohio river and took the cars for Indianapolis at 7 A.M. marched two miles to the Soldiers home and got breakfast. Took the train for Belle Fountain at 9 or 10 A.M. Lieut. J.F. Kent was very sick and I procured him a berth in a sleeping car where about fifteen confederate officers were with the federal officer in charge. They were all drunk, Yankees, Rebs. And all, except Kent and myself. Arrived at Belle Fountain at 12 midnight and lay over till morning. Got breakfast at a hotel where some "copperheads" alias peace democrats, alias, sensible men wanted and offered to pay for our breakfast and did pay the bills of some prisoners who were without money. Left Bell Fountain at 10 A.M. and reached Sandusky City at dark, took a boat and in half an hour were at Johnson's Island, and at 9 ½ o'clock we entered the pen amid cries of "where are you from?" "Fresh Fish!" "What did you come here for?" etc. from the prisoners who lined the doors and windows of the different barracks. We were taken to Block 7, up stairs where we slept on the floor. This was on the night of the 7th of December, 1863. The next morning I arose bright and early and found myself in a pen, some 16 or 18 acres in extent, surrounded by a high wall, on which armed sentinels were pacing their rounds. Thirteen blocks, two stories high even numbers were on one side and the odd on the other (except block 13 which was situated in the middle of the space between blocks 11 and 12) were the quarters for prisoners. Block 6 was the hospital. In the center of the yard between the buildings are the walls from which water was forced by means of pumps, washed my face on that morning and began to hunt for a "bunk". I went up stairs in Block 5 and found Bolvar Edwards, W.C. and J.G. McGinney, all old friends and schoolmates, whom I was glad to meet. Through them I found and obtained a bunk and began life in prison. For over fourteen months I have remained here, have met many old friends and formed some acquaintances whom I shall ever remember with pleasure and affection.

Back in Georgia, on the northern side of Rocky Face Ridge federal camps occupied the land from Ringgold to Charleston, Tennessee on the Hiawassee River. Following his march to Knoxville's relief,

Sherman had rejoined Grant in Chattanooga where they began preparing three armies for the campaign to capture Atlanta with the coming spring.

Chattanooga remained the headquarters of these armies over the winter of 1863/64. The government poured more and more supplies via the railroad and river into the warehouses that now lined the streets close to the river. The town was transformed into an armed camp full of uniformed troops and warehouses full of supplies necessary for armies on active campaign.

Dr. Thomas McCallie, the twenty three year old Pastor of Presbyterian Church of Chattanooga, was permitted to occupy his home with his family by the Union Command. He held services there whenever possible. He described the Christmas of 1863 thusly:

"I shall never forget the Christmas of 1863. Christmas Eve came. All without was winter. It was winter in the city and winter in the State. War had desolated everything. Our church was still used for a hospital and no bell rang out on the air telling us of God, His house, His worship. There was no Sunday school. There was no day school. The churches were all closed, the pastors, except myself, were gone. The old citizens had gone to the South or been sent to the North. Only a few families remained and they very infrequently saw each other. There were no stores open, no markets of any kind, no carriages on the streets, no civil officers, and no taxes or collectors, fortunately. Strangers filled our streets, highways and houses. The rattle of spurs of the officers and the tramp of soldiers fell constantly on our ears. The town was white with tents; tents, tents everywhere, soldiers' tents, sutlers' tents, with precious little in them, tents for negroes or 'Freedmen' as they were called. It was winter in the home except for a few precious rays of sunshine. We had no milk, no butter, no cheese, scarcely any fruit; but we had bacon, bread, such as could be made without milk or yeast, a little coffee, some sugar, and a barrel of pickles in brine but no vinegar to put with them. The rays of sunshine were good health, powerful divine protection, keeping us in peace when so many were being sent away from their homes, and a sense of God's forgiveness and watchful care of us."

During Confederate occupation of the town, Dr. McCallie had made a practice of praying for the Confederate president, Jefferson Davis, and bravely continued to pray for him after the city changed hands, even though Federal soldiers and officers attended his services. He was eventually arrested for this practice. The Military commander harshly reprimanded him before releasing him. Pastor McCallie stubbornly continued to pray for Davis.

The Regimental History of the 78th Pennsylvania published in 1905 described the unit's occupation of Lookout Mountain the first of December and remaining on its ridgeline until May.

> On the 28th of November we left Negley and returned to our encampment; and on the 29th of November, at 4 O'clock, we left our encampment and marched to the summit of Lookout Mountain. On the first of December we (marched) ten miles southward, countermarched some distance and encamped within nine miles of Summerville. On the second we marched about two miles south and halted in a place where there had been a confederate encampment. On the third we marched back to Summerville and went into camp, where we remained until the first of May. During the next five months in our camp on Lookout Mountain, we had our most delightful army experiences. During the months of December and January it was sometimes very cold, especially when we were on picket duty at night. The summit of Lookout Mountain is the highest point of land within a radius of many miles, and the wind blew frequently at the rate of from twenty to fifty miles an hour. It is hardly necessary to say that we dreaded picket duty on a windy night.

On January 6th, 1864 Samuel Hoffman of the 18th Ohio wrote to his sister to inform her that they were now receiving ample supplies and rations. He was assigned as part of General Steadman's body guard and the regiment had been conducting numerous patrols in the hills surrounding Chattanooga.

Chattanooga Tenn
Jan. 6 1864
Dear Sister,
> *I have been wanting to write to the folks but I have not had*

time to do it. I am sitting in a log shanty with a big fire in front of General Steadman's Head Quarters. We are his body guards. The regiment was out on a raid and just got back on Sunday morning with out any one hurt. It is snowing down here now but it melts as soon as it hits the ground, but the mud is knee deep in the streets. The hills is full of rebels. We went over to chop wood. We had a camp of about 80 men in it and we passed by them before we seen them until we had stacked our guns and (they) could (have) took us all prisoners...   ... before they had time to do anything. they had 45 men. They (were) making a plan to burn the bridge that the government had built. It cost one hundred thousand dollars to build it. One of the rebels told it, and we took them up to head quarters, disarmed them and put them in the military prison.

I am getting stronger and fat and healther every day. I fell (feel) as if I was at home. We have nothing to do but patrols, guards every three days. We have quarters large enough for four plenty to eat, wear, wood, blankets. We don't sleep on the ground, we sleep on boards. Lent Phillips has resigned and is going home. He is a fraid he will get killed if he don't. their not much hope if he does. For all the boys hates him.

Tell mother and father that they can pay Henry S. Lewis what they owe him on the lot out of my money, If they wish make him give you a receipt for it to and (if) there is any left you can live off it. if you want and raise onions, you can sell them in Cincinnati for 50 cents per dozens. If Hufnagle has not sent that box to Harry, send my hat. I must close my letter by telling all the boys and girls that enquires about me to write to me. Give my love to all. My friends, father and sisters and brothers. Tell Bill to play Bonaparts retreat for me all tho I will be far a way. Direct your letters to the 18th O.V.I. of Chattanooga Tenn.

Dear Maggie or William Wells, I received your kind and welcomed letter a few days ago and was very glad to hear from you and that you are well and enjoying all good health. to William wells & Maggie Harmon of Ohio a quick note to a friend's sister and not to waste paper and yes there were to and that's in the letters.

By the end of January the supplies and reinforcements were flowing into the city and soldiers were once again receiving full rations and recovering from their ordeals. Charlie Caley of the 105th Ohio wrote home to his wife telling her he wished he'd come home when wounded last year because he doesn't think he'll be able to get a furlough; those were going to three year enlistments that were coming up. If the men reenlisted they would get a bonus and a furlough home.

Chattanooga Tenn.
Jan. 31st 1864
My dear Juliaett,

I reseived two leters from you since I last rote. I am as usual wel and hope this wil find you enjoying the same blessing. the box you sent has not got here yet or had not yesterday after noon. I was at the express office to see if I could hear from it but could learn nothing about it. It may come yet but I am afraid it is lost. it continues warm and pleasant. our camp is fixed up and I think we have one of the nicest camps in town. to morrow one of our Lut. (Lieutenant) and the drivers start for Nashville for horses. I don't know whether I am a driver or not yet. if I don't have to go I am going to send in applications for a furlow but am afraid in all unless as there is so many gon from the company now. those gon are men whos time had expired and have reinlisted and getting furlows of from thirty to sixty days it seems to me as ift I had aught to have one. if any one has earnt one I think I have now. foolish I was when in the hospital (a) year ago last fall wounded that I did not runaway from the hospital and go home. they could of done nothing with me for it but its to late to think of that now and I was afraid to risk then.

I have heard of the spree that Co. F had Newyears eve and don't think it very strange of Nelson King. He don't know any to much any way and I guess its nothing nu for him. he is a mean low lifed scamp. Guess I have never told you about his striking a boy belonging to Co. H whilst on university hill. he got in a quarrel with him and stuck him with a club. nearly killing him and the fellow is not in his right mind yet. It would have ben a hard job for Nel if he had of ben found out. Don't say any thing about it. it has ben kept very still and I should not like to have the name of letting it ben known.

Wel Juliaett you say you want to see me. I dar say you do and I want to see you but if I cant get a chance to go home I must get along as wel as I can the rest of my time and that wel be half out next Saturday any way and if I have my health that wil soon pass. we are getting plenty to eat now and wil soon have plenty of cloathing. a rugeder (more rugged) set of men I never saw than has ben in Chattanooga for the last four month.

I wish you could see a negro regiment that is campt near us. if they don't put on stile then no soldiers ever did. When they go out on dress parade the regiment takes off their hats to salute the Col. And for all the stile (you) ever saw they can beat it . (14th U.S.C.T.)

I do not think when I began to rite that I should fill up a sheat but got it ful before I knowed it.

The 105th is getting a good many recruits now days. The sick that was in the hospitals are coming up and (I heard) some nu enlisted men are coming yesterday. twenty five came and some have come before. wel I guess I have riten about all I can for this time and wil now stop by biding you good by.

From Your husband Charley

On the 7th of February Charley responded to a letter his dear Juliaette had written the same day he had written to her last. He was still searching for the care package she had sent him a month ago and wistfully hoping for a furlough.

Chattanooga. Tenn.
Feb. 7 1864
My dear Juliaett

I reseived your leter of the 31st of jan. this morning and see by the post mark that it was mailed the 2nd making but five days for it to be on the road. I also reseived one from Thomas which was riten on the 2nd. he was at Mareys when he rote it. his health he says is very good this winter. He had got through working for Stephen Carroll at present. Stephen wanted to hire him for a year but he thinks he can do beter. he is going to work for Harmon Carroll this winter an thinks that he can get beter wages next sumar than he could to hire out by the year.

I reseived the fu lines that you rote last wednsday. I have spoken to the lieut. about getting a furlow but am afraid I cant succeed in getting it.   there is so many of the oald hands inn this company that is reinlisting and they of course have to have a furlow that I am afraid that I cant get) on(e).   The Lut. Says he wil do all he can towards helping me get one.   I was at the express office yesterday to see if I could find any thing of my box but could not.   there is hundreds of boxes at the office but none of them for me or this company. I saw Tom Casey at the express office. he wont reinlist. he is inn the 20th Ohio battery and says he wil serve the rest of his time out before he is fastened for three years longer.

We have ben having some very nice warm days here but it is coald and yesterday it snowed some but not enough to cover the ground and today it is clear but the wind blows quite coald. The depot inn town burnt down last night. it was filled up with nue cloathing for the armey inn the front and is very heavy loss to the soldiers as they are inn need of cloaths.

I guess I shall have to tel you about our inspection that we had this fore noon.   we have to get out inn time on the parade ground with our shoes blacked and clean cloaths on.   also every man has to have on his haver sack and canteen and have our tents all cleaned and blankets foaled and every thing has to be as clean as they can be made.

Wel Juliaett I have not much to rite this time. So I shal have to ask you to excuse this short leter on account of not knowin what to rite and my ink is very poor   so bad that I can Hardly rite atall

I wil now bid you good by and rite soon again. rite often to your husband

> *C.C. Caley*

their seems to be a great deal of talk of the 105th going to Cinncinati to be provo guard this sumar.

By the end of February the life of winter camp was taking a toll on Charlie Gano of the 21st Ohio. While the officers kept the men busy and rotating patrols broke the monotony of camp life, soldiers like Charlie had too much time to think of home and the loved ones they were missing. He wrote the following to his brother.

Chattanooga Tenn.
Feb. 23/64
Dear brother Henry,
*   I this evening (I) indever to address an answer to your kind letter that I received three days ago as I receive but few letters from home it is a comfort to me to hear from you all that remain at home. alow me to say that there is no place like home although I think that it is my dutey to stay my time out but still I appreciate society very much and hope that I may have the privedge off that happy day. but it is unsertain. well I have but little to write as I have so much duty to do at this time I must cut my letter short but inform you that my helth is good at this present time. I was glad to hear that you was all well with the exceptions off colds & hope that these few lines may find you all well. Oh Henrey it is a thing to be so long in the survices and cut out off (from) society. Well Henrey you must not think hard off me for not writing more this time as it is bed time and we are going on a three days out and start at five O'Clock in the morning. I have no news to write about the war but may have when I return if I do return. I think that there is sum Rebels that must be routed sum ware but they had better git out in time. I close by biding you good night hoping to hear from you often. Give my best wishes to all and you have the same with you.*
I remain as ever your friend and brother

C. M. Gano 21st Ohio
to Henrey W. Hill
Direct as before

With the massive buildup of troops and animals in Chattanooga, water for all purposes was scarce so a reservoir was built on the slope of Cameron Hill which was filled by a pump station near the river that constantly maintained its level. Gravity then delivered the water to the various outlets in town in order to meet the needs of the military and civilian populations. A gristmill was even constructed next to the pipeline that fed the city's water and the power of the water flowing downhill kept its stones grinding continually.

A shipyard was constructed near the pumping station. It built and maintained all manner of steamboats, barges and gunboats throughout the balance of the war.

The incredible quantities of materials needed to maintain armies the size of those operating in this war required fast, reliable transportation for hundreds of cars in order to sustain their missions. The Western and Atlantic Railroad became the central highway for Federal troops advancing south, deep into Georgia from Chattanooga in 1864. It also served the same purpose for what had now become Joseph E. Johnston's Army of Tennessee as his line of communications running north from Atlanta.

To keep the rails running, the Federal Government built a rolling mill and foundry in Chattanooga early in 1864. A traveler, who visited the community after the war, remarked that among the first things to be seen, as the train came around the foot of Lookout Mountain was the "lurid glare upon the black waters (of the Tennessee River) of sparks and flame sent out from the chimneys of a rolling mill that was busy day and night in turning railroad iron to replace the waste of war."[1]

Almost every vacant space in and around the community was converted to wagon and artillery parks, as well as pens for hogs, cattle and army transport animals. Homes and businesses became offices and barracks for various departments of the army. Churches were turned into the likes of ordnance depots and prisons.

In 1861 the Confederates had removed James R. Hood from the editor's desk of the Chattanooga Gazette due to his Union sympathies. Now, with the Yankee occupation, he returned to his desk and the first issue was published on Feb. 29, 1864. Army news was featured and extreme policies toward Confederate sympathizers were advocated.

Chapter Fifteen

Union Hospitals

Of equal importance to the building of this immense military depot was the care for sick and wounded soldiers. Immediately after the battle of Chickamauga, churches and hotels were added to the growing list of facilities the Confederates had previously developed to serve as hospitals. Now that Chattanooga was secure, additional buildings were constructed for hospitals and convalescent camps.

The Office of the Superintendent and Director of Hospitals listed 24 separate hospitals and their length of operation in Chattanooga. These hospitals were opened from between September 9, 1863 and July 19, 1865. A number of these hospitals were short lived while treating wounded from Chickamauga and the breakout in November, but six hospitals remained in service through the end of the war and beyond.

Hospital No. 1 - General Hospital Chattanooga Tenn. Opened September 17, 1863 and closed November 14, 1863 Located in wooden barracks, skirts of town near R.R. Depot on hill previously "Bragg Hospital" as Confederate Hospital. Being nearest to the depot. Sick cases were brought here as also the bodies of those who had died in the cars in route.

Hospital No. 2 - General Hospital Chattanooga Tenn. Opened September 20, 1863. Became the 1st of the 4th Army Corps Hospital September 28, 1863. Closed November 14, 1863. Temporarily used November 20 to November 25, 1863. Located in wooden barracks number 2201. Used by Confederates as a receiving Hospital.

Hospital No. 3 - General Hospital Chattanooga Tenn. Opened September 20, 1863 Continued as Division 3 of General Hospital. Location in the Crutchfield Hotel skirts of town.

Hospital No. 4 - General Hospital Chattanooga Tenn. Opened September 20, 1863. Transformed as Division Hospital 4th Army Corps Hospital September 28, 1863. October 17, 1863 Military Hospital added. Closed January 28, 1864. Located in three churches on Main Street. October 17, 1863 added a row of buildings on main street. (formally Hospitals 5 & 6), added Commissary store house October 21, 1863.

Hospital No. 5 - General Hospital Chattanooga Tenn. (Temporary Hospital) Opened September 20, 1863. Closed February 64. Location in lofts over Commissary store house on main street. September 25, 1863 to Division Hospital 14th Army Corps. October of 1863 made the convalescent Hospital until December 15, 1863. Closed February 1864.

Hospital No. 6 - General Hospital Chattanooga Tenn. Opened September 20, 1863. Building on Main street. Closed February 1864

Hospital No. 7 - General Hospital Chattanooga Tenn (officers). Opened September 15, 1863. Location a private house in suburbs formerly Johnson House. Closed February 1864.

Hospital No. 7 - General Hospital (non-officer) unknown location opened October 1863. Closed January 6, 1864.

Hospital No. 8 - General Hospital Tenn. Opened October 1863. Closed February 8, 1864. In location of brick Church on Main Street.

Hospital No. 8 - Officers Hospital No. 2 Chattanooga Tenn. Opened September 20, 1863. Closed October 6, 1863. Located in Private houses in town.

Hospital No. 9 - General Hospital Chattanooga Tenn.- Opened October 1863. Closed October 22, 1863. Location in frame building skirts of town and stores on main street.

Hospital No. 10 - General Hospital Chattanooga Tenn. Opened December 1863. Closed January 22, 1864. Location unknown.

Reorganized General Hospital No. 1. Opened June 17, 1864. Closed November 7, 1865. Last hospital that remained opened in Chattanooga. Location in wooden positions with a brick building as the Executive office near the site of old No. 1 General Hospital on Academy Hill.

Reorganized General Hospital No. 2. Organized and opened June 17, 1864. Closed March 15, 1865. Mainly in tents, skirts of the town near old Fort Wood.

Reorganized General Hospital No. 3- Lookout Mountain. Opened June 16, 1864. Closed October 5 1865.

General Hospital Lookout Mountain near Chattanooga. Open in May 1864- 405 patients. Closed July 9, 1864. Location unknown.

No. 4 General hospital. Colored and small pox. Opened September 30, 1864. Closed August 26, 1865. In parts of the buildings formerly the General Field Hospital.

Officers General Hospital (Lookout Mountain)- Opened May 7, 1864. Moved here from the town (Chattanooga). Location in three large buildings (two of them formerly Hotels) and some smaller buildings near Summertown on the summit of the Mountain.

Military Prison Hospital Chattanooga Tenn. Opened August 1863. Closed December 1863. Attached to the old No. 4 G. H.

General Field Hospital (Army of the Cumberland) Opened September 1863. Broken up October 14, 1864. In tents and wooden barracks south side of town, near Kelly's Ferry. September 1863 each of the 2 divisions of the Army of the Cumberland formed a field Hospital in Dry Valley where light cases were treated and no records kept prior to October. November 9, 1863 the site was changed to south of town and nearer the town. One ward was for contrabands and the other for small pox cases.

Provisional Hospital Chattanooga Tenn. (temporary Hospital) opened July 3, 1864 and closed October 15, 1864. In wooden barracks that were previously part of the G.F.H. General Hospital Chattanooga Tenn. Opened June 1, 1864. Closed March 1865. Barracks used as G.H.S.

Post Hospital Chattanooga Tenn. Opened November 3, 1865. Closed April 12, 1879.

Soldiers Home Chattanooga Tenn. A place of rest and refreshment for soldiers on the transit.

Joseph King of the 6th Indiana was wounded on the 19th of September during the battle of Chickamauga. One of the fortunate "walking wounded", he was able to evacuate himself and ended up in one of the general field hospitals near Chattanooga. He wrote the following to his parents.

General Field hospital near Chattanooga
Sept. 27 1863
Dear Father and mother,
I am getting along fine as could be except I was wounded Saturday Sept. 19 at sundown just below the right knee. It did not brake the bone, nor it affected me much, I was able to walk off the field of action a half a mile. The ball passed through the front part of my leg. It glanced around the shin bone. If it had went straight throw it

would have broke it I think. It was an Enfield ball that hit me. I have very good care taking of me here

I saw the captain last night. He says Daniel is well in the hospital. That I am 1 in three is five out of our company. Their names are orderly Paterson and Henry Hooker both wounded below the right knee by buck shot. Henry is a talking of going back to the company. He is out and walking now. Paterson is not so well, the shot passed through the shin bone. I guess it didn't break, it slivered it some.

Phillips leg is broke and slivered up badly. I haven't saw him yet. I will give you a list of the wounded as well as I can, G.C. Monroe right arm, Samuel C. Swift in the arm. E. Clemens in the hand and thigh not broken. Walter Truddle flesh wound in the thigh. Thomas Monroe slightly wounded. Wesley Die- David Rodaybough and John Dickson are missing. The total in our company wounded and missing is 11.

We went into the fight with about 30 men as near as I can recollect. I cannot tell you how much of the first day. We held our own on the first. We were ordered forward when I was wounded. Our men in front were falling back and as they passed our regiment, we were ordered forward, we checked them. It being to dark to see we drawed off that night a little ways. I guess you have heard all of the news before this time. You need be the least bit uneasy about me for I am not very bad wounded. This was the first chance I got to write. I have got my knapsack and all my things. I could write a good more but I guess it is sent (isn't) nessesary.

There is no fighting a going on today that I can hear of. I am a bout two miles from Chattanooga. Our lines are formed on the other side of Chattanooga. The rebels are here in great force. We are ready for them. I wish I was able to go and try them a gain. I don't know where to tell you to write to. I get the letters from the regiment. Yet if we stay here it will do to direct them as you always have

You son
Joseph King

Assistant Surgeon Dallas Bache completed his Memoranda of Events in the campaigns of the Army of the Cumberland about Chattanooga as a report on the execution of the medical department's duties from

Murfreesboro through January of 1864. The excerpt below begins with the army's position prior to the Battle of Chickamauga and continues through February of 1864.

..." *On the 7th (of September) headquarters reached Trenton, where it remained until the morning of the 9th, when the enemy, having evacuated his position at Chattanooga, it was removed to that point. During this time, since the crossing of the river, there had been but little sickness, most of the sick remaining with their commands, but few requiring to be sent to the rear. Immediately after the occupation of Chattanooga, orders were issued for the preparation of one thousand beds in the various buildings in the town, some of which had been previously constructed and used by the Confederates for hospital purposes; but as this communication was as yet both long and difficult, much difficulty and delay was experienced in obtaining even a meager supply of things the most needed.*

The Fourteenth and Twentieth Corps in debouching into the valley in the east of the Lookout Range, found themselves confronted by the enemy in superior force, and were, in turn, obliged to withdraw through the gaps, and marching down the Lookout Valley, to recross the mountains nearer Chattanooga. The Twenty-first Corps was at this time moved out to Ringgold, in order to effect a junction with the remainder of the army. The enemy at this time being reinforced, had turned his face to the north and offered battle, moving with the intention of turning our left and gaining the main route through Rossville to Chattanooga. Headquarters moved on the 16th to Gardiner's Mills, remaining there until the morning of the 18th, when the battle of Chickamauga opened. During the stay at Gardner's, as a battle was certain, orders were issued to the medical directors of corps directing the proper disposition of supplies, and the immediate selection of positions suitable for the temporary field hospitals. This selection was the more difficult as this country was poorly watered, and the changing nature of the battle might leave the hospitals of one day too far to the right in the next. Crawfish Spring, affording a large and excellent supply of water, was designated as the position of the hospital on the right, then held by part of the Twentieth and Twenty-first Corp, the medical director of the Fourteenth Corps choosing for his divisions such points as his judgment dictated and circumstances required. During the battle of the 18th, headquarters was situated at Widow Glenn's, only changing when, on the 19th, the right wing being drawn back, it was removed to Chattanooga. Our loss during the engagement of the first day was probably five thousand; on the second, five thousand five hundred. On the night of the 18th, it being found impracticable to find proper places in the centre and left for the hospitals, the officer commanding ordered all the wounded to be removed to Crawfish Spring, giving directions at the same time that all empty wagons should be drawn to that point, loaded with sick and wounded, and thence sent to Chattanooga. But few of the wounded of the battle of the 20th reached this point, as the enemy turned and forced back our right a few hours after the action commenced, cutting off all access to that portion of the field. The cavalry under Brigadier General R. B. Mitchell had been ordered to protect the wounded at the depot of Crawfish Spring, and remained there faithfully until the morning of the 21st, repulsing all attempts of the enemy to force their position and prevent the removal of the wounded. As soon as the rout of the right occurred, orders were given by Surgeon Perin, medical director, to load all ambulances, and seek as many of the wounded as possible by the Rossville road and send them to Chattanooga, which order was faithfully obeyed, only such of the wounded remaining on the field as would not bear transportation. On the evening of the 20th, the army retired in good order to Rossville, and on the 21st, assumed their position around Chattanooga, throwing up rough lines of defense, consisting of rifle-pits and barriers of logs and earth. Our loss in this series of actions was about sixteen thousand, of whom eleven thousand were killed and wounded, and the remainder taken prisoners. All lists of killed are of necessity very inaccurate, as it was found impossible to separate those supposed to be killed from those reported missing. In many instances those reported killed in the report of the assistant adjutant general were found either in the hospitals or among the number of wounded subsequently exchanged by the enemy. The force engaged in this battle was probably forty-six thousand infantry and artillery, and six thousand cavalry. The force of the enemy was estimated at seventy-five thousand of all arms, and his loss at eighteen thousand, of whom two thousand and three were prisoners. In the removal of the wounded from Crawfish Spring, those whose injuries were mortal, or too serious to allow the fatigue of transportation, were left behind in charge of the medical officers stationed at that point. Fifty-two surgeons and assistant surgeons were detailed for this purpose, and the wounded remaining numbering two thousand, they found constant employment. Most of the hospital tents that had been in use at this spring were left by order, and such medicines and supplies as were on hand sufficient for ten days. It is to be regretted that the facilities afforded and the confusion of the movement prevented ta complete list of these wounded from being taken and transmitted to our lines. The wounds inflicted in this battle were principally by the conical leaden ball at short range, the fire of the enemy's artillery being at no time severe. The wounded were rapidly distributed among the various organized hospitals in Chattanooga, then under the superintendence of Surgeon I. Moses, U. S. V.; but as their utmost capacity was soon reached, it became necessary to open new buildings, and to organize on a larger scale a hospital in the field. For the latter purpose, a well watered slope was chosen on the north side of the Tennessee, about one and a half miles from Chattanooga, and the medical directors of the corps ordered each to superintend the erection of shelter and the care of his own wounded. In this manner, by collecting all hospital and other tents, pavilions, and by the erection of bowers or branches and leaves, nearly two thousand wounded were comfortably sheltered. On the 21st, anticipating the confusion that would occur in the attempt of the slightly wounded to get to the rear on their way to Stevenson and Nashville, the medical director had medical officers stationed at the entrance to the pontoon bridge, with orders to examine every man that was wounded, and if his injury was very slight to send him to his command, or, if sever to forward him to the north. In spite of all precautions, some of each class escaped attention, and were afterwards found in the number of those sent on foot to Stevenson. Nearly three thousand slightly wounded men reached Stevenson in this way, a detail of medical officers and sufficient food being sent to accompany them. The distance they travelled was not less than forty to forty-five miles, over an almost impassable mountain road. No greater tribute could be paid to the cheerful endurance of our soldiers than the simple recital of this march of wounded men. On arriving at Stevenson their wounds were attended to in the general field hospital at that point, and, as rapidly as possible, they were forwarded to

Nashville, Tennessee. From the nature of most of the buildings occupied by the wounded in Chattanooga, and their necessarily crowded condition, the mortality was much greater than would probably have occurred under more favorable conditions, as at no time previously had the physical condition of the men been so good. Many secondary amputations and operations had to be performed, as the immediate removal of the wounded from the field was a matter of pressing necessity, and left no time for surgical interference. Owing to the deficient transportation, the line of commination being nearly sixty miles over a mountain road, supplies of all kinds were exceedingly limited, the chief dependence for medicines being on the medicine wagons, some fifteen in number, which had been supplied to some regiments before leaving Murfreesboro, or soon after. The cooking utensils in them were of particular service. Great difficulty was found at first in getting material to fill the bed-sacks, in order to remove the sick and wounded from the ground or floor; but fortunately some two hundred bales of cotton were found in the town, and details of upholsterers being made from the various commands, mattresses were speedily furnished, nearly three thousand being made in this manner. About a week after the battle, negotiations were opened by Major General Rosecrans for the exchange of wounded and a number of surgeons equal to those we held. As we held only about fifty of their wounded, most of ours were to be counted in future exchanges. In this way we received, on September 29th and October 1st and 2d, one thousand seven hundred of the sick and wounded left on the field, accompanied by four medical offers. A few of the wounded still remained at Crawfish Spring unable to be removed. The transfer of the wounded to Stevenson was a matter of grave consideration and much difficulty. The enemy had complete possession of the roads on the south side of the Tennessee, and commanded also the river or Haley Trace road on the opposite bank, making it necessary to make a wide detour over Walden's Ridge, either by the Anderson road, or some new route over the ridge, and thence down the Sequatchie Valley. Any road in this direction was full of difficulties – leading over the mountains, affording no forage, and the journey and restarts occupying nearly two weeks. All the available ambulances were collected and organized into trains, and from time to time were filled with sick and wounded, and sent under proper charge to Stevenson. Wagon trains going to this point for supplies were, when practicable, also used for this purpose. In this manner the hospitals were finally depleted. Sanitary agents were stationed at various points along this route, making a species of entre pointst for the aid of the passing ambulance trains, or such soldiers as might be returning to their commands; and in this way much assistance was rendered. From scarcity of forage, the animals at length were reduced by starvation both in strength and numbers, so that it became no longer possible to send the wounded in this manner, and it became a subject of doubt whether, in case of a forced evacuation of our position, it would be necessary to abandon the remaining sick and wounded, about sixteen hundred, to the enemy. Happily this necessity never came. On October 29th, by a brilliant and successful movement, the enemy's lines at Brown's Ferry were penetrated, and the south side of the Tennessee occupied from Bridgeport to that point. On the night of the 29th, a severe attack was made by General Wood's rebel division upon the division of General Geary of the Twelfth Corps, which had that evening reached Wauhautchie Station, on the line of railroad from Bridgeport to Chattanooga. This attack was gallantly repulsed, with a loss to the enemy of two hundred prisoners and a thousand stand of small arms. Our loss in the engagement was three hundred killed and wounded. The possession of the river to this point enabled the boats to ascend the river either to Kelly's Ferry or to Brown's. As the river was difficult to navigate above the former ferry on account of the rapids, cargoes were generally discharged at that point and wagoned over the narrow neck of land to Brown's thence across a pontoon bridge to the north side of the river, the road skirting along the bank until opposite to Chattanooga, where a second pontoon bridge completed the route. Supplies in this way soon became more plenty, and the stress upon the hospitals was soon relieved. A depot of transit for the sick and wounded was immediately established at Kelly's Ferry, and the boats carried them from that point to the railroad terminus at Bridgeport, whence they were taken in the hospital train to Nashville. As all mention of this train has been previously omitted in this paper, it is necessary to devote a few words to its organization and results. Before leaving Murfreesboro, two ordinary passenger cars had been fitted up with bunks, and the same number unaltered, with the addition of a box-car for cooking purposes, had been organized by the

302

medical director as a train exclusively for the transportation of the sick. At the same time measures had been taken to build for the government two first class cars, fitted up inside with berths suspended from elastic rings, in order to lessen the motion of the cars. The latter cars were put upon the road about the middle of September. A competent medical officer, with a detail of nurses and cooks, are in constant attendance during the entire time. The train at present is capable of conveying sixty bed patients, and the same number sitting up. As the number of patients gradually decreased, the field hospital on the north side of the river was broken up, and a site having been selected about one mile from Chattanooga, on Chattanooga Creek, it was re-established in the new situation. The field hospital at Stevenson was also about this time broken up, and orders given to bring all the tents, stores, etc., to Chattanooga; but owing to the inability of the boats, only three in number, to carry all the freight, much delay was experienced in forwarding them to their destination. It was intended to unite these hospitals with the one in Chattanooga, and thus make a hospital with a capacity of about two thousand beds. This hospital at that time had seven hundred beds ready for the occupation of sick. In the middle of November it became evident, from the nature of the preparations around, that a movement against the enemy was intended, and the medical director began his preparations accordingly. Supplies, in addition to those already on hand, were ordered from Nashville, and such of the churches and available buildings as had been previously completed were again refitted for the occupation of the wounded. An estimate was made for the accommodation of five thousand, and the means at hand expended for that end. It is not necessary to attempt a description of the battle of Missionary Ridge, which resulted in perfect victory to our arms, but only to mention the leading features of medical interest in and after the engagement. The wounded men were more readily and rapidly cared for than at any previous battle of that army. The ambulance trains moved rapidly from the town to the front, only a distance of two or three miles, and returned with their loads. In this way all were comfortably housed, except here and there some severely wounded man who had found his way to some house, and was unable to report his situation. The loss of the army of the Cumberland in this battle was three hundred and eighty-five killed and three thousand two hundred *and thirteen wounded, and the loss of the Fifteenth Corps, under Major General Sherman, probably eighteen hundred more. The loss of the enemy is reported in their papers as twenty-five hundred in killed and wounded, and the lists of the provost marshal of the department of the Cumberland show the names of nearly seven thousand prisoners. Here admirable opportunity was offered for the prompt exercise of surgical skill in primary operations, but the previous health of the men had been so much lowered by deficient food, that the success was in no wise flattering in the subsequent treatment and results. The hospitals were very much overcrowded, as only those able to bear exposure and fatigue could be safely sent to the rear by the journey of boat and cars. Hospital gangrene now manifested itself attacking, with few exceptions, all the stumps. The treatment by bromine, elaborated by Surgeon Goldsmith's care, was tried in nearly all the cases, with what final result I do not know. Although the line of railroad was now entirely in our possession, it was not until the middle of January that the trains commenced their regular trips from Nashville, and the hospital train could be used to deplete the crowded hospitals. In the meantime, on account of the severe weather, it was impossible to send any more sick or wounded by the regular way, so that all were held in Chattanooga until the completion of the road afforded the proper means. About four hundred rebel wounded and thirteen of their medical officers fell into our hands at this battle. They were assigned to several buildings and one of their number placed in charge of the whole. They kept their hospitals in the filthy condition that seems necessary to their comfort, and showed a want of interest in the care of their patients, that was attended with the usual results. The addition of the Fifteenth Corps taxed our supplies to the utmost, as it was anticipated that their own stores were ample, and no estimate for their wants had been made; and still heavier calls were made upon our stores at this time, necessitated by the transfer of the Fourth Corps, under General Gordon Granger, to operate in east Tennessee, and also by the urgent wants of the troops of General Burnside in that department. Medicines and stores for one thousand beds and ten thousand troops were in this way supplied. Three additional boats having been built at Bridgeport, the means of transportation made the supply of the things most needed ample enough for the wants of the hospitals, and no further difficulty was felt either in the supplying the*

command at Chattanooga or Knoxville.   About January 1st, the new
supply table was issued upon the basis of a brigade organization, the
table being nearly in all respects the same as that previously in use by
the army of the Potomac. At the same time the organization of the
ambulance corps was completed and rapidly pushed into practice
throughout the army. It was also the intention of the medical director
to supply each regiment with one double pannier set, and medicine
cases to the batteries of each division, relying on the supply in the
brigade medicine wagons for the emergencies of battle and the care of
the hospitals in the field. The allowance of hospital and wall tents for
the brigade hospitals was also apportioned – one hospital tent for
every three hundred and fifty men, and one wall tent for the brigade –
and the necessary orders were issued regulating the detail of nurses an
cooks. The general field hospital on Chattanooga Creek, under the
superintendence of Assistant Surgeon R. Bartholow, U. S. A., is now
reorganized on a basis of two thousand beds, the tents being stretched
over substantial frames and floored. A hospital for five hundred beds,
and a large convalescent camp, to be situated at Summertown or
Lookout Mountain, are also under consideration. The railroad being
open through to Nashville, the hospital train made three trips a week,
so that the work of emptying and closing the hospitals in town was
almost complete by the middle of February. It was then the intention
of the medical director to concentrate all the patients who were either
unable to bear transportation or who did not need a transfer in the
field hospitals, to the Crutchfield Hotel, and a pavilion hospital built by
the confederates, and capable of holding four hundred patients. With
the hospital already established in Nashville, and a capacity of
extension of five thousand beds, the hospitals in Louisville,
Jeffersonville and New Albany, and those in Chattanooga, it was
expected that every emergency would be readily met.

Another general hospital patient, John Dunmore of the 96th Illinois,
wrote to his mother on January 2nd about his bout with the mumps
and subsequent hospitalization.

Chattanooga
January 2, 1864
Dear Father and Mother

I now take my pen in hand to wright you a few lines. I have been on the move for the last four days. We camped at Mission Ridge last night. This morning when I waked up on the cold ground I found that my face was swelled up with the mumps. I whent and seen the doctor and he sent me back to Chattanooga to the field hospital. I just got there in time. the rain pord down in torant in five minutes after I got here. I have a good bed.....

.....sent back to Bridgeport I have not hurd from him since but I suppose he has rote to you I have not received any letter from you yet and I begin to think you have not wrote any. thare is $285 on the way to you that belongs to me and $280 that belongs to Jacob and I am ancious to hear wheather you have received it. Write soon. Don't delay John R Dunmore

In a post script to his brother Dunmore seemed in good spirits.

General Field Hospital near Chattanooga Tennessee Ward 2 Brother..I will make you a present of my necti (neck tie). You must keep it nice till I see you for I want to see how you look with it on. John your brother.

Dr. Mary Edward Walker came to the Union army at Chattanooga at the time of the battle of Chickamauga. She was employed as a civilian - Contract Acting Assistant Surgeon - by the Army of the Cumberland. Ultimately General Thomas appointed her as assistant surgeon for the 52nd Ohio Infantry.

Mary Walker had completed her medical degree in 1855 at Syracuse Medical College in New York and was a pronounced abolitionist and suffragette. Dr. Walker had volunteered as a surgeon in Washington, D.C. but the army refused to accept her as a surgeon as a woman. Rather than accept a position as a paid nurse she worked as a surgeon on a voluntary basis serving as such through the aftermath of the battles of First Bull Run and Fredericksburg before receiving the aforementioned contract with the Army of the Cumberland. Upon being appointed as surgeon for the 52nd Ohio Volunteer Infantry, she was the first female to receive employment as a surgeon for the U. S. army.

Dr. Mary Walker often crossed battle lines or stayed with wounded soldiers as lines moved back and forth. She also crossed battle lines to treat sick civilians and during one such incident on April 10, 1864 she was captured by the Confederates and arrested as a spy. Ironically, she had just finished helping a Confederate surgeon perform an amputation. She remained a prisoner until exchanged for a Confederate Surgeon on August 12, four months later.

Walker went on to serve as supervisor of a female prison in Louisville, Kentucky and as the head of an orphanage in Tennessee.

Dr. Mary Edward Walker was the first and only woman to become a recipient of the Medal of Honor.

Axel Reed who had been seriously wounded in the arm during the assault of Missionary Ridge recorded the following notes in his diary regarding the initial struggle and horror immediately following the battle, his gratitude to the surgeon that saved him and rejoining his regiment.

It is impossible for me to give any thing of an idea of the incidents and scenes of horror that fell under my own eyes, during my two months of hospital life in Chattanooga, Tenn. About twelve died in the ward (room) I was in, out of twenty-one of the wounded that were put in there.

January 26th, I was so far recovered that Dr. Soelheim, of the 9th Ohio, to whom I give the credit for saving my life (by his kind and skillful attention to me especially) permitted me to receive a hospital furlough.

Chicago, March 12th. I left Rochester, N. Y., March 3d, and arrived here the 5th via Buffalo, Cleveland, Crestline and Fort Wayne. I heard that my regiment was on its way from Fort Snelling (to the front at Chattanooga), where they had been spending a 'veteran furlough' for two months or more. Stayed here waiting for them until the 11th, when I started for Minnesota, and met them at Minnesota Junction in

Wisconsin, where I turned back, to go with them to Chattanooga and was glad and happy to meet the boys again.

Surgeon John Moore produced a highly detailed report to the Surgeon General of the United States Army regarding the operations of the Medical Department at the Battle of Chattanooga. His report not only describes the medical department's actions during the battle but provides keen insights into the contributing factors to the overall health of an army due to camp conditions, extensive marching and overall exertion.

General: The following report of the battle of Chattanooga, as far as participated in by the army of the Tennessee, is respectfully submitted. This long delay is owing to the fact that, from the day following the battle to January 1ˢᵗ, we were constantly on the march, and that in one week afterward I was ordered on business to Vicksburg and Memphis, and only returned on February 26ᵗʰ. At the time I left, the reports of casualties from division surgeons had not been received. The troops engaged in the battle were four divisions, forming the Fifteenth Corps, under the command of Major General W. T. Sherman, and making an aggregate of twenty thousand men. After the surrender of Vicksburg these troops were encamped along the Big Black River about twenty miles in rear of the town, a locality considered by the inhabitants to be very unhealthy. The percentage of sick in this command has been throughout the summer, higher than that of the troops stationed in Vicksburg. On September 28ᵗʰ, they were put on transports and brought to Memphis. All serious cases of sick had been previously sent on board the hospital steamers R. C. Wood and Charles McDougal, both of which arrived before the embarkation. On arrival at Memphis, all who were not able to undergo a march of twenty miles a day were ordered to convalescent camp or hospital. From Memphis a portion of the command went by rail to Iuka, one hundred and twenty miles, and the remainder marched. On October 27ᵗʰ, orders were received to cross the Tennessee River at Eastport, and march to Chattanooga by roads on the north or western side. The route was through Florence, Alabama, Fayetteville and Winchester, Tennessee, to Bridgeport, Alabama, the point at which the Memphis and Charleston railroad crosses the Tennessee River, and thence to Chattanooga, which was reached on November 23d. The command, without crossing, moved four miles up and camped on the western side. The country marched through was fertile, well cultivated, and beautifully variegated. Supplies were found of all kinds in abundance, and were freely taken. As a result of this, the whole command had very much improved in health. Several hundred men, who on the beginning of the march, were found unable to keep with the column and had to be carried in the ambulances, were now in vigorous health. Before daylight on November 24th, one division had crossed the river, and thrown up intrenchments to serve as a Tete-du-pont for the pontoons. This was begun at daylight and completed before noon, when the whole corps crossed, and, forming on the eastern side, marched in three columns to the attack of that part of Missionary Ridge, immediately to the west of Tunnel Hill. The hill was in our possession before four o'clock in the afternoon, with no other casualty than a severe flesh wound in the arm of General Giles Smith. Up to this time it had not been decided whether the hospital should be established on the eastern or western side of the river. The great convenience of having them on the same side as the troops engaged was, of course, obvious; but it was feared they would be under fire. But when we had possession of a portion of the ridge, and saw the range of the enemy's shot, it was decided to place hospitals in suitable position near the bridge, about five miles above Chattanooga and two in rear of our line of battle. Directions to this effect were given to the division surgeons, and the wagons and ambulances containing the regimental hospital tents and hospital property were driven to the points indicated, and their erection pushed forward as rapidly as possible. About nine o'clock the following morning, portions of the corps were constantly engaged near the rebel intrenched position at Tunnel Hill, from this time until about four in the afternoon, with short intervals and on the close approach of our troops to the enemy's intrenchments, great numbers were killed and wounded. As soon as the action commenced, the ambulances, of which there were two to a regiment, with their stretcher-bearers, were sent out to the front. Owing to the fact that the firing of the enemy was nearly parallel with the direction of the ridge, the ambulances came safely to the foot of it, thus getting much nearer than is usual during the continuance of an engagement, and in this way greatly facilitating the removal of the wounded. On the return of the ambulances to their respective divisions, the wounded were taken in charge by the surgeons detailed for that purpose. These were organized substantially on the plan adopted more than a year since by Surgeon J. Letterman, U. S. A., and found to work well in the army of the Potomac. One medical officer was retained with each regiment, who with hospital knapsack and pocket case, was prepared to attend to cases requiring immediate care, and to direct such as were slightly wounded the way to the field hospital. All the wounded were brought off before night, except a small number who fell so near the rebel intrenchments that they could not be reached. But all these were brought off before ten o'clock that night, when it was found that the enemy had abandoned his position. Several of the regiments had large medicine wagons, which, although ill adapted on account of their great weight for marches over bad roads, yet on this occasion, were found of very great service. The cooking stoves and operating table were at once put to important uses. A sufficient amount of beef essence, and all needed stimulants were on hand for use during the day, and, on the following day, a large supply of both these important articles, together with one thousand two hundred blankets, arrived from Nashville in charge of a medical officer, who had been dispatched for that purpose a week before the battle. Straw was found in abundance in the neighborhood, and the tents being thickly littered with it made a comfortable bed, which was improved in all severely injured cases, by spreading a blanket or gutta-percha cloth over the straw and laying the wounded man on this. In two of the divisions the tents were inadequate for the accommodation of their wounded, and temporary shelters, made of lumber taken from vacant buildings in the neighborhood, were improvised, which answered the purpose very well. The weather for the first two or three days after the battle was warm and clear, and fires were not needed to make the hospitals comfortable. This time was improved to the utmost in extending and improving the appliances for cooking, by the erection of temporary kitchens out of poles, and covering them with tent flies or boards, as well as in collecting from houses in the neighborhood such large pots as were not essential for the use of the inhabitants. It should be added here that these articles were either returned to the owners or left on breaking up the hospitals. At the same time lumber was collected for the construction of bunks or forms to raise the men from the ground, and, in a few days, enough of these were made to accommodate all who were so severely hurt as to be compelled to keep their beds on these bunks, sacks filled with straw were laid, thus making a very comfortable bed. On the day following the battle, the corps was ordered in pursuit of the retreating enemy, and all the medical officer that could be spared from the hospitals were ordered away with their respective regiments. As another engagement was expected, the details for hospitals, both as to medical officers and attendants, was much more limited than would have been if no advance had been made, and for this reason the more credit is due to the surgeons in charge for getting their men quite comfortable with what, under ordinary circumstances, would be considered inadequate assistance. Supplies composed of the ordinary soldiers' ration were obtained from Chattanooga. This was varied and improved during the first ten days by additions in the way of mutton, chicken, and beef brought in by enterprising foraging parties from the surrounding country. These predatory excursions were then stopped by orders from the department commander. About eight days after the battle, the weather became very cold, and as heating stoves were not to be had, other expeditions for warming had to be resorted to. Where brick was obtainable it was used for the construction of chimneys or such and when this failed chimneys were built of sticks and mud, or flues made through the tents by digging a small trench from the outside through the tent terminating from five to eight feet beyond the opposite side. This trench was then covered with flat stones an inch or two of earth thrown over these, and a chimney or flue some eight or ten feet high erected at one end, and the fire made in the other. Where railroad iron can be procured, as often occurs, the rails may be used instead of stones to make the top of the flues. When properly covered with clay, this makes an admirable heating arrangement; the same flue then can be run through several tents. The hospital under charge of Surgeon Joslyn, U. S. V., was considered by many who saw it as one of the best they had seen in the field; he displayed uncommon energy and aptitude in conducting it. Surgeon E. O. F. Roler, 55th Illinois Volunteers, acting inspector Fifteenth Corps, who was ordered back from the march to have a general supervision of all the division hospitals, as well as to Assistant Surgeon D. L. Huntington, U. S. A. who has been in my office as assistant medical director since July last, and who arriving the day after the battle, was ordered to remain and assist in looking after the hospitals. His zeal and intelligent industry, as well as his acquaintance with most of the staff officers of the department of the Cumberland, through whom supplies for our wounded were necessarily obtained, enabled him to render very important aid to those in immediate charge. On the morning of the 25th, I met Dr. Newberry, of the U. S. Sanitary Commission, who kindly offered many luxuries for the wounded that were not obtainable elsewhere, and of course the offer was thankfully accepted. And, while speaking of this, I may add, that it has often been my experience in this department to find the U. S. Sanitary Commission prepared to furnish hospitals, not only with luxuries, not to be expected from the subsistence department, but with vegetables of an indispensable character, as potatoes and dried fruits, which were not to be had of the commissaries for the reason as alleged, they could not be brought through for want of transportation. This was the case for months in Vicksburg last summer, and is true of this place at the present time. It is mortifying to be dependent upon an outside charitable organization for important supplies, acknowledged to be a legitimate part of the ration. The three division field hospitals established above Chattanooga were continued for twenty-five days after the battle. The success of treatment in these hospitals was much more gratifying than in those established in houses in Chattanooga, to which the wounded of the army of the Cumberland were taken. Erysipelas, hospital gangrene, and other adynamic diseases prevailed among those to an enormous extent, while in the field hospitals there was not a single case of gangrene, and but one slight one of erysipelas. This immunity in the wounded of the Fifteenth Corps was probably due to two causes. In the first place, it has been proven by experience on many occasions in this war, that men recover more rapidly from wounds when placed comfortably in tents, where they get an abundance of fresh air, than in such hospitals as are usually improvised from the houses of a town, taken promiscuously; and probably quite as well as in the majority of our general hospitals, where it is almost impossible to prevent more or less contamination of the atmosphere, into which evaporations are continually passing from a large aggregation of open suppurating wounds. In the second place, the men of the army of the Tennessee, although, exposed to malarious influences during the proceeding summer, had entirely recovered from its effects, during their long march from Memphis, through a fruitful and interesting country; they went into the battle in vigorous health, and exultant from previous military successes; whereas, the army of the Cumberland, after the repulse at Chickamauga and return to Chattanooga, in addition to very arduous duties, was for many days, on reduced rations; for several days in fact, corn on the ear was issued in lieu of bread or flour. The 1st division of the Fifteenth Corps having been separated from the rest of the command by the accidental breaking of a pontoon bridge across the Tennessee River, was attached to the command of General Hooker, and fought at Lookout Mountain on the 24th, Missionary Ridge on the 25th, and at the mountain pass near Ringgold, Georgia, on the 27th. The field hospital was established below Chattanooga, near the scene of the first day's fight, and all the wounded except about thirty, who were sent to the hospitals in the town, were sent to this place from the three battles in which the division was engaged. On the return of the different divisions from the pursuit, the hospitals were relieved of all cases that could be taken care of in the regiments.

Through the kind assistance of Surgeon G. Perin, U. S. A., medical director, army of the Cumberland, the little steamers on the river were put at the disposal of Surgeon E. O. F. Roler, 55th Illinois Volunteers, who was then superintending our hospitals, and permission being given to send all cases to the hospitals in Nashville that were in condition to be sent. During the 21st and 22nd of December, these were sent on board the boats to Bridgeport, accompanied by nurses and medical officers. At Bridgeport they were taken in ambulances to the receiving field hospital of that place, and in a day or two sent by comfortable hospital cars to Nashville. The kindness, patience and care shown to the wounded by the surgeons and nurses on these cars excited my admiration. Those not in condition to be sent to Nashville, were sent to the camp hospital near Chattanooga, established by Surgeon Perin, where they could be much more easily supplied; surgeons and attendants were sent with them. Some of the surgeons showed skill in the performance of operations and on the whole, as well as I could ascertain, this part of their duties was very well performed. None were permitted to operate but those previously selected, for their known or presumed knowledge in this branch of surgery. No cases of tetanus have been reported. Chloroform was administered in all except two of the important operations performed. Two amputations of the thigh appear from the tabular report to have been performed without anesthetics. No reason for this has been assigned. It is probable the shock was so great as, in the opinion of the surgeon, to render its administration hazardous. This objection I believe is not considered valid by the majority of good authorities. No casualty resulted from its administration in one hundred and thirty-six cases. Sixteen cases of secondary hemorrhage occurred. The attempts at conservative surgery in wounds of the knee-joint were not encouraging. Of sixteen cases reported as occurring in the 2d, 3d, and 4th divisions, seven underwent primary amputation, and seven were treated without amputation. On the 25th day, one case not amputated had died, and but two were reported as favorable for recovery without loss of leg. From these same divisions I have received the following tabular summary of important operations, giving results up to 25th day after battle. It was compiled by Surgeon Roler, 55th Illinois Volunteers , in general charge of the hospitals. Amputations of leg, seven; of which six were primary and one secondary operations; one death resulted from primary operations; amputations of the thigh, twenty-one; of which seventeen were primary and four secondary operations; three deaths resulted from primary and two from secondary operations. Amputations of arm and forearm twenty-one; of which nineteen were primary and two secondary operations; one death resulted from secondary operation. On the whole there was as little suffering from delay or want in this battle as is likely to ever occur; and this is due to the following causes: The day was fine; the roads for the ambulances good; those in charge of bearing off the wounded did their duty; the battle was expected; began in the morning and terminated before night; the hospital tents were ready before the wounded began to arrive; and supplies sent for to Nashville arrived at the proper time; and lastly Surgeon G. Perin, U. S. A., medical director army of the Cumberland, was ever prompt to furnish anything he had to spare from his own supplies. I regret that the surgical statistics I send are so meagre and unsatisfactory. Where the medical force left in the hospitals is barely sufficient to attend to the wants of those under their care, it requires more zeal in the interests of science, and generally more knowledge of what is of interest to note, than is found among the majority of army surgeons, to induce them to keep any intelligent record of important cases. In future I hope to improve the report in this respect by directing special attention to certain classes of wounds, and if possible, have some man of known fitness to overlook, and endeavor to excite some little interest, even among the indifferent; but I cannot work miracles, and shall not pledge myself to accomplish a great deal. In the three of the western States, surgeons are admitted and assigned to regiments without any form of examination whatever. Of course among these are men whose ignorance is disgraceful to the profession, and whose stupidity and blunders tend to cast a stigma upon the whole medical staff of the army. Very much is lost for want of men of sufficient professional intelligence to know what to observe particularly, and also for lack of industry to record their observations. And while on this subject I would respectfully suggest that, in my opinion, the form of tabular statement of gunshot wounds furnished from the office in Washington is, in some respects, susceptible of improvement, a single case may appear as three or four, if he have, as often happens, as many wounds in different parts of the body. Surgeon C. W. McMillin, 1st Tennessee Volunteers, medical director Fifteenth Corps, in his report says the want of proper instruments for exsections is very much felt by the operating staff, and very properly suggests the propriety of furnishing a complete case of exsecting instruments to each surgeon in chief of a division. At present, I believe they are only furnished to medical officers of the regular army. As an addendum to this report, I will complete the history of the corps up to December 31st, 1863. As before stated, the pursuit of the rebels was taken up the morning after the battle; this was continued for two days, with occasional unimportant skirmishing with the enemy's rear guard, when the pursuit was abandoned. Two divisions were then ordered back to vicinity of Chattanooga; and the other two, in conjunction with the Eleventh Corps, under General Howard, and part of the Fourth, under General Gordon Granger, were ordered to march as rapidly as possible to Knoxville to relieve General Burnside, who was closely besieged by Longstreet. The distance was one hundred and twenty miles; the troops had but three days' rations and the Eleventh and Fifteenth Corps were almost without tents or camp and garrison equipage of any kind. The weather turned very cold, and for several days the roads were frozen hard. The march was made. The siege was abandoned the day before our arrival, and on the following day the return march began. On December 20th, arrived at Chattanooga, after a continuous march of eighteen days. The three days' rations were made to answer for eighteen by being eked out from the forced contributions of the farmers in the beautiful and fertile valleys of East Tennessee. On the return march several hundred men were entirely barefooted. The weather was cold, and the roads frequently frozen during the forenoon. Notwithstanding this, but few of them complained or asked to be relieved from marching. A truthful account of their heroic fortitude would place them on a level with the soldiers of the Revolution, of whose patriotism we have such glowing accounts, because a few of them were barefooted when the ground was covered with snow. Supplies were obtained at Chattanooga, and the march continued to Huntsville, Alabama, which was reached January 1, 1864. Since October 1st, this corps has marched not less than seven hundred and fifty miles; and notwithstanding all these seeming privations and fatigues, came into camp with but few sick; and that all the exposure these troops underwent has had no depressing or unhealthy tendency, is proven by the fact that the ratio of sick for January and February been less than five per cent. Accompanying the report is a topographical map of that part of battle-field embraced in the operations of the army of the Tennessee, except in the 1st division, which was accidentally detached as before mentioned.

> *John Moore,*
> *Surgeon U. S. Army, Medical Director of the Department of the Tennessee. To the Surgeon General U. S. Army."*

In August of 1864 a sick soldier of the 89th Ohio was in Hospital No. 2 in Chattanooga, detached from his regiment that was closing in on Atlanta. He wrote to his wife to tell of his current condition and provides a good explanation of what life in the hospital was like for an ambulatory patient. He wanted to return to his regiment as soon as he could.

Chattanooga Tenn
Sunday Oct 23 1864

Beloved Wife,

    I take my pencil this pleasant Sabbath day to address you again. Feeling very lonely this morning. I got up pretty early and strolled down to the Bank of the Tennessee River before Breakfast. I have been quite unwell for several days. I reported myself sick on Thursday morning and went Before the surgeon and he sent me to the hospital. It is called Hospital No 2. Large tents little cotts. just large enough for one man. There are 5 cotts in each tent. I came to the Hospital on Thursday afternoon and staid all night on Thursday night & Friday & Friday night & until Saturday noon. The doctor called around on Saturday morning at 8 o'clock. I am troubled with a bad cold and a pain in my breast and my spine troubles me pretty smart & I also have a very large boil on the back of my neck which has troubled me a good deal all last week but is now gitting Better. I was tranfered out of the tent I first went to into the one I now am in on yesterday at noon and attached to a Squad called a Working Squad on what they call light duty. Thos. Kerns is in the same tent with me. he is the only man in the tent that I am acquainted with. we have not seen or herd from Jos. Blomcett or Thos. Kelsey since we left the company camp on last Thursday. It is Reported here in the Hospital Camp that they have started for the front at Atlanta Georgia about 155 miles further south. We do not know how long they will keep Kerns & me here in the Hospital Camp. I feel Better this morning than I have for some days and as soon as I can I want to start on to our Regiment at Atlanta. They are their doing guard duty. We get pretty poor fare here. Nothing but Bread & poor coffee. Then we have to fall in two ranks outside of the Eating House when they sound the Bugle. then sutch crowding and jamming like (a) drove of hogs. I want you to get Benjamin to take the size of the pipes of your little stove & the length of it and let him send to the city and get pipe enough to put up the little stove in the parlor so that you can burn cole in it. I want you to use the money I left with you to buy your flower & meat and sutch things as you have to have. also get you a good pair of Calf Skin shoes and also some good stockings and keep yourself warm and comfortable. I can draw clothing when I kneed any. I have moor now up here by every train. We have hard sckratching in this camp to get wood enough to cook our grub and then have to carry it about ¾ mile. We do not know when we will have to leave here. I want you to take good care of yourself and live comfortable. have someone to stay with you Especely at night and have them saw you plenty of wood and have plenty to eat. I do not want you to pay any Body any money If (you owe) any body any money on debts until I come home or I give you further orders. If anyone wants you to pay them any money tell them you cannot until I come home.

Tell Frank not to buy any one anything or medicines or anything else with out my orders. Give my respects to my father and I want you to be kind to him. Console him in his declining age. Show this to all. I must close for it is getting late. I will wright soon

When you wright to me direct your letter to Chattanooga Tenn. Comp F 82 Ohio Vol. Infanty. 20th Army Corps.

Farewell for this time From your aft. (affectionate) husband

A Baldwin

P S Send me 25cts in postage stamps

Chapter Sixteen

Chattanooga in 1864

Throughout Sherman's Campaign for Atlanta, Chattanooga remained the supply depot, primary general hospital and rendezvous point for troops going to or coming from the front. As Sherman advanced his three armies toward Atlanta, the Western & Atlantic Railroad served as the lifeline for supplies, rations and ammunition. Although he moved away from this vital line to utilize flanking maneuvers against Joseph Johnston, he never strayed far and always returned when supplies started to wane.

Meanwhile, Chattanooga was consumed with everything military. Regular business almost completely dried up while sutlers and traders set up shop in every available space where a tent may be erected or a tin shed put up. Some took residence in larger permanent structures. Suffice to say the modest civilian population of Chattanooga was completely overrun by the U.S. Army and its related components.

Prices on all goods, military or civilian, necessity or luxury began to rise to excess and by December of 1864 the Post Command published a list of prices for all items which was to be posted with every sutler and adhered to without exception. New items and prices were added as they became known to be available.

After armies from both sides had ravaged the countryside there was little food and forage for humans and animals in the winter of 1863-64. Benefit associations were formed in Eastern Tennessee and sent north to secure donations and food for the population. Northerners were happy to oblige as long as "no part of the bounty" was given to Confederate sympathizers of military age. Garden seeds were included in the provisions so that the people could plant and provide for themselves in the spring.

In the summer of 1864, refugees started pouring into Chattanooga. Black and white alike came to the community in terrible condition seeking food and safety. By November, 4000 rations were issued to the starving each day in the city and surrounding territory.

The Federal forces had driven the Confederates from almost every corner of Tennessee by 1864 and Andrew Johnson was appointed military governor of the state. With the 1864 presidential election coming in November, citizens began to wonder if they were or weren't considered part of the Union and eligible to vote. At the Maryland convention in June, Tennessee sent a number of delegates with this question in mind. When Andrew Johnson was proposed and accepted as Lincoln's running mate the answer was clear. On November 9, The Gazette reported that Lincoln and Johnson had carried the vote in Chattanooga. On the eleventh, it reported that Lincoln had swept every state in the Union. The Congress threw out the electoral votes from Tennessee but Johnson was sworn in as Vice President. This signaled that Tennessee was not considered a state.

Chapter Seventeen

United States Colored Troops

When the Emancipation Proclamation went into effect in January of 1863 the recruitment and enlistment of African-American (Colored) troops began in earnest. By the end of the war, 175 regiments of colored troops had been formed making up approximately ten percent of the northern army's total enlistments. Fifteen African-American soldiers would receive the Medal of Honor.

Following the battle of Chickamauga and the securing of Chattanooga, there were a high number of potential recruits in southeast Tennessee for these regiments. The commissioner for Organization of Colored Troops, Colonel R. D. Massey, determined to form four regiments in this area. They were to be the 14th, 15th, 16th and 17th United States Colored Troops (USCT).

Two of the African-American regiments based in Chattanooga were the 14th and 16th USCT. The experiences of the two regiments during the war could not have been more different.

14th USCT

Lieutenant Thomas J. Morgan was a strong supporter of black troops and having been accepted as an officer in the USCT he began recruiting for the 14th in Gallatin, Tennessee, twenty nine miles northeast of Nashville. Many of the recruits came from slaves who had come to do labor for the Union army. Upon gathering the required recruits for a regiment, Morgan was promoted to Lt. Colonel of the regiment and began the school of instruction of the soldier. It should be noted that all USCT regiments were led by white officers. Blacks could not rise above the non-commissioned ranks.

From the General Orders book for the regiment the following standing orders were posted for the regiment on December 17th.

Head Qtrs 14th US C Troops
Gallatin, Tenn. Dec 17th 1863
For the general system and discipline of the Regiment the following until further orders, will be strictly adhered to by each

Company officer; and each Company Commander will be held responsible for the enforcement of this order in his company.

I.   *Reveille*

         6:30 A. M.

(1)1st Sergeants will be prompt in getting every able bodied man on the Co. Parade ground for roll call.[2] Roll call will be invariably superintended by a company officer.[3] Every man will wash, comb and put himself in neat order.[4] Every blanket will be well shaken, & aired and tenets properly arranged. (5) Each company will by detail, police thoroughly the company grounds, commencing at the color front, and the same space to the Rear guard line.

II.   *Breakfast*

         7:00 A. M.

III.   *Adjutant's Call*

         7:15 A. M.

1st Sergeants will in person take to the Adjutant's office the Co. Report, with his own signature, and that of the Company Commander clearly written in the proper place.

IV.   *Sick Call*

         7:30 A. M.

1st Sergeants will see that a correct report of all sick are reported promptly to the Surgeon.[2] The sick report must be made by one of sergeants.

V.   *Guard Mounting (1st Call)*

         8:15 A. M.

1st Sergeants will assemble, on company parade ground the force detailed.[2] Every man for guard will appear with ammo, accouterments and clothing in neat order.

VI.   *Guard Mounting (2nd Call)*

         8:30 A.M.

1st Sergeants will march their detail force to color line.

VII.   *Squad Drill*
                    9.   " "
Company officers will strictly superintend their exercises; and observe that Squads under the Non commissioned officers are faithfully exercised in the School of the Soldier and manual of arms.

VIII.   *Recall from Drill*
                    11. A. M.
IX.   *Dinner*
                    12.   M

X.   *Roll Call as at reveille*
                    1.   P.M.
XI.   *Company Drill*
                    2. P. M.
Company officers, with every man able or not otherwise employed will invariably attend this exercise. Excuses will be granted to no officer or soldier except in extreme cases.

XII.   *Recall from Drill*

XIII.   *Dress Parade (1st Call)*
                    3:30 P. M.
Companies will assemble on their respective Company parade grounds with clothing arms and accouterments in neat order, overcoats worn only in very cold or stormy weather.

XIV.   *Dress Parade (2nd Call)*
                    4.   P. M.
Companies will with order, and regard to proper formation of Battalion take their respective place on Color line.

XV.   *Supper*
                    4:30 P. M.
XVI.   *Tattoo*
                    7:45 P. M.

> Roll call as at Reveille. [2] Every man present at Roll call will make speedy preparations to retire.

XVII.   Taps

> 8:00 P.M.
>
> Every man will retire and every light in mens quarters will be extinguished – No lights in mens tents or kitchens fires will allowed except in special cases and by permission of the Officer Commanding Regiment – No whooping singing or any other boisterous noise will be allowed.
>
> > By order of
> >
> > Thomas J. Morgan <u>Lt. Col</u>
> >
> > Commanding Regt.
> >
> > (sig)   W. H. H. Avery, Addjutant

Special Order number 2 shows Morgan's dedication to treating the regiment with the discipline and bearing of a fully engaged military unit.

Head Quarters, 14th U. S. Colored Troops
Gallatin, Tenn 24th Dec 1863
Special Orders
No. 2

> The Report of the weekly inspection of quarters, etc. made in the 1st Batt. 14th U.S.C.T. at Bridgeport, Ala on the 20th Dec. 1863 has been received. The Lieut. Col. Comd'g compliments the officers and men of "A" Company for the excellent condition in which their quarters, streets, cooking arrangements, etc. were found, as shown by the Report.

> Cleanliness is a cardinal virtue. Every soldier should be taught to keep his person, his arms, his clothing, his bed and his tent always clean.

> > By order of
> >
> > Thos. J. Morgan Lieut. Col
> >
> > Comd'g Reg't
> >
> > > W. C. C. Avery, Adjutant

Special Order number 3 addresses the discipline expected in the treatment of private property and the company commanders' responsibilities to assure that this order is followed without exception.

Head Quarters 14th U. S. Colored Troops
Gallatin, Tenn 23rd Dec 1863
Special Orders

No. 3

        The Lt. Colonel commanding regrets that any soldier under his command should be guilty of destruction of property. The taking of lumber, burning of rails and all such acts, must be unscrupulously avoided. The Company Commanders will see that the men are supplied with lumber for making their tents comfortable, and with plenty of wood, and with everything that the Government allows to insure the comfort of soldiers. Whatever soldiers are entitled to they must have, otherwise they must do without.

        Any soldier violating this order will be punished. It will be read at the head of each company and Company Officers will be held responsible for the enforcement.

                    By order of
                    Tho's. J. Morgan, Lt. Colonel
                    Comd'g Regiment
                            W. C. C. Avery, Adjutant

On December 31, 1863 the 14th was included in the forces of Brigadier General Eleazer A. Paine in the Gallatin area then transferred to Chattanooga in February. While many USCT regiments were deemed worthy only for labor, Morgan was adamant that his troops be used in combat roles.

Initially, 4 companies of the regiment had been assigned as work details in Bridgeport, Alabama. In mid-February they were reunited with the bulk of the regiment when it reached Chattanooga in order to guard and protect the hospitals and supply line vital to Sherman's efforts.

14th U.S. Colored Troops
Chattanooga Tenn.

13th Feb. 1864General Orders   no. 4
        The commanding Officer congratulates the Regt. upon being complete and at last united. He instructs that nothing may transpire to mar the good feeling that should exist between the different parts of the same Regiment. It should be one in feeling name and in action. He hopes the intercourse between the officers will be marked by the gentleness courtesy and respect for each other that characterize the well-bred gentleman and officer. That they will treat their men as soldiers, and as men remembering that discipline is not incompatible with kindness and he wishes the men to treat each other as brothers united in a holy cause.
        To major Corbin and the officers with him, he tenders his gratitude for the excellent and satisfactory manner in which the affairs of the 1st Battalion have been conducted and he thanks the men for their good behavior during the time they have been absent from him.

By order of
Thomas J. Morgan Lt. Col.
Comd'g Regiment

W.H.H Avery Adjutant.

General Order number five instructed all companies to have morning roll call with arms and sergeants in full uniform and side arms as well. This was further evidence of Morgan's commitment to military discipline and keeping the men battle ready. Beyond being combat ready, Morgan believed that the duty of his officers was to prepare their men for life after the war. A crucial part of that preparedness was teaching them to read, write and spell. On the same day, General Order No. 6 both complimented the men and reported the progress of the regiment.

Headquarters 14 U.S. Colored Troops
Chattanooga Tenn.

21st Feb. 1864

General order}   No. 5

111- At each roll call every company will turn out under arms, and in all cases a non-commissioned officer must be present in proper uniform and with side arms.

> *By order of*
> *Thomas J. Morgan Colonel*
> *Comd'g Regiment*

> *W.H.H. Avery Adjutant*

General Order No. 6 }

Major General Thomas directs the Colonel Comd.g to say to the officers and men of the 14th U.S. Colored Troops, that he was well pleased on the 20th inst. to see the progress they had made, and the skill with which the men used their arms.

One of the first tasks given to the officers of the 14th U.S.C.T. was to teach the enlisted men to spell, read and write. By February 21st 1864 about half of the men were now able to read write and spell.

General Order No. 7 contained the current results of the regiment toward the goal of each man becoming competent in reading, writing and spelling along with a compliment from the chaplain. Colonel Morgan admonished the officers to earn their respect through honorable actions.

Head Quarters 14th U.S.C. Troops
Chattanooga, Ten, Febry 21st, 1864
General Orders
No 7
Extract

The Colonel Commanding takes pleasure in Communicating to the Regiment the following Report.

	Present Attainments			No. Taught since Nov 20th 1863		
Co.	Spell	Read	Write	Spell	Read	Write
A	50	1	3	31	1	3
B	44	15	5	40	12	4
C	40	13	21	30	12	2
D	70	15	1	10	12	1
E	36	15	1	30	12	1
F	48	11	3	40	9	3
G	35	15	7	23	11	4
H	20	10	1	18	10	1
I	21	6	2	16	1	1
K	55	16	30	30	9	2
		122	33	318	94	27

Remarks -The men show great anxiety to learn, more books are daily called for. Not a case of drunkenness has come to my attention since the organization of the regiment. Profane and improper language is rapidly decreasing, while kindness thoughtfulness and soldiering habits are fast gaining ground.

Respectfully Submitted
WM. Elgin
Chaplin

We earnestly hope that at the end of another quarter every man in the command will be able to spell-and large number of them able to read. Learning to read is one of the first steps toward that higher manhood to which these men are hastening- for those who were lately slaves to be U.S. soldiers and freeman, they should be intelligent, thoughtful, and self reliant

He calls on every Officer and man in the regiment to devote himself earnestly to the work of education. He would suggest that an increase of knowledge relating to their specific duties, and the higher positions to which at any time an officer is liable to be called and that information reaching beyond the sphere of the soldier will not be in vain. But will fit them for the higher and responsible duties of the

American Officer and that without such knowledge no officer can claim from others that consideration and respect that attaches to his position. It is an empty honor that is given to rank only. Every officer should seek rather to reflect honor upon his rank then to expect it to reflect honor upon himself.

> *By order of*
> *Thomas F Morgan*
> *Col. Commanding Regt.*

General Order No. 40 was an example of disciplinary action ordered to be taken against slovenly soldiers. This order both exposed them to public humiliation before the regiment and impacted their pay by charging them for new issue clothing prior to an official refitting of equipment.

Head Qrts 14th U. S. C. T. Infy
Chattanooga Tenn July 31st 1864
General Orders
No 40

In order to correct, if possible, a great evil, it is ordered that at company inspection preceding Dress Parade, those men, who from their own carelessness, and unfit to appear at Parade, shall be sent to the Officer of the Day, who shall cause them to be paraded under charge of a non-commissioned officer, twenty paces from the left of the line.

The non-commissioned officer in charge will repair to the center with the 1st Sergeants and report – "Dirty squad, __ men present." The names of each man will be sent to the Adjutant, and by him be publicly announced.

Such men will be supplied by their commanding officer with new clothing, if necessary, to the full extent of their pay, and enter such extra issues as are made, upon the Pay Roll.

"Cleanliness is next to Godliness"

> *By order of Tho's J. Morgan*
> *Col. 14th U.S. Colored Inf'y*
> *W. N. N. Avery, Lt and Adjt.*

General Order No. 41 addressed guard mount and how important it was for the soldiers assigned to this duty to understand the requisite character and attention to detail the assignment demands.

Head Qrs 14th U.S. C. Infantry
Chattanooga Tenn Aug 4th 1864
General Orders
No 41

Guard Mounting is a test of the attainments of a regiment. There is no reason why the Guard Mounting in this regiment should not be brought to the highest perfection. To this end, the following directions will be observed.

Only those men will be detailed for guard who are in the habit of keeping themselves neat and doing their duty soldierly for sentinels being few in numbers and guard duty being lighter than fatigue, it is proper to make this discrimination against the unsoldierly.

Sentinel duty is among the most important that a soldier performs, and never should be imposed as a punishment.

First Sergeants should make detail for guard the preceding evening, allow the entire time before Guard Mounting to those detailed, for preparation and improve the full time between calls in fitting the men for duty; 1st they will inspect the detail to ascertain if their arms and accoutrements are perfectly clean, if their clothing is neat, if they have clean gloves, if they possess the requisite amount of ammunition. 2nd, They will exercise them in the manual of the piece, so far as it is need upon Guard Mounting, including them especially in <u>steadiness in ranks</u> and maintaining carefully, when required the position of "Attention". Hereafter no man will be sent back to his quarters from Guard Mounting; he will be sent under charge of 1st Sergeants to Comd'g Officer of regiment, who will award to both Sergeant and man such punishment as the case merits.

By a little care on the part of all concerned, Guard Mounting can be made unexceptionally beautiful.

By order of Thos. J. Morgan
Col 14th U.S. C. Inf'y

W. H. H. Avery, Lt and Adjt

It is clear to see that Morgan and his officers worked tirelessly to prepare the men for action. The 14th's first opportunity to participate in that military action came in August of 1864 when they were sent along with others to reinforce a Federal force at Dalton, Georgia that was under attack from Confederate Cavalryman, Joseph Wheeler. Morgan later wrote of the fight:

"Dalton… was occupied by a small detachment of Union troops belonging to the 2nd Missouri, under command of Colonel Laibold. General Steadman went to Laibold's aid, and forming line of battle attacked and routed the Southern force. My regiment formed on the left of the 51st Indiana Infantry, under command of Col. A. D. Streight… Just before going into the fight, Lieutenant Keinborts said to his men: 'Boys, some of you may be killed, but remember you are fighting for liberty.' Henry Price replied, 'I am ready to die for liberty.' In fifteen minutes he lay dead, a rifle ball through the heart, - a willing martyr."

"The fight was short," Colonel Morgan continued, *"and not at all severe. The regiment was all exposed to fire. One private was killed, one lost a leg, and one was wounded in the right hand. Company B, on the skirmish line, killed five of the enemy and wounded others. To us it was a great battle, and a glorious victory. The regiment had been recognized as soldiers; it had taken its place side by side with a white regiment; it had been under fire. The men behaved gallantly. A colored soldier had died for liberty. Others had shed their blood in the great cause."* [1]

Following this action the 14th returned briefly to Chattanooga before being sent to Murfreesboro to subdue cavalry raids in the area before moving to Huntsville, Alabama while pursuing Wheeler's cavalry. This consumed the first half of the month of September.

On September 17th, the 14th along with the 16th USCT were engaged again at Pulaski, Tennessee. They had moved to the area by rail to reinforce Major General Rousseau's Cavalry in their efforts to thwart General Nathan Bedford Forrest's Confederate cavalry raids. Upon disembarking from the train, Morgan advanced his force toward the sound of artillery and musketry. Finding Rousseau, he was ordered to form the 14th into a skirmish line with a battle line behind it. As

Rousseau's men retreated through his line, Morgan and the 14th held Forest at bay. Eventually Forest withdrew his men. There were only a few minor casualties in this conflict but they had held against Forrest's vaunted cavalry.

Late in October, the 14th left Chattanooga to support Colonel Charles C. Dolittle in Decatur, Alabama. Dolittle had been attacked by General John B. Hood's army as Hood was moving into Tennessee with the intent of capturing Nashville. Once again, as soon as the 14th arrived on the scene they were thrown into action.

"Lt. Gillett, of Company G, was mortally wounded by a cannon ball, and several others hurt. One brave private of Company B climbed a tree and began firing as a sharpshooter. Soon his right hand was broken by an enemy ball. His captain shouted up to him to climb down and go to the rear and find the hospital. The solider replied that he could shoot with his left hand and remained in the tree, firing until darkness set in.

The next day, October 28th, the 14th charged and captured an enemy battery, capturing 14 prisoners. The white troops present commented on their bravery, determination and precision in carrying the works." [2]

In this engagement the 14th suffered 2 killed, 52 wounded and one missing for a total of 55 casualties. The commanding general, R. S. Granger said the following of the 14th's performance.

"The action of the colored troops under Colonel Morgan was everything that could be expected or desired of soldiers. They were cool, brave, and determined; and under the heaviest fire of the enemy exhibited no signs of confusion." [3]

On November 2nd, Colonel Morgan gave heartfelt congratulations to the regiment in General Orders No. 50. He was profoundly proud of their performance at Decatur and praised them for their professionalism and success on the battlefield.

Head Qrs. 14th U.S. C. Infantry
Chattanooga, Tenn Nov 2nd 1864
General Orders
No 50

The Colonel commanding desires to express to the officers and men of the 14th US. Colored Infantry, his entire satisfaction with their conduct during the 27th, 28th, 29th and 30th days of October in the defense of Decatur, Ala. On the march, on the skirmish line, in the charge, they proved themselves soldiers. Their conduct has gained for the regiment an enviable reputation in the Western Army noted for its fighting qualities. The blood of those who fell has hushed the mouths of our enemies, while the conduct of those who live elicited praises and cheers from all who witnessed it. It is no small event for a black regiment to receive the hearty cheers from a regiment of white men; and yet the 14th deserved the compliment.

It is sad to lose the officers and men that have been so long intimately connected with the regiment; but it had been better for all to have gone with them to honorable graves, than for the regiment to have failed to do its duty.

There were many instances of personal bravery and devotion to the regiment shown by the enlisted men. The Colonel was especially pleased with these, and will not forget those who thus distinguished themselves. – Sergeant Major <u>*George Griffith,*</u> *Sergeant* <u>*Thomas McClellan,*</u> *Sergeant* <u>*King,*</u> *Sergeant* <u>*Graffenberg,*</u> *Corporal* <u>*Senter*</u> *and those who bore and stood by the Colors, did admirably. Companies "F" and "G" never before had been under fire, and yet they behaved like veteran soldiers.*

One year ago the regiment was unknown, and it was considered by most of the Army and a large number of the people of the United States very doubtful whether negroes would make good soldiers, and it was esteemed no honor to be an officer in a black regiment. Today, the 14th is known throughout the army and the north; and is honored. The Colonel commanding is proud of the regiment, and would not exchange its command for that of the best white regiment in the United States service.

He again thanks the men for their bravery and the earnestness they have manifested in their work, and the Officers for their ready cooperation with him in advancing the interests of the comman, but he cautions them that very much remains to be done.

By order of Thomas J. Morgan, Colonel
14th US. Colored Infantry
Wm H. H. Avery, Lt. and Adjutant

On the 23rd Morgan commended the men of Company G for having raised three hundred and sixty dollars for a monument to their fallen Lieutenant during the battle.

Head Qrs 14th US. C. Infantry
Chattanooga, Tenn Nov 23rd 1864
General Orders
No 51
   The Colonel commanding takes pleasure in calling attention to the benevolence and public spirit manifested by the members of "G" Company, 14th U.S. Colored Infantry, in contributing Three Hundred and Sixty Dollars ($360) for the erection of a suitable monument over the grave of their lamented Lieutenant – the brave and good <u>Frank Gillett,</u> who fell in battle at Decatur Alabama on October 28th 1864.
   Their example is worthy of <u>imitation.</u>
      By order of Thomas J. Morgan Colonel
      14th US. Colored Infantry
        Wm H. H. Avery Lt. and Adjutant

After returning to Chattanooga following this action, the regiment was sent on November 30th to reinforce General Thomas in Nashville. Hood's attacking Confederate army had been severely wounded that same day at Franklin, Tennessee. Although Union General Schofield had held his position and delivered devastating losses to the Army of Tennessee, Hood continued to drive toward Nashville in hopes of wresting the place from Thomas.

During transit to Nashville, General Nathan Bedford Forrest attacked one of the trains that were carrying two companies of the 14th USCT. The train was derailed and two of the 14th members were killed, five wounded and 18 missing a result.

The closing act of Hood's ill-fated Tennessee campaign was the battle of Nashville on December 15th and 16th. The 14th USCT participated in the battle, losing four killed, 41 wounded and 20 missing. Their first assault on the Rebel line had been unsuccessful but they took a different breastwork in their second attempt during the first day of the battle. During the second day of fighting they served as support of an artillery battery in reserve.

The 14th was part of the pursuing Union forces trying to mop up the remnants of Hood's army as they retreated back into Alabama. This duty consumed the next two months with the 14th reporting at Bridgeport, Alabama on February 12, 1865.

By this time Colonel Morgan was commanding the brigade which contained the 14th. They returned to Chattanooga and on April 30th the brigade was turned over to Colonel Lewis Johnson after Morgan was promoted to Brigadier General and sent to another command.

The 14th USCT served as occupation forces in east Tennessee until March 26, 1866 when they were mustered out of service. Many chose to remain in Chattanooga as their home.

16th USCT

Shortly after the battle of Chickamauga, the formation of what would become the 16th USCT was begun in Clarksville, Tennessee and completed in Nashville early in 1864. The regiment was assigned to working on the fortifications around Chattanooga, arriving there on May 30th with 26 officers and 638 enlisted men.

In contrast to Colonel Morgan's treatment and development of the 14th USCT as professional fighting men, the commander of the 16th, William B. Gaw, did not seem interested in training his regiment to fight or in placing them or himself in combat roles. Neither did he put any effort into preparing the men for civilian life after the war. He was content in their use as laborers for the army. Hence they predominantly worked on defenses, building roads and other such projects.

Regardless of Gaw's wish to keep his regiment from fighting, they were pressed into service as soldiers in September of 1864. Detailed to Loudon, Tennessee, one of the companies under Captain Gordon was ordered to destroy ferry boats and patrol the river against any further action by General Joseph Wheeler's cavalry that had recently made a raid in that region. The rest of the regiment went along with the 14th USCT on their mission to Murfreesboro and on to Huntsville, Alabama as previously noted.

After a brief redeployment to Tullahoma, Tennessee to guard the Nashville and Chattanooga Railroad they were ordered to return to Chattanooga in mid-November.

On November 30 the regiment joined Morgan's First Colored Brigade as part of Major General James B. Steedman's division and sent to Nashville in preparation for Hood's advance on that city. While involved in near constant skirmishing during this two week period, they were not in any pitched battles. On December 14th Morgan received orders to move forward on the left of the Union line but Gaw had made arrangements to have the 16th taken out of the brigade and moved to the rear in order to assist a group of engineers service a pontoon bridge over Rutherford's Creek. This maneuver kept him out of harm's way and kept the 16th from participating in the Battle of Nashville on December 15-16, 1864.

On December 21, 1864, Gaw ordered the 16th to return to Chattanooga where it served out the balance of the war and its enlistment as garrison and occupational forces. The regiment was mustered out on April 30, 1866.

Chapter Eighteen

Chattanooga and the Close of the War

Following the national election in November of 1864 a new governor for the state of Tennessee was required. A convention was convened in December, dominated by East Tennessee Unionists. Not only did they ultimately install their candidate, Parson Brownlow for governor, they took on the legislative role of reversing all that the Confederate government had put into place in the state. The Ordinance of Secession was repealed, all acts of the Confederate legislature nullified and slavery was outlawed in an amendment to the state constitution. The qualifications for voting included proof of being a Union Loyalist and while the turnout for the ratification vote was low Brownlow won his race and the amendment was accepted.

In the spring of 1865, the closing of the war was imminent and civilian businesses began to resurface and thrive in the city. With the fall of Richmond 100 canon were fired in salute from the hills that ringed the city. When Lee surrendered at Appomattox 200 guns were fired in rapid succession. On April 15 the elation came to a quick halt with the assassination of President Lincoln. Artillerist Jenkin Lloyd Jones wrote in his diary:

"Tis night, a beautiful day has just closed. But alas! A dark pall hangs over our camp. The soldier mourns the loss of the noblest American of the day. President Abraham Lincoln has fallen by the hands of a traitorous assassin. 2 P.M we started out to graze, each and all lighthearted and merry. But lo! While out near the foot of Mission Ridge, the stars and stripes over Fort Creighton were seen to descend to half-mast, and the news reached us as if by magic of the fall of our noble president. A gloom was cast upon every one, and silently we returned to camp, still hoping for a contradiction. But it was too true. The scene that followed was one very seldom seen in the tented field. But a soldier is not, as many think, wholly void of feeling. All regarded the loss of him as of a near and dear relative. Terrible were the oaths and imprecations uttered through clenched teeth against the vile perpetrators."

The next day, he noted:

"The whole town was draped in mourning, flags tied with black, and white crepe exhibited in all parts of the town, while the 100 pounder Parrotts high up on Cameron Hill fired half-hour guns from 5 A.M. till 6 P.M. The gloom of yesterday still hangs over the camp.[1]

Getting mustered out and sent home was the most fervent thought on each soldier's mind. But the necessity of maintaining order and making a transition from war to peace takes time and routine duty continued for many of the troops posted in Chattanooga. Jones and his companions looked for every positive sign that they would soon go home. On May 5th, he wrote in his diary,

"Ration day. Drew two days' rations of bread and three of hard-tack, no more soft bread to be issued. They want us to eat the surplus hard-tack. This is considered significant."

He also commented about returning Confederate veterans passing though.

"Many of them were quite splendidly dressed, having the finest uniforms I have ever seen with them. I talked with many of them in a friendly strain, astonished to find them so ignorant of the last year. But most of them are heartily tired of war, and say they are willing to bide the will of the United States, but fear Andy Johnson's severity. One poor fellow in a sad strain said he 'was going to the place where his home once was, but God knows where it is now. I have not heard from any of them for ten months.' They were commanded by one of the most desperate, wild-looking colonels I have ever seen.... He wore a large, warm home-made cloak, plaited around the waist like an old fashioned wammus, hanging clear to his heels, and a coarse white hat with a brim a foot wide, and greasy hair below his shoulders."

As Demobilization began public auctions were held to sell off the massive quantities of materials needed for an army and stored in the warehouses along the river. Everything imaginable including buildings, steamboats, harness and nose bags, cut stone and more were sold. The waterworks was sold to private owners and the railroads returned to their owners but in bad repair. A considerable amount of time would be needed to return them to reliable and dependable condition. The quartermasters repaired the churches and returned them to their original mission.

Many Union soldiers who had been mustered out determined to stay in Chattanooga and previous residents began to return. David M. Key, who had been a prominent lawyer before the war and served as a Confederate officer questioned whether he would be welcomed home under the changed demographics of the city. He wrote to a friend who had been a Union Sympathizer, William Crutchfield, asking if he should bring his family back to town. Crutchfield replied:

"Maj. Key's deportment was such as far as I have been informed to treat all men kindly, courteously & gentlemanly regardless of their political opinions – any man in the Rebel Army deporting himself thus – has nothing to fear from an honorable high minded intelligent community. As an officer in the Army I presume he is aware of the various proclamations and the many difficulties on the path of a prominent Rebel.

In this section, I can assure you, Maj. Key would be kindly treated and such help as can be rendered by me and mine and all his old friends shall be freely, frankly, & cheerfully given." [2]

This promise of tolerance was fulfilled upon Key's return in November of 1865. Years later, Key wrote, *"A friend gave us a house, rent free. My health was wretched. Our Confederate money was worthless, and we had none other. The people of the neighborhood were wonderful kind to us. One furnished us his best milch cow. Another who owned a mill, sent us breadstuffs and all were generous. I cultivated a good garden, about six acres in corn and a half acre in potatoes... The Negroes who had been in the Federal lines began to return to their former homes, bringing with them some greenbacks and were anxious to purchase some finery for their families. My wife disposed of a great deal of her wardrobe to them for whatever she could get, and some money was raised in this way. One fellow took quite a fancy to my uniform and my wife sold it to him at quite a low figure..."*[3] *Key was granted a full pardon for his participation in "the rebellion" by President Johnson.)*

A census of November 1865 indicated that the population of Chattanooga consisted of 3,119 white men, women and children and 2,657 black men, women and children for a total of 5,776. There were also 3,000 Union soldiers still stationed in town. The work of dismantling the forts that ringed the city was completed during the winter of 1865-66. 2,000 pieces of artillery and several hundred tons of ammunition were hauled to the depot and from there transported to Northern arsenals.

By April 1866, Chattanooga was practically cleared of troops. The difficult task of ramping up the rebuilding of the community and healing the wounds of war, both physical and mental continued in earnest.

Chapter Nineteen

Chattanooga National Cemetery

Following the battles of Chickamauga and Chattanooga, it was necessary to acquire appropriate land for burial of the Union dead.

In the official history of the Army of the Cumberland, the decision on the designated property and Thomas's order were detailed as such:

"During the battle, which resulted in the dislodgement of General Bragg's army from Missionary Ridge, a reserve force in line over a hill near the field position of General Thomas, revealed its beautiful contour and suggested its use as a National Cemetery. This hill, conical in general outline, but fruitful in lateral hillocks and varied in expression from every point of view, is located equidistant from Cameron hill, which rise abruptly from the Tennessee river, where it turns toward Lookout Mountain and Missionary Ridge on the east, and is central between General Hooker's point of attack on Lookout Mountain and General Sherman's on the northern summit of Missionary Ridge. Thus it is the center of this complex battle-field."

(General Orders, No. 296)

Chattanooga, Tenn., December 25, 1863
It is ordered that a National Cemetery be founded at this place, in commemoration of the battles at Chattanooga, fought November 23d, 24th, 25th, 26th and 27th, and to provide a proper resting-place for the remains of the brave men who fell upon the fields fought over upon those days, and for the remains of such as may hereafter give up their lives in this region in defending their country against treason and rebellion.

The ground selected for the cemetery is the hill lying beyond the Western and Atlantic railroad, in a southeasterly direction from the town.

It is proposed to erect a monument upon the summit of the hill of such materials as are to be obtained in this vicinity, which, like all the work upon the cemetery, shall be exclusively done by the troops of the Army of the Cumberland.

Plans for the monument are invited to be sent in to these headquarters. When the ground is prepared, notice will be given, and all interments of soldiers will thereafter be made in the cemetery, and all now buried in and around the town removed to that place.

By command of Major-General George H. Thomas,

(signed,)   WM. D. WHIPPLE

Assistant Adjutant-General.

As remains were brought to the cemetery they were buried without regard to units or states. When asked why this was so, General Thomas, who had ordered it, replied:

"I am tired of States' Rights. Let's have a national cemetery." [1]

The monument requested by Thomas was never erected and circumstances of the spring campaign for Atlanta, defense of Nashville and the March to the Sea prevented the Army of Cumberland from completing the burial tasks. The United States Quartermaster's department completed the work after the war. Subsequent cemeteries were established for the relocation of Union dead in and around Stones River, Nashville and Marietta. 40,000 Union Civil War dead are buried in these 4 cemeteries.

(Extract from General Orders, NO. 8)

Headquarters Army of the Cumberland
Chattanooga, Tenn. January 8, 1864

Commanding officers of regiments in this department will furnish, on the application of Chaplain Thomas B. Van Horne, 13th O.V.I., in charge of the Mortuary Record of the National Cemetery at this place, full information in regard to the full name, rank, company, native state, date, age, marital state, date of enlistment, address of nearest friends, number of engagements participated in, soldierly character, special circumstances of death, if killed in action, and whatever else is worthy of their history of record, of all soldiers who may be interred in the National Cemetery at Chattanooga.

By Command of Major-General Thomas:

WM D WHIPPLE, Assistant Adjutant-General.

Official: Wm McMichael Assistant Adjutant-General

By 1870 more than 12,800 Union soldiers were laid to rest in the Chattanooga National Cemetery. 8,685 are identified and 4,189 were unknown. The first ever recipients of the Medal of Honor, four of the members of Andrews Raiders, are buried in the Chattanooga National Cemetery.

Chattanooga National Cemetery circa

(image courtesy of the Library of Congress)

Contributing Soldiers' Biographies

Asahe Baldwin   82nd **Ohio Volunteer Infantry**

1st Brigade   **3rd Division**   **XI Corps**
Hooker's Command   **United States**

Asahe enlisted September 26, 1864 having been payed as a substitute. He mustered out of service June 18, 1865.

Adelbert Childs   33rd **Ohio Volunteer Infantry**

1st Brigade   **1st Division**   **14th Corps**
Army of the Cumberland   **United States**

Childs was 20 when he enlisted on September 16, 1861 for a three year term. He was wounded October 8, 1862 at the Battle of Perryville, Kentucky. He died October 20, 1862 as a result of those wounds.

Adelbert Hauman   104th **Illinois Volunteer Infantry**

1st Brigade   **2nd Division** **14th Corps**
Army of the Cumberland   **United States**

Hauman enlisted in Company B in Putnam County Illinois on August 27th, 1861. He was Killed November 23, 1863 during the attack on Missionary Ridge. He is buried in an unknown grave in the Chattanooga National Cemetery.

Addison Searles   21st **Ohio Volunteer Infantry**

3rd Brigade   **2nd Division** **14th Corps**
Army of the Cumberland   **United States**

Serales enlisted September 21, 1861 at the age of 21. He died of disease at Hospital Number 1 in Chattanooga. He is buried in the Chattanooga National Cemetery. Section A, Grave 257

Alfred Searles   **21st Ohio Volunteer Infantry**

3rd Brigade   2nd Division   14th Corps
Army of the Cumberland   United States

The older brother of Addison, Alfred enlisted on September 2, 1861 at the age of 27. He died July 7, 1864 at a hospital in Columbus, Ohio and is buried in Green Lawn Cemetery in that city.

Axel Reed   **2nd Minnesota Volunteer Infantry**

3rd Brigade   3rd Division   14th Corps
Army of the Cumberland   United States

Axel enlisted in Company K of the regiment August 26, 1861. He reenlisted as a veteran on February 18, 1863. He was promoted to sergeant on August 28, 1863. Reed was wounded November 25th, 1863 during the attack on Missionary Ridge. Consequently his arm was amputated. He mustered out of service August 17, 1864

Benjamin Mason   **137th New York Volunteer Infantry**

3rd Brigade   2nd Diviison   XII Corps
Hooker's Command   United States

Benjamin was from Union County New York and enlisted in Company B June 9, 1861 at the age of 19. He was promoted to corporal on August 9, 1862. He was killed November 24, 1863 at the Battle of Lookout Mountain. He is buried in the Chattanooga National Cemetery. Section B, Grave 576.

Charles Roberts   **Mississippi Light Artillery**
Cheatham's Division   **Polk's Corp**
Army of Tennessee   **Confederate States**

Charles enlisted May 16, 1863 and paroled May 1, 1865 at Greensboro North Carolina following the surrender of Johnston's army.

Charles Caley   **105th Ohio Volunteer Infantry**

1st Brigade   **5th Division**   **XIV Corps**
Army of the Cumberland   **United States**

Charles enlisted on September 21, 1861. He was first wounded October 8, 1862 at the Battle of Perryville Kentucky. He was then captured December 31, 1862 at the Battle of Stones River, then paroled on January 3, 1863. Charles was wounded in the right foot at the Battle of Chickamauga on September 20, 1863.

Dennis Murphy   **104th Illinois Volunteer Infantry**

1st Brigade   **2nd Division**   **XIV Corps**
Army of the Cumberland   **United States**

Dennis enlisted on August 27, 1862 in Ottawa County Illinois. He died in Chattanooga on November 1, 1863 from wounds received September 19, 1863 during the Battle of Chickamauga. He is buried in Chattanooga National Cemetery. Section A. Grave 77

1st Brigade   **1st Division**   **XXI Corps**
Army of the Cumberland   **United States**

Our Brethren are on the Field

Dr. D. L. Strait   6th **South Carolina Infantry**

Jenkin's Brigade   Hood's Division   **Longstreet's Command**
Army of Northern Virginia   **Confederate States**

Dr. Strait served with Company A as well as the field and staff of the 6th beginning June 19, 1861. He was present with the regiment through all of its moves for the entire war. He was paroled May 2, 1865

E.P. Daniels   5th **Georgia Volunteer Infantry**

Jackson's Brigade   **Cheatham's Division**   **Polk's Corps**
Army of Tennessee   **Confederate States**

E.P. Enlisted at Macon Georgia on May 1, 1861. On May 8, 1862 he was promoted to 1st sergeant. He was promoted to Captain of company B before being promoted again to major by General Joseph E. Johnston on July 8, 1863. He surrendered to Union forces at Greensboro South Carolina May 1, 1865.

Edward Hutsell   75th **Indiana Volunteer Infantry**

2nd Brigade   4th **Division**   **XIV Corps**
Army of the Cumberland   **United States**

Edward left his home in New Holland Indiana to enlist on July 21, 1862. He died at Chattanooga June 29, 1864. He is buried in the Chattanooga National Cemetery. Section D. Grave 12548

Our Brethren are on the Field

G. Foster   **51ˢᵗ Illinois Volunteer Infantry**

3ʳᵈ Brigade   3ʳᵈ Division   XX Corps
Army of the Cumberland   United States

Foster enlisted in Company F July 18, 1862 in Bath County Illinois. He was promoted to sergeant prior to being killed on September 19, 1863 at Chickamauga. He is buried in the Chattanooga National Cemetery in an unknown grave.

George Dobson   **10ᵗʰ Mississippi Volunteer Infantry**

Anderson's Brigade   Hindman's Division   Polk's Corps
Army of Tennessee   Confederate States

George enlisted as a private on April 17, 1861 and was promoted to captain March 6, 1862. He became a veteran volunteer June 3, 1862. He spent much of the later years of the war detached from action as a guard of Union prisoners, both in Georgia and North Carolina.

George Smith   **111ᵗʰ Pennsylvania Volunteer Infantry**

2ⁿᵈ Brigade   2ⁿᵈ Division   XII Corps
Hooker's Command   United States

George enlisted July 17, 1863 as a substitute. He was killed at Dallas Georgia May 31, 1864 and is buried in the Marietta National Cemetery. Section A. Grave 733

George Thorn   **13ᵗʰ Ohio Volunteer Infantry**

2ⁿᵈ Brigade   3ʳᵈ Division   XXI Corps
Army of the Cumberland   United States

George enlisted at the age of 33 on June 21, 1861 for a three year term. He was killed at Lovejoy Station, Georgia September 5, 1864.

George H. Burns **34th Georgia Volunteer Infantry**

Cummings Brigade
Army of Tennessee **Confederate States**

George enlisted in Company A as the regiment was being initially formed on May 15, 1862 and was elected musician. He was captured at Vicksburg, Mississippi on July 4, 1863 and was paroled on July 8th. He returned to the regiment on July 30, 1863. He was reported in the General Hospital at Charlotte, North Carolina on February 13, 1865. He surrendered and was paroled May 5th, 1865.

Given Campbell **Forrest's Cavalry**

Henry Robison **104th Illinois Volunteer Infantry**

1st Brigade **2nd Division** **XIV Corps**
Army of the Cumberland **United States**

Henry enlisted at Lasalle County, Illinois on August 27, 1862. Surviving the war, he mustered out on June 6, 1865.

Joseph Dewater **13th Michigan Infantry**

1st Brigade **1st Division** **XXI Corps**
Army of the Cumberland **United States**

Joseph enlisted at the age of 33 at Kalamazoo County on June 2, 1861. He was promoted to corporal on November 2, 1862 and wounded at Stones River on December 31, 1862. He died of disease at the Hospital on Lookout Mountain. He is buried in the Chattanooga National Cemetery. Section C. Grave 1299.

Joseph O'Bryan   **1ˢᵗ Tennessee Volunteer Infantry**

Maney's Brigade   Cheatham's Division   Polk's Corps
Army of Tennessee   Confederate States

Joseph enlisted in Company B June 30, 1861. He was promoted to sergeant on October 2, 1861. He reenlisted as a veteran Volunteer on January 9, 1864 and mustered out of service May 5, 1865.

John Baker   **96ᵗʰ Illinois Volunteer Infantry**

1ˢᵗ Brigade   1ˢᵗ Division   Granger's Reserve Corps
Army of the Cumberland   United States

John enlisted September 6, 1862 in Company G and died at Estelle Springs, Tennessee exactly one year later on September 6, 1863.

John Bennett   **74ᵗʰ Indiana Volunteer Infantry**

2ⁿᵈ Brigade   3ʳᵈ Division   XIV Corps
Army of the Cumberland   United States

John enlisted in Company H at Flint County Indiana on August 7, 1862. He was killed at Chickamauga on September 19ᵗʰ, 1863.

John Dunmore   **96ᵗʰ Illinois Volunteer Infantry**

1ˢᵗ Brigade   1ˢᵗ Division   Granger's Reserve Corps
Army of the Cumberland   United States

John enlisted in Company D on December 23, 1863 at Benton County Illinois. He Died in Chattanooga, Tennessee on July 1, 1864. He is buried in Chattanooga National Cemetery. Section E. Grave 11676

John Ellis   16th **Louisiana Volunteer Infantry**

Adam's Brigade   **Breckinridge's Division   Hill's Corps**
Army of Tennessee   **Confederate States**

John enlisted December 2nd, 1861. No further information.

John Magee   **Stanford's Battery – Mississippi LA**

Artillery   **Cheatham's Division   Polk's Corps**
Army of Tennessee   **Confederate States**

John enlisted at the age of 20 on November 16, 1861. He had dark
hair and a dark complexion, standing 5 feet 6 inches tall. He was
wounded December 31, 1862 at the Battle of Stones River. He
deserted the Confederate army on June 1, 1864. He was captured at
Seniker, Ohio and took the oath of allegiance on June 3, 1864. He had
to remain north of the Ohio River for the remainder of the war, being
released on May 12, 1865.

John Hagan   29th **Georgia Volunteer Infantry**

Wilson's Brigade   Walker's Division   **Walker's Reserve Corps**
Army of Tennessee   **Confederate States**

John enlisted in Company K June 21, 1862. He was captured near
Atlanta, Georgia July 20, 1864 eventually being sent to Camp Chase in
Columbus, Ohio. He was paroled and released March 4, 1865.

Jonas Hollem   74th **Illinois Volunteer Infantry**

1st Brigade   1st Division   XX Corps
Army of the Cumberland   **United States**

Jonas enlisted at Rockford Illinois, September 4, 1862. He died at
Chattanooga, Tennessee August 8, 1864 of wounds received June 27
of that year. He is buried in Chattanooga National Cemetery. Section
E. Grave 11761

Joseph King   **6th Indiana Volunteer Infantry**

3rd Brigade   2nd Division   XX Corps
Army of the Cumberland   United States

Joseph enlisted in Company A on September 20, 1865. He was wounded and captured at Allatoona Pass, Georgia on May 27, 1864. He was paroled on June 18, 1864 and mustered out of service on June 19, 1865.

Joseph Vangundy   **26th Ohio Volunteer Infantry**

1st Brigade   1st Division   XXI Corps
Army of the Cumberland   United States

Joseph enlisted in Company B at the age of 21 on June 21, 1861. He was killed September 19, 1863 at the Battle of Chickamauga. He is buried in the Chattanooga National Cemetery in an unknown grave.

Loyal B. Wort   **21st Ohio Volunteer Infantry**

3rd Brigade   2nd Division   XIV Corps
Army of the Cumberland   United States

Loyal enlisted on August 29, 1861 at the age of 31. He was captured at the battle of Stones River on December 31, 1862 and paroled on March14, 1863. He returned to the regiment on April 21, 1862. He was discharged on September 19, 1864 on expiration of his term of service.

Maurice Williams   **36th Indiana Volunteer Infantry**

3rd Brigade   2nd Division   XXI Corps
Army of the Cumberland   United States

Maurice enlisted on October 23, 1861 at Union County Indiana. He was killed September 19, 1863 at the Battle of Chickamauga.

Osso Quiggle   14th **Ohio Volunteer Infantry**

2nd Brigade   3rd Division   XIV Corps
Army of Cumberland   United States

Osso enlisted September 5, 1861 at the age of 18. He was killed in a skirmish near Milledgeville, Georgia during Sherman's march to the sea.

Otis Baker   10th **Mississippi Volunteer Infantry**

Anderson's Brigade   Hindman's Division   Polk's Corps
Army of Tennessee   Confederate States

Otis enlisted as a lieutenant on March 1, 1862 at Natchez, Mississippi at the age of 21. He was described as being 5 feet 9 inches tall, with gray eyes, light hair and fair complexion. He was wounded at Michens Ridge near Corinth, Mississippi on April 24, 1862. He was wounded again near Atlanta, Georgia on July 28, 1864. He mustered out of service on March 28, 1865.

Robert Woody   9th **Tennessee Battalion**

Forest's Brigade   Armstrong's Division   Forest's Cavalry Corps
Army of Tennessee   Confederate States

Robert enlisted June 30, 1864 and served until December 31, 1864.

Samuel Hoffman **18th Ohio Volunteer Infantry**

2nd Brigade 2nd Division XIV Corps
Army of the Cumberland United States

Samuel enlisted in Company A September 15, 1861 at the age of 18. He was discharged May 19, 1865 at Chattanooga on a certificate of disability but never returned home. He died on May 24, 1865 while still in Chattanooga. He is buried in Chattanooga National Cemetery. Section G. Grave 8546.

Samuel Withrow **22nd Indiana Volunteer Infantry**

1st Brigade 1st Division XX Corps
Army of the Cumberland United States

Samuel enlisted in Company K on August 15, 1862 and died in Chattanooga on May 5, 1865. He is buried in Chattanooga National Cemetery. Section G. Grave 8735

Vincent Messler **115th Illinois Volunteer Infantry**

1st Brigade 1st Division Granger's Reserve Corps
Army of the Cumberland United States

Vincent enlisted September 13, 1862 in Richmond County Illinois. He died at Chattanooga, Tennessee on November 4, 1863 from wounds received September 20th during the Battle of Chickamauga. He is buried in Chattanooga National Cemetery. Section B. Grave 1015

W. H. Reynolds **5th Georgia Volunteer Infantry**

Jackson's Brigade Cheatham's Division Polk's Corps
Army of Tennessee Confederate States

W. H. enlisted in Company K on September 19, 1862 in Atlanta. He was promoted to captain September 22, 1864. He was discharged at Camp Douglas, Illinois on May 12, 1865 having been a prisoner of war.

W. R. Stilwell   **53rd Georgia Volunteer Infantry**

Bryan's Brigade   McLaw's Division
Longstreet's Command   **Confederate States**

On May 21, 1861 Stilwell enlisted in Company F at Henry County Georgia. He was slightly wounded in the right foot at the battle of Cedar Creek Virginia and captured at Strasburg Virginia October 19, 1864. He was sent to the prisoner of war camp at Point Lookout Maryland, arriving there on October 29, 1864. He was exchanged on October 30, 1864 and mustered out of service on May 2, 1864.

Wesley Connor   **Cherokee Artillery**

Cheatham's Division   **Polk's Corps**
Army of Tennessee   **Confederate States**

Wesley enlisted June 17, 1861 and was captured at Vicksburg, Mississippi on July 9, 1863. Captured again, he was paroled June 1, 1865.

William Talley   **14th Georgia Artillery**

Cheatham's Division   **Polk's Corps**
Army of Tennessee   **Confederate States**

William enlisted at the age of 22 near Griffin, Georgia on April 27, 1861. Served for four years of the war.

W. W. Carnes   **Stevens Artillery**

Army of Tennessee   **Confederate States**

Carnes enlisted August 17, 1861 at New Madrid Missouri. He was promoted to 1st lieutenant on August 18, 1861 and captain on June 26, 1862. He resigned December 18, 1863 to accept a commission as Major in the Confederate States Navy. He served there until March 21, 1864 when he returned to the artillery at Dalton Georgia. He was paroled June 21, 1865 at the end of the war.

Acknowledgements

Brad and Dick want to thank Robert Moran for the hours he spent pulling records and photographing letters at the National Archives over nine separate trips to Washington D.C. His work provided a significant number of the letters found in the book.

Dick would also like to acknowledge Brad for being the backbone of each of these projects and a tremendous source of material as well as inspiration for the many, many hours spent compiling the letters and diaries and creating a narrative to make it all flow. I would also like to thank my precious wife, Mary Rubin, for her help in reviewing the manuscript, suggestions and final edits. I extend that gratitude as well to my father-in-law, David Sharrock for his efforts in reviewing the manuscript and offering input.

We also want to thank and acknowledge Hal Jespersen for providing the maps used in the book. His excellence in cartography provides a visual guide that helps the reader make sense of the descriptions of campaigns and battles recorded in the book. His work is indispensable in that regard.

We cannot fail to acknowledge the assistance provided by the Chattanooga and Chickamauga National Battle Park and Jim Ogden in particular for their assistance in sharing letters and diaries from Confederate Soldiers who served and fought in this as well as other regions of the conflict.

Notes

(1) History of Hamilton County and Chattanooga
Tennessee. Volume II – Armstrong pages 28 & 29

Chapter Three

(1) *New York Times* June 30, 1861
(2) C.W. Anderson "After the Fall of Fort Donelson" –
Confederate Veteran IV Pgs 289-290
(3) *Ibid.*, page 290
(4) Key Collection

Chapter Six

(1) James Street Jr *The Struggle for Tennessee – Tupelo
to Stones River* Time Life pg 149

Chapter Eight

(1) Capt. S.S. Canfield *History of the 21st Regiment Ohio
Volunteer Infantry in the War of the Rebellion* pgs
104-106

Chapter Nine

(1) Jerry Korn *The Fight for Chattanooga 0
Chickamauga to Missionary Ridge* Time Life Pg 69
(2) Capt. S.S. Canfield *History of the 21st Regiment Ohio
Volunteer Infantry in the War of the Rebellion* pg
132
(3) Jerry Korn *The Fight for Chattanooga 0
Chickamauga to Missionary Ridge* Time Life Pg 73

Chapter Fourteen

(1) Sir John Kennaway *On Sherman's Track* Pg 91

Chapter 17

(1) E. Raymond Evans *Contributions By United States Colored Troops (USCT) of Chattanooga and North Georgia during the American Civil War Reconstruction and Formation of Chattanooga* Pg 127

(2) E. Raymond Evans *Contributions By United States Colored Troops (USCT) of Chattanooga and North Georgia during the American Civil War Reconstruction and Formation of Chattanooga* Pg 131

(3) E. Raymond Evans *Contributions By United States Colored Troops (USCT) of Chattanooga and North Georgia during the American Civil War Reconstruction and Formation of Chattanooga* Pg 132

Chapter Eighteen

(1) Jones: *opcit* pg 323

(2) "W. Crutchfield to S. A. Key Aug 28 1865" *Key Collection*

(3) *Key Collection*

Chapter 19

(1) *O.R. Series 1XXX1 Part 3*, page 487

Bibliography

E. Raymond Evans *Contributions by United States Colored Troops (USCT) of Chattanooga and North Georgia During the American Civil War Reconstruction and Formation of Chattanooga* Rock Springs: Beverly, Catherine Mitchell Foster Press 2003

Captain S. S. Canfield *History of the 21st Ohio Volunteer Infantry in the War of the Rebellion* Vrooman, Anderson & Bateman, Printers 1893

James Street Jr. *The Struggle for Tennessee* The Civil War Time Life 1985

Jerry Korn *The Fight for Chattanooga* The Civil War Time Life 1985

Peter Cozzens The Battle of Stones River *No Better Place To Die* University of Illinois Press 1991

Peter Cozzens *The Battle of Chickamauga This Terrible Sound* University of Illinois Press 1996

Ronald Mosely *The Stilwell Letters, A Georgian in Longstreet's Corps* William, Ross Stilwell, Mollie Stilwell, Ronald H. Mosely. Macon Georgia Mercer University Press 2002

Wikipedia *Union Order of Battle – Perryville, Confederate Order of Battle – Perryville, Union Order of Battle – Stones River, Confederate Order of Battle- Stones River, Union Order of Battle – Tullahoma, Confederate Order of Battle – Tullahoma, Union Order of Battle – Chickamauga, Confederate Order of Battle – Chickamauga, Union Order of Battle – Missionary Ridge, Confederate Order of Battle Missionary Ridge*

Thomas Van Horn *History of the Army of the Cumberland Vol II* The Clarke & Co. Cincinnati, Ohio 1875

Confederate Veteran Volume IV Cunningham Press 1893-1932

Govan and Livingood *The Chattnooga Country 1540-1951* New York Dutton 1952

Kate Cumming *Kate: Journal of A Confederate Nurse* Louisiana State University Press

Zella Armstrong *History of Hamilton County and Chattanooga Tennessee Volume II* Overmountain Press 1993

National *Archives Appended Documents – Western Armies 1863* Pg 286